SECURITY
BY OTHER MEANS

SECURITY
BY OTHER MEANS

Foreign Assistance,
Global Poverty, and
American Leadership

Lael Brainard
editor

CENTER FOR STRATEGIC AND
INTERNATIONAL STUDIES

BROOKINGS INSTITUTION PRESS
Washington, D.C.

Copyright © 2007
THE BROOKINGS INSTITUTION
1775 Massachusetts Avenue, N.W., Washington, D.C. 20036
www.brookings.edu

Library of Congress Cataloging-in-Publication data

Security by other means : foreign assistance, global poverty, and American leadership / Lael Brainard, editor.
   p.   cm.
  Summary: "Assesses the current structures of foreign assistance and makes recommendations for efficient coordination. Drawing on expertise from the full range of foreign aid agencies, examines foreign assistance across four categories: security, economic, humanitarian, and political"—Provided by publisher.
  Includes bibliographical references and index.
  ISBN-13: 978-0-8157-1362-3 (cloth : alk. paper)
  ISBN-10: 0-8157-1362-2 (cloth : alk. paper)
  ISBN-13: 978-0-8157-1361-6 (pbk. : alk. paper)
  ISBN-10: 0-8157-1361-4 (pbk. : alk. paper)
  1. Economic assistance, American. 2. Technical assistance, American. 3. United States—Foreign relations. I. Brainard, Lael.
  HC60.S4135 2006
  338.91'73—dc22   2006037241

9 8 7 6 5 4 3 2 1
The paper used in this publication meets minimum requirements of the American National Standard for Information Sciences—Permanence of Paper for Printed Library Materials: ANSI Z39.48-1992.

Typeset in Minion

Composition by Circle Graphics
Columbia, Maryland

Printed by R. R. Donnelley
Harrisonburg, Virginia

Contents

Members of the Brookings-CSIS Task Force
on Transforming Foreign Assistance in the 21st Century

Codirectors

Lael Brainard, vice president, Brookings Institution

Patrick Cronin, director of studies, International Institute for Strategic Studies

Members

Gordon Adams, professor of the Practice of International Affairs and director of the Security Policy Studies Program, George Washington University

Owen Barder, senior program associate, Center for Global Development, and former director of Information, Communications, and Knowledge, U.K. Department for International Development

Rand Beers, former special assistant to the president and senior director for Combating Terrorism, National Security Council, and current president of the Coalition for American Leadership and Security

Rodney Bent, deputy chief executive officer and vice president, Department of Policy and International Relations, Millennium Challenge Corporation

Tish Butler, senior associate, Booz Allen Hamilton

Paul Clayman, chief counsel, Foreign Relations Committee, U.S. Senate

Nisha Desai, Democratic clerk, Committee on Appropriations, Subcommittee on Foreign Operations, Export Financing and Related Programs, U.S. House of Representatives, and former director of public policy, InterAction

Charles Flickner, former staff director, Committee on Appropriations, Subcommittee on Foreign Operations, Export Financing and Related Programs, U.S. House of Representatives

Steven Hansch, senior associate, Georgetown University Institute for the Study of International Migration

George Ingram, executive director, Academy for Educational Development

Carol Lancaster, director, Mortara Center for International Studies, Georgetown University

Mark Lippert, foreign policy adviser, Office of Senator Barack Obama, U.S. Senate

Mary McClymont, former president and chief executive officer, InterAction

Matthew McLean, chief of Staff, Millennium Challenge Corporation

Bruce McNamer, president, Technoserve

Allen Moore, senior fellow, Global Health Council

See Appendix A for a list of all those involved with the task force and its work.

J. Stephen Morrison, director, Africa Program, Center for Strategic and International Studies, and executive director, HIV/AIDS Task Force

Sean Mulvaney, senior legislative assistant, Office of Representative Jim Kolbe, U.S. House of Representatives

Larry Nowels, specialist in foreign affairs, Congressional Research Service

Paul L. Oostburg Sanz, Democratic deputy chief counsel, Committee on International Relations, U.S. House of Representatives

Steven Radelet, senior fellow, Center for Global Development, and former deputy assistant secretary of the U.S. Treasury for Africa, the Middle East, and Asia

Anne Richard, vice president, Government Relations and Advocacy, International Rescue Committee

Ann Van Dusen, adjunct professor, Georgetown University

Foreword

In a world transformed by globalization and challenged by terrorism, foreign aid has assumed renewed importance as a foreign policy tool. With hard power assets stretched thin and facing twenty-first century threats from global poverty, pandemics, and terrorism, the United States must deploy the other tools of national power more effectively. Doing so will require a major overhaul of America's weak aid infrastructure.

The urgent demands of postconflict reconstruction and humanitarian disasters have led to a faster rate of expansion of foreign assistance dollars in the last six years than at any point since the onset of the cold war. Ambitious new international assistance programs have been launched, such as the President's Emergency Plan for AIDS Relief and the Millennium Challenge Corporation. The impact of such programs will not be commensurate with dollars expended as long as America's soft power apparatus is debilitated by incoherence.

U.S. foreign assistance is not guided by a coherent strategic framework but is instead allocated haphazardly to meet successive presidential and congressional imperatives. Within the U.S. government, fifty separate units deliver aid, with a dizzying array of over fifty objectives, ranging from narcotics eradication to refugee assistance. Different agencies pursue overlapping objectives with shockingly poor communication and even worse coordination between them. At best, the lack of integration means that the United States fails to take advantage of potential synergies; at worst, these disparate efforts work at cross-purposes. As a result the United States punches well below its weight class in the international arena—which should be unmatched measured in absolute aid dollars.

Troubled by the risks and costs associated with this incoherence in organization and policy, several distinguished leaders in the field of foreign assistance called for the establishment of an independent, bipartisan Task Force on Transforming Foreign Assistance in the 21st Century. Lael Brainard, vice president of the Brookings Institution, and Patrick Cronin, formerly director of studies at the Center for Strategic and International Studies (CSIS) and currently director of studies at the International Institute for Strategic Studies, assembled a bipartisan, multidisciplinary group of leading experts, including political appointees in the executive branch from successive administrations, congressional staff from both authorizing and appropriating committees in both the House and Senate, academics, practitioners with extensive experience in the field, and representatives of nongovernmental organizations (NGOs) and the private sector. Over a period of fifteen months, the Task Force's deliberations and presentations by current national security and development officials afforded a unique opportunity to test new ideas, to learn from past successes and failures in the field and from the experiences of other donors, and to work toward agreement on best practices in foreign assistance policymaking. The Task Force, under the leadership of Brainard and Cronin, provided a forum for the critical review of papers submitted for publication in this volume, which unifies issues of organizational structure and strategy, policy and operations, congressional and executive branch objectives, and finally, national security and long-term development goals.

The findings of the Task Force have been compiled into *Security by Other Means: Foreign Assistance, Global Poverty, and American Leadership*, edited by Lael Brainard. It includes submissions by Owen Barder (recently of the U.K. Department for International Development), Patrick Cronin, Charles Flickner (recently of the House Appropriations Committee), Stephen Morrison (CSIS), Steve Radelet (Center for Global Development), Steven Hansch (Georgetown University), and Larry Nowels (Congressional Research Service).

The book comes at an opportune time as the Bush administration and members of Congress are contemplating organizational changes to make foreign assistance more effective. We believe this volume offers useful suggestions for members of Congress and the administration, and could serve efforts such as the HELP Commission, as well as the private sector, advocacy groups, and the NGO community. Our chief hope is that it will help lead to meaningful changes in the way the United States provides aid to the citizens of poor nations struggling to achieve a brighter future.

The authors benefited from the collaboration and expertise of many colleagues throughout the course of the project, including the members of the Task Force on Transforming Foreign Assistance, participants in discussions, presentations, and interviews, many of whom are listed in appendix A, and other colleagues and friends. Special thanks are due to George Ingram, Paul Clayman, Nisha Desai, Mary McClymont, Paul Oostburg Sanz, Smita Singh, and Ann Van Dusen for their wisdom and their commitment to the project.

Special thanks are also due to J. Stephen Morrison, who picked up responsibilities for CSIS upon Patrick Cronin's departure, to Benjamin Landy and Zoe Konovalov for their outstanding contributions as associate directors of the Task Force on Transforming Foreign Assistance, to James Pickett as associate editor, and to Tarek Ghani, Katherine Smyth, Eric Haven, Inbal Hasbani, Sarah Zalud, Tristan Reed, Kristie Latulippe, Sarah Cannon, and Emily McWithey for their research and editing assistance.

The authors also wish to thank Starr Belsky and Anthony Nathe for excellent (and rapid) editing and Janet Walker and Susan Woollen of the Brookings Institution Press. The authors remain responsible for the manuscript and its content and any errors or omissions. All the authors or Task Force members do not necessarily agree with all the recommendations in this volume.

This book is part of the Foreign Assistance for the 21st Century Project, coordinated by the Center for Strategic and International Studies and the Brookings Institution in Washington, D.C., and was made possible by a generous grant from the William and Flora Hewlett Foundation, for which we are very grateful. Its contents represent the views, findings, and opinions of the authors and are not necessarily those of the Center for Strategic and International Studies, the Brookings Institution, or the William and Flora Hewlett Foundation.

STROBE TALBOTT
President
The Brookings Institution

JOHN HAMRE
President
Center for Strategic and
International Studies

CHAPTER 1

A Unified Framework for U.S. Foreign Assistance

Lael Brainard

The tragic events of September 11, 2001, together with the protracted unfolding tragedy of the HIV/AIDS pandemic have catapulted America's relations with poor nations to a high priority on our national security agenda. Heightened attention to the plight of the hundreds of millions living in poverty and more than 500 million threatened by infectious disease was discernible both at the highest levels of government and in public discourse in the late 1990s, but it took a fundamental disruption to the security environment to produce bipartisan support for commitment of substantially greater resources.[1]

Since that time funding has grown, and programs and offices responsible for formulating and implementing U.S. policy toward poor nations have proliferated, but with little clarity of purpose and no comprehensive organizational design. Indeed, while development nominally has been elevated to coequal status with diplomacy and defense as part of the president's national security strategy triad, in reality a growing preponderance of funding is directed at postconflict reconstruction, strategic and security objectives, and humanitarian crises. Despite this multiplicity of objectives, critics loudly lament the poor "development" outcomes of assistance never originally designed nor deployed for purposes of long-term development.

Nation-states have been providing official assistance to other states as far back as the 1700s, for much of that time as a means of strengthening security allies. In fact, America first experienced foreign aid as a beneficiary,

I am grateful to Zoe Konovalov for outstanding assistance in writing this chapter. I am also indebted to Charlie Flickner, Patrick Cronin, George Ingram, Eric Lief, and Ben Landy for invaluable insights and suggestions.

when it went hat in hand to request French assistance in the fight against the British.[2] But the notion of using taxpayer monies to promote economic growth in foreign lands is a relatively recent one. The U.S. foreign aid enterprise got into full swing only in the wake of two world wars and with the threat of the cold war looming. Indeed, as Owen Barder points out in chapter 10, even in Britain it was not until the 1920s that British politicians began to debate directing resource flows into their much poorer colonies for development, in sharp contrast to the traditional emphasis on imperial security and markets for British trade. For the United States, the development enterprise did not begin in earnest until the Marshall Plan, where a complex mix of motives can be discerned, including the moral impulse but also the desire to build strong bulwarks against communism in Europe and to restore the critical trade relationships that were so vital to American manufacturing. Today that same mix of interests can be seen.

Foreign assistance is an instrument, not an end in itself. Foreign assistance variously serves to advance national security, national interests, and national values. It works best when there is clarity about the strategic objective it is designed to serve and well aligned with the other instruments of American power: military power, economic exchange, and diplomacy. Unfortunately, at present that sort of clarity and alignment is the exception rather than the rule.

Today, U.S. interests in the developing world have never been greater—in economic, security, and humanitarian terms. Tomorrow, U.S. interests in the developing world will be greater still, as demographic trends project the fastest population growth in those nations least capable of providing adequate economic opportunity, health care, and education to their citizens. A tectonic shift is under way in the global balance of power, as measured in population and resource use. Over the next four decades, the earth's population will grow by 40 percent, and developing countries will account for all of that increase, swelling their ranks to nearly 8 billion—86 percent of the world's population.[3] Moreover, both developed and developing nations confront threats to their security that were scarcely imagined when America's foreign assistance statutory framework was enacted. Yet the United States continues to deploy its primary "soft power" tool through obsolete cold war–era structures. It is high time to step back from the urgent task of moving money out the door and focus on the important enterprise of reorienting American foreign assistance away from cold war tools and concepts and toward twenty-first century realities. This book seeks to respond to that need, starting in this chapter by constructing a unified conceptual framework for U.S. foreign assistance that encompasses strategic and humanitarian objectives and long-term development.

Back in the Spotlight

The international community has increasingly recognized the vital importance of foreign assistance in recent years. An ever-growing chorus of voices has mobilized to prod political leaders toward greater generosity, running the gamut from Christian evangelical groups to human rights activists. The Jubilee 2000 Campaign for third world debt relief was the first major example of the "big-tent" approach, whose success paved the way for subsequent campaigns, including the ONE Campaign in the United States against global AIDS and poverty, and the "Make Poverty History" movement in the United Kingdom.[4]

Celebrity appeal has helped to transform foreign aid from a decidedly unglamorous bureaucratic backwater to one of the hippest topics around. The tireless work of Bono (from the rock group U2) against poverty earned him a Nobel Peace Prize nomination; Irish musician Bob Geldof staged six "Live 8" rockstravaganzas in advance of the 2005 G-8 summit; and MTV broadcast "The Diary of Angelina Jolie and Dr. Jeffrey Sachs in Africa." Public figures have also lent their personal renown to the cause, with Nelson Mandela urging young people to wear white armbands to demonstrate their commitment to combating poverty and Bill Clinton inaugurating the high-profile poverty-centered Clinton Global Initiative in New York City.

Many political leaders are heeding the call. In 2005 alone a trio of key international meetings centered on the fight against global poverty: the Gleneagles Group of Eight (G-8) Summit in July, where British prime minister Tony Blair pledged to put Africa's challenges front and center; the United Nations General Assembly's review of the Millennium Development Goals in September; and the World Trade Organization's ministerial meeting in December, where the fate of the Doha Development Agenda hung in the balance.

But celebrity appeal, international pressure, and powerful advocacy existed before the growing mobilization of foreign assistance in the United States. So too did alarm about the humanitarian calamity of HIV/AIDS and commitment at the highest levels of the U.S. government to combat global poverty, as demonstrated by U.S. support for the Highly Indebted Poor Countries initiative; the UN special session on HIV/AIDS; establishment of the Global Fund to Fight AIDS, Tuberculosis, and Malaria; and agreement on the UN Millennium Development Goals. Yet political impediments proved more powerful still, such as the widely shared skepticism articulated by former U.S. Senate Foreign Relations Committee chairman Jesse Helms when he noted that foreign aid only "lined the pockets of corrupt dictators, while funding the salaries of a growing, bloated bureaucracy."[5]

Indeed, it took the tragedy of September 11, 2001, to unite lawmakers across the political spectrum in support of a sizable increase in American foreign assistance. Two major military interventions, whose scope and duration have not been seen since America's occupation of Japan and Germany, and a succession of humanitarian disasters, including the East Asian tsunami and the Pakistan earthquake, have led to massive increases in U.S. assistance. For the first time since the cold war ended, national security strategists and military experts are making the case that America has vital security interests in effective governance abroad. Indeed, one of the most persuasive advocates of deep U.S. engagement in the least developed reaches of the planet comes not from the development community but from the Naval War College. Thomas P. M. Barnett writes, "If a country is either losing out to globalization or rejecting much of the content flows associated with its advance, there is a far greater chance that the United States will end up sending military forces there at some point."[6]

Although it would have been impossible to discern any interest in the subject from the campaign positions and early foreign policy statements of President George W. Bush, his administration has presided over a virtual doubling of foreign assistance and the creation of new federal entities to administer it, including the Millennium Challenge Corporation, the Office of the Global AIDS Coordinator, the Iraq Coalition Provisional Authority, and the State Department's Office of the Coordinator for Reconstruction and Stabilization. Most recently, the position of director of U.S. foreign assistance was established to oversee all aid funding and programs in the State Department and the U.S. Agency for International Development (USAID).[7]

Despite these important new missions, U.S. government mechanisms for designing and delivering aid have not adjusted to new realities. In fact, the underlying bureaucratic structure of foreign aid delivery has not changed since the 1960s, when John F. Kennedy made overhaul of foreign assistance a key presidential priority and instituted the USAID to rationalize "a haphazard and irrational structure covering at least four departments and several other agencies."[8] Today the U.S. government is struggling with an even greater proliferation of priorities and programs established outside USAID, all the while lacking a single locus for decisionmaking and coordination on aid and unprepared to accommodate the growing importance of nonaid instruments.[9]

But simply moving around the boxes will do nothing to improve the effectiveness and impact of foreign assistance unless the goals to be accomplished are clearly defined and there is broad and deep buy-in. This theme emerges clearly from Larry Nowels' analysis of previous reform efforts.[10] Before any plans for aligning government structures, budgets, and programs can be considered, there must first be agreement on a coherent strategic framework to establish the principal objectives that U.S. foreign assistance is intended to advance and the design of programs to achieve those foreign aid objectives. Indeed, clarity about purpose and strategy is a prerequisite to finding sensible answers to current debates about how much aid is enough, whether the United States is a stingy or generous hegemon, and whether there is a smarter alternative to the traditional approach that delivers short-term stability without long-term reform.[11]

Unified Framework for U.S. Foreign Assistance

Establishing a coherent conceptual framework requires bridging two professional communities engaged in aid policymaking and analysis that start with sharply contrasting frames of reference. National security professionals and political scientists tend to view foreign assistance as a "soft power" tool designed to achieve diplomatic and strategic ends, often through an implicit bargain with the recipient government. In contrast, development practitioners and economic officials tend to view foreign assistance as a resource flow for poverty alleviation and development, implying that assistance should be allocated according to recipients' policy environment and needs. The development community also often favors a quid pro quo but for very different ends: to leverage policies conducive to growth and poverty alleviation. The national security and development communities often talk past each other and sometimes disagree—for instance, during the 1998 financial crisis debate over committing financial stabilization resources to a strategically important but economically feckless country such as Russia.

The strategic framework for U.S. foreign assistance proposed below seeks to integrate these two perspectives by posing two fundamental questions: what is at stake for the United States, and what are the needs and capacities of the country in question? (See figure 1-1.) While potential recipients are identified by their strategic position vis-à-vis U.S. national

Figure 1-1 A Unified Framework for U.S. Foreign Assistance

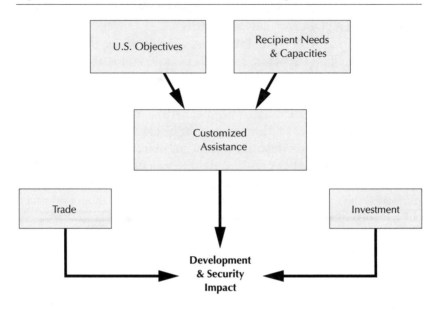

interests, the amount and type of assistance and to whom and how it is distributed are determined by the development efficiency of the investment.

If the first defining dimension of the conceptual framework consists of U.S. objectives, then the second equally important dimension concerns the condition of the intended recipient nations, as defined by the extent of human need and the capacity of national governments to govern and invest aid funds effectively—and where this is lacking, the capacity of subnational or nongovernmental organizations (NGOs) to undertake social investments, governance promotion, and humanitarian interventions. This is clearest in the case of development assistance intended primarily to boost growth and alleviate poverty. Experience suggests and research confirms that development returns are greatest in countries with transparent and accountable governments that are committed to sound fiscal and monetary policies, removing unnecessary impediments to commerce, and investing in primary education and basic health. Achieving the best results from development assistance requires customizing the approach to each recipient's capacity, for instance, by increasing local ownership and control as capacity rises. But even in cases where the United States is pursuing a different primary strategic objective—for example, combating a transnational threat such as HIV/AIDS—recipient capacity should still be the primary determinant of whether foreign aid is distributed directly to the government or through NGOs, whether it is delivered in the form of project assistance or program assistance, and what amount of assistance can be absorbed.

Some aid advocates would argue instead for making the sectoral focus of aid the primary dimension of analysis, noting that the U.S. foreign assistance budget allocations are already divided along primarily sectoral lines, such as child survival and health or counternarcotics operations. The political rationale for such an approach is compelling since the most effective foreign aid advocacy often focuses on concrete results in particular sectors, such as immunization or universal primary education. Sectorwide approaches also hold out the potential for developing powerful solutions to challenges that transcend national borders—such as developing immunizations against tropical infectious diseases or new crop varieties for tropical agriculture. Indeed, I strongly support building deep technical expertise in select sectors, taking advantage of sector-specific transnational public-private partnerships, and greatly expanding investments in research and development that could yield solutions to common problems faced by many poor nations, as happened with the Green Revolution.

Nonetheless, history provides little support for sectoral silver bullets in generating and sustaining accelerated countrywide development. And U.S. interests vis-à-vis its foreign partners are only rarely served by sectoral interventions alone. Thus it makes sense to include sectorwide investments in expertise, technology, and partnerships as a third dimension to the conceptual matrix, while maintaining strategic objectives and capacity as the two primary building blocks. That is not to say that the United States must address the full set of development and poverty challenges in each nation—indeed, there may be compelling reasons for the United States to develop a comparative advantage in certain sectors while leaving other specialties to donors such as the World Bank or the U.K. Department for International Development. But U.S. foreign assistance strategy must begin with a clearheaded assessment of a recipient's full set of interlocking challenges rather than starting with stovepiped U.S. capacity or budget accounts in particular sectors and then trying to make country strategies fit the predetermined capacity.

Once these foundations are mapped out, other important dimensions can be added to the matrix, such as funding modalities and the relationship of assistance to other soft power instruments, including trade or investment policy. Disaggregating the various dimensions of foreign assistance in this way makes clear, for instance, that the degree of over-sight and restrictions on U.S. funds should be influenced more by the quality of the recipient government than by the U.S. program from whence funds are expended, as is the case at present.

U.S. Objectives

The starting point for establishing a coherent approach to foreign assistance must be a clear delineation of the specific objectives to be achieved.[12] As simple and obvious as this might seem, it is remarkable how elusive it has proven in practice, as new missions have been piled on top of old ones. A recent Brookings analysis counted over fifty such objectives among various statutes and agency mission statements—which is tantamount to ensuring few will be performed effectively.[13] What is more, this laundry list is not ordered in any consistent hierarchy.

Aid donors deemed to be the most effective and generous, such as Norway or Denmark, are lauded for their singular focus on economic development. Yet those countries are burdened with neither the colonial history nor strategic entanglements that animate foreign assistance decisionmaking for several important donors, including the United States. As a global power, therefore, the United States deploys foreign assistance to advance several strategic and other objectives in addition to long-term development, but the number of such objectives should be on the order of four or five—well below fifty.

The aid debate evidences considerable confusion on the goals of foreign assistance. Most of the research assesses foreign assistance on the basis of economic development and poverty outcomes—in essence treating all aid as *development* assistance. However, a look at the U.S. foreign assistance budget in any given year makes it clear that only a small fraction of funds is allocated strictly according to economic and poverty criteria—less than 15 percent.[14] The remainder is *allocated* to countries on the basis of other criteria related to America's broader security and other interests or to humanitarian values—or in response to domestic pressures—with a portion of it *spent* on promoting development. For instance, Egypt receives $27 per person in aid from the United States while Ghana receives less than $4 per person, despite the fact that its per capita GDP is approximately half that of Egypt. USAID is perhaps the best symbol of this confusion: America's only agency with "international development" in its title is now devoting about 60 percent of its resources to postconflict reconstruction and humanitarian relief, while the flagship U.S. program that both allocates and spends resources according to development criteria—the Millennium Challenge Corporation (MCC)—is housed elsewhere.[15]

Why this confusion of objectives? Partly it is due to the different professional communities involved in foreign assistance, as discussed above; partly it is attributable to uneven congressional oversight of foreign assistance (see the discussion by Charles Flickner in chapter 8); and in part it is a result of the explosion of presidential initiatives layered on top of existing programs. Sometimes this confusion reflects the gap between the rationale needed to win public and political support and the one that drives policy behind the scenes. Ambiguity often serves the interests of diplomacy even as it muddles the intended outcomes of aid dollars. It would have been impolite at best and damaging at worst to have stated baldly in early 2002 that the aid spigot for Pakistan was turned on to the tune of $3 billion over the next five years in return for critical concessions in draining Afghanistan's murderous swamp—despite strong suspicions that these funds would be invested no more effectively than the $22 billion of past assistance that has yielded neither sustained growth nor democratization.[16] But few would seriously dispute the implicit quid pro quo.

The U.S. foreign aid taps did not get turned on systematically until the global conflagrations of the twentieth century, when the United States used forgiveness of official wartime debts as a backdoor entrance into the aid business. The notion of advancing foreign economic development in its own right did not emerge until the Marshall Plan, which proved a fundamental turning point, raising the ambition and volume of U.S. aid to levels never before seen.[17]

For the subsequent decades, the fight against communism was at the core of U.S. foreign assistance. The presidency of John Kennedy upped the ante with the Alliance for Progress and the creation of the Peace Corps and USAID. Additional goals were layered on during the 1970s and 1980s, when Israel and Egypt became large beneficiaries as part of U.S. strategic engagement in the Middle East. As the cold war wound down into the 1990s, U.S. assistance was increasingly directed toward facilitating transition in Eastern Europe and the former Soviet Union as well as toward humanitarian relief, counternarcotics efforts in the Andean countries, and global health challenges, instead of rewarding sometimes unsavory cold war allies as it had in the past.

Today, the United States confronts new global threats and opportunities associated with the growing importance of developing nations.

Below I propose encapsulating them in five strategic objectives to guide foreign aid:
—supporting the emergence of capable partners,
—countering security threats from poorly performing states,
—countering security threats with foreign partners,
—countering humanitarian threats, and
—countering transnational threats.

These are the subjects of subsequent chapters of this book. Figure 1-2 provides a strategic map of the world that shows broadly how these strategic objectives correspond to America's engagement (or lack thereof) in particular countries and regions.

Supporting the Emergence of Capable Partners

For an important group of developing nations, there is a subtle and often not well articulated U.S. strategic priority at play: the goal of strengthening the capacity of states imprinted with similar values and economic and political systems. Nations with similar systems and values advance America's national interest and national security by virtue of their intrinsic nature rather than through sometimes short-lived bargains. They act as stabilizers and economic anchors within their regions. They also fill the role of like-minded associates, taking similar positions in international negotiations and often partnering in international endeavors. Indeed, nowhere was this strategic objective clearer than in the Marshall Plan, where America sought not only to strengthen European economies but also to ensure that European nations would share America's systems of liberal democracy and market economy as well as antipathy to communism.

Viewed in this broader perspective, America deploys foreign assistance as a primary tool in a set of policies designed to strengthen societies with shared values and similar economic and political systems. Technical assistance and trade and investment policies also figure prominently. The implicit aim, shared with like-minded allies, is to nurture a community of nations broadly oriented toward peaceful coexistence, open markets, and liberal democratic governance and sharing similar impulses regarding questions of global governance, international cooperation and exchange, and national rights and responsibilities. Economic development lies at the core of this enterprise; citizens of nations that provide economic and political opportunity, as well as security, are far more likely to share common values and interests and to demand and sustain democratic reform.

Figure 1-2 Strategic Map of the World

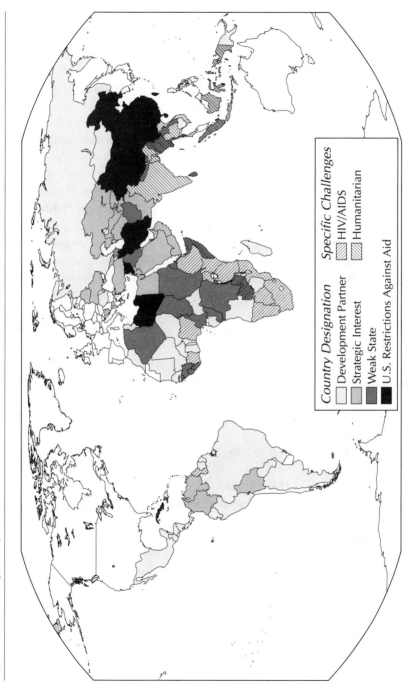

Source: Author's rankings based on data from the United Nations and the World Bank and from U.S. budget documents.

Paradoxically, although these are the nations where U.S. values and interests are most closely aligned and where development investments are likely to have the most sustained payoffs, this category of assistance accounts for a relatively small share of the overall pie. Bilateral development assistance—defined as funding that is both *allocated* and *spent* according to poverty and development impact rather than political criteria—accounts for only about 15 percent of the total foreign assistance budget.[18]

Indeed, U.S. bilateral foreign aid has played only an indirect role (arguably through the Green Revolution) in the ascent out of poverty of hundreds of millions of people in India and China in recent years. The cases of China, India, and Vietnam are useful reminders of the complicated set of drivers that determine U.S. foreign assistance allocations, with the development and poverty impact only one of several considerations.

The international donor community is in growing agreement on a set of principles for making such development assistance maximally effective:

—To achieve commitment and buy-in, recipient governments rather than donors should "own" the setting of priorities and the design and implementation of programs.

—Stakeholders should be involved in prioritization through a transparent process.

—Monitoring and evaluation should be a part of the program design from the start rather than an afterthought added halfway into the program.

—Funding modalities should be differentiated so that flexibility can increase along with the capacity, openness, and accountability of the recipient government.[19]

One international donor currently attempting to observe many of these principles is the Global Fund to Fight AIDS, Tuberculosis, and Malaria. Unfortunately, in the United States, there is a tension between implementation of these principles and congressional and public support for a sectoral approach to assistance, such as targeting funding to child survival, education, or trade capacity building.

Perhaps the most important principle is that development assistance should be differentiated according to the capacity of the recipients. For the group of poor nations that performs best, development assistance should be allocated according to some metric of efficiency or effectiveness. In the U.S. aid system, the Millennium Challenge Corporation most closely approximates such an approach, determining eligibility—although not aid allocations—according to transparent measures of capacity (or more accurately, policy virtue) and need. With the MCC up and running, it is critical for the United States to focus greater attention and resources on strengthening the middle and bottom tiers within this strategic category. Many populous countries in Africa, in particular, fall into a middle tier where state capacity is moving in the right direction but is uneven and vulnerable to reversals. And the poor nations with fragile state capacity also merit more sustained development attention than they receive currently, lest they cycle back into conflict and possibly join that group of poorly performing states that poses security threats. Carefully customized investments in these less capable states are currently an area of near neglect despite important potential benefits.

Democracy or Governance?

During the second term of the Bush administration, the agenda of spreading shared values and institutions was progressively narrowed down to democratization, variously labeled as "the freedom agenda" and "transformational diplomacy." Secretary of State Condoleezza Rice has elevated transformational diplomacy to a primary principle of U.S. foreign policy. "The Secretary's objective of transformational diplomacy, articulated in remarks at the Georgetown School of Foreign Service on January 18, 2006, is to 'work with our many partners around the world to build and sustain democratic, well-governed states that will respond to the needs of their people—and conduct themselves responsibly in the international system.' "[20]

While there is broad support and mounting evidence for the virtues of liberal democracies that emerge organically on the foundations of robust political and societal institutions, there is nonetheless controversy surrounding the ability of foreign powers to transplant democracy into societies where existing institutional foundations are weak. Indeed, administration officials have acknowledged the uncertainties of elevating democratization to the primary organizing principle for diplomacy and foreign assistance. In the words of one administration official, "On this question of . . . not having a theory . . . it's true. This is a very hard problem and we don't have a clear theory about how to go about it. Do we need organic change in which we have to do everything at once? Can we identify certain key sectors? Can we isolate some sectors?"[21]

The success of Hamas—considered an extremist group in the United States—in the Palestinian elections shortly after Secretary Rice enshrined transformational diplomacy as a primary principle of foreign policy served to dramatize the inherent contradictions in this agenda. The

complexity of the task before the United States is summarized thought-
fully by Francis Fukuyama:

> The final area that needs rethinking, and the one that will be the most contested
> in the coming months and years, is the place of democracy promotion in Amer-
> ican foreign policy. . . . The United States has played an often decisive role in
> helping along many recent democratic transitions. . . . But the overarching les-
> son that emerges from these cases is that the United States does not get to decide
> when and where democracy comes about. By definition, outsiders can't "impose"
> democracy on a country that doesn't want it; demand for democracy and reform
> must be domestic. Democracy promotion is therefore a long-term and oppor-
> tunistic process that has to await the gradual ripening of political and economic
> conditions to be effective.[22]

There is strong evidence that healthy economies are vitally important
for vibrant democracies, although scholarly research remains divided over
democracy's contribution to economic development.[23] According to Adam
Przeworski,

> The evidence is overwhelming that if democracy emerges in a country that is
> already [economically] modern, then it is much more likely to survive. No
> democracy ever fell in a country with a per capita income higher than that of
> Argentina in 1975—US$6,055. This is a startling fact given that throughout
> history about 70 democracies have collapsed in poorer countries. In contrast,
> 35 democracies spent a total of 1,000 years under more affluent conditions, and
> not one collapsed. Affluent democracies survived wars, riots, scandals, and eco-
> nomic and governmental crises.[24]

Historically, the United States government has supported democratization through different means under different circumstances and with very
different degrees of success. In important cases, such as Taiwan and South
Korea, strong and prosperous democracies have emerged after decades of
channeling substantial economic assistance to decidedly undemocratic
regimes. The United States also assisted successful democratization in the
Philippines, Chile, and a series of Eastern European nations and former
Soviet republics. But in other nations benefiting from substantial aid flows,
such as Egypt and Ethiopia, neither economic development nor democracy has emerged on a sustained basis.[25]

By contrast, there are no such complications associated with the objective of strengthening *governance*—loosely defined as transparent and
accountable government, predictable and fair administration of laws and
regulations, and restraint on corruption. Good governance is a sine qua non
of the development process and essential for a variety of other objectives,
including reducing conflict and containing transnational threats such as

pandemics, illegal narcotics, and weapons proliferation. The World Bank and the broader research community have measured and tested a wide variety of institutional features that differentiate the governance environment in various countries, with results that are starting to provide concrete guidance for practitioners in the field.[26] In recent years America increasingly has used foreign assistance to pursue governance reforms either through program content or conditions for eligibility. Indeed, the newest U.S. development agency, the Millennium Challenge Corporation, for the first time makes progress on corruption and "ruling justly"—although not democracy per se—an explicit criterion for eligibility. Nonetheless, actually achieving good governance remains an implementation challenge.

Countering Security Threats from Poorly Performing States

At the other end of the spectrum lies the foreign assistance most visibly related to national security, deployed to counter threats to the United States, its allies and partners, and the international order in general. Such threats encompass not only the traditional security concerns about terrorism and proliferation of weapons of mass destruction but also activities that jeopardize supplies of vital resources, such as energy. Conceptually, countering security threats can be treated as a single objective, but in reality there are two sets of challenges that merit separate analysis and program design. The first set arises from working around governments—and often with nonstate entities—to fill a dangerous void created by a weak state or to head off conflict. The second set arises from working with foreign governments whose goals are aligned with specific U.S. objectives, for instance on counterterrorism or counternarcotics, and whose capacities are sufficient to make them effective.

The terrorist attacks of September 11 initiated a paradigm shift in foreign aid no less than that occurring in national security and a far-ranging debate on the nature of the existential threats facing the nation. The destruction of the World Trade Center in New York was followed quickly by the destruction of the comfortable myth that dysfunctional states abroad were of little concern to the United States.

Within a three-year time span, the same president who as a candidate had derided nation building would be engaged in two nation-building efforts whose scope had not been seen since MacArthur's heyday in Japan and Germany. For Afghanistan alone the U.S. foreign assistance operations budget would double, driven by an ambitious effort to fundamentally transform the society, political system, and economy of a conflict-ridden state that had been abandoned a decade earlier after it no longer was central to the cold war.[27]

When state institutions weaken or dissolve in the face of protracted conflict, a power vacuum often occurs that facilitates the growth of terrorism and transnational threats. Poorly performing states often contribute to humanitarian crises and damage stability in their regions. When measured in dollar terms, countering the threats that emanate from dysfunctional states has become the highest priority of foreign assistance in the early twenty-first century. Estimates of the number and importance of states that are highly vulnerable to conflict and failure suggest this will remain a high priority into the foreseeable future.[28] Although the recent attention to the dangers posed by poorly performing states is welcome, not all such states pose equal or indeed in some cases material—threats to U.S. security. Thus, within this category, it is important to be precise about where American vital interests might be threatened.

This category of foreign assistance has two components: prevention of conflict and postconflict stabilization and reconstruction. In part because the U.S. government has not systematically or effectively invested in the first, it is now engaged knee deep in dealing with the second.

Despite being involved in a myriad of postconflict interventions in recent years, of varying levels of ambition and commitment (Somalia, Bosnia, Kosovo, East Timor, Afghanistan, Liberia, and Iraq), the U.S. government remains surprisingly poorly organized for such engagements— especially on the civilian side.[29] Thus, at the close of 2005, the Bush administration for the first time released parallel directives seeking to strengthen the dual civilian and military pillars of reconstruction operations.

The U.S. capacity to prevent conflict is even weaker, as evidenced by the repeated cycling of many countries (such as Haiti, Liberia, and Ethiopia) in and out of conflict over long periods of time, despite U.S. involvement. Here the urgent tends to crowd out the important, despite expert analysis that suggests that preventive assistance to provide economic opportunity, address abject poverty, and strengthen governance would be far less costly than stabilizing and reconstructing the same country after it has succumbed to conflict.[30]

Increasingly, there is recognition that the United States would be far more effective if it mounted a sustained effort to address this set of security threats. In past efforts a fresh U.S. interagency apparatus has been invented anew to deal with each successive country in conflict, treating each situation as a unique case.[31] Of late, however, there is a growing appreciation—within the administration, among the expert and practitioner communities, and among some dedicated members of Congress—of the value of dealing with this set of potential threats in a systematic manner that would engender institutional learning and a growing body of tested analytical and operational approaches.

Countering Security Threats with Foreign Partners

The terrorist attacks elevated the importance of a related set of national security concerns, which Patrick Cronin and Tarek Ghani dub the four C's: counterterrorism, counterproliferation, counternarcotics, and coalition building.[32] The difference between countering dysfunctional states and addressing this broader set of security threats lies in the degree to which the U.S. government works with or against foreign governments. The United States generally deploys security or strategic assistance to advance the four C's by working *with* governments rather than *against* or *around* them in order to achieve the desired goals. But providing support to often repressive governments in order to achieve short-term vital interests frequently conflicts with America's longer-term interests in promoting open and democratic societies—a paradox that is prompting a major rethinking of the traditional approach to security and strategic assistance.

Counterterrorism has received the greatest attention since September 11, and funding for it has increased substantially. It has also evolved in interesting directions. As narrowly defined, counterterrorism still entails security assistance to governments to help strengthen their capacities for counterterror cooperation. However, its scope has broadened to include assistance designed to bring greater economic and political opportunity to areas where political and economic stagnation increase susceptibility to extremist ideology.

Traditionally, U.S. security and strategic assistance programs—which ranged from cash payments and debt relief to training and equipping the militaries of strategic allies—promoted stability rather than potentially destabilizing reform. During the cold war, the main objective of containing the Soviet Union was advanced by military and other assistance to nations based on their opposition to Soviet policies, regardless of their own record on domestic political freedom. In the wake of September 11, that approach is undergoing revision, as security strategists increasingly believe that open and democratic societies are the only sure long-term weapon against terrorism, which thrives in the dank corners of closed and repressive societies. This is reflected in the National Intelligence Council's 2020 report: "A counterterrorism strategy that approaches the problem on multiple fronts offers the greatest chance of containing—and ultimately reducing—the terrorist threat. The development of more open political systems and representation, broader economic opportunities, and empowerment of Muslim reformers would be viewed positively by the broad Muslim communities who do not support the radical agenda of Islamic extremists."[33]

But as discussed earlier, the "freedom agenda" is a path fraught with uncertainties because of the inherent tension between the principle of supporting open, democratic societies and the practical need to work with existing regimes on urgent problems. This tension between short-term stability and longer-term reform in the U.S. security agenda cannot easily be resolved, as pointed out by Francis Fukuyama: "We need in the first instance to understand that promoting democracy and modernization in the Middle East is not a solution to the problem of jihadist terrorism; in all likelihood it will make the short-term problem worse, as we have seen in the case of the Palestinian election bringing Hamas to power."[34]

In dollar terms America continues to place far greater emphasis on bribing nondemocratic states than on promoting their democratization. For example, funding for the president's signature Middle East Partnership Initiative, which focuses on economic, educational, and political reform, was only 2 percent of overall U.S. economic assistance to the Middle East in fiscal year 2005.[35] Thus a strategically important government resisting reform, such as Egypt, can still count on receiving the great majority of its aid package intact. Despite ranking in the bottom twentieth percentile of the World Bank's governance indicators, Egypt receives nearly $30 per person in U.S. foreign assistance. In contrast, India has better governance than over half of all other countries by this same measure, yet receives 16 cents per person. In fact, as shown in figure 1-3, countries with better governance ratings actually receive less U.S. assistance on average.

Rewarding foreign nations for strategic cooperation is the oldest purpose of foreign aid. Shoring up alliances and foreign support more generally remains a potent motivation for aid in dollar terms, encompassing both direct military assistance and indirect economic assistance. During the Bush administration, much of this activity has come under the rubric of "coalition building"—whether in taking on the Taliban in Afghanistan or enforcing the peace in Iraq. With coalition building no less than with

Figure 1-3 Foreign Assistance Is Not Given to Countries That Will Use It Well[a]

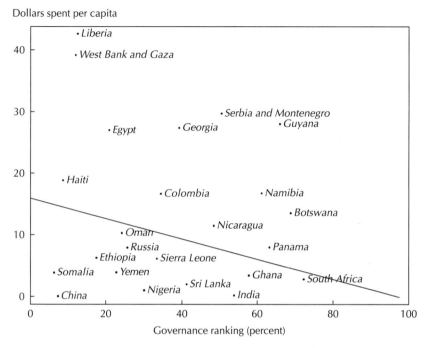

Dollars spent per capita

Governance ranking (percent)

Source: Per capita foreign aid spending data are based on USAID, "U.S. Overseas Loans and Grants [Greenbook]" (qesdb.cdie.org/gbk/index.html [August 2006]). Governance rankings are determined from World Bank, "Governance Indicators: 1996–2004" (www.worldbank.org/wbi/governance/govdata/index.html [August 2006]).
a. The graph shows a subset of countries for purposes of clarity. The correlation line is based on the entire sample (Israel and Micronesia are excluded). Notable countries excluded from the picture but not from the sample include Iraq, with per capita aid of $309 and governance indicator of 4.4, and Afghanistan, with $65 in per capita aid and a governance score of 65.4.

counterterrorism, there is often the uncomfortable necessity to address urgent security goals by cooperating with regimes—such as those in Uzbekistan and Pakistan—that violate human rights or democratic norms. This puts the United States in the contradictory position of relying on cooperation with an unsavory regime at the same time it is seeking to circumvent it by strengthening the forces of reform.

After the September 11 attacks, Americans woke up to the potentially catastrophic consequences of weapons of mass destruction falling into the hands of terrorists—arguably, the single most potent threat to national security today. This injected fresh urgency into counterproliferation efforts, in particular the farsighted Nunn-Lugar Cooperative Threat Reduction Program, created in the 1990s to address the potential for proliferation of weapons of mass destruction from the new states of the former Soviet Union. New and nascent nuclear powers hostile to the United States pose an equally chilling threat, one where foreign assistance would become relevant only if a diplomatic solution were to emerge, as for instance, in the case of Libya.[36]

Finally, the United States uses both trade and foreign assistance to help strengthen resistance to the illegal narcotics trade in developing nations. Both the funding and priority assigned to this objective have grown sharply in recent years, along with increased recognition that the illegal narcotics trade poses serious national security threats by enriching and empowering criminal syndicates and possibly terrorist groups and thereby undermining legitimate governments, breeding chaos and instability. U.S. counternarcotics strategy is focused in particular on the illegal cocaine and heroin trade from Colombia and Afghanistan. Here, as in other areas of foreign assistance geared toward security ends, there is an ongoing debate between short-term expediency and longer-term investments—in this case in regard to the relative emphasis to be placed on the short-term agenda of eradication and interdiction as opposed to the longer-term agenda of building vibrant economic alternatives and strong, accountable governments.

Countering Humanitarian Threats

While national security motivations for official foreign aid resonate with lawmakers and opinion leaders in Washington, the American people are moved by generosity of spirit and moral conviction. The level of private giving testifies to the strength of this impulse: during the 2004 tsunami relief effort, U.S. private donations of $1.9 billion eclipsed U.S. government donations of $656 million.[37] More generally, private giving for humanitarian emergencies is roughly equally to U.S. official assistance.

Strong public support translates into strong congressional support and substantial budget allocations. As a result this is one area of foreign assistance where the U.S. truly shines, bumping up against its spending ceiling in donations to most U.N. humanitarian aid categories. The United States is by far the biggest single humanitarian donor in the world and among the most effective and technically well equipped. While development assistance has declined in real terms over the past two decades, humanitarian assistance has grown strongly.[38] Steven Hansch estimates that humanitarian assistance could represent half of total foreign assistance in ten years if current trends continue.[39] A key challenge for the powerful advocacy groups, rock stars, public figures, and faith-based groups is to help extend the visceral emotional connection that many Americans feel with foreigners afflicted by humanitarian disasters to other types of giving, particularly longer-term development aid.

America's strong demonstration of humanitarian generosity is all the more remarkable considering that a purely altruistic motivation for official foreign aid is a relatively recent historical phenomenon. Nation-states have long given each other aid, true, but traditionally in the name of their own self-interest—whether in developing the productive capacity of a colony, rewarding a partner in a military alliance, or stimulating foreign export markets.[40]

Humanitarian assistance is a cost-effective endeavor, measured in a variety of ways, and has evolved toward an increasingly evidence-based and scientifically equipped enterprise. Indeed, in a little-known success, deaths from famines have almost vanished, thanks to a sophisticated famine early warning system developed by the United States.[41]

Although both wars and deaths from wars have declined, complex emergencies—those involving violent conflict—are expected to place an increasing demand on humanitarian relief in the years ahead. Yet one of foreign aid's weakest links is in regard to transitions into and out of complex emergencies: preventing a country from slipping over the edge in the first place and supporting the transition from humanitarian relief to long-term economic and political development. This is partly due to the inherent difficulty of bringing order and stability to conflict-threatened societies. But it also reflects the reactive and sporadic attention of political leaders and the American public alike, who demonstrate an outpouring of generosity for tsunami victims while at the same time seeming indifferent to the silent tragedy of the far more numerous deaths from preventable infectious diseases and the suffering endured by the more than 1 billion people living on less than $1 a day.[42]

Countering Transnational Threats: The HIV/AIDS Pandemic

Globalization has elevated the profile of so-called transnational threats—those that defy containment within national borders and require concerted action to combat effectively. Within that category infectious diseases, such as avian flu, pose one of the greatest natural threats confronting humanity in the twenty-first century, despite enormous advances in science and technology. Perhaps nowhere are the consequences more evident today than in the HIV/AIDS pandemic, which is not only a humanitarian crisis but also threatens the long-term development prospects, health and education sectors, government capacity, and security of poor nations.

The U.S. response to the global HIV/AIDS pandemic was thwarted for many years by political dissension due to the nature of the disease and its uncomfortably close connection to issues of sexuality and, in the eyes of some, morality. It was also limited by the high cost of effective treatment and uncertainty about the ability of health systems in poor countries to implement complicated treatment regimes over a sustained period. However, over time the cost of antiretroviral drugs declined, and evidence of effective treatment in poor communities emerged. In addition, in an important shift, the evangelical community decided to join with committed advocates across the political spectrum in support of U.S. engagement in the global fight against HIV/AIDS. These changes catalyzed a realignment of political forces that enabled a massive increase in U.S. assistance.[43]

Even though the U.S. aid response to HIV/AIDS is in a category of its own, it presents a fascinating case study of many of the issues concerning U.S. foreign assistance. The breadth and intensity of the coalition supporting the effort is both a blessing and a curse, as deep-seated divisions over issues such as condom use lead to life-threatening delays in program design. As its name suggests, the President's Emergency Plan for AIDS Relief (PEPFAR) is a signature presidential initiative whose design bears distinctive marks associated with the proclivities of a particular president and the person he chose to lead the effort. There are questions about the staying power of a program that has the qualities of a sprint-like emergency operation and yet embodies an American promise to provide a growing population of foreigners with life-saving treatment for an indefinite period at considerable cost. As a single-disease program, PEPFAR benefits from the clarity of purpose, intensity of support, and measurable results of a vertical approach, but its format precludes the synergies that come from collaborating with the broader health sector and the governance strengthening engendered by an integrated, horizontal approach. Assertively bilateral, PEPFAR sits uneasily alongside the multilateral Global Fund to Fight AIDS, Tuberculosis, and Malaria, which was established with considerable U.S. support two years earlier to address the same problem—a situation that underscores the administration's frequent impatience with multilateral institutions. And the uneasy coexistence of the office administering PEPFAR within the State

Department is an interesting test case, which early on demonstrated some of the limitations of seeking operational support from a primarily policy-oriented organization.

Multilateral and Bilateral Approaches

With all of its foreign assistance programs, the United States faces a choice of providing aid directly to recipients through bilateral programs or using its substantial leverage through the multilateral development banks (chief among them the World Bank), as well as through UN aid programs. Despite its instrumental role in creating these multilateral institutions and its out-sized role in funding and directing them, the United States harbors sub-stantial ambivalence about going the multilateral route. Of course, in particular circumstances, multilateral assistance may be poorly suited to the pursuit of America's most vital strategic interests, especially where security assistance is concerned or where there is an important quid pro quo involved. But multilateralism would seem to be a very attractive alterna-tive where interests among donors are well aligned, for instance, in help-ing states vulnerable to conflict, tackling humanitarian emergencies and HIV/AIDS, and, especially, promoting long-term development. Despite this, the current administration has shown a decided aversion to multi-lateral approaches, especially in the latter two categories where major new bilateral programs have been initiated.

Yet, in principle, more reliance on multilateral institutions for devel-opment assistance could be more efficient and effective for several reasons. First, in principle, the multilateral development banks should be less sus-ceptible to idiosyncratic political considerations and therefore more likely to direct funding to the highest-returning investments—those in countries with accountable governance and virtuous policies—although there are many exceptions in practice. Second, lack of donor coordination is one of the great drains on recipient government managerial resources: the more donors, the greater the number of idiosyncratic conditions to meet, sepa-rate funds to administer, and forms to fill out.

Recipient Capacity and Needs

Thus far in this discussion the focus has been on delineating the various *strategic objectives* that foreign assistance is designed to serve. Now it is time to examine the second critical component of a conceptual framework for foreign aid: *recipient capacities* and *needs*. Indeed, as is clear from the discussion of countering security threats, state and broader societal capacity are tightly interwoven with considerations of strategy.

Consideration of U.S. national security interests and values is inevitable in allocating assistance, but it is also critical to assess recipients along a continuum of capacity and need to ensure that aid dollars have the best chance of achieving their ends. For those developing nations that are viewed primarily through a development lens, such assessments can help limit the amount of political interference in aid allocations. Even for those countries whose strategic importance guarantees them some amount of aid, detailed assessments of need and capacity can help determine how aid dollars should be spent—whether through the national government, NGOs, or subnational governments, and whether on social or productive sectors—as well as shape funding arrangements, such as degree of flexibility and type of oversight.

A strict focus on development and poverty impact, with no reference to strategic importance, would argue strongly for allocating aid according to a formula based on measures of need and effectiveness alone.[44] Several aid organizations already use fairly formulaic approaches to determine eligibility and country rankings, although less so to determine amounts of aid. The Millennium Challenge Corporation uses a relatively transparent formula to determine eligibility—although not amounts of funding—based on performance relative to the median for sixteen indicators measuring control of corruption, ruling justly, providing economic opportunity, and investing in people.[45] The World Bank employs a somewhat more analytically grounded approach with its performance-based allocation system, which is based on country policy and institutional assessments scores measuring sixteen policy and institutional components. Unlike the MCC the World Bank uses its formula to determine the *amount* of funding among the poorest countries. Paul Collier and David Dollar have developed a formula to measure the "poverty efficiency" of an aid dollar invested in different countries and propose allocating aid according to its imputed poverty efficiency.[46]

There is substantial research on aid effectiveness that provides metrics for categorizing recipient capacity and need. The international community teems with indicators designed to measure almost every aspect of developing country needs and capabilities, and substantial empirical research analyzes the relationship between different capacity measures and the contribution of assistance to growth.

The simplest unitary metric of needs is per capita income, which the World Bank uses to separate countries into categories eligible for different types of financing. The MCC also applies this metric to determine the pool of countries to be considered for eligibility. The UN has created a more multidimensional metric, the Human Development Index, an assessment based on several criteria including life expectancy, knowledge (measured by literacy and school enrollment), and standard of living (measured by GDP per capita). And most recently, the eighteen targets included in the UN Millennium Development Goals provide internationally agreed-upon measures of developing country progress, based on various indicators. In measuring government capabilities, the World Bank has become a primary resource for data relating to governance, voice and accountability, rule of law, corruption, days to start a business, and regulatory quality. Transparency International publishes a widely used Corruption Perceptions Index, while Freedom House rates countries on their civil liberties.[47]

Figure 1-4 provides a simple look at the relationship between recipient needs and capabilities, using the UN Human Development Index to proxy the extent of need and an index based on World Bank governance indicators to proxy government capacity. It shows that countries afflicted with poor governance also generally suffer the most severe human needs; this relationship is robust to a different choice of capacity measure and to controlling for population size.

Patience and Opportunity

U.S. foreign assistance needs to be characterized by patience and commitment while also being sufficiently flexible to capitalize on strategic windows of opportunity. A great deal of U.S. foreign assistance has been on autopilot for a decade or more, remaining stable from year to year, with modest increments or declines off the baseline, and then shifting into overdrive to cope with the latest humanitarian emergency. But the long-term nature of development argues for greater patience and more extended disbursement of funds than is generally seen today and for maintaining a commitment to a region until the job is done.

However, it is also important to be able to deploy assistance rapidly to capitalize on those windows of opportunity that have truly transformational potential. The clearest examples are cases where a country has emerged from conflict into a fragile peace or where newly elected leaders in a young democracy must quickly demonstrate some type of democracy

Figure 1-4 Poor Governance and Humanitarian Need Go Hand in Hand[a]

Governance capacity

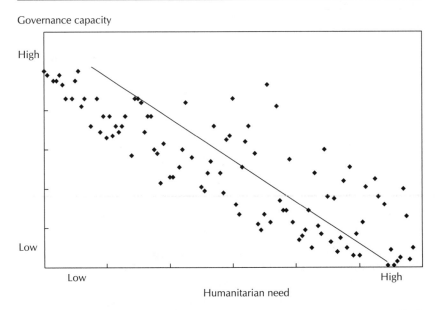

Humanitarian need

Source: Governance capacity is measured by the Rule of Law Index from World Bank, *2004: Worldwide Governance Research Indicators Dataset* (Washington: 2004). Humanitarian need is based on the UN Human Development Index; see United Nations Development Program, "Human Development Report 2005" (hdr.undp.org/reports/global/2005 [August 2006]).
   a. Correlation statistics: $R^2 = 0.67$; population-weighted $R^2 = 0.74$.

dividend to impatient constituents with unrealistic expectations. As has been recognized by some members of Congress, the U.S. government needs a more robust capacity to anticipate these opportunities and to quickly commit technical assistance, including security assistance, as well as funding, trade preferences, investment guarantees, and debt relief where appropriate.

The Right Tool for Some Circumstances—But Not All

Although foreign assistance is a critical tool in advancing American values, interests, and security, an old aphorism reminds us that having a hammer in hand creates a temptation to treat all problems as nails.[48] Foreign assistance is not an appropriate tool for all circumstances and may sometimes be counterproductive or impotent or profitably replaced with trade or technical assistance. Most obviously, while foreign assistance may be critical in promoting reform in resource-poor countries in the Middle East, it is the wrong tool for promoting such economic and political modernization in oil-rich countries.

As middle-income countries such as Brazil and Mexico develop increasingly sophisticated production capacities and economic systems, favorable access to the global marketplace through trade and investment opportunities and technical assistance on policy, legal, and regulatory frameworks are far more powerful drivers of transformation than bilateral foreign assistance. (Nonetheless, a case can be made for limited, targeted foreign assistance in some middle-income countries that are home to large concentrations of the world's poorest citizens.) More broadly, advancing economic and political modernization in the developing world increasingly requires a seamless web of policies encompassing foreign assistance (where appropriate), along with trade and investment, technical assistance, debt relief, and financial stabilization. To be an effective partner, the U.S. government will need a much more coherent approach, not only across its foreign assistance programs but also across the entire portfolio of policies affecting the prospects of developing countries.

A Unified Approach to Foreign Assistance for the Twenty-First Century

The very utility of foreign aid has been challenged, not only by politicians but by academic experts who have questioned the contribution of aid to growth and poverty alleviation.[49] And yet some researchers have found average returns of up to 30 percent on development aid projects.[50] But setting even this fact aside, this debate focuses too narrowly on the effects of development-targeted aid as measured by GDP growth and ignores the many other criteria for determining the success of aid: the lives saved due to mass immunization campaigns and oral rehydration therapy, the immeasurable benefits of peace, the famines averted thanks to USAID's Famine Early Warning System, and the hunger and malnutrition averted due to the Green Revolution.

The United States faces enormously different challenges and opportunities in dealing with developing nations today compared with twenty or even ten years ago. And yet, U.S. foreign assistance is hampered by a lack of clarity about its strategic aims and has failed to customize aid approaches appropriately and set realistic goals. Thus the moment has come to constitute a new, unified political conception of the purpose and design of U.S. foreign assistance. Only in so doing will it be possible to improve coherence across the executive branch, establish a productive executive-legislative partnership, and gain public support for the critical role of foreign assistance in advancing America's security, interests, and values.

The unified framework proposed here attempts to integrate America's twenty-first century objectives—supporting capable foreign partners and countering security, humanitarian, and transnational threats—with the particular needs and capacities of poor countries. Promising sectoral approaches can also be accommodated as a third cross-cutting dimension to this framework. Without such a unified framework, it is pointless to rearrange organizational boxes or redefine budget accounts. With it in place, however, seemingly intractable questions of design, structure, and organization start to suggest their own solutions. With clarity of purpose, not only will the U.S. government be better equipped to assess performance, but the critical tool of foreign assistance will be rendered far more powerful.

Notes

1. The figure of 500 million includes global figures for people with tuberculosis (15,430,000), malaria (408,388,001), HIV/AIDS (40,300,000), as well as other diseases. See "Data by Topic" (www.globalhealthfacts.org/bytopic.jsp?va=1 [May 2006]).

2. See "American Revolution," in *Columbia Encyclopedia*, 6th ed. (Columbia University Press, 2005), 1: 276–78.

3. The 2004 revision of the official United Nations population estimates and projections estimated that the world's population will grow from 6.5 billion today to 9.1 billion in 2050. All of that growth will come from developing countries; the population of developed nations will hold stable at 1.2 billion. United Nations, *State of World Population 2005* (New York, 2005).

4. For more information on these movements, see Third World Traveler, "Jubilee 2000 Campaign" (www.thirdworldtraveler.com/Reforming_System/Jubilee_2000.html [April 2006]); "ONE: The Campaign to Make Poverty History" (www.one.org [April 2006]); and "Make Poverty History" (www.makepovertyhistory.org [April 2006]).

5. Jesse Helms, "Towards a Compassionate Conservative Foreign Policy," speech given at the American Enterprise Institute, Washington, January 11, 2001.

6. Thomas P. M. Barnett, *The Pentagon's New Map: War and Peace in the Twenty-First Century* (New York: Putnam's Sons, 2004).

7. U.S. Department of State, "Director of U.S. Foreign Assistance" (www.state.gov/f/ [November 2006]). In January 2006 Ambassador Randall L. Tobias was named the nation's first U.S. foreign assistance director while serving concurrently as administrator of USAID with a rank equivalent to deputy secretary. He is charged with "directing

the transformation of the U.S. Government approach to foreign assistance." When this book went to press, the nature and scope of this transformation were still unknown.

8. John F. Kennedy, "Special Message to the Congress on Foreign Aid," March 22, 1961, in *Public Papers of the President: John F. Kennedy, 1961* (Government Printing Office, 1962), pp. 203–12.

9. See Lael Brainard, chapter 2 this volume.

10. See chapter 9 in this volume.

11. Although the U.S. government is currently the top donor in absolute terms, contributing $16.3 billion or just under 25 percent of the $69 billion in development assistance given by the world's twenty-two top donors in 2003, critics argue that this share is far below America's 40 percent share of total donor income. See David Roodman, "An Index of Donor Performance," Working Paper 67 (Washington: Center for Global Development, August 2005). One oft-quoted statistic is that when aid is measured as a share of national income, the United States ranks last among developed countries at 0.15 percent. (Top givers include Norway, at 0.92 percent; Denmark, at 0.84 percent; Belgium, at 0.60 percent; and Germany, at 0.28 percent.) See online database at Organization for Economic Cooperation and Development (www.oecd.org/dac/stats [May 2006]). When measured in per capita terms, U.S. aid comes to $51 per citizen, ranking it sixteenth among donor countries. Some argue that when the calculations include the substantial private donations from U.S. citizens, the United States is far more generous than its ranking would suggest. Others would go further, arguing that U.S. military and strategic support for international peacekeeping should also count toward its foreign aid contribution.

12. See Lael Brainard, "Compassionate Conservatism Confronts Global Poverty," *Washington Quarterly* 26, no. 2 (2003): 149–69.

13. See Lael Brainard and others, *The Other War: Global Poverty and the Millennium Challenge Account* (Brookings, 2003).

14. Based on the sum of aid assigned to development assistance, the Millennium Challenge Account, and multilateral development banks. See Department of State, "FY 2005 International Affairs (Function 150) Budget Request," February 2, 2004 (www.state.gov/s/d/rm/rls/iab/2005). Even this figure is an overestimate; consider the case of aid to Pakistan, discussed below, and purportedly assigned to the development assistance account.

15. See USAID, "Congressional Budget Justification FY 2005" (www.usaid.gov/policy/budget/cbj2005 [May 2005]). Even the Millennium Challenge Corporation, arguably the most fair and transparent U.S. development aid program, has been criticized for using political considerations to allocate aid, notably in the case of Georgia. A Center for Global Development paper stated, "Apparently, the MCC Board wanted to support Georgia's political transition and newly elected president, Mikhail Saakashvili. While this goal is certainly justifiable from a U.S. foreign policy perspective, it is not an appropriate use of MCA [Millennium Challenge Account] funds. It would have been much more appropriate to support Georgia with resources from the State Department's Economic Support Fund (ESF) that is targeted for such purposes, instead of through the MCA that is aimed for countries with a demonstrated commitment to strong policies and institutions." See Sarah Lucas and Steve Radelet, "An MCA Scorecard: Who Qualified, Who Did Not, and the MCC Board's Use of Discretion," May 2004 (www.cgdev.org/doc/commentary/MCAScorecard_0528.pdf [April 2006]).

16. See Department of State, "Remarks with Pakistan Foreign Minister Mian Kursheed Mehmood Kasuri," Islamabad, Pakistan, March 18, 2004 (www.state.gov/secretary/former/powell/remarks/30540.htm [April 2006]). See also Mumtaz Anwar and Katharina Michaelowa, "The Political Economy of U.S. Aid to Pakistan," Discussion Paper 302 (Hamburg Institute of International Economics, November 2004), table 1.

17. See Robert Wood, "Book Review: Bipartisan Strategy: Selling the Marshall Plan," *Naval War College Review* 57, no. 1 (2004): 1–6; Diane Kunz, "The Marshall Plan Reconsidered: A Complex of Motives," *Foreign Affairs* 76, no. 3 (1997): 162–70; David Ellwood, "You Too Can Be Like Us: Selling the Marshall Plan," *History Today* 48, no. 10 (1998): 33–39.

18. This figure is necessarily imprecise since the current format of the U.S. International Affairs Budget (also known as the "150 Account") lumps together both politically motivated and developmental aid.

19. These principles and their applicability to U.S. foreign assistance are analyzed by Steve Radelet in chapter 4.

20. Department of State, "Secretary of State Condoleezza Rice" (www.state.gov/secretary/ [April 2006]).

21. See comments of Stephen Krasner in Center for Global Development, "Transformational Diplomacy," transcript, January 20, 2006 (www.cgdev.org/doc/event%20docs/Krasner%20Transcript.pdf [April 2006]).

22. Francis Fukuyama, "After Neoconservatism," *New York Times Magazine,* February 19, 2006, pp. 10–19.

23. See, for instance, the differing viewpoints of Fareed Zakaria, *The Future of Freedom: Illiberal Democracy at Home and Abroad* (New York: W. W. Norton, 2003), and Mort Halperin, Joe Siegle, and Michael Weinstein, *The Democracy Advantage: How Democracies Promote Prosperity and Peace* (New York: Routledge, December 2004).

24. Adam Przeworski, "A Flawed Blueprint: The Covert Politicization of Development Economics," *Harvard International Review* 25, no. 1 (2003): 42–47.

25. In another example, in more recent years, all U.S. assistance to Zimbabwe has been channeled through nonprofits and other private actors to avoid government control. In 2002 Congress passed the Zimbabwe Democracy and Economic Recovery Act to require that nation's government to reform its conduct before the U.S. representative at the World Bank would vote for new aid to Zimbabwe.

26. See Daniel Kaufmann, "Back to Basics—10 Myths about Governance and Corruption," *Finance and Development* 42, no. 3 (2005): 41–43. See also R. Gaston Gelos and Shang-Jin Wei, "Transparency and International Portfolio Holdings," *Journal of Finance* 60, no. 6 (2005): 2987–3020.

27. Emergency supplemental spending for Afghanistan compared for 2000 to 2003 period. See Department of State, "FY 2005 International Affairs."

28. Paul Collier and Anke Hoeffler, "Aid, Policy and Growth in Post-Conflict Societies," *European Economic Review* 48, no. 5 (2004): 1125–45.

29. See the discussion by Patrick Cronin in chapter 6 of this volume.

30. See Carnegie Commission, *Report on Preventing Deadly Conflict* (New York: Carnegie Press, September 1997); *Report of the Panel on United Nations Peace Operations* (New York: United Nations, August 21, 2000); *Prevention of Armed Conflict, Report of the Secretary-General* (New York: United Nations, June 7, 2001).

31. Steven D. Krasner and Carlos Pascual, "Addressing State Failure," *Foreign Affairs* 84, no. 4 (2005): 26–35.

32. See chapter 7 in this volume.

33. National Intelligence Council, *Mapping the Global Future: Report of the National Intelligence Council's 2020 Project* (Government Printing Office, December, 2004).

34. Francis Fukuyama, "After Neoconservatism," *New York Times Magazine,* February 19, 2006, p. 10–19.

35. Jeremy M. Sharp, "U.S. Foreign Assistance to the Middle East: Historical Background, Recent Trends, and the FY2006 Request," Report RL32260 (Congressional Research Service, Library of Congress, June 13, 2005).

36. World Food Programme, "Libya's Desert Corridor—Realising a Logistical Dream," December 22, 2005 (www.wfp.org/english/?ModuleID=137&Key=1961 [April 2006]).

37. USAID, "Fact Sheet: Tsunami Assistance, One Year Later," December 21, 2005 (www.usaid.gov/press/factsheets/2005/fs051221.html [April 2006]).

38. For a discussion of the decline in development assistance, see Curt Tarnoff and Larry Nowels, "Foreign Aid: An Introductory Overview of U.S. Programs and Policy," Report 98-916 (Congressional Research Service, Library of Congress, April 15, 2004).

39. See chapter 5 in this volume.

40. The first instance of official U.S. humanitarian assistance was a grant to Colombian earthquake victims in 1812.

41. See chapter 5.

42. World Bank, *World Development Indicators 2005* (Washington, 2005).

43. The evolution of the resulting U.S. foreign assistance initiative is examined by Stephen Morrison in chapter 3 of this volume.

44. For a more detailed exploration, see Radelet in chapter 4.

45. For analysis of the pros and cons of this median-based methodology, see Brainard and others, *The Other War;* Lael Brainard and Allison Driscoll, "Making the Millennium Challenge Account Work for Africa," Policy Brief 123 (Brookings, September 2003); and Steven Radelet, *Challenging Foreign Aid: A Policymaker's Guide to the Millennium Challenge Account* (Washington: Center for Global Development, 2003).

46. David Dollar and Paul Collier, "Aid Allocation and Poverty Reduction," Working Paper 2041 (Washington: World Bank, 1999).

47. See Transparency International, "Corruption Perceptions Index 2005" (www.transparansi.or.id/cpi/2005/media_pack_en.pdf [April 2006]); Freedom House, "Freedom in the World 2006" (www.freedomhouse.org/uploads/pdf/Charts2006.pdf [April 2006]).

48. Attributed variously to either psychologist Abraham Maslow or to the financier and statesman Bernard Baruch.

49. See Craig Burnside and David Dollar, "Aid, Policies, and Growth," *American Economic Review* 90, no. 4 (2000): 847–68; Radelet and Bhavnani, "Counting Chickens When They Hatch: The Short-Term Effect of Aid on Growth," Working Paper 44 (Washington: Center for Global Development, July 2004); and Raghuram G. Rajan and Arvind Subramanian, "What Undermines Aid's Impact on Growth?" Working Paper (Washington: International Monetary Fund, June 2005).

50. Carl-Johan Dalgaard and Henrik Hansen, "The Return to Foreign Aid," Working Paper 609 (Washington: World Bank, May 2005).

CHAPTER 2

Organizing U.S. Foreign Assistance to Meet Twenty-First Century Challenges

Lael Brainard

The smartest policy and the biggest increase in resources in the world will not improve the success of America's aid enterprise without fundamental organizational and operational transformation. Well-meaning increases in resources could be vitiated by the realities of bureaucratic turf battles, lack of coordination with international efforts, and contradictory approaches across the many U.S. policies affecting countries receiving U.S. assistance.

At any given time, in any particular developing country, any or all of over fifty separate government units could be operating separate aid activities with distinct objectives, implementing authorities, reporting requirements, and local points of contact.[1] Figure 2-1 lists a subset of government organizations involved in foreign aid and links them to a bewildering array of objectives (see appendix B for a full list). Some U.S. ambassadors coordinate the aid efforts under their nominal authority, but most do not. Yet coordination in the field looks enviably simple when compared with the overlapping jurisdictions in Washington.

In recent years there has been a breathtaking succession of new foreign assistance imperatives. While congressional appropriations earmarks

The author wishes to thank Zoe Konovalov for outstanding research assistance, Charlie Flickner and George Ingram for thoughtful suggestions, and members of the Brookings–Center for Strategic and International Studies Task Force on Transforming Foreign Assistance in the Twenty-First Century for their insights and expertise.

Figure 2-1 U.S. Foreign Assistance Objectives and Organizations

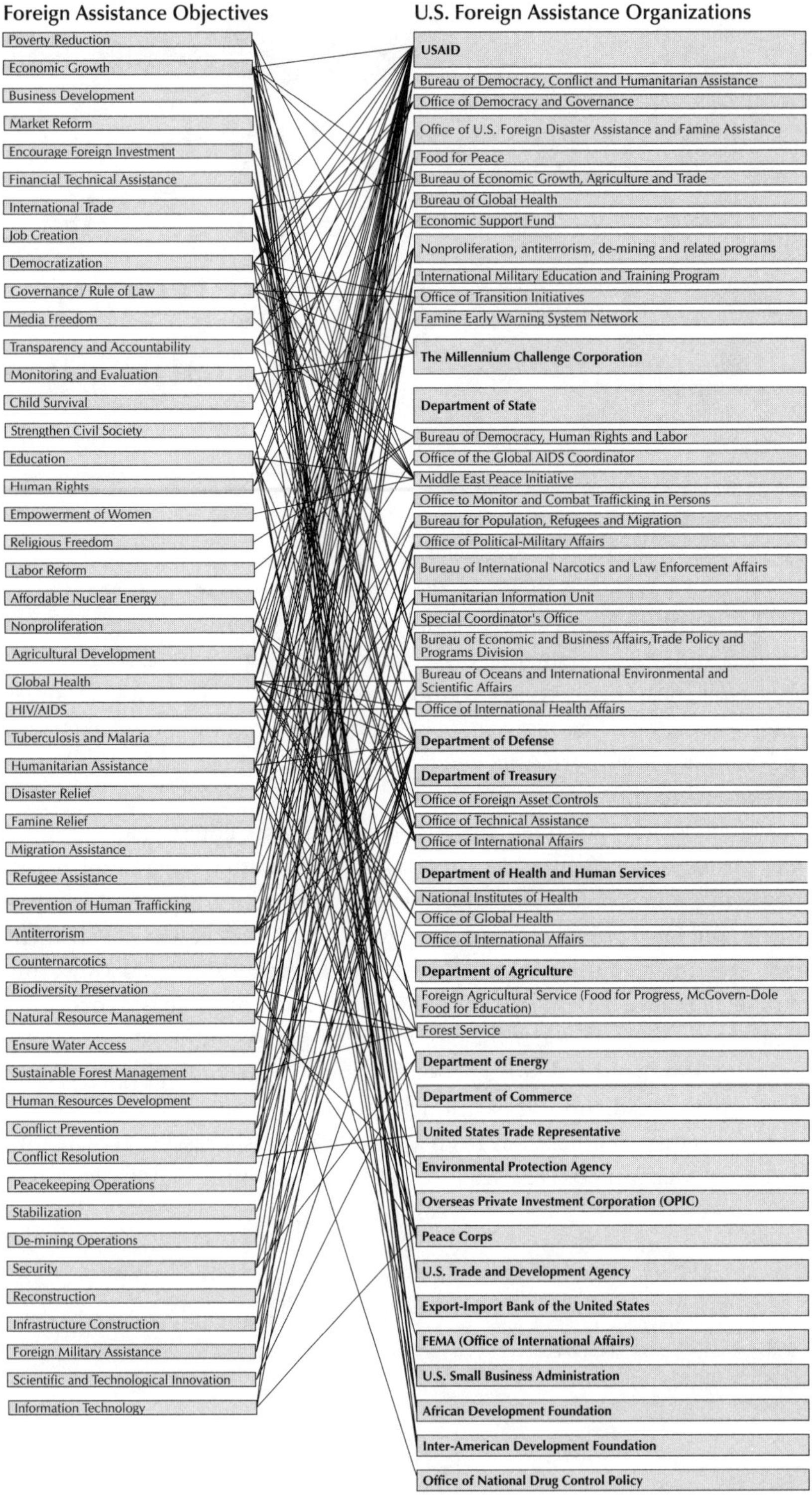

Foreign Assistance Objectives

- Poverty Reduction
- Economic Growth
- Business Development
- Market Reform
- Encourage Foreign Investment
- Financial Technical Assistance
- International Trade
- Job Creation
- Democratization
- Governance / Rule of Law
- Media Freedom
- Transparency and Accountability
- Monitoring and Evaluation
- Child Survival
- Strengthen Civil Society
- Education
- Human Rights
- Empowerment of Women
- Religious Freedom
- Labor Reform
- Affordable Nuclear Energy
- Nonproliferation
- Agricultural Development
- Global Health
- HIV/AIDS
- Tuberculosis and Malaria
- Humanitarian Assistance
- Disaster Relief
- Famine Relief
- Migration Assistance
- Refugee Assistance
- Prevention of Human Trafficking
- Antiterrorism
- Counternarcotics
- Biodiversity Preservation
- Natural Resource Management
- Ensure Water Access
- Sustainable Forest Management
- Human Resources Development
- Conflict Prevention
- Conflict Resolution
- Peacekeeping Operations
- Stabilization
- De-mining Operations
- Security
- Reconstruction
- Infrastructure Construction
- Foreign Military Assistance
- Scientific and Technological Innovation
- Information Technology

U.S. Foreign Assistance Organizations

USAID
- Bureau of Democracy, Conflict and Humanitarian Assistance
- Office of Democracy and Governance
- Office of U.S. Foreign Disaster Assistance and Famine Assistance
- Food for Peace
- Bureau of Economic Growth, Agriculture and Trade
- Bureau of Global Health
- Economic Support Fund
- Nonproliferation, antiterrorism, de-mining and related programs
- International Military Education and Training Program
- Office of Transition Initiatives
- Famine Early Warning System Network

The Millennium Challenge Corporation

Department of State
- Bureau of Democracy, Human Rights and Labor
- Office of the Global AIDS Coordinator
- Middle East Peace Initiative
- Office to Monitor and Combat Trafficking in Persons
- Bureau for Population, Refugees and Migration
- Office of Political-Military Affairs
- Bureau of International Narcotics and Law Enforcement Affairs
- Humanitarian Information Unit
- Special Coordinator's Office
- Bureau of Economic and Business Affairs, Trade Policy and Programs Division
- Bureau of Oceans and International Environmental and Scientific Affairs
- Office of International Health Affairs

Department of Defense

Department of Treasury
- Office of Foreign Asset Controls
- Office of Technical Assistance
- Office of International Affairs

Department of Health and Human Services
- National Institutes of Health
- Office of Global Health
- Office of International Affairs

Department of Agriculture
- Foreign Agricultural Service (Food for Progress, McGovern-Dole Food for Education)
- Forest Service

Department of Energy

Department of Commerce

United States Trade Representative

Environmental Protection Agency

Overseas Private Investment Corporation (OPIC)

Peace Corps

U.S. Trade and Development Agency

Export-Import Bank of the United States

FEMA (Office of International Affairs)

U.S. Small Business Administration

African Development Foundation

Inter-American Development Foundation

Office of National Drug Control Policy

and committee report directives pose a relatively constant set of complications, a whole new level of complexity has arisen from the recent proliferation of presidential initiatives lodged in a confusing array of new offices without any pruning of existing mandates and programs.

Why has this confusion been allowed to progress, and how difficult would it be to overcome? The history of U.S. foreign assistance reforms is sobering.[2] As is clear from the recent creation of the Department of Homeland Security, fundamental organizational overhaul is achieved only once every few decades at significant political cost and often with initially mixed results.[3]

Are new challenges in the international environment sufficiently important and the existing bureaucracy sufficiently besieged to warrant the major political investment required for a fundamental organizational shake-up? I believe the answer is yes, although I suspect there is no political momentum for such a change yet. Indeed, in the Organization for Economic Cooperation and Development (OECD), nearly half of the twenty-two members of the Development Assistance Committee have undertaken a major reorganization of foreign assistance in the last decade.[4] For example, the creation of the Department for International Development (DFID) in the United Kingdom points to circumstances where major organizational changes can yield significant improvements in policy and operations while also giving a powerful boost to a donor's influence on the international stage.[5]

The British DFID experience as well as the old dictum that form follows function serve as reminders that a successful organizational overhaul must be premised on clarity of purpose and supported by a growing political consensus—neither of which yet exists.[6] For that reason I recommend using the Bush administration's recent recognition of the need for reform as a welcome opening to kick off a process of deliberations and congressional engagement akin to the process undertaken in the years leading up to the 1986 Goldwater-Nichols Act mandating defense reorganization.

Below I suggest seven principles that should guide an organizational transformation: clarity of mission; speaking with a unified voice; realization of synergies across policy instruments; alignment of policy, operations, and budget; focus on core competencies; investment in knowledge for development; and elevation of the development mission. I then lay out four possible models for organizing foreign assistance to fulfill the unified framework laid out in chapter 1, evaluate each model for its ability to address the aforementioned principles, and make recommendations about improving foreign aid effectiveness, both on the margins and more fundamentally if an opportunity arises.

Principles for Effective Organizational Design

The last fundamental overhaul of the foreign assistance structure took place in 1961, when President John F. Kennedy instituted the U.S. Agency for International Development (USAID) by gathering together a myriad of aid programs.[7] President Kennedy set out the many failings of U.S. foreign assistance in a special message to Congress:

> No objective supporter of foreign aid can be satisfied with the existing program—actually a multiplicity of programs. Bureaucratically fragmented, awkward and slow, its administration is diffused over a haphazard and irrational structure covering at least four departments and several other agencies. The program is based on a series of legislative measures and administrative procedures conceived at different times and for different purposes, many of them now obsolete, inconsistent and unduly rigid and thus unsuited for our present needs and purposes. Its weaknesses have begun to undermine confidence in our effort both here and abroad.[8]

Four decades later, President Kennedy's critique applies with even greater force. The problems he described have returned in more acute form, with a fungus-like proliferation of programs and priorities, the absence of a single locus of decisionmaking and coordination on aid, and the lack of coherence across aid and increasingly important nonaid instruments. The sweeping reform undertaken by Kennedy also holds important lessons for today. It required personal commitment and political capital on the part of the nation's chief executive to fundamentally transform the system. The reform embodied an emerging bipartisan consensus about the strategic challenges confronting the nation and the important role of foreign assistance in addressing them. Transformation was undertaken to realign U.S. government structures and operations against profound new challenges as the United States and its allies moved beyond postwar reconstruction to cold war containment.

The last successful effort to significantly overhaul the Foreign Assistance Act occurred in 1973. Since that time new programs have been instituted either through the appropriations process, such as the Plan Colombia/Andean Counterdrug Initiative of 2000 and the Millennium Challenge Act of 2004, or through stand-alone authorizations, such as the Support for Eastern European Democracy Act of 1989, the "Nunn-Lugar"

Soviet Nuclear Threat Reduction Act of 1991 and Cooperative Threat Reduction Act of 1993, the Freedom Support Act of 1992, and the Leadership against Global HIV/AIDS, Tuberculosis, and Malaria Act of 2003. In areas not covered by these new initiatives, the cold war–era Foreign Assistance Act continues to govern most foreign assistance, despite the breathtaking changes to the international landscape that have taken place since it was enacted in 1961.[9]

Principle 1: Rationalize Agencies and Clarify Missions

Recent foreign assistance objectives have been accommodated through new programs and new institutions without reforming or reorganizing the existing structure, which was designed for different challenges in a different era. Partly as a result, the OECD now counts as many as fifty separate units in the U.S. government that deliver aid.[10] There also has been a notable expansion of involvement by the Department of Defense in foreign assistance activities ranging from humanitarian assistance to policing to postconflict reconstruction without concomitant expansion of the coordinating structures and rules to ensure effective civilian and military collaboration.[11]

Max Weber's ideal of a modern bureaucracy involves a division of labor into fixed jurisdictions, a clear chain of command, and stable, specialized, and consistent rules.[12] By contrast, America's foreign assistance bureaucracy has mutable jurisdictions, an unclear chain of command, and inconsistent rules and policies. For example, the assistance programs under the Support for Eastern European Democracy Act (which targets central and eastern Europe) and the Freedom Support Act (which targets the components of the former Soviet Union) are implemented by more than a dozen U.S. agencies and coordinated by a state department official whose authority is confined to his own department and USAID.

Recent years have witnessed a proliferation of new presidential initiatives, many housed in policy rather than operational agencies. The design of the new Office of the Global AIDS Coordinator would seem to confound every tenet of good organizational design. In the words of former USAID administrator M. Peter McPherson, "How does one explain the HIV/AIDS program? What would Peter Drucker say about being able to hold anyone accountable when the money is in HHS, the policy in the Department of State, and the implementation in both AID and HHS?"[13] Meanwhile, the new and largest assistance program to promote development, the Millennium Challenge Corporation, has been housed in a new stand-alone agency while the existing agency with "international development" in its name, USAID, has been increasingly redirected to postconflict reconstruction and assistance for strategic states.

Indeed, it is common for agencies to suffer from mission creep as their responsibilities undergo de facto changes. For example, the Office of Transition Initiatives within USAID was created by President Clinton to help navigate the transition from short-term emergency relief and stabilization to longer-term reconstruction, but it subsequently gravitated toward activities related to civil society and governance, leaving an important gap in U.S. capabilities.[14] Belated recognition of the critical need for a coordinated U.S. strategy for anticipating, preventing, and responding to complex emergencies resulted in the creation of yet another new office in August 2004, the Coordinator for Reconstruction and Stabilization (CRS), this time placed within the State Department.[15] Over a year later, in December 2005, National Security Presidential Directive 44 clarified the State Department's role as the lead civilian coordinator in planning and executing stabilization and reconstruction operations.[16] Yet despite filling a clear need identified by senior Senate authorizers and supported by the administration, operational funding for the CRS was rejected by congressional appropriators, who requested a comprehensive coherent strategy detailing how the CRS will function.[17]

Policymakers have struggled with some of these problems for years, but a combination of unwillingness to expend political capital at the highest levels and political pressures has stymied policymakers' abilities to fight bureaucratic inertia.[18] Poor communication between the executive branch and Congress has exacerbated the problem.[19]

Recent experience suggests it is much easier to add a new program, office, or even agency than to tame the existing morass of competing centers. In an effort to wrestle with the growing sprawl of initiatives, the secretary of state in January 2006 designated the administrator of USAID as the director of foreign assistance with the rank (although not position) of deputy secretary of state and the mandate to provide strategic direction, coordination, and guidance over U.S. foreign assistance.[20] Yet the new director of foreign assistance lacks formal, statutory authority even over the Offices of the Coordinator for Reconstruction and Stabilization and the Global AIDS Coordinator within the State Department—let alone over assistance programs administered by the Departments of Defense or Agriculture, for instance, or the myriad of other U.S. foreign assistance activities housed in other agencies.[21]

A bolder effort will ultimately be required. The number of players within the executive branch must be rationalized, a clear division of labor among them defined, and the power to coordinate among them assigned and enforced. Reducing the number of players, eliminating overlapping jurisdictions, and bringing coherence to the overall effort is critical to achieving better value for the growing fiscal resources directed to foreign assistance in an environment of fiscal belt tightening.

It is difficult to imagine that a reorganization process could be successfully led by one of the competing agencies—although the elevation of one agency over others might logically be the outcome. The bureaucratic infighting over the best home for the Millennium Challenge Account illustrates how difficult it is to leave aside agency loyalties in determinations of this type.[22] Within the executive branch, only the president is capable of assigning responsibilities and defining a clear chain of command

Ideally, the White House would lead an executive branch process to review each of the objectives foreign assistance is designed to achieve and assign prime responsibility for each to a single agency or office. The president can delegate ongoing interagency coordination to one of the agencies involved, but White House senior staff must play an active role in setting out the overall framework for decisionmaking and implementation. Failing a deliberate strategic process, at minimum there should be a moratorium on the creation of new offices or agencies associated with foreign assistance unless an existing office is closed down for each new entity created.

Congress also has an integral role in clarifying missions and imposing organizational discipline. By holding hearings, mandating Government Accountability Office analysis of the current structure, requesting expert input on alternative organizational structures, and holding the line on creating new organizational entities to house additional presidential initiatives, Congress could play a much more active and constructive role in shaping the organization and delivery of U.S. foreign assistance.

Principle 2: Speak with a Single Voice

The current sprawl of different agency roles and responsibilities generates confusion as to which official speaks for the U.S. government on foreign assistance issues in the field and international forums, where negotiations and agreements frequently cut across U.S. agency responsibilities. At a time when coordination of assistance among donors has been recognized as one of the most important principles for increasing aid effectiveness, the

United States appears to be moving in the other direction—lacking coordination within its own ranks and often de facto requiring recipients to navigate a maze of different sets of program criteria and reporting requirements associated with different offices and agencies within the U.S. government.[23] For instance, with funding for U.S. bilateral HIV/AIDS programs variously coming from the State Department, USAID, the Department of Health and Human Services, or the Centers for Disease Control, one could legitimately be confused as to which of these agencies represents the official U.S. position at an international HIV/AIDS conference or where to turn to discuss U.S. policy.[24] The situation is reputedly better for security assistance, where the U.S. regional commanders or the NATO structure bring more discipline to military assistance in key countries.

Recent years have seen greatly increased international emphasis on donor coordination as a key principle in making development assistance more effective. The costs associated with multiple donors include the transaction costs of arranging ministry visits, staff time consumed in detailed reporting according to each donor's specification, and often the need to reconcile different donors' competing priorities. A plethora of donor organizations in a region, with their need for skilled local personnel, often poach sorely needed workers from the local bureaucracy, creating a "brain drain." In an attempt to measure this phenomenon, Stephen Knack and Aminur Rahman found that donor fragmentation was predictive of lower recipient bureaucratic quality.[25]

A study conducted in the 1990s found that a typical African country prepared 2,400 donor reports every quarter and hosted 1,000 meetings a year; for some countries, such as Tanzania, the estimate is far greater.[26] Suggesting that the marginal cost of accepting aid equaled its marginal benefit, in 2003 Tanzania declared April through July to be a "quiet time," during which only the most urgent visits would be accepted from donor officials.[27] Agreements within the OECD and the 2003 Rome Declaration on Harmonization commit donors to support the priorities and objectives embodied in national strategies developed by recipient nations themselves, to coordinate and cooperate with other donors in providing support, and to support recipient governments' own systems for planning, implementation, and evaluation rather than creating burdensome parallel mechanisms.[28]

Given this context, the United States must undertake a concerted effort to coordinate its own internal practices and procedures. This means doing the hard work of resolving interagency inconsistencies internally rather than leaving it to recipient nations to navigate them. It means creating a system of one-stop shopping in recipient nations, with clear coordination among different program staff in the field and a simplified set of reporting requirements so that the United States does not impose undue burdens on limited recipient capacity. Ultimately, it means developing unified U.S. government-wide approaches for each recipient nation.

Indeed, the critical need for internal coordination on the civilian side of the U.S. foreign assistance enterprise has been one of the major themes emerging from the ongoing postconflict operations in both Iraq and Afghanistan. Defense officials, finding themselves increasingly drawn into foreign assistance, scratch their heads at the jumble of civilian agencies at the table and lament the absence of a primary counterpart on the civilian side.[29] Reflecting these experiences, several task force reports have recommended changes to make the civilian side of postconflict operations a more unified and operationally capable partner.[30]

Only when it acts as a single coordinated donor can the United States engage effectively with other donors. Speaking with a single voice would also boost American influence in the international development debate over the terms, conditions, and purposes of foreign assistance. For example, by concentrating authority over development policy in an independent agency vested with cabinet status, the United Kingdom not only elevated the stature of development within its own government but also boosted U.K. influence in framing the international debate on assistance disproportionately to its international donor ranking.[31] The reverse is probably true of the United States today: it wields international influence below what one might expect of the world's largest donor, in part because of the multiple competing entities representing America abroad. In one of many recent examples of unconventional roles, the U.S. Defense Department comptroller led the international effort to raise funds for assistance to Afghanistan.

Principle 3: Achieve Synergies across Policies

At a time when the international community has identified policy coherence as a second core principle for aid effectiveness, the United States continues to stovepipe decisions on the key policy instruments affecting nations it seeks to support. More often than not, the United States underutilizes its weight in the soft power arena because coordination across different development policy instruments is ad hoc at best and frequently simply absent.

Foreign assistance is but one of several increasingly important tools that implement U.S. policies toward developing countries; others include trade agreements and disputes, investment provisions, financial stabilization policies, debt relief, and economic sanctions. Indeed, for many middle-income countries with sizable poor populations and for countries such as China, where there are political strictures, foreign assistance has long since given way to trade and investment policies as America's primary soft power levers.

Although there could be important synergies among the various policy instruments, they are often used in isolation, without reference to each other. Thus, for example, determinations on investments in rural infrastructure and agricultural extension in cotton-growing parts of Africa are made by USAID, determinations on subsidies for American cotton farmers are made by the Department of Agriculture and Congress, and determinations on America cotton trade barriers are made by the Office of the U.S. Trade Representative (USTR)—all separately, as if they had no bearing on one another. More generally, decisions regarding the multiple policies jointly affecting the development prospects of poor nations are made by different agencies within the U.S. government according to different criteria in an uncoordinated manner. The Department of the Treasury determines debt and financial stabilization policies and U.S. positions on multilateral lending through its guidance over the international financial institutions; the USTR determines trade policy and international intellectual property enforcement primarily based on commercial objectives; the Department of Agriculture and Congress are dominant in setting U.S. agricultural policy and food aid; and the Commerce Department wields influence over U.S. trade remedies affecting imports from developing countries. Significantly, neither USAID nor the Millennium Challenge Corporation (MCC) has the official standing to influence any of these nonaid instruments, although the inclusion of the secretary of the treasury and the U.S. trade representative on the MCC board is a positive step.

While foreign assistance is increasingly important, it is only one tool in a larger toolkit that includes debt policies, volunteer services, trade and investment agreements, and military support for peacekeeping and humanitarian missions. Even without becoming the world's most generous official donor relative to its income, the United States could wield greater influence per aid dollar spent than any other nation simply by deploying its influence in world trade and investment and debt and financial policies in a deliberate manner as a force multiplier. Ideally, decisions on each policy should be made with a view to ensuring the entire package is mutually reinforcing and more powerful than the sum of its parts.

In principle, for any set of decisions surrounding policy that materially affects developing countries, all relevant agencies should be at the table—including an entity that represents America's interests in economic development and poverty alleviation. White House coordination is the best way of ensuring that everyone is at the table, formulating a unified and internally consistent policy, and bestowing primacy on one particular agency to carry out the policy. But often when the White House provides direction through the official deputy secretary and cabinet-level decisionmaking processes, key players, most notably USAID, MCC, and USTR, do not have the official standing that guarantees their participation.[32] These critical players depend on the goodwill of the convener and must expend time lobbying and cajoling to secure a place at the table. Moreover, as recent experience has shown, the White House staff is generally stretched thin and can be consumed by crises. Thus White House coordination can be expected for the highest priority issues, but for decisionmaking that requires sustained attention and also for joint planning and operations, effective mechanisms for both coordination and integration must be empowered at lower levels at a designated agency.

In contrast, the reorganization of foreign assistance undertaken by the United Kingdom officially assigned the cabinet-level Department for International Development the lead on development issues that cross ministry jurisdictions, empowering it to represent the interests of developing countries in the trade policymaking process and providing incentives such as extra budgetary resources for cross-ministry collaboration.[33] This has institutionalized a powerful position for DFID within the cabinet structure rather than making its status dependent on the kindness of competing bureaucracies and the prime minister's staff.

Thus regularized mechanisms for coordination and integration of policy are critical—either across agencies or by providing authority to a single empowered agency. But integration across agencies is just as critical at the level of planning and operations, as illustrated by recent experiences with postconflict reconstruction. Integration of operations and planning across agencies will require removal of disincentives and creation of incentive mechanisms, such as reserving special budgetary funds to reward effective interagency collaboration on priority goals and tying

career advancement to interagency rotations and participation in interagency joint operations.

Principle 4: Align Policy, Operations, and Budget

Getting foreign assistance right hinges fundamentally on operational effectiveness. The current system defies basic management principles by sepa-
rating policy from operations and both from budgeting. Currently, there
is clear separation of policymaking from implementation for a large share
of foreign assistance programming. For many categories of foreign assistance, policy is determined by a set of decisionmakers at the State Department while implementation is in the hands of a wholly separate set of
USAID officials. Perhaps the best example is the Economic Support Fund,
where the secretary of state makes the allocation decision among countries, her regional bureaus seek to make detailed programming decisions,
and the administrator of USAID is held responsible for the performance of
the country programs. Similarly, the Treasury Department determines
U.S. positions in the International Monetary Fund and the World Bank
boards on both financial stabilization programs and debt relief with no
requirement to consult USAID in the affected countries, despite the reality
that USAID may have valuable familiarity with conditions on the ground
and important program investments at stake. The divide between policy
and operations is particularly acute at the highest levels of executive branch
decisionmaking—the principal and deputy secretary levels—where the policy agencies (State and Treasury Departments) have a seat at the table and
the implementing agencies (USAID, MCC) do not.

Although this kind of separation can be understood as a reasonable
accommodation of competing bureaucratic claims, no organizational textbook would recommend it. Implicitly, it assumes that aid decisions can be
made solely on the basis of policy considerations—such as U.S. objectives—
without regard to the technical aspects of the particular sectoral or functional activity or to feedback from implementers in the field. In the words
of former USAID administrator M. Peter McPherson, "I question the whole
idea that policy can generally be separated organizationally from the implementation. How do you decide that a road should be built as a matter of
policy without having the technical input or the capacity to understand
such input as to the practicality of the road?"[34] This process is further complicated because the State Department and USAID budget offices track
funding with two different systems that cannot easily be cross-referenced:

the State Department uses a country-based system, and USAID uses one based on accounts.

In addition to fully integrating policy and operations, it is critical to reconnect U.S. budget resources with the mission that the assistance is intended to achieve in each country. A decade ago, with fewer programs and agencies, there was somewhat greater alignment between budget accounts and objectives. Since then strategic, development, and humanitarian funds have been intermingled, with individual projects often in receipt of money from several types of accounts. Increasingly, the State Department has found it necessary to allocate foreign assistance under its control in a cumbersome process. First it determines targets by country or region.[35] Then it attempts to meet the targets by distributing funds made available from several budget accounts after congressional and administrative earmarks are satisfied.[36]

The resulting concoction may reflect the requirements of U.S. funding systems more than the needs of a given country, since the budget account structure is not closely tied to policy objectives at the country level, and different accounts designed for specific purposes offer different degrees of flexibility. For instance, development assistance is most constrained, the Economic Support Fund is moderately constrained, and disaster assistance–transition initiatives are least constrained by law and regulation. To complicate matters further, funds with a high degree of flexibility directed at high-priority development sectors—the Child Survival and Health Fund, the Global AIDS Initiative, and the Millennium Challenge Corporation—are allocated among countries in independent processes.

Any management textbook would recommend the alignment of authority with responsibility, of policy with operations. This principle must be reflected to a much greater degree in the foreign assistance enterprise. Foreign assistance is about getting a job done; it is by nature an operational function—informed by policy but not a policymaking function per se. The U.S. organizations entrusted with managing foreign assistance must recruit personnel with the right kind of technical, operational, and project management skills; reward effective performance; and work relentlessly to improve on-the-ground results.

A diminished focus on operational effectiveness is one of the biggest risks associated with undertaking a development or reconstruction mission within an agency that has a majority culture dominated by policymaking, diplomacy, and international negotiations, as is the case with the State or Treasury Departments. There are, of course, talented individuals who thrive equally in the give-and-take of policy deliberations and in overseeing a logistically complex emergency operation, but the organizations' overall cultures and missions are likely to be starkly different, with fundamentally different recruiting needs, incentives, and training systems.

The quality of both policy and implementation is likely to be greatly enhanced when they are closely integrated and there is a tight feedback loop informing both. It is critical to elevate the operational function of foreign assistance and provide a seat for it at the policymaking table. This could be achieved while preserving current divisions of responsibilities when effective. An example would be U.S. participation in UN humanitarian interventions, where the division of responsibilities between the State Department, as chief U.S. interlocutor at the UN, and USAID, as chief implementing agency, appears to be relatively effective.[37] In addition, there is a strong push within the administration to restructure budget accounts so that each country program could be crafted from within a single budget account rather than cobbling together a patchwork of funds from different account structures. Indeed, the position of director of foreign assistance was proposed in part as a mechanism for bootstrapping this kind of reform without having to invest in lengthy negotiations with Congress to formally redefine account structures. While there is a value to reforming both budget accounts and funding modalities to make them more consistent with current challenges and opportunities, this would be far more compelling as a logical outcome of a process that began with establishing agreement around a new unified framework for foreign assistance and the best organizational structure for making it operational.

Principle 5: Focus on Core Competencies

Drilling further down into operations reveals another consequential trend: USAID is moving more and more money with fewer and fewer people, in effect outsourcing most of its operations. If the current trends of loss of policy control and outsourcing of operations continue to squeeze USAID from two directions, the aid agency risks being reduced to a contracting entity. According to former USAID administrator M. Peter McPherson, the number of professional staff at USAID has fallen by a third since 1990 during a time when assistance flows have grown in real terms. Between 1998 and 2006, reductions in direct-hire staff were accompanied by a sharp increase in foreign assistance spending, with the result that aid disbursement per staff member grew by 46 percent to $2 million, with most overseas managers implementing far larger programs.[38]

The inevitable result of reduced staffing accompanied by increased foreign assistance is growing reliance on outsourcing. Indeed, a recent USAID report includes the recommendation that mission directors should resume using agency staff to design and manage programs rather than relying on contractors, which is astonishing for what it suggests about current practices.[39] In their 2005 analysis of U.S. foreign aid, Carol Lancaster and Ann Van Dusen write, "In many cases, USAID has become a wholesaler to wholesalers—letting large contracts for aid work, usually to consulting firms, which then subcontract much of the work to other firms or NGOs."[40] This trend toward greater and greater outsourcing of megacontracts may undercut the value of USAID's field presence—traditionally a key comparative advantage among its peer donor organizations. The outsourcing trend exacerbates the disconnect between policy and firsthand understanding of the challenges and lessons associated with implementation, leading to a loss of institutional memory and important learning opportunities so that the same mistakes are repeated. In addition, assistance funds can be consumed by additional administrative and indirect costs incurred by multiple layers of management.

Currently, there is some tension about whether USAID will remain an implementing agency or will continue evolving in the direction of a "wholesaler of wholesalers," passing on increasingly large-scale projects and programs to contractors, who then turn over much of the work to subcontractors. Growing reliance on megacontracts is both cause and consequence of diminishing personnel and field presence. Similar challenges face the MCC and security assistance programs.

Although there are many benefits from outsourcing appropriate functions, organizational effectiveness requires retaining core competencies in house. The primary development, humanitarian, and civilian postconflict operations agency within the U.S. government should undertake a deliberate process of determining which functions are central to its core missions and invest in the right mix of skills and personnel systems as well as the right field structure to ensure excellence in those missions. That would argue for a professional staff with a mix of granular country knowledge, general management and operational skills, and deep technical expertise in priority sectors and functions. Many worry that the mix within USAID has evolved excessively away from technical expertise, in keeping with greater reliance on outsourcing. I would argue that the knowledge-intensive nature of effective foreign assistance demands much greater emphasis on technical expertise and on systematically tapping into expert knowledge networks.

While U.S. competencies are clearly world class in some priority areas such as humanitarian assistance and public-private partnerships, key capabilities critical to boosting the productive capacities of poor economies have atrophied, infrastructure chief among them.[41] In contrast to its early years, when USAID was deeply engaged in supporting transportation, energy, and communications infrastructure, an astonishingly low 3 percent of the agency's technical experts are now engineers.[42]

Economists have long emphasized the role of infrastructure in promoting economic growth. Indeed, the earliest focus of U.S. foreign aid was infrastructure financing. After the success of the Marshall Plan, which included many projects to rebuild Europe's devastated buildings and transportation infrastructure, President Harry Truman announced in his 1949 presidential inaugural address a "Point Four" program that would provide similar assistance to developing countries.[43]

The U.S. government subsequently got out of the foreign infrastructure business for some good reasons, which also led to a change in focus by the World Bank and regional development banks. Large, expensive, long-term public works projects involving multiple contracts, opaque costs, and limited accountability offer tempting opportunities for corruption and political gaming. Given the frequent recriminations over "bridges to nowhere" that happen even in the most developed countries, it is no surprise that countries with weaker institutional infrastructure and less transparency and accountability have difficulty managing such projects well.[44]

Yet despite implementation challenges, infrastructure investment is as important today as it was in the 1940s. Indeed, it is estimated that the infrastructure investment needed to keep up with projected growth is between 5 to 9 percent of developing countries' GDP annually, evenly split between new projects and maintenance. Yet the governments of developing nations are currently spending only 2 to 4 percent of GDP on such projects, with the gap particularly severe in Latin America and Africa.[45] In places like Nigeria, where 2006 road density is one-seventh that of 1950 India, simple investments in roads to connect farmers with markets for their products and supplies of fertilizer can make a huge difference.[46] The United Kingdom's Commission for Africa has declared, "Despite its clear benefits, African governments and development partners sharply reduced, over the

1990s, the share of resources allocated to infrastructure. . . . In retrospect, this was a policy mistake founded in a new dogma of the 1980s and 1990s asserting that infrastructure would now be financed by the private sector."[47] But important advances in public-private partnerships for developing and managing infrastructure on an ongoing basis now provide mechanisms to surmount some of those problems, which should prompt new attention to this area, as recommended by the Commission for Africa.

The U.S. government needs to build its capabilities in a few core areas that include police and judicial training and local governance as well as rural development and infrastructure. For those functions outside the core that are determined on the basis of systematic analysis to be best accomplished through outsourcing, emphasis should be placed on improving the foreign assistance contracting function. USAID procurement relies heavily on skills and systems developed for the Department of Defense and NASA to navigate the federal acquisitions regulations, which have been shaped around the highest value procurers in the federal government. Career USAID officials point out, however, that the Defense Department and NASA have experience in procuring goods and equipment but not the services that constitute the larger share of USAID contracts.[48]

Principle 6: Invest in Learning

In a related area, an effective institutional design for foreign assistance should focus not only on doing but also learning—investing in operational research as well as new knowledge targeted to developing nation challenges. This is particularly true of the development enterprise, where many of the greatest success stories—whether the Green Revolution, the eradication of smallpox, or the Famine Early Warning System—involved adapting science and technology to address the particular challenges facing developing countries. Given the range of institutional capacities, recipient countries have achieved greater success in absorbing knowledge in areas such as medicine, nutrition, family planning, education, and agriculture than in raising overall productivity, which seems to be more sensitive to the institutional environment.[49] The case is compelling for developing and sharing know-how in the areas of the environment, energy, family planning, agriculture, and health as well as operational research to mitigate regional conflict or to help rehabilitate ungoverned states. Moreover, investments in these types of knowledge need not be as constrained by absorptive capacity in poor countries as are some other types of development investments.

But paradoxically, at a time when technological advances hold great promise for addressing important development challenges, USAID has been reducing technical expertise in favor of generalist management skills.[50] This trend is exacerbated by a bias in Congress and elsewhere in favor of service delivery as opposed to more abstract investments in research and development. For example, a bill currently under review in the Senate would limit malaria funds used for research to "not more than 5 percent . . . including basic research or operational research or vaccine and therapeutic research and development."[51]

From USAID's earliest days, scientists, engineers, and technical experts were central to its mission, operating out of both specialized functional offices and regional bureaus and missions. In the early 1980s, the role of specialized knowledge was boosted further by the creation of the Bureau of Science and Technology, which remained strong throughout the decade. In 1990 it was renamed the Global Bureau. According to a National Academies of Sciences report, the dilution of its focus together with personnel cuts in the 1990s led to the loss of substantial technical expertise and the diminution of the status of such specialized knowledge.[52]

According to a USAID report, of 1,821 professionals at the agency in 2004, roughly 55 percent were working in civil society, general development, or other general areas.[53] Experts note that both economic analysis and program evaluation capabilities have declined considerably, and both are critical to the organization's capacity to learn from its vast experiences and enhance operations based on that learning.[54]

USAID and the MCC have inadequate capacity to support research and innovation on problems related to their mission.[55] Similarly, the research budgets of the National Institutes of Health and the Department of Agriculture only allocate minimal funds for addressing the challenges facing developing countries. This deprives the U.S. government of the opportunity to foster groundbreaking research and to make potentially useful contacts with the research community in the U.S. and overseas. Such networks could provide valuable new ideas and feedback—as they did with the pathbreaking development of the Green Revolution.[56]

The paucity of American public support for research for development contrasts with the situation in the United Kingdom, where the Central Research Department of the Department for International Development has a budget projected to grow significantly. The DFID mission statement is a good description of what the United States government should be doing in the realm of foreign assistance, including commissioning research and working to shape university and private sector research agendas more generally:

> New science, technologies and ideas are crucial for the achievement of the Millennium Development Goals, but global research investments are insufficient to match needs and do not focus on the priorities of the poor. . . . DFID's Central Research Department (CRD) commissions research to help fill this gap, aiming to ensure tangible outcomes on the livelihoods of the poor. CRD seeks to influence the international and U.K. research agendas, putting poverty reduction and the needs of the poor at the forefront of global research efforts.[57]

Since the social value of many innovations targeted to the needs of poor countries far outstrips the market value, funding is the natural province of government and philanthropy. The United States should have a unique advantage in this area based on the depth and breadth of its research and development infrastructure, the strength of its private sector applied research, its strong tradition of venture philanthropy, and its notable successes funded by government and philanthropic support. America's development agenda should greatly expand the official emphasis on generating and disseminating knowledge for development purposes by establishing a research grant-making operation and actively investing in networks of researchers from both developing and rich countries.[58] This is a missed opportunity to engage institutions of higher learning in the challenge of global poverty as well as to inspire students to invest their energy and creativity in solving some of the most important problems facing humanity.

There is also enormous value in operational research—especially through independent evaluations—to improve development interventions based on their impact. Yet evaluation has been one of the weakest areas for U.S. assistance, which generally relies on process or input accounting rather than true impact analysis, and is often undertaken in a perfunctory or defensive manner. Ideally, the emphasis should be redirected toward using operational research and evaluations to foster a learning environment incorporating lessons from the field.

To improve the value of evaluation, the U.S. foreign assistance enterprise should pioneer new techniques. In a promising new development, researchers are evaluating impact using randomized field trials analogous to clinical trials conducted by medical researchers, including the use of control groups.[59] Mexico inadvertently pioneered this approach when it rolled out Progresa/Oportunidades, a government-funded program that provided mothers with cash grants and health interventions as an inducement to send their children to school. The program made a virtue out of necessity.

When initial funding permitted the program to reach only 500 out of a potential pool of 50,000 poor communities, it selected the initial recipients through a randomized process and made data on the program accessible to the research community.[60]

This fascinating transplant from the field of medicine underscores a point that is made far too rarely: foreign assistance is an area of experimentation and risk taking. We need to raise the tolerance for risk and expect failure, publicize it, and learn from it. The spotty record of development and training of courts and security forces in postconflict states should come as no surprise given the inherent complexity and diversity of the institutional environments involved. This argues for more experimentation, not less, and a much more systematic and research-based approach to evaluation.[61]

Fortunately, the former USAID administrator highlighted some of the glaring deficiencies discussed here and proposed measures to begin addressing them, such as hiring a part-time scientific adviser and establishing a new program for evaluation.[62] However, bolder efforts are needed in a faster time frame.

Principle 7: Elevate the Development Mission

The development community cheered when the 2002 National Security Strategy recognized development alongside defense and diplomacy as a third critically important and independent pillar of national security.[63] Increasingly, however, and especially with the 2006 decisions to bring the director of foreign assistance formally within the State Department structure, advocates worry that development is being subordinated to diplomacy.[64] State Department officials have argued that the reverse is more accurate, that foreign service officers are increasingly recognizing that U.S. vital interests are best served by influencing the domestic policies of foreign governments in ways that favor economic development and democratization.

While greater appreciation of democratization, security, and development challenges may indeed be permeating the ranks of the career foreign service, that does not in itself alleviate the potential tension between the diplomatic and development functions of the U.S. government. First, the primary function of diplomacy is state-to-state relations whereas development and especially democratization often require working around foreign governments and sometimes with groups opposed to them. Indeed, in many cases, diplomats benefit from being able to "blame" unwelcome aid decisions on an independent agency, while foreign aid officials can sometimes be more effective by not bearing direct responsibility for U.S. foreign policy. Second, U.S. relations with many developing nations are still characterized by a tension between short-term strategic objectives and the longer-term agenda of economic and political reform.[65] Maintaining the integrity of independent diplomatic and development functions makes those tensions far easier to manage than blending the two.

If there is one principle that applies above all others to the revitalization of the U.S. foreign assistance enterprise, it is that the development mission—broadly construed to include security and good governance—must be elevated to coequal status with defense and diplomacy—not just in principle but also in practice. Indeed, a growing number in the Defense Department are strong advocates for the importance of sustaining core development capabilities in a civilian agency. The sense of mission—vital to America's interests as well as to global peace and prosperity—must be restored and with it both the stature of the enterprise and the morale of the personnel engaged in it.

Success will only be achieved if there is a clearly defined operational mission. A mission that is clear and inspiring is also critical for purposes of morale and the ability to attract and retain the most talented professionals in the field. One of the greatest advantages enjoyed by the relatively small-scale Peace Corps is its strong professional ethos, clarity of mission, and the identification of its members with that mission.[66] Indeed, one of the strongest arguments for setting up the Millennium Challenge Corporation independently rather than within USAID or the State Department was to create a strong organizational culture and ethos that would attract top talent and fuel an ethic of delivering concrete results unburdened by past baggage.

Can a much larger organization with a complex mission attain that same sense of purpose and commitment? Numerous examples in the private sector and in other parts of the U.S. government are reassuring on that score.[67] But it requires strong leadership and vigilance about taking on new missions. It may also require fundamental organizational renewal at long intervals—rather than the frequent "reorganizations" that afflict both the World Bank and USAID that do not appear to achieve notably greater clarity of purpose or commitment on the part of stakeholders. And it may well require a strong independent organization that does not depend on more powerful agencies to represent it in interagency deliberations and is not viewed merely as the implementation arm of more powerful entities that retain authority over budget allocations and policy.

Alternative Organizational Models

When considering the "right" organizational model for U.S. foreign assistance, we can turn to a comparative analysis of programs in other donor countries that suggests two important trends: there has been substantial organizational overhaul in the past decade, and this has converged, broadly speaking, on four or five different organizational models, each with its own virtues and drawbacks. These models vary in the degree of centralization of the foreign assistance function, in the stature assigned to it, and in the degree of control by the ministry of foreign affairs. Table 2-1 groups many of the leading donor nations into the four main organizational forms in operation today.

This taxonomy is useful for introducing the possible organizational options for the United States, some of that would require only administrative changes to existing structures and others that would require major

Table 2-1 Organization of Foreign Assistance Activities: Comparison of OECD Countries

Format	Examples
Multiple aid entities	Germany Japan United States
Separate implementing arm of foreign affairs ministry	Norway Sweden Austria Belgium Luxembourg
Merged into foreign affairs ministry	Denmark Finland Ireland Netherlands
Cabinet agency	United Kingdom Canada

Source: Author's analysis based on Development Assistance Committee, *Management and Study Practices for Development Cooperation in DAC Member Countries* (Paris: OECD, 2004), p. 40.

bureaucratic and statutory overhaul. Each is evaluated below in terms of the principles proposed above; a summary is presented in table 2-2.

Option 1: Improved Status Quo—Coordination of Multiple Aid Entities

By far the easiest improvement would be to superimpose a strong inter-agency coordination structure on the existing constellation of foreign assistance and international economic policy players. As suggested above, this could mean beefing up the existing White House policy and budget coordination mechanisms with more regular and extensive oversight of both the foreign assistance decisionmaking process and decisions on policy instruments—such as trade, investment, and debt relief—that might have important implications for developing nations. The Department of State's recent changes would be fully consistent with this approach, which would require greater coordination not only at the highest levels of executive branch decisionmaking but also mid-level interagency coordination led by designated agencies.

To make this model a significant improvement over the existing situation would require not only high-level policy coordination but also true

Table 2-2 Ability of Alternative Organizational Models to Meet Criteria for Effective Organizational Design[a]

	Organizational criteria						
Principal organizational model	Clarifies and rationalizes agency roles	Speaks with single voice	Achieves policy synergies	Aligns policy and operations	Strengthens core competencies	Invests in learning	Boosts stature and morale
Status quo plus	M	M	M	L	L	L	L
USAID as implementation arm of State Department	L	M	L	L	L	L	L
USAID merged into State Department	M	M	L	H	L	L	M
New Empowered Department of Global Development	H	H	H	H	H	H	H

a. The table is intended as a preliminary assessment of each organizational model. H = high; M = moderate; L = low.

collaboration in planning and operations among agencies, as discussed above in the sections on coordination (speaking with one voice) and coherence (achieving synergies). It would require creating budgetary and career advancement incentives and removing the disincentives for joint interagency work as well as for interagency personnel rotations—not only within the State Department–USAID complex but also extending to the Pentagon, the MCC, and the Treasury Department.

The political capital required for such a change would be fairly modest. It requires no new statutory authorities or indeed even consultations with Congress to effect. Mostly, it would need personal commitment on the part of the president and senior White House staff as well as the heads of the agencies being "coordinated."

If undertaken with such high-level commitment, this approach could significantly improve the current situation in terms of policy coherence, enabling the United States to act as a more coordinated donor and clarifying the division of labor among agencies. It would do nothing, however, to fundamentally improve the core value of the foreign assistance enterprise, to integrate policy and operations, or to elevate the development mission. It is worth noting that the United States would remain in a category with only a handful of donors, notably Japan and Germany, who are among the most significant in dollar terms but are not known for shaping the broader development agenda.

Option 2: USAID as Implementation Subsidiary of the State Department

A second modification of the status quo would be to strengthen the trend of more clearly defining USAID as an implementation arm of the State Department. This would continue a trajectory set in the 1990s partly in response to congressional pressure, although it would go a significant step further by formalizing and clarifying the role of USAID as the implementing agency vis-à-vis the State Department.

This approach would put the United States in good company with countries such as Norway and Sweden, two donors that are influential in the international development community and seen as quite effective. A modified Swedish model might include a high-level interagency policy group to oversee coordination of nonaid policy instruments, comparable to that overseeing the MCC, while clarifying and elevating USAID as the lead implementation agency for foreign assistance.

This would have the virtue of clarifying agency roles and could lead to better coordination among policies as well as fewer U.S. government voices. It would be further strengthened by the kind of interagency integration of planning and operations described above and the creation of incentives for rotating between USAID and the State Department and for acquiring operational skills.

On the other hand, it would only address coordination problems within the USAID–State Department complex and do nothing to address coordination with the myriad other offices and agencies delivering foreign aid, chief among them the MCC. It would further solidify the divide between policy and operations, and absent major changes within USAID and in the way Congress interacts with it, would do little to boost investment in U.S. core operational capacity for foreign assistance or in knowledge for development. Perhaps most important, there are risks in carrying the Norwegian and Swedish analogies too far. Because the diplomatic and defense missions have much greater relative importance within the U.S. system than in northern Europe, the risk of lowering the stature and morale of the development mission by subordinating it to the diplomatic mission would seem to be much greater in the U.S. context.

Option 3: Merger of USAID into the State Department

A more ambitious reform would go still further by formally merging USAID into the State Department while elevating the stature of the head of USAID within the department's hierarchy and providing explicit guidelines for the division of authority. Here, too, this reform would put the United States in good company alongside the Danes and the Dutch, among others. However, in reality a considerable amount of the foreign assistance apparatus would remain outside State Department control unless there were a bolder consolidation that incorporated the MCC, other independent entities, and programs operated by other agencies.

Merger would eliminate one important set of overlapping jurisdictions and essentially bring to its logical conclusion a process that has been gathering momentum over the past decade. It could help spread appreciation of the importance of the development mission among career foreign service officers and lead to greater cross-fertilization of ideas and experience between the two groups of professionals.

The primary arguments against placing USAID solely under the authority of the State Department, however, are those that were made in the 1990s, when there was considerable pressure from a leading member of Congress to merge USAID into the State Department. First, despite its considerable foreign policy expertise, the department has limited development experience, little operational (as opposed to policy) experience in the regional bureaus, and no capacity to administer a program budget as large as that of USAID. Second, merging USAID into the Department of State could risk the appearance—and possibly the reality—of subordination of the development mission to foreign policy imperatives in the allocation of long-term development assistance. The concerns that were raised in the 1990s debate are likely to have greater force a second time around, since the experience with merging the U.S. Information Agency has been widely judged a consequential failure.[68] And it would do nothing to fundamentally upgrade the quality and stature of the foreign assistance enterprise within the U.S. government nor to address coordination with the myriad other offices and agencies delivering foreign aid, chief among them the MCC.

Option 4: New Empowered Department of Global Development

By far the most ambitious reform would be to establish a new cabinet-level agency that would have overarching responsibility for the development pillar of U.S. policy. Such a "department of global development" would either administer directly or have authority over the foreign assistance activities of the U.S. government and would represent the development mission in the formulation of policies with particular salience, such as those affecting trade, debt relief, investment, and agriculture. Most likely, the new department for global development would include the Millennium Challenge Corporation as a relatively independent flagship operation and extend the MCC's most successful features more broadly, such as nonearmarked funding, recipient design and ownership, grant-based financing for the poorest, and transparent eligibility criteria.[69] It also might logically include such functions as overseeing U.S. policy toward the World Bank and regional development banks and some core security assistance functions, such as police training, while assuming no responsibility for military-to-military assistance, for example.

This model, which has been adopted by both the United Kingdom and Canada, has powerful potential benefits for the efficient functioning of the U.S. government, for aid recipients, and for America's influence in the international community. It is the most ambitious reform with regard to rationalizing agencies, ensuring a single U.S. voice, achieving coherence across aid and nonaid policies, and aligning policy and operations. It holds out great promise for reforming the operations of foreign assistance to ensure greater effectiveness, more focus on core competencies, and greater investment in knowledge for development.

Perhaps most important, a new cabinet-level agency holds out the greatest hope of catapulting development into coequal status with defense and diplomacy, in line with the president's National Security Strategy. One of the interesting by-products of creating DFID in the United Kingdom was that over the course of a few years development work became the top choice for new entrants into the British civil service, surpassing both Treasury and the Foreign Office combined.[70] Largely as a result of the reform, and the political consensus supporting it, DFID has become a magnet for top talent and one of the most influential actors in the foreign assistance arena.

But despite the great promise this approach holds, the downsides are equally daunting. This reform would require enormous political capital to elicit the necessary broad and deep political support for authorizing legislation. There would be considerable, possibly insurmountable, opposition from many quarters, including from within the administration and in Congress, to a reform of this nature. It would lead to substantial disruption during the transition.

Prospects and Constraints

A significant reform of the current sprawl of foreign assistance activities to achieve greater coherence and efficiency would require significant political capital, fundamental organizational overhaul, and probably new legislation. Based on the analysis of previous U.S. reforms and the recent U.K. reform, a major overhaul of U.S. foreign assistance would likely require at least one and possibly most of the following five conditions:

—a crisis,

—an emerging political consensus that foreign assistance reform is central to advancing vital national interests in the face of new international challenges,

—personal commitment on the part of the president,

—congressional championship, or

—a concerted, sustained, and well-organized advocacy campaign spanning the political spectrum and uniting the disparate interests of coalition members around a clear and compelling goal.[71]

Since the terrorist attacks of September 11, 2001, and the unfolding lethality of the HIV/AIDS pandemic have generated new challenges of epic proportions, the first condition (a crisis) would seem to have been met. And in the wake of these events, the importance of underperforming governments in impoverished areas has become more apparent, thus highlighting the critical role of foreign assistance and at least laying the groundwork for meeting the second condition (political consensus).

President George W. Bush's foreign policy agenda was profoundly reshaped by the aforementioned events. But after a period of internal deliberation and consideration of the significant political capital likely to be required for a major overhaul of U.S. foreign assistance, the administration's response has been to pursue a course of marginal reform. Some of the proposed changes should lead to improved coordination between the State Department and USAID, but they will not yield fundamental progress toward institutionalizing many of the organizational principles laid out above. And given the president's preferred approach of addressing new challenges by layering a progression of new initiatives on top of the existing structure, rather than attempting fundamental reform, the third condition (presidential commitment) has not been met.

Indeed, it is difficult for any administration in midstream to propose fundamental changes that threaten existing bureaucratic boundaries. Such changes are far easier to evaluate objectively and to implement during a change of administrations. Currently, even deeply committed members of Congress lack the traction to champion more fundamental reforms, as the fourth condition requires.

Thus it is apparent that the likelihood of fundamental change will remain low as long as there is no political payoff. This is where condition five can be pivotal: it is critical that the advocacy community, which has proven immensely successful in recent years in support of debt relief and vastly increased sums for the fight against HIV/AIDS, undertake a major effort to place foreign assistance transformation high on campaign agendas. After all, the creation of DFID was a plank of Britain's New Labour platform, which gained unstoppable political impetus when Tony Blair swept into office.[72] At the moment it is hard to imagine the status of U.S. foreign assistance meriting even a mention in a presidential debate, let alone becoming a core tenet of a candidate's agenda. But strong support from key advocacy groups and other nongovernmental organizations could generate the requisite political will for reform. For lessons to be learned from an earlier, ultimately successful attempt at major governmental reform, see box 2-1.

> ### BOX 2-1 Goldwater-Nichols: Lessons for Reforming U.S. Foreign Assistance
>
> In 1986 the Goldwater-Nichols Department of Defense Reorganization Act was signed into law, instituting a joint chain of command for the uniformed military. It is widely believed to be the most significant national security reform since the National Security Act of 1947.[1]
>
> The Goldwater-Nichols Act holds some lessons for the substance of foreign assistance reform; it is generally credited with creating the institutional underpinnings for systematically joining the different services in all aspects of planning and operations (while getting lower marks on resource allocation issues). But the most important lessons for foreign assistance concern the reorganization process.
>
> Against a backdrop of growing concern about dysfunctional interservice rivalry stemming from experiences in Vietnam, the failed Iranian hostage rescue mission, and the invasion of Grenada, a 1982 article written by a retiring chairman of the Joint Chiefs of Staff critiquing the existing structure and recommending reforms set off the process.[2] Defense reorganization was given added impetus when the successor chairman announced his support and called for more ambitious reforms. Despite opposition from the Reagan administration, reform proposals were taken up in hearings by the House Committee on Armed Services. A Senate staff study analyzing the existing organizational structure was undertaken, and a parallel process of hearings began in the Senate Armed Services Committee. Defense reorganization legislation was proposed and failed in each of the three years preceding the passage in 1986 of the far-reaching legislation championed by Senator Barry Goldwater and Representative Bill Nichols.
>
> ---
>
> 1. Thomas L. McNaugher, *Improving Military Coordination: The Goldwater-Nichols Reorganization of the Department of Defense* (Brookings, 1994); Clark A. Murdock and Michele A. Flournoy, *Beyond Goldwater-Nichols: U.S. Government and Defense Reform for a New Strategic Era—Phase 2 Report* (Washington: Center for Strategic and International Studies, July 2005).
>
> 2. See Peter W. Chiarelli, "Beyond Goldwater-Nichols," *JFQ: Joint Forces Quarterly,* Autumn, 1993, pp. 71–81.

Recommendations

Brilliant policies and increased funding are not enough, in and of themselves, to improve the effectiveness of America's aid enterprise unless they are accompanied by fundamental organizational and operational transformation. Such change would be best guided by seven simple principles:

—Rationalize agencies and clarify missions.

—Speak with a single U.S. voice.

—Realize synergies across policy instruments.

—Align policy, operations, and budgeting.

—Focus on core competencies.

—Invest in learning.

—Elevate the development mission.

In addition, four models of aid organization, suggested by recent trends among OECD donors, should be evaluated as possible alternatives, taking into account the unique global position of the United States as well as its defining political culture. These models include coordination among multiple decentralized agencies, USAID as the implementation arm of State, USAID merger into State, and a new department of global development.

Most of the conditions necessary for this kind of fundamental overhaul—including an emergent political consensus surrounding the urgency of the mission and personal commitment on the part of the president or key congressional champions—are not currently present and are unlikely to be during the remainder of a second-term presidency. But it is still possible at this time to make improvements by instituting a clear system of coordination led at the highest levels out of the White House, with authority delegated to appropriate agency leads for planning and operations.

In parallel, it is critical for Congress and organizations outside of government to lay the groundwork for and build broad agreement around a more profound vision for reform, in a process akin to that leading up to the Goldwater-Nichols Defense Reorganization Act of 1986 (which is described above in box 2-1). The HELP Commission established by Representative Frank Wolf provides one such vehicle, and congressional authorizers could commission studies from the Government Accountability Office and CRS as well as hold hearings to deepen understanding of the challenges and begin to build the foundations for lasting solutions.[73]

Outside advocacy groups and nongovernmental organizations should also undertake a campaign to highlight the importance of more effective aid and the key mechanisms for achieving it. Without such mobilization and the articulation of a clear, compelling goal, sufficient political momentum for reform will not emerge.

Ultimately, a new, empowered department of global development is likely to be the model that holds the greatest promise of transforming the U.S. foreign assistance enterprise to lead in addressing the challenges of the twenty-first century. The analysis of the various organizational models discussed in this chapter suggests that a new department of global development comes closer than any of the other options to achieving key principles of aid effectiveness. Only a new cabinet agency will be able to boost the stature and morale of the development mission and attract the next generation of top talent within the U.S. government. Only an independent department will be able to realize the president's vision of elevating development as the third pillar, alongside diplomacy and defense, underpinning America's international leadership.

Notes

1. Organization for Economic Cooperation and Development, Development Assistance Committee, "United States (2002), Development Co-operation Review," *DAC Journal* 3, no. 4 (2002): 11.

2. See Larry Nowels, chapter 9 in this volume.

3. Michael D'Arcy, and others, *Protecting the Homeland 2006/2007* (Brookings, 2006).

4. Development Assistance Committee, *Managing Aid: Practices of DAC Member Countries* (Paris: OECD, 2005), p. 11.

5. See Owen Barder, chapter 10 in this volume.

6. In regard to clarity of purpose, see Lael Brainard in chapter 1 of this volume for discussion of a unified framework.

7. See "USAID History: Summary" (www.usaid.gov/about_usaid/usaidhist.html [May 2006]).

8. John F. Kennedy, "Special Message to the Congress on Foreign Aid," March 22, 1961, in *Public Papers of the Presidents of the United States: John. F. Kennedy, 1961* (Government Printing Office, 1961).

9. See Nowels, chapter 9.

10. OECD, Development Assistance Committee, "United States (2002)."

11. Department of Defense, "Directive 3000.05: Military Support for Stability, Security, Transition, and Reconstruction (SSTR) Operations," November 28, 2005 (www.dtic.mil/whs/directives/corres/pdf/d300005_112805/d300005p.pdf).

12. Max Weber, *The Theory of Social and Economic Organization,* trans. A. M. Henderson and Talcott Parsons (New York: Free Press, 1947).

13. Letter to Secretary of State Condoleezza Rice, from M. Peter McPherson, President, National Association of State Universities and Land-Grant Colleges, Washington, January 2006.

14. See Steven Hansch, chapter 5 in this volume.

15. Department of State, "Office of the Coordinator for Reconstruction and Stabilization" (www.state.gov/s/crs [May 2006]).

16. White House, "National Security Presidential Directive/NSPD-44," Washington, D.C., December 7, 2005 (www.fas.org/irp/offdocs/nspd/nspd-44.html).

17. *Making Appropriations for Foreign Operations, Export Financing, and Related Programs for the Fiscal Year Ending September 30, 2006, and for Other Purposes,* H. Rept. 109-265, 109 Cong. 2 sess. (Government Printing Office, 2006).

18. See Nowels, chapter 9.

19. See Charles Flickner, chapter 8 in this volume.

20. Department of State, "Background Briefing: Two Senior State Department Officials on Foreign Assistance," January 19, 2006 (www.state.gov/r/pa/prs/ps/2006/59426.htm).

21. Lael Brainard and Charlie Flickner, "Transformational Diplomacy," January 23, 2006 (www.brookings.org/views/op-ed/brainard/20060123.htm).

22. Lael Brainard and others, *The Other War: Global Poverty and the Millennium Challenge Account* (Brookings, 2003).

23. Arnab Acharya, Ana de Lima, and Mick Moore, "Proliferation and Fragmentation: Transactions Costs and the Value of Aid," *Journal of Development Studies* 42, no. 1 (2006): 1–21; Arnab Acharya, Ana Fuzzo de Lima, and Mick Moore, "Aid Proliferation: How Responsible Are the Donors?" Working Paper 214 (Brighton, United Kingdom: Institute of Development Studies, January 2004).

24. Department of State, "General Policy Guidance for All Bilateral Programs" (www.state.gov/s/gac/partners/guide/bilat [May 2006]).

25. Stephen Knack and Aminur Rahman, "Donor Fragmentation and Bureaucratic Quality in Aid Recipients," Policy Research Working Paper 3186 (Washington: World Bank, January 2004).

26. Nicolas Van de Walle and Timothy A. Johnston, *Improving Aid to Africa,* (Johns Hopkins University Press, 1996). p. 50. As David Roodman notes in "Aid Project Proliferation and Absorptive Capacity" (Center for Global Development Working Paper 75, 2006, p. 4), Tanzania is often incorrectly cited as having to submit 2,400 donor reports every quarter and conduct 1,000 donor meetings a year. Those numbers are in fact an average for all of Africa; Tanzania's figures are, in fact, far higher, making the country an even more striking example of the inefficiency of aid agency proliferation.

27. Nancy Birdsall and Brian Deese, "Hard Currency," *Washington Monthly,* March 2004, p. 39.

28. See Development Assistance Committee, *Harmonising Donor Practices for Effective Aid Delivery* (Paris: OECD, 2003). See also Aid Harmonization and Alignment, "Rome High-Level Forum (2003)" (www.aidharmonization.org/secondary-pages/editable?key=106 [May 2006]).

29. This assessment arose from discussions of the Brookings–Center for Strategic and International Studies Task Force on Transforming Foreign Assistance for the Twenty-First Century. See also Patrick Cronin, chapter 6 in this volume.

30. Clark A. Murdock and Michele A. Flournoy, *Beyond Goldwater-Nichols: U.S. Government and Defense Reform for a New Strategic Era—Phase 2 Report* (Washington: Center for Strategic and International Studies, July 2005); Samuel R. Berger and Brent Scowcroft, chairs, *In the Wake of War: Improving U.S. Post-Conflict Capabilities,* Independent Task Force Report 55 (Washington: Council on Foreign Relations, 2005).

31. See Barder, chapter 10.

32. USAID does not have cabinet status. Although the USTR most often has cabinet status, it is at the discretion of the president, and it is not considered one of the core economic or security agencies for purposes of National Security Council coordination.

33. See Barder, chapter 10.

34. Letter to Secretary of State Condoleezza Rice from M. Peter McPherson, January 2006.

35. Often the country or regional level of funding has already been set by Congress.

36. Numerous Congressional earmarks and directives must be satisfied during this process, with the result that a country needing help with malaria may obtain instead education or counternarcotics assistance.

37. See Hansch, chapter 5.

38. USAID, "Budget Justification to Congress, Fiscal Year 2006" (www.usaid.gov/policy/budget/cbj2006 [April 2006]).

39. USAID Administrator, *Report of World Wide Mission Directors Conference,* May 17–20, 2005, cited in Committee on Science and Technology in Foreign Assistance, National Research Council, *The Fundamental Role of Science and Technology in International Development: An Imperative for the U.S. Agency for International Development* (Washington: National Academies Press, 2006), p. 68.

40. Carol Lancaster and Ann Van Dusen, *Organizing U.S. Foreign Aid: Confronting the Challenges of the Twenty-First Century* (Brookings, 2005).

41. For a discussion on U.S. competencies in humanitarian assistance, see Hansch, chapter 5. For a discussion of the U.S. role in public-private partnerships, see Larry Cooley, "2 + 2 = 5: A Pragmatic View of Partnerships between Official Donors and Multinational Corporations," in *Transforming the Development Landscape: The Role of the Private Sector,* edited by Lael Brainard (Brookings, forthcoming).

42. USAID, "USAID Primer: What We Do and How We Do It," January 2006 (www.usaid.gov/about_usaid/PDACG100.pdf).

43. See Wilfred Owen, *Distance and Development* (Brookings, 1968), p. 58.

44. Incentive problems for infrastructure projects include temptations for politicians to overstate the price of these projects to maximize their kickbacks (usually on commission), and subpar construction work associated with contracts awarded on the basis of connections rather than merit. Furthermore, political capital is usually gained from high-profile announcements but not expenditures on maintenance, creating an incentive to generate new projects but abandon ones that have been started. See OECD, *A Policy Framework for Investment: Infrastructure and Financial Services* (Rio de Janeiro: World Bank, 2005), pp. 3–5.

45. World Bank, *Infrastructure and the World Bank* (Washington, 2005), pp. 3–4.

46. UN Millennium Project 2005, *Halving Hunger: It Can Be Done,* Task Force Report on Hunger (London: Earthscan, 2005).

47. Commission for Africa, "Going for Growth and Poverty Reduction," in *Our Common Interest: Report of the Commission for Africa* (London, 2005,) pp. 233–34.

48. Interviews with Janet C. Ballantyne and Phyllis Forbes, former senior USAID officials, cited in Brainard and others, *The Other War,* p. 142.

49. Lael Brainard, "The Role for Health in the Fight against International Poverty," in *Biological Security and Global Public Health: In Search of a Global Treatment,* Kurt Campbell and Philip Zellikow, editors (Washington: Aspen Institute, 2003), pp. 73–84; Charles Kenny, "Why Are We Worried about Income? Nearly Everything that Matters Is Converging," *World Development* 33, no. 1 (2005): 1–19.

50. Lancaster and Dusen, *Organizing U.S. Foreign Aid.*

51. 109th Congress, "S. 950: A bill to provide assistance to combat tuberculosis, malaria, and other infectious diseases, and for other purposes," introduced by Senator Samuel Brownback (R-Kans.).

52. Committee on Science and Technology, *The Fundamental Role of Science and Technology,* p. 62.

53. USAID, "USAID Primer: What We Do and How We Do It" (www.usaid.gov/about_usaid/primer.html [January 2006]).

54. Committee on Science and Technology, *Fundamental Role of Science and Technology.*

55. Ibid.

56. Kalil, Thomas, "A Broader Vision for Government Research," *Issues in Science and Technology* 19, no. 3 (2003): 29–37.

57. Department for International Development, "DFID and Research," April 27, 2006 (www.dfid.gov.uk/research).

58. Lael Brainard, "Investing in Knowledge for Development: The Role of Science and Technology in the Fight against Global Poverty," Thirtieth Annual American Association for Advancement of Science Forum on Science and Technology Policy, Washington, April 21–22, 2005.

59. See Michael Kremer, "Randomized Evaluations of Educational Programs in Developing Countries: Some Lessons," *American Economic Review Papers and Proceedings* 93, no. 2 (2003): 102–15. See also Michael Kremer and Esther Duflo, "Use of Randomization in the Evaluation of Development Effectiveness," presented at the World Bank Operations Evaluation Department Conference on Evaluation and Development Effectiveness, Washington, July 15–16, 2003.

60. For an in-depth discussion of Progresa/Oportunidades program, see Santiago Levy, *Progress against Poverty: Sustaining Mexico's Progresa-Oportunidades Program* (Brookings, 2006).

61. Brainard, "Investing in Knowledge."

62. Committee on Science and Technology, *The Fundamental Role of Science and Technology,* p. 71.

63. White House, "The National Security Strategy of the United States of America," September 17, 2002 (www.whitehouse.gov/nsc/nssall.html).

64. Carol Lancaster, "Bush's Foreign Aid Reforms Do Not Go Far Enough," *Financial Times,* January 19, 2006 (registration.ft.com/registration/barrier?referer=http://news.ft.com/home/us&location=http%3A//news.ft.com/cms/s/aef26d86-891e-11da-94a6-0000779e2340.html).

65. See chapters 1 and 7.

66. Lex Rieffel, "Reconsidering the Peace Corps," Policy Brief 127 (Brookings, December 2003).

67. Such examples include General Electric, Microsoft, and the military services.

68. Lancaster, "Bush's Foreign Aid."

69. Despite increasing emphasis in recent years on grant-based financing for the poorest countries—a trend that the United States has supported at the World Bank and implemented in the context of the MCC—USAID funding remains heavily loan based.

70. See Barder, chapter 10.

71. See Nowels, chapter 9, and Barder, chapter 10.

72. See Barder, chapter 10.

73. For a summary of the HELP Commission, see Frank Wolf, "Helping Enhance the Livelihood of People (HELP) around the Globe Commission Act" (www.house.gov/wolf/news/2003/FAEC_Summary_and_Section.htm [May 2006]).

CHAPTER 3

What Role for U.S. Assistance in the Fight against Global HIV/AIDS?

J. Stephen Morrison

The President's Emergency Plan for AIDS Relief (PEPFAR), announced by President George Bush at the January 28, 2003, State of the Union Address, is a compelling, signature White House foreign assistance initiative intended to address, on an urgent basis, a single global infectious disease.[1] In its early phase, it has begun to reveal what is possible and to suggest what the future implications might be when the White House launches a foreign assistance innovation that carries the imprimatur, personality, and prestige of that singularly iconic institution.

Most fundamentally, PEPFAR is an unprecedented, unexpected, high-risk presidential foreign policy commitment in the field of global public health.[2] *In effect, the president of the United States declared that a foreign policy priority would be the placement of 2 million vulnerable individuals, living with the human immunodeficiency virus—for which there is no cure,*

In preparing this chapter, I have benefited enormously from the work of my colleagues on the Center for Strategic and International Studies Task Force on HIV/AIDS. The Task Force's four working committees—on gender, prevention, security, and, more recently, PEPFAR implementation—have generated invaluable insights and published important analyses on prevention indicators, gender programming, routine testing, and emergency models, among other topics. Each committee has helped advance discussion of how to strengthen PEPFAR and helped inform my views. Moreover, the Task Force's multiple expert missions to Nigeria, Ethiopia, India, Russia, and China, in which I was fortunate to participate, also offered invaluable background and insights. Last, I am indebted to the many staff members at the Office of the Global AIDS Coordinator, the Department of Health and Human Services and Centers for Disease Control, and the U.S. Agency for International Development for their friendship and insights, and to the many U.S. ambassadors and agency directors in the PEPFAR focal countries who were generously ready to share their views, frequently on short notice.

no vaccine, and neither in sight—on life-extending care for an indefinite period. The long-term challenges that grow out of this commitment—operational, financial, moral, and at the highest political levels—are just beginning to be understood and confronted.

PEPFAR arrived in a burst of activity that was striking in multiple ways: for its hubris, its close association with the Bush administration's overall controversial foreign policy aims, its scale, its narrow focus upon a single disease, HIV/AIDS, and its equally narrow focus on a finite subset of fourteen (now fifteen) focus countries.[3] It confronted considerable unknowns, was overwhelmingly bilateral in character, put itself into tension and conflict with the Global Fund to Fight AIDS, Tuberculosis and Malaria (Global Fund), and suddenly elevated HIV/AIDS into the mainstream discourse on evolving U.S. global security interests in the post–September 11 era. It attracted and stoked political tensions and controversy over prevention strategies, procurement of generics, and the proper balance between bilateral and multilateral approaches. And the administration moved swiftly in winning passage of supporting legislation in Congress, recruiting and confirming an empowered U.S. global AIDS coordinator, Ambassador Randall Tobias, and disbursing cash.

The president promised significant resources, more than any other donor or international organization had been able to muster, much less countenance: $15 billion over five years. That single step, along with the advent in 2002 of the Global Fund, abruptly shifted the parameters of action and catalyzed other donors. Aggregate global flows dedicated to international HIV/AIDS programs jumped from $1 billion in 2000 to an estimated $8.3 billion in 2005.

The president directed that the resources be dedicated to a single disease through a highly vertical set of interventions. The centerpiece, for which not less than 55 percent of fiscal year 2006 through 2008 PEPFAR appropriations are earmarked, is provision of antiretroviral treatment (ART) and related care to 2 million persons in fifteen focus countries.[4] This was a dramatic turn of policy: over the previous fifteen years, the U.S. approach had been almost entirely prevention oriented. Critical to this change was the radical reduction in per capita annual costs for the provision of ART, from $10,000 at the beginning of the decade to below $1,000, and the emergence of well-organized international campaigns dedicated to expanding access to treatment in developing countries.[5]

This chapter examines PEPFAR's genesis, its early promising start-up, lessons revealed thus far about such a White House–driven foreign assistance initiative, and outstanding issues that will influence the sustainability of PEPFAR into the future. However, because PEPFAR is still very much in its early stage, the analysis and conclusions contained in this essay should be regarded as preliminary. PEPFAR has been operational, as of the end of 2005, for less than two years. The report from the congressionally mandated interim review of PEPFAR, undertaken by the Institute of Medicine, is not due to be completed until fall 2006, and even then, it will offer only preliminary conclusions. A Government Accountability Office review of PEPFAR prevention efforts is currently under way and expected to be released by April 2006. Still, the data available are often too limited to permit fully informed conclusions. Decisions and actions are spread across the Office of the Global AIDS Coordinator (OGAC, based at the Department of State), multiple implementing executive agencies, and fifteen countries—more if you incorporate nonfocal countries with growing programs such as Cambodia, Zimbabwe, China, and India. And a unified, transparent monitoring and evaluation system has not yet been put in place by OGAC. Under these circumstances, while it is advisable to begin careful consideration of PEPFAR's experience (debate in Congress will accelerate in spring 2006 and intensify in the following year), it is at the same time prudent to resist the temptation to rush to judgment.

One additional comment must be made at this point. A deep impression from the past year—shared, I believe, very widely across diverse independent observers of PEPFAR—is of the exceptional intensity and dedication of those in the U.S. government and among nongovernmental partners who are charged with actually setting up programs, in the face of relentlessly urgent demands, considerable uncertainty, and senior staff turnover within OGAC. This exceptional level of commitment has been conspicuous in OGAC, the implementing agencies, and among U.S. embassy personnel overseas. The early success achieved thus far belongs to them and their in-country partners. It has come, however, at the price of high staff fatigue and threat of burnout, both in Washington and the U.S. embassies in focal countries. A more tenable, durable staffing structure is essential to preserving and consolidating early, promising gains.

Genesis of the Emergency Plan

At the outset of the Bush administration, no one would have predicted that President Bush would select the global HIV/AIDS pandemic to be the focus of an expensive, high-profile, signature White House initiative. One of the first reorganizing steps taken in 2001 by then-National Security Adviser Condoleezza Rice was to eliminate the senior National Security Council slot dedicated to global infectious diseases and bioterrorism, on the grounds that this position reflected the "soft security" concept favored by the Clinton administration.[6] In this period, Vice President Dick Cheney and other senior officials questioned whether HIV/AIDS constituted an international security threat that should concern the U.S. government.

What changed in the interim? What conditions led to the launch of the Emergency Plan a short two years after President Bush first entered office? Four broad factors came into play.

Visibly Disturbing Progression of the HIV/AIDS Epidemic

As the new decade began, the rising humanitarian toll of HIV/AIDS was accelerating and becoming far more manifest, especially in Africa, a function of the quickly maturing epidemic entering an advanced stage. The huge spike in new infections in the early 1990s quickly began to translate, a decade later, into millions of persons symptomatic with AIDS, concentrated in southern and eastern Africa. Death rates rose steeply, with potentially destabilizing effects. At the same time, popular pressures intensified for access to life-extending treatment, as Paul Farmer, founder of Partners in Health, and others demonstrated that complex treatment could work in very poor countries such as Haiti.[7]

In the most gravely affected countries, it was becoming more and more evident that the epidemic was reversing a generation of gains in human development, hitting young and middle-aged adults of all socioeconomic classes and leaving a dangerous youth bulge. The annual cost in forgone economic growth climbed to 1 to 2 percent. Life expectancy began dropping precipitously, to as low as twenty-five years.[8] Losses among key professional groups, such as educators and health providers, rose to dangerously high levels. As the pandemic damaged national economies, undermined communities, and destroyed the livelihoods of households, it visibly worsened poverty and raised the specter that provision of basic services by some national governments might become infeasible.[9]

This sharpened focus on the epidemic's progression and its impacts was advanced substantially by the high media interest accorded HIV/AIDS during and after the July 2000 International Conference on AIDS in Durban, South Africa. It also was shaped by much improved, convergent data compiled by the Joint United Nations Program on HIV/AIDS (UNAIDS), the U.S. Bureau of the Census, the U.S. National Intelligence Council, and others.

White House Response to the Altered Security Context after September 11

Paradoxically, the experience of terror combined with the lead-up to the Iraq war elevated the strategic importance of HIV/AIDS and created a critical impetus for PEPFAR. The president, emerging in this period with exceptional leeway to act and gain acceptance for his strategic choices from Congress and the American people, was well positioned to leverage the White House's expansive authority to push for acceptance of this program. After Republicans regained control of the Senate in the 2002 elections, the White House was further buoyed by the consolidation of predominant Republican power in both executive and legislative branches (a trend that only deepened after the 2004 elections). In sum, once the president elected to launch PEPFAR, it moved forward rapidly, initially encountering few serious obstacles.

September 11 forced an urgent, wholesale rethinking of global security within the administration, which soon placed surprisingly heavy emphasis on global health and the imperative to check the destructive power of runaway global infectious diseases, especially HIV/AIDS, in developing countries. A revised security doctrine that gave priority of place to global infectious disease was spelled out most explicitly and completely in the September 2002 National Security Strategy.[10] That document laid the analytical groundwork for the 2003 State of the Union address, which asserted that the president's HIV/AIDS initiative would serve the dual purposes of meeting global moral obligations and stemming new transnational security threats.

Parallel with this shift in strategic thinking, the administration in mid-2002 had begun formulating a large initiative—something "big"— that would counterbalance the ongoing U.S. military intervention in Afghanistan and the coming intervention in Iraq, planning for which accelerated in the second half of 2002. The program unveiled in January 2003 fit that requirement: it provided a dramatic "soft" offset to the "hard" projection of U.S. military might. PEPFAR would be concentrated in Africa, the continent historically of least strategic significance to the United States but of greatest global significance in terms of the humanitarian toll and threat to societies and national economies posed by HIV/AIDS. It was to be a single-disease campaign, drawing on the historical experience that narrowly focused disease campaigns have the greatest chance of capturing public attention and support (for example, the eradication campaigns against smallpox and polio).

Attitudinal Shift in America's Religious Conservative Community

In the late 1990s and into the present decade, this constituency, an integral part of the Bush administration's core electoral base, swung surprisingly strongly in favor of an activist international engagement to combat HIV/AIDS. It became increasingly engaged in international human rights, with a special focus on religious persecution, through the newly formed National Commission on International Religious Freedom and other forums. It took a lead role in pressing for high-level White House engagement in ending Sudan's internal war. In this period the constituency also began to hear impassioned appeals increasingly from Africa-based mission affiliates who stressed the dire threat that HIV/AIDS posed to their communities and requested expanded U.S. assistance. Important American personalities, notably Reverend Franklin Graham and Senator Jesse Helms, publicly took up their cause, drawing attention to the special threat that HIV/AIDS posed to the "innocent" categories of mothers, infants, and orphaned children.[11] Their efforts were buoyed by the increased feasibility of ART treatment and the development of prevention interventions based on abstinence and faithfulness. Such a focus at least temporarily altered the public face of HIV/AIDS and lowered the volume of discussion about the sexual and other behaviors of stigmatized high-risk core transmission groups (for example, men who have sex with men, injection drug users, and commercial sex workers) that, in reality, drive the pandemic.

Favorable Public Opinion and Bipartisan Governmental Support

In post–September 11 America, HIV/AIDS inherently resonated with the public's new, raw consciousness of terror.[12] Here was a disease with special, pernicious properties: it lay unseen, spreading quietly for years. When it struck, it shocked, creating a vast humanitarian toll and threatening the viability of societies in weak, ill-prepared states. For Americans also, there was a national narrative that resonated and could be tapped: we had a national experience of living with and containing the threat of HIV/AIDS, and we possessed a depth of technology and knowledge that could be mobilized to benefit others under threat outside our borders.

Even before September 11, the executive and legislative branches of the government were leaning toward a greater role for the United States in the global fight against HIV/AIDS. The Clinton administration, near the conclusion of its second term, mobilized bipartisan support in Congress for the $100 million LIFE (Leadership and Investment in Fighting an Epidemic) Initiative, proving that White House leadership on HIV/AIDS could leverage sentiment in favor of expanding U.S. efforts to combat HIV/AIDS in poor and middle-income countries.[13] The Bush administration, early on, built upon that initiative with additional increases.

This consensus was reinforced by opinion surveys, including a joint Center for Strategic and International Studies (CSIS)–UN Foundation survey in 2002 that demonstrated rising popular awareness of the pandemic, increasing compassion, and receptivity to an enlarged U.S. leadership role.[14] Also in 2002 Senators John Kerry and Bill Frist, original cochairs of the CSIS Task Force on HIV/AIDS, moved through the Senate their bill to fund AIDS prevention programs and investment in vaccine development, as well as to create a long-term strategy for dealing with the pandemic.[15]

When in 2003 the White House sought passage in Congress of authorizing legislation, it drew consciously on these earlier initiatives, confronted few barriers, and was quickly successful. That locked in a legislative success that could subsequently be used, to good effect, in the 2004 presidential elections.

The White House Style of Decisionmaking

A signature White House foreign assistance initiative entails a distinct style of decisionmaking, with certain institutional and political implications. Indeed, how decisions are made at the outset by the White House is often more significant than the content of the decisions themselves.

In mid-2002 President Bush mandated a select number of senior officials to devise PEPFAR, in relative secrecy and on an urgent basis, for launch by year's end. Information was tightly held; operational agency input was sought only on a highly selective basis, from one agency at a time; and external consultations with nongovernmental American public health authorities and international organizations were minimal.

The plan that emerged, not surprisingly, bore the markings of the Bush White House initiative. It was a top-down enterprise, calling for vesting exceptional powers in a State Department–based global AIDS coordinator— as an extension of the president—and it was overwhelmingly bilateral in character. Up to this point, U.S. leadership and funding had been critical to the launch of the Global Fund to Fight AIDS, Tuberculosis, and Malaria. The arrival of PEPFAR, which led to the proposal to earmark only $200 million a year for the Global Fund (less than half of the initial U.S. contribution in 2002) signaled a significant decrease in the priority assigned to the fund.[16]

The plan was heavily bounded and results centered: it confined itself to a single disease, set mass targets (2 million people on antiretroviral treatment, 7 million infections prevented, care for 10 million), and confined itself to fourteen (now fifteen) focal countries. Congressional earmarks were accepted, perhaps even encouraged—55 percent to treatment, 25 percent to care, 20 percent to prevention—that locked in ART as the initiative's centerpiece, in contrast to the established programs already being implemented by the U.S. Agency for International Development (USAID), Centers for Disease Control, and others that were overwhelmingly prevention oriented.[17]

This design, with its imperative to achieve quantifiable, verifiable results, was consciously adopted to ward off the skeptics, within the administration and Congress, who continued to question whether a high-profile, White House initiative on HIV/AIDS could truly achieve meaningful, concrete results in the short or medium term. It was meant to answer just how PEPFAR would prove that it could avoid the traps that had historically bedeviled foreign assistance—corruption, weak or decayed institutions, and feckless national leadership.

The Launch

The first year of PEPFAR operation showed promising results, detailed in the global AIDS coordinator's March 2005 report to Congress.[18] Country operational plans were developed, on a crash basis. By early 2005 the administration claimed that it had moved hundreds of millions of dollars in resources, contributed to placing over 230,000 persons on ART, and accelerated the delivery of treatment and prevention programs.[19] Some of these achievements were, at least in part, also the result of other investments by African governments and of U.S. corporate and foundation support for treatment programs.[20] Strong high-level executive leadership was pivotal to achieving these early positive outcomes.

To propel matters forward, Ambassador Tobias drew on his considerable senior corporate management experience, took full advantage of his White House mandate and a few new statutory authorities, and generated a blaze of activity. He wisely decided early on that embassy teams needed to be empowered to lead in the refinement and execution of strategies; embassies would not be forced to conform to centralized contracting mechanisms directed from Washington. He enforced a new level of unprecedented interagency cooperation; overrode select instances of embassy-based resistance; earned the personal confidence of many seasoned, activist U.S. ambassadors already in place in several of the focal countries; expedited the secondment to OGAC of critical staff from USAID, the Centers for Disease Control, and elsewhere; and quickly dispatched interagency expert teams to aid in the development of country plans. He established and led three extended consultations that brought together Washington and Atlanta personnel with embassy teams from the focal countries: in Gaborone, Botswana, in October 2003; Johannesburg, South Africa, in June 2004; and Addis Ababa, Ethiopia, in May 2005. Over time, these sessions became highly important in advancing direct face-to-face communications, building trust, and promoting cross-fertilization of programs. In 2004 Tobias also established Washington-based "core teams" assigned to liaise with counterpart embassy teams in the focus countries.[21]

As plans were formulated and implementation began, disclosure of data was controlled, in part because of congressional notification considerations and because no system for disclosure was in place, but also to minimize outside scrutiny in this delicate phase. Lack of early transparency dampened outside demands for explanations and allowed a concentrated focus on the immediate requirements of setting up programs. It also fed frustration and suspicion, including within Congress and the implementing agencies themselves, and meant that when speculative or otherwise ill-informed accounts of decisions began to surface, accurate data were often not immediately available to inform discourse.

It took the administration six crucial months to reach consensus on guidance for prevention policy. What resulted, in March 2005, was a careful, balanced statement, achieved after hard internal debate—testimony to Ambassador Tobias's ability to navigate intense political cross-currents.[22] Others were not as adept at avoiding the political shoals. For example, some embassies, in weighing early decisions on prevention, chose to lower their perceived political exposure—unnecessarily in retrospect—by retreating from a serious commitment to condom distribution and work with commercial sex workers. Mid-level and senior personnel at some embassies feared retribution, both from Congress and the administration.

In the first year of start-up, Ambassador Tobias also consciously postponed certain critical decisions for later resolution. The issue of whether generic medications would qualify for ART programs was deferred by placing it in the hands of a newly created Food and Drug Administration fast-track authority in 2004.[23] The first such generic drug was approved in May 2005; seven had been approved by the end of 2005 (approximately fifteen would be required before a full complement of generics could begin to be deployed). The operating assumption was that this channel could settle the question in a timely enough fashion, before programmatic demands for high volumes of low-cost quality medications accelerated steeply in year two. In the short term, the decision eased immediate political pressures, and different short-term treatment strategies were pursued (for example, winning Nigeria's permission to begin treatment in year one of 15,000 individuals with branded drugs and providing second-line therapies in Zambia). By mid-2005, however, this approach was becoming openly problematic and threatened to constrain future progress gravely. With no clear plan yet in place for how the administration was to deliver—reliably, safely, and in adequate volumes— low-cost generic medications (optimally, single-dose triple therapies), U.S. embassies were by mid-2005 "in a black box," in the words of one ambassador, when attempting to explain to their staff and their host governments how they intended to meet their ambitious targets for expanded treatment.[24]

Similarly, OGAC delayed consideration of its long-term institutional and staffing structure, including possible special legislative authorities. During year one the assumption was that an adequate ad hoc team had been assembled and that in time more careful consideration of institutional requirements could be pursued. That decision underestimated the level of fatigue that Washington and embassy personnel would experience.

The State Department had been selected as the institutional home for OGAC to signal PEPFAR's significance to U.S. foreign policy and to position it to broker relations with the Department of Health and Human Services and USAID. That the Department of State did not have a good record as an operational agency—an obvious concern—was not considered an impediment at the time.

However, in 2004 it became apparent that this was an imperfect solution. Identification with the State Department failed to deliver several anticipated advantages, nor did OGAC acquire strong diplomatic capacities.

Early in the Bush administration's first term, Secretary of State Colin Powell had been a powerful advocate for greater U.S. involvement in fighting HIV/AIDS; yet later he was only minimally enlisted in support of PEPFAR's start-up. Only rarely were his deputies called upon by Ambassador Tobias to provide assistance in breaking bureaucratic logjams. The regional bureaus' senior leadership in Washington, most importantly that of the Bureau of African Affairs, played virtually no role in policy formulation and implementation. It was the ambassadors in key African embassies who were integral and in the lead; the bureau in Washington was often largely unaware of what was unfolding. The international health office in the Bureau of Oceans and International Environmental and Scientific Affairs was largely marginalized as OGAC took form. As a matter of departmental policy, no decision was made to create and place in the embassies of focal countries foreign service officers with expertise in both global health and coordination; over time, this knowledge gap would become problematic.

There were other actions taken that also weakened OGAC's linkages to the foreign policy establishment. Its offices were physically located outside the State Department; the diplomatic deputy slot was eliminated in 2004 and only restored at the end of 2005; and most of its work was to be performed outside normal departmental cable channels, relying instead largely on e-mail and other unclassified, uncleared communications.

However, OGAC did make important adjustments in its first year. In particular, operations in three areas that initially received insufficient attention and showed weak outcomes—diplomacy, gender issues, and the role of the military—were subsequently improved.

Diplomacy

The Fifteenth International AIDS Conference in Bangkok, Thailand, in July 2004 was a diplomatic and public relations nadir. Ill-prepared and defensive, the administration came across in the international media as inwardly focused and antagonistic to the Global Fund and other international organizations. Little credit was given to U.S. government efforts, and heated criticisms dominated much of the media coverage and commentary. This experience came two years after the Fourteenth International AIDS Conference, held in Barcelona, Spain, in 2002, where U.S. Health and Human Services Secretary Tommy Thompson was heckled and booed on stage while delivering a keynote address.[25]

However, diplomatic gains were made during this same period. In Washington in April 2004, OGAC joined UNAIDS, the Global Fund, and Britain to launch "The Three Ones." This was a commitment, prompted by demands from overtaxed recipient governments, that donors work collaboratively with them to agree upon one national plan, one coordinating mechanism, and one monitoring and evaluation system for each country.[26] However, follow-up implementation has been slow. Further diplomatic progress was seen at the Davos World Economic Forum in January 2005, when the United States, UNAIDS, and the Global Fund documented in a single consensus statement the rising numbers of persons with access to antiretroviral treatment.[27]

Gender Issues

Over the course of 2004 and into 2005, the administration began to pay more serious attention to the structural factors that account for the acute vulnerability of young women and girls to HIV/AIDS. Initially, OGAC downplayed this dimension. In the five-year strategy, issued in the spring of 2004, and the first-year review issued a year later, there was open and detailed acknowledgment of the centrality of gender and the need to translate that awareness into effective programs and policies.[28] However, integrating these issues into operations, as with instituting stronger international coordination mechanisms, has proven difficult and slow.

Role of the Military

Last, as planning proceeded in 2004, the administration moved to make greater use of military-to-military programs, tapping capacities and interest in the U.S. European Command, Walter Reed Army Medical Center, and the Naval Health Unit in San Diego. In fiscal year 2005, PEPFAR underwrote the costs of a rising number of military-to-military treatment, care, and prevention programs across the fifteen focus countries, at an aggregate commitment of over $30 million.

Lessons Learned Thus Far

In the short span of its existence, PEPFAR has revealed five compelling realities. These center on the pivotal role of White House leadership; the virtues and pitfalls of rapid and strong implementation; the new obstacles encountered over time; the need for a clear, stable balance between bilateral and multilateral approaches; and the need to accommodate the evolving situation on the ground.

White House Leadership Is Essential to Quick Major Results—and to Future Sustainability

Substantial early progress in the launch phase (early 2004 to the present) has relied overwhelmingly on strong White House leadership, backed by the promise of major new resources and an urgent, strategic purpose. It was essential for mobilizing Congress, multiple agencies, scattered embassies, and recipient governments. Without this factor, the initiative never would have taken off.

A Good Beginning Draws Praise—and Recurrent, Increasingly Partisan Criticism

PEPFAR has drawn praise from diverse quarters for its determined approach and early impressive results. It has also drawn persistent criticisms that the program

—was introduced without adequate prior consultations with recipient governments, American public health experts, and international organizations already actively engaged in providing HIV/AIDS services;

—follows an overwhelmingly bilateral approach that undervalues the integration of U.S. efforts with others and dangerously downgrades U.S. commitment to the new multilateral financing instrument, the Global Fund;

—focuses narrowly on the provision of medical treatment and too little on the need to build a sustainable public health infrastructure that brings broad benefits and on the means to overcome the mounting shortfall in skilled health workers; and

—is hostile to the use of condoms and harm reduction strategies for drug-injecting populations, and does not take a comprehensive enough view of prevention.[29]

Alternatively, among political conservatives, especially the religious conservative community, a counterview is that the "Abstinence, Be faithful, and Condoms" (ABC) prevention approach places excessive reliance on the mass distribution of condoms.

Formidable Obstacles to Sustainability Become More Visible over Time

Regarding *mass treatment,* there are considerable unknowns related to the true cost of universal procurement, as well as the difficulties of providing treatment on a mass scale. There are also nagging questions, such as how to overcome Africa's growing deficit of skilled health workers and how to mitigate the skewing of health services that will result when a sudden, massive investment is made in HIV/AIDS services.

There is deep uncertainty as to whether it will be possible to ensure a reliable, unbroken logistics chain of affordable ART medications to 2 million individuals residing in fifteen countries. These countries often have weak institutions that are vulnerable to corruption. Also, no one can reliably predict the true, long-term costs of sustaining this program. It will be essential to account increasingly for individuals who start therapy on less expensive drug regimens and then later require far more expensive, second-line therapy after they have developed side effects or resistance to first-line drugs.

There is also continued confusion over how U.S. procurement of medications for treatment, both patented and generic, will be coordinated with that of the Global Fund, the World Bank, the U.K.'s Department for International Development, and others. With no proven record of delivering low-cost generic medications reliably, safely, and in adequate volumes, U.S. embassies are hard pressed to explain, to their staff and to host governments, how they will expedite meeting their ambitious targets for expanded treatment as popular expectations continue to rise.

There is the daunting macroissue of what will be the true cost for expanded treatment to meet dramatically expanded demand in the developing world and how these costs will be met. It is wholly plausible that the future costs of delivering and sustaining treatment to an ever larger population in developing countries will be several times that of current levels. A premise of UNAIDS estimates for future requirements is that ART will account for an increasing share of total expenditures, assuming that new HIV infections continue at the current high rates and that significantly higher numbers of people living with HIV will demand and gain access to treatment, extend their lives as a result, and add steadily to a population on treatment in the developing world for an indefinite period. Such a scenario suggests that we may very well be on the verge of an explosive demand for ART in the developing world and a sharp ratcheting upward of long-term carrying costs. These shifts, if they result in widening funding gaps, could heighten tensions between poor countries acutely affected by HIV/AIDS and the United States and other wealthy Western donors. For the United States, this scenario argues strongly in favor of engaging Congress early on the likely escalating costs for mass treatment and what might be a "fair share" for the United States. It also argues for aggressive early outreach to other donors and countries affected by HIV/AIDS to seek a concerted approach to future escalating demands.

Skilled workforce shortages are also a profound obstacle to delivery of HIV/AIDS services on a national scale in Africa. Africa will need to more than double its current number of skilled health workers (doctors, nurses, laboratory technicians, and managers) if it is to fulfill the program's treatment goals. Greatly expanded training is essential, but the challenge reaches far beyond that. It requires countering the international commercial recruitment of skilled personnel from Africa by establishing retention policies that redress poor pay, unsafe working conditions, and weak management. Furthermore, there must be a strategy to minimize the subsequent distortion of health services: a sudden surge of funding for HIV/AIDS can deplete assistance in other critical areas, such as child vaccination and diarrhea treatment and prevention programs, worsening mortality risks. Donors, the United States included, have up to now been ill prepared to deal with this stark trade-off, either through bilateral programs or in concert through multilateral initiatives.

In the *prevention arena,* a worsening political polarization threatens effective action and overall sustainability of HIV/AIDS programs. If the spread of the pandemic is truly to be reversed, then prevention must be a priority. The only way that mass treatment can be sustained, moreover, is if the number of new infections is curbed through effective prevention. But ensuring that prevention is a genuine priority and that prevention services are really effective are formidable challenges. Making the case for providing treatment to extend the lives of persons living with HIV is inherently more compelling than advocating prevention of HIV infections: the former delivers a tangible service—with observable results—that restores hope for individuals; the latter, when successful, is a nonevent. Furthermore, while much is known about what works to reduce the spread of HIV, a strong consensus is lacking on how to apply such strategies. Indeed, much of the HIV prevention arena is highly contested societal terrain that inherently invites escalating conflicts around moral and cultural values. At its base, any consideration of HIV/AIDS prevention entails changing the behaviors of adults and adolescents, and this requires an often uncomfortable confrontation with intimate aspects of human sexuality—and in some countries, with the interaction of sex, illicit drug use, and alcohol. It means inexorably grappling with gender violence and inequality, and the behavior of stigmatized high-risk groups such as commercial sex workers, men who have sex with men, and injection drug users.

The prevention issue has been further complicated by the intensifying suspicion and criticism of PEPFAR emanating from groups who subscribe to a diverse range of ideologies and perspectives and whose information is frequently grounded in anecdotes or otherwise thin data. Much of the conflict has centered on the clash between advocates of condoms versus advocates of "abstinence only" as a preferred prevention intervention. A related controversy arose in early 2005 when Tommy Thompson, then-secretary of Health and Human Services, announced that nongovernmental organization grantees would have to sign a statement condemning commercial sex work.[30] This, in turn, triggered a lawsuit by DKT International after it lost U.S. funding for prevention programs in Vietnam because it refused to comply with this requirement.[31]

The burgeoning conflict between the different perspectives toward prevention came into full view in late August 2005 when AIDS activists alleged that Uganda was experiencing a dire shortage of condoms that was "being driven and exacerbated by PEPFAR and by the extreme policies that the administration in the United States is now pursuing."[32] This incited immediate public counterattacks by U.S. conservatives on American funding for the distribution of condoms.[33] These episodes have created a loud background noise that has hardened opinion and conjured false choices; edged out consideration of many important prevention issues such as gender, alcohol abuse, and injection drug use; and obscured the debate over PEPFAR's long-term requirements.

This escalating confrontation could move in two directions. The two new de facto partners in support of expanded HIV/AIDS programs—secular and religious—could find sufficient common purpose, manage their differences, and strengthen the bipartisan compact that made PEPFAR possible. Alternatively, they could grow more antagonistic as implementation proceeds, battling over strategies via the airwaves and in Congress. Under the latter scenario, the political center will ultimately fray, weakening prospects for future, high-level U.S. leadership in the fight to control HIV/AIDS.

Without a Clear, Stable Balance between U.S. Bilateralism and Multilateral Options, Conflict Increases

The Global Fund to Fight AIDS, Tuberculosis, and Malaria, an independent, international financing instrument, was launched in 2002 with heavy U.S. political and financial backing.[34] It seeks to cover a financing gap— estimated at $7 to $9 billion in 2002—for controlling these diseases. By summer 2005 the Global Fund had committed $3.7 billion to over 300 programs in 127 countries. Sixty percent of its funds went to Africa, and 55 percent were allocated to fight HIV/AIDS. As of September 2005, the Global Fund had moved $1.5 billion to field projects, contributing to 220,000 persons receiving ART, 600,000 people receiving treatment for tuberculosis, and 1.1 million people being treated for malaria.

With the launch of PEPFAR in 2003, the Global Fund's relationship with the United States became more complicated and at times difficult. The administration has publicly acknowledged the Global Fund's special strengths and capacities and its value as a partner. The fund can leverage resources from multiple sources, finance tuberculosis and malaria programs in PEPFAR focus countries, and support a range of infectious disease programs in countries that matter to the United States but fall outside of PEPFAR's purview.

Tensions are inherent in the relationship, however, since the Global Fund and PEPFAR are in competition for scarce dollars. That competition appears increasingly zero-sum, especially as PEPFAR programs rapidly expand and require ever more funding at the same time that pressures intensify on the Global Fund to graduate to the scale of operations originally envisioned for it by its founders. This inherent competition prompted skeptics within the administration to emphasize the Global Fund's slow disbursement rates and criticize its other flaws. It lacks operational or technical capacities and is wholly reliant on in-country partners. It also lacks a track record for control over corruption, initially had weak fundraising success with European donors and the Japanese, and is vulnerable to multiple political pressures. To the Global Fund's credit, its management sought to answer each of these concerns promptly, as best it could during the fund's start-up phase, and quickly set up on its website impressive, transparent reporting mechanisms, superior to those of virtually all bilateral donors, including the United States.

In the initial allocation plan for PEPFAR's $15 billion, annual contributions to the Global Fund were set at $200 million, far less than the $300 million committed in the fund's start-up year between 2001 and 2002, or the $322 million committed in 2003. Beginning in 2003, finding a proper balance between the U.S. bilateral program and the Global Fund fell to congressional appropriators, who were generous and protective of the Global Fund (allocating $458 million in 2004 and $435 million in 2005).

Beginning in fiscal year 2004, Congress also officially mandated that the U.S. contribution could not exceed one-third of the total funds raised.[35] That prompted the Global Fund's leadership to become more aggressive in fundraising, scoring major gains from the Japanese, Canadians, French, and Germans in the lead-up to the 2005 G8 Summit at Gleneagles in Perthshire, Scotland. But achieving these results has become increasingly problematic. At the September 2005 meeting to replenish funding for the Global Fund's existing projects, donors pledged only $3.7 billion toward the estimated requirement of $7.1 billion.[36] While European donations were up significantly, most notably from the French (and also the Japanese), the U.S. annual contribution, at $300 million for each of the next two years, amounted to far less than one-third of funds pledged. It now remains to be seen whether Congress increases that amount significantly. The disappointing replenishment outcome not only called into question the "fair shares" compact, but it also challenged the ability of the Global Fund to sustain its existing project commitments and, beyond that, to fund new projects to meet emerging demands in the next two years.

Evolving On-the-Ground Realities in the Focus Countries Will Shape PEPFAR's Future Outcomes

Over time, U.S. policies, funding levels, and programs will have to accommodate the changing situations in the focus countries. During the first year of operations, the difference in outcomes among the fifteen focal countries became increasingly manifest. Among small or mid-sized stable African states with reasonably good leadership, established national policies, working relations with donor governments and implementing organizations, and established operational platforms, it has been comparatively straightforward to plan for and begin operation of expanded treatment, care, and prevention programs. Within this promising pool are Uganda, Kenya, Tanzania, Botswana, Mozambique, Rwanda, Zambia, and Namibia. In most of these countries, the administration has had U.S. ambassadors and agency directors who have considerable field knowledge and experience in HIV/AIDS, and a strong passion to do more.

South Africa has posed a paradoxical challenge. Despite exceptional capacities in government, industry, the private health sector, and the nongovernmental sector, it continues to be led by a recalcitrant national government that does not embrace the urgent priority of advancing HIV/AIDS programs. The U.S. embassy there—prescient, well led, and staffed with an unusual depth of public health expertise—foresaw these challenges early and developed arguably the most comprehensive and sophisticated strategy to circumnavigate South Africa's special obstacles. A robust civil society and an independent judiciary in South Africa also acted to overcome the government's resistance to providing a broad-scale treatment program. South Africa now spends more than any other African country on HIV/AIDS.[37]

At the other end of the spectrum are weak or failing states (for example, Côte d'Ivoire and Haiti) where few favorable conditions exist for PEPFAR to take root. Guyana, though less overtly conflicted, nonetheless remains weak and unpromising.

Ethiopia and Nigeria present their own exceptional challenges: large populations (70 million and 130 million, respectively), nonexistent or greatly decayed public health systems, delayed action in launching national policies on HIV/AIDS, minimal strength within the nongovernmental sector, and inherent instability—born of pervasive corruption in Nigeria and a structural vulnerability to mass famine in Ethiopia. In these two instances, progress in achieving early and mid-term goals in treatment, care, and prevention is not out of the question but is not likely to be near the scale envisioned in the initial targets set by PEPFAR.

Vietnam, selected as the fifteenth focal country in 2004, is still at an early point in the development of PEPFAR programs. It is the sole focal country with an epidemic that is predominantly driven by injection drug use, and for that reason decisions regarding U.S. policies and approaches in Vietnam will set important precedents, especially with respect to substitution therapies and access to injection drug users and commercial sex workers seeking care and transition support out of rehabilitation centers. At present, OGAC has not issued policy guidelines for providing ART to injection drug users.

Elements of a Sustainable U.S. Approach

It is still early in the PEPFAR process, and yet much uncertainty hangs over its future sustainability. Several strains are increasingly a factor: worsening budget deficits; clashes between secular and religious constituencies and their respective allies within Congress; outsized expectations, especially regarding treatment; uncertainties over the future carrying costs for programs; tensions between PEPFAR and the Global Fund; and pressures for greater transparency in the disclosure of information. All of these will come into play as Congress in 2006 and 2007 considers reauthorizing the programs beyond the first five-year period, which ends in fiscal year 2008. A number of key conditions will be essential to a sustained, effective U.S. AIDS policy.

Continued White House leadership will be strategic to an effective U.S. approach. Much of the success achieved thus far has rested on the quality and forcefulness of leadership choices made in the early start-up phase. A critical next decision, with regard to sustaining White House engagement, will be the selection of a dynamic successor to Ambassador Tobias. On policy grounds a critical test will be whether the president makes the case for a balanced approach between bilateral programs and multilateral approaches, one that forcefully reaffirms the U.S. commitment to doing its fair share to sustain *both* PEPFAR and the Global Fund. A weak or failing Global Fund will only weaken U.S. bilateral efforts and threaten overall global mobilization. In the near future lies the test of what the president will argue before Congress as the U.S. vision beyond fiscal year 2008. And beyond 2008 lies the challenge of guaranteeing that the next U.S. president attaches equal importance to global control of HIV/AIDS and builds that priority explicitly into his or her foreign policy agenda.

The administration will need to articulate a long-term, broadened vision and action plan that surmounts emerging challenges. Congress and the American people need to be convinced that the U.S. commitment on battling HIV/AIDS is a lengthy enterprise that will stretch well into the coming decade and will require multiple robust instruments.

On the treatment side, an effective U.S. strategy will require review of true input costs and a realistic assessment of the pressures that are building to increase the U.S. commitment to make ART available to an expanding population of persons living with HIV in developing countries. Part of making the case to the American people will be demonstrating convincingly that the commitments made thus far are indeed achieving results and that other donors are contributing their escalating "fair share."

Future success in sustaining U.S. leadership will also require speedy resolution of critical procurement issues, including expediting procurement contracts and determining which producers of generic single dose therapies qualify for U.S. purchase and can reliably meet growing demands. Beyond these immediate concerns, more effort is needed to lower the risk of major future production and supply disruptions and to encourage corporate investment in the next generation of antiretroviral medications.

On the prevention side, there will be a continued pressing need, well into the future, for the administration to make explicit that prevention is indeed a genuine top priority, backed by money, strategy, and pronouncements. Twenty percent of aggregate resources is simply too little for effective prevention efforts. Standards and prevention targets need better definition, and the official strategy must be broadened beyond "ABC" to encompass a comprehensive approach that addresses the different routes of transmission (including alcohol and injection drug use) and the underlying issues, such as gender inequality.

For all programs, PEPFAR's future requires an increasing investment in skilled personnel. A more systematic, far-reaching plan of action is needed to expand training and retention programs, improve projections of future skill needs, and track future progress. This will entail strategic planning in concert with African governments, other donors, and international organizations. This process will be strengthened by increasingly linking U.S. investments to the creation of enduring health care capacities in African countries and by broadening the focus of U.S. efforts to include malaria, tuberculosis, and other acute infectious diseases.

Strengthening U.S. coordination with other agencies, especially the Global Fund and the World Bank, will be key to building up broad-based public health systems in Africa. It will also serve to develop viable international schemes to offset the drain of medical talent out of Africa by offering new training and retention programs.

The future will require giving higher priority to strengthening capacities within the Office of the Global AIDS Coordinator and U.S. embassies and taking steps to more closely integrate the Department of State's Office of International Health Affairs with OGAC. OGAC will need a stronger diplomatic team to leverage higher commitments from other donors, manage relations with host governments, and integrate policy initiatives with the Global Fund, UNAIDS, and other entities. Giving priority to strengthening OGAC will help enlist the resources of the State Department, which are today marginal to PEPFAR's work, and bind the secretary of state more intimately to PEPFAR's mission. Likewise the Department of State will need to create professional incentives and the structure necessary to integrate global health issues into U.S. foreign policy, for instance, by establishing a global health career track.

The United States has reason to be proud of its achievements in recent years in mobilizing the political will and bringing substantial new resources forward to combat HIV/AIDS in the developing world. Anyone who visits a focus country knows how the White House's PEPFAR initiative has touched the lives of people living with HIV as well as the lives of their loved ones. Anyone who has friends among the frontline personnel responsible for moving programs knows of their intense dedication and resolve. This is not easy work.

There is also reason for humility and caution. As the United States and its partners have moved from the euphoric launch phase earlier in the decade to the operational implementation phase of the past two years, it has become far clearer just how daunting and complex the essential interventions are. The process of discovery has often been rude and disquieting. It has also become clearer how fragile is the process of preserving bipartisan support at home and building the legitimacy of U.S. efforts abroad. A White House signature initiative benefited enormously from the power and prestige of that institution. Substantial, quick, early gains generated considerable good will and political space. But not for long. This White House initiative was also a conspicuous foreign assistance innovation focused on a disease grounded in sexuality and a pandemic that is still in its ascendance. No less important, it was introduced in a period of rising political and cultural polarization at home and abroad, for which the White House, fairly or unfairly, was often called to account. More courage and creativity will be needed into the future to navigate these shoals and sustain U.S. commitments. That is where transformational diplomacy will be tested at its core.

Notes

1. George Bush, "State of the Union Address," Washington, D.C., January 28, 2003.

2. On May 27, 2003, President Bush signed P.L. 108-25, the *United States Leadership against Global HIV/AIDS, Tuberculosis, and Malaria Act of 2003,* which provided the legislative authorization for PEPFAR.

3. President Bush's original plan included Botswana, Ethiopia, Guyana, Haiti, Côte d'Ivoire, Kenya, Mozambique, Namibia, Nigeria, Rwanda, South Africa, Tanzania, Uganda, and Zambia. In November 2003 Congress required that an additional country, outside Africa and the Caribbean, be designated. Ambassador Tobias announced the selection of Vietnam as the fifteenth focus country in June 2004.

4. P.L. 108-25, sec. 403.

5. See Yazdan Yazdanpanah, "Costs Associated with Combination Antiretroviral Therapy in HIV-Infected Patients," *Journal of Antimicrobial Chemotherapy* 53, no. 4 (2004): 558-61; UNICEF–UNAIDS Secretariat–WHO–Médecins sans Frontières, *Sources and Prices of Selected Medicines and Diagnostics for People Living with HIV/AIDS* (June 2004).

6. See Tom Malinowski, "The Epidemic and the Administration," *Washington Post,* February 9, 2001, p. A29.

7. See Jennifer Moeller, "Success in Haiti—One Program at a Time," *Christian Science Monitor* (www.csmonitor.com/2005/0926/p13s02-lire.html [September 26, 2005]).

8. U.S. Agency for International Development, "Life Expectancy Will Drop Worldwide Due to AIDS," Press Release 2002-068 (July 8, 2002).

9. UNAIDS and World Bank, "AIDS Hindering Economic Growth, Worsening Poverty in Hard-Hit Countries," Press Release (July 11, 2000).

10. See White House, *The National Security Strategy of the United States of America* (www.whitehouse.gov/nsc/nss.pdf [September 2002]).

11. See Holly Burkhalter, "The Politics of AIDS: Engaging Conservative Activists," *Foreign Affairs* 83 (January/February 2004): 8-14; CBS News, "Jesse Helms to Tackle AIDS" (cbsnews.cbs.com/stories/2002/02/26/politics/main502106.shtml [February 21, 2002]).

12. See "The Worldwide Threat in 2003: Evolving Dangers in a Complex World," Testimony of CIA Director George Tenet before the Senate Select Committee on Intelligence, February 11, 2003 (www.cia.gov/cia/public_affairs/speeches/2003/dci_speech_02112003.html [February 2006]).

13. See White House, Office of the Vice President, "Vice President Gore Announces Administration Will Seek $100 Million Initiative—a Record Increase—in Funds to Fight Global AIDS," Press Release (January 19, 1999).

14. Public Opinion Strategies and Greenberg Quinlan Rosner Research; Bill McInturff, partner; Bob Boorstin, partner; Lori Weigel, partner; CSIS HIV/AIDS Task Force, *The Global AIDS Crisis: A National Survey of Likely Voters and a Survey of Foreign Policy Experts In-Depth Interviews* (April 2002). The survey was commissioned by the Better World Campaign to support the CSIS Task Force on HIV/AIDS, cochaired by Senators William Frist (R-Tenn.) and Russell Feingold (D-Wisc.).

15. *U.S. Leadership against HIV/AIDS, TB and Malaria Act of 2002,* S. Rept. 10-206, 107 Cong. 2 sess. (June 26, 2002).

16. U.S. Department of State, Office of the Spokesman, "Global Fund to Fight AIDS, Tuberculosis, and Malaria (revised) Fact Sheet" (March 3, 2003).

17. P.L. 108-25, sec. 403.

18. U.S. Department of State, Office of the U.S. Global AIDS Coordinator, *Engendering Bold Leadership: The President's Emergency Plan for AIDS Relief. First Annual Report to Congress* (March 2005).

19. For the fifteen PEPFAR focus countries, the administration moved $350 million in early 2004, $515 million in mid-2004, and just under $1.4 billion in mid-2005. Other funds flowed simultaneously to the Global Fund, other bilateral programs, and research. Ibid.

20. See Craig Timberg, "Botswana's Gains against AIDS Put U.S. Claims to Test," *Washington Post,* July 1, 2005, p. A1.

21. See Department of State, *Engendering Bold Leadership,* chap. 10 (www.state.gov/s/gac/rl/43967.htm [May 23, 2005]).

22. For more information on OGAC prevention policies, see U.S. State Department, "Sexual Transmission of HIV and the ABC Approach to Prevention" (www.state.gov/documents/organization/58270.pdf [December 2005]).

23. *Federal Drug Administration Modernization Act of 1997,* P.L. 105-115, sec. 112.

24. In late September 2005, the administration awarded a three-year, $77 million contract to the Partnership for Supply Chain Management—a network comprising fifteen groups—to manage the supply of treatment drugs and related supplies estimated at $500 million in value. See U.S. Department of State, "Public-Private Partnership to Enhance Delivery of AIDS Drugs," Press Release 2005-082 (September 27, 2005).

25. See Sanjay Gupta, "Bush's Thompson Booed at AIDS Conference" (archives.cnn.com/2002/ALLPOLITICS/07/09/thompson.aids.conference [July 9, 2002]).

26. On April 25, 2004, UNAIDS, the United States, and the United Kingdom cohosted a high-level meeting in Washington to launch "The Three Ones." See UNAIDS, "The Three Ones" (www.unaids.org/en/Coordination/Initiatives/three_ones.asp [February 2006]).

27. See World Health Organization, "700,000 People Living with AIDS in Developing Countries Now Receiving Treatment," Press Release (www.who.int/mediacentre/news/releases/2005/pr07/en [January 26, 2005]).

28. See U.S. Department of State, Office of the U.S. Global AIDS Coordinator, *The President's Emergency Plan for AIDS Relief: U.S. Five-Year Global HIV/AIDS Strategy* (February 2004); Department of State, *Engendering Bold Leadership.*

29. See "News: International AIDS Conference Roundup," *Global Fund Observer Newsletter,* no. 30, July 16, 2004.

30. Brennan Center for Justice, NYU School of Law, "Constitutionality of Anti-Prostitution Pledge in the AIDS Act," Memorandum, June 13, 2005 (www.nswp.org/pdf/BRENNAN-USAID.PDF[February 2006]).

31. "AIDS, Aid and Prostitution," *Economist,* August 18, 2005.

32. This comment by Stephen Lewis, the UN secretary general's special envoy for HIV/AIDS in Africa, was based on allegations laid out by Jodi Jacobson of the Center for Health and Gender Equity. See Lawrence K. Altman, "U.S. Blamed for Condom Shortage in Fighting AIDS in Uganda," *New York Times,* August 30, 2005, p. A4.

33. James Dobson, head of Focus on the Family, condemned the U.S.-based group, Advocates for Youth, for promoting condom use in Uganda and reasserted that the dramatic drop in that nation's HIV prevalence was due to abstinence. In a related development, Senator Tom Coburn (R-Okla.) demanded that the United States cease financing a prevention program by Population Services International in Central America that promoted condom use. See William Fisher, "Politics: U.S. Conservatives Step Up Fight against Condom Programs," *Inter Press Service,* September 1, 2005.

34. Global Fund for AIDS, Tuberculosis and Malaria, "History of the Fund in Detail" (www.theglobalfund.org/en/about/road/history/default.asp [January 24, 2005]).

35. Global Fund for AIDS, Tuberculosis and Malaria, "Global Fund Receives Pledges of U.S. $3.7 Billion for 2006–2007," Press Release (September 6, 2005).

36. U.S. Department of State, "U.S. Challenges Other Donors to Support Global Disease Fund" (usinfo.state.gov/gi/Archive/2004/Aug/20-550748.html [August 19, 2004]).

37. UNAIDS, "South Africa" (www.unaids.org/en/Regions_Countries/Countries/south_africa.asp [January 25, 2006]).

CHAPTER 4

Strengthening U.S. Development Assistance

Steven Radelet

Beginning in the early 1990s, two major trends in the world economy led to renewed debate about development assistance, its purposes, and how to make it more effective. First, with the end of the cold war, many aid programs lost their raison d'être and much of their political support. Second, the resolution of the widespread macroeconomic crises that had led to the ascendancy of International Monetary Fund (IMF) and World Bank stabilization and structural adjustment programs led to a deep rethinking about the IMF and World Bank approach. While these programs had clearly helped many countries achieve macroeconomic stability, critics charged that they had had little impact on growth and poverty reduction, and in some cases appeared to have been a detriment to development. Broad-based program aid based on strict donor-driven policies and demands for reform seemed to have failed, at least in many countries.

Criticisms of aid grew sharply, with detractors from left and right arguing that aid programs were heavily bureaucratic, unfocused, poorly managed, and ineffective in supporting development. U.S. foreign aid was criticized for having far too many objectives (often conflicting), being too disorganized across too many implementing agencies, laboring under too many restrictions from Congress, and having too large a bureaucracy.[1]

While many of these criticisms were valid and there is little doubt that aid could be improved, these problems should not be overstated. It would be incorrect to conclude (as some have) that the entire U.S. aid program has been a failure. There have been several important accomplishments, such as the U.S. Agency for International Development's contributions to the Green Revolution, its role in developing oral rehydration therapy, involvement in the campaign to reduce river blindness, work on population and family planning, and more recent efforts in support of innovative microfinance and HIV/AIDS programs. Recent research has shown that aid (from all donors) that actually has been aimed at supporting economic growth has largely had a positive impact, and several studies have concluded that aid has worked well in countries with strong policies and good governance, although other research has challenged that result.[2] The strong pessimism about aid expressed by some is unfounded. Aid has been successful in countries like Korea, Botswana, Indonesia, and, more recently, Uganda, Tanzania, and Mozambique, and has had a large impact on improving global health.[3] But there is little doubt that it has been less successful in many others countries—and in some countries has done damage.

Given these mixed results, there is little question that U.S. development aid could be improved dramatically. Much aid is wasted on countries with governments that are not serious about development, on projects that are poorly designed, and on heavy bureaucracy that ensures that a large proportion of aid money never gets close to its intended recipients. Part of the problem lies with the internal structure and culture of the U.S. Agency for International Development (USAID) and other agencies as well. Much of the problem also lies with the elaborate web of legislation and directives from Congress under which the agency labors. To get a sense of the complexity, consider the U.S. Foreign Assistance Act of 1961, which, as amended, specifies a remarkable 33 different goals, 75 priority areas, and 247 directives. These multiple goals are more than just an administrative burden: they make it very difficult for USAID to achieve clear results. In particular, when USAID is asked to provide funds to strategic and diplomatic partners to meet important national security objectives, the impact of its programs on economic development and poverty reduction can suffer as a result.

Foreign assistance has assumed a much stronger position in U.S. foreign policy in recent years. The Bush administration made development one of the three cornerstones of its National Security Strategy alongside diplomacy and defense. U.S. spending on assistance, which began rising in 1998, has accelerated in recent years with the launch of the Millennium Challenge Corporation (MCC), the President's Emergency Plan for AIDS Relief (PEPFAR), and other initiatives.

U.S. foreign assistance stands at an important crossroads, and the opportunity exists to take steps to improve the way the United States provides assistance. This chapter begins by examining some of the most important changes in global donor practices in response to the criticisms of aid and their implications for the U.S. government. It then explores three critical ways in which U.S. development assistance could be strengthened:

—first, improving allocation of aid dollars by providing more to countries that need it most and can use it well;

—second, developing a broader range of approaches for providing development assistance and delivering it differently to countries, depending on the quality of their governance and policies; and

—third, improving monitoring and evaluation and moving more toward managing for results.

Evolving Practices

In response to the growing criticisms of aid in the 1990s, foreign donors have begun to change how they deliver aid in several key ways. Many of these changes are central to efforts to improve the effectiveness of U.S. assistance programs. Five key changes are most relevant.

Improving Aid Allocation

Donors are beginning to change how they allocate aid in order to provide more to countries that can use it well and less to those that are less likely to show strong results. Many donors, particularly the United States, France, Belgium, and several others, tend to provide disproportionately large amounts of aid to political allies and middle-income countries that have much less poverty than low-income countries. They also give too much aid to countries that do not have policies and institutions conducive to sustained development. Research has shown that aid could be more effective in supporting growth and reducing poverty if it were allocated to countries that have both a large share of people living in poverty and relatively strong policies and institutions conducive to economic growth.[4]

The World Bank and regional development banks have started using "performance-based allocation" systems to distribute aid based on country need and policy and institutional performance. Some European donors have moved toward a performance- and needs-based system. The United States has taken some big steps in this direction, most preeminently through the MCC but also to some extent through PEPFAR, which allocated much of its assistance based on need, as gauged by HIV prevalence rates. But, as discussed in the first chapter, most U.S. assistance is not allocated in this way.[5]

Increased Country Ownership and Broader Participation

In some cases assistance programs fail because they do not reflect local priorities and do not sufficiently involve recipients in their design. Many donors, especially the United States, earmark significant funds for specific purposes that reflect the donor's priorities but may not be most appropriate in local settings. One high-profile example is PEPFAR, which allocates specific percentages of HIV/AIDS funding for programs on prevention, abstinence, treatment, care, and orphans, but the mix determined in Washington many not be appropriate in recipient countries. More involvement and ownership by the recipient government, both in setting priorities and designing specific programs, along with greater participation in program design and execution by nongovernmental organizations (NGOs), civil society groups, and the private sector, could enhance local commitment and increase aid effectiveness.[6] In this view, recipients should take the lead in developing and implementing their development strategies through a broad consultative process and translate these strategies into specific programs. While this approach might slow program development, the idea is that it will help build institutions and local commitment over time, thus improving long-term results. And more donors have started to use this approach.

The shift toward greater ownership and broader participation began with the World Bank and IMF's Poverty Reduction Strategy Paper (PRSP) approach, in which governments, NGOs, civil society groups, and private sector representatives collectively provide input into a national strategy to fight poverty, which in turn provides the basis for IMF and World Bank programs. Greater local ownership and participation also has been taken very seriously by some new donor organizations such as the Global Fund to Fight AIDS, Tuberculosis, and Malaria. In the United States, the MCC has introduced a strong element of country ownership and broader participation, but there has been much less shift in this direction by other U.S. agencies. As discussed below, however, this approach may be appropriate in some but not all circumstances. Strong country ownership makes sense in well-governed nations where the governments have a track record of relatively sound development policies, but it makes much less sense in corrupt autocracies with little interest in spurring development. Thus U.S. programs should be designed with this distinction in mind.

Stronger Results-Based Management

Most donors are talking about being more results oriented in their aid programs, and some are actually doing it in practice. In most aid agencies, including those of the United States, monitoring and evaluation systems are weak, and aid disbursements bear little relationship to performance. Donors rarely measure results, so there is little historical, systematic information about which programs work well and which do not. USAID evaluates most of its projects, but this information often is not publicly available, and there are few feedback loops to allow these evaluations to inform policymakers' decisions about future programs. This lack of information makes it harder to allocate new funds efficiently and increases the perception that aid is ineffective.

Some donors—for example, the Global Fund and the Global Alliance for Vaccines and Immunizations—are trying to move toward more results-based management. Many others, such as the MCC, state that they intend to be more results based, but it is too early too tell whether this, in fact, will be the case. Going forward, however, there seems little doubt that U.S. programs will have to do a better job of demonstrating their impact if they are to receive sustained and increased funding over time.

Increased Program and Budget Support

Many European donors, especially the United Kingdom, the Netherlands, and the Nordic countries, along with the World Bank and some other multilateral development banks, have begun to provide broad-based program, budget, or sector support, usually for a select group of countries deemed to have shown a stronger commitment to sound development policies. These donors now offer financing for education or health through sector-wide approaches (SWAps), which provide pooled funding to support sector-specific strategies. In some cases donors jointly contribute to a "basket" of funds aimed at specific purposes. These "horizontal" approaches have a number of advantages. They

—reduce overhead and bureaucratic costs,

—provide greater flexibility for recipients to allocate funding for their highest priority and adapt to changing needs,

—allow recipients to finance recurrent as well as capital costs,

—have the potential to make aid-financed activities more consistent with the government's development strategy (since the budget should provide the blueprint for allocating public sector resources) and more easily integrate aid with government financial resources aimed at development activities, and

—provide the opportunity—only sometimes embraced—for donors to focus on helping countries build stronger, more transparent, and more accountable public finance systems.

However, this approach tends to complicate financial oversight since funds go directly to the national budget, and it is harder to connect specific dollars to specific activities. Monitoring and evaluation generally are more difficult though not impossible. Donors can still expect to see a certain number of kilometers of roads built or children immunized, but it is more difficult to attribute those changes to specific donor funds. In these programs, therefore, the objective tends to be the more general one of supporting governments that are continuing to show broad progress in achieving key development goals. Most donors that have moved in this direction tend to do so mainly in countries they believe are better governed. This makes sense: this kind of approach is most appropriate in countries with strong institutions and good governance but not in countries with widespread corruption and poor or destructive policies.

Generally, the United States does not embrace this approach in its bilateral programs (although in the 1970s and 1980s, a significant share of U.S. aid was provided in similar ways). Except for the Heavily Indebted Poor Countries initiative, the United States has been only a reluctant supporter of World Bank moves in this direction. Under certain limited circumstances, a shift toward some budget support might be appropriate, as discussed below.

Increased Single-Purpose Funds

Several new initiatives provide funding for very specific purposes, in some ways a move in almost the opposite direction from program and budget support. The most prominent of these are for health, especially the Global Fund, the Global Alliance for Vaccines and Immunizations, and PEPFAR. The Fast-Track Initiative for Education for All as well as the Global Environmental Facility also share some of these characteristics. These "vertical" funds have several advantages. They

—provide a narrower focus of activities and clearer goals, and therefore are more amenable to results-based management approaches;

—usually (but not always) require a smaller bureaucracy; and

—are often able to elicit stronger financial support than broader aid programs because of their clearer and more understandable mission.

However, they are criticized for focusing too narrowly, thus missing other important issues, and for not concentrating on building broader systems and institutions. Some believe that a narrow focus on HIV/AIDS could undermine efforts to combat childhood diarrheal diseases, for example, and divert attention away from building broader health care systems.

Single-purpose funds are not new (many UN agencies, such as UNICEF, got their start this way), but there has been a small resurgence of this approach in recent years. The MCC shares some of these characteristics with its stand-alone bureaucracy, somewhat narrower range of activities (although broader in the activities it funds than typical single-purpose facilities), and focus on achieving measurable results. Generally speaking, the United States tends to be more comfortable with this more "vertical" approach than are other donors.

There is room for both horizontal and vertical approaches in donor assistance, depending on the circumstances on the ground in specific recipient countries. Horizontal approaches make most sense when donors are supporting a broad spectrum of activities within a development strategy and are focusing on building systems and institutions. Vertical approaches make sense either when specific issues require a large scale-up in resources or in countries with very weak governance where broad-based support may be unwise or infeasible, and also when donors wish to support more clearly defined activities. In some circumstances, both approaches may be warranted, such as in a well-governed country that can utilize broad-based support effectively but may require particularly large resources in one area, such as dealing with HIV/AIDS.

Key Steps to Improve Effectiveness of U.S. Development Assistance

Drawing from these recent changes in foreign assistance, there are several ways in which the U.S. government could enhance the effectiveness of its aid programs. While there is a long list of possible changes, here the focus is on three critical ones: improving the allocation of aid so that more funding goes to countries that can use it well; altering the mechanisms by which aid is delivered so that it is provided to different countries in different ways, depending on their characteristics; and managing for results so that more aid is given where it works and less where it does not.[7]

Improve Aid Allocation

Because there is such a strong overlay of strategic and security goals, as described in earlier chapters, current U.S. assistance is poorly allocated to achieve the goals of supporting economic growth and poverty reduction in the world's poorest countries. Significant amounts of aid go to middle-income countries that have access to private sector capital and have graduated from other aid programs such as the World Bank's concessional International Development Association. Middle-income Macedonia received U.S. assistance amounting to an average of $28 per person per year between 2002 and 2004, while much poorer Nicaragua received just $12. Cyprus received $14 per person while Bangladesh received just $0.46 per person.[8]

In addition, U.S. assistance goes almost as much to poorly governed countries with weak policies as it does to countries with stronger governance, better policies, and a demonstrated commitment to development. Relatively well governed Tanzania received just $2 in aid per person from the United States, on average, between 2002 and 2004, while poorly governed Angola received more than four times as much at $9 per person. Ghana, another relatively well governed country, received only about $4 per person, while Eritrea received $17 per person.[9] Although these patterns should improve as the MCC gets up to full speed, most U.S. aid agencies do not allocate aid based on where it could have the greatest impact on poverty reduction.

The most striking pattern is the difference in aid provided to middle-income countries relative to low-income countries, as shown in table 4-1. Between 2002 and 2004, for the eighty-one countries classified by the World Bank as low income (with per capita incomes below about $1,500), the median amount of assistance provided by the U.S. was about $3.50 per person per year in the recipient country.[10] For thirty lower-middle-income countries (with per capita incomes between approximately $1,500 and $3,000), the median received was $5.43 per person. For countries with incomes greater than $3,000, there were fifteen that received more than $5 million in U.S. assistance, and the median amount received in these countries was $10.56 per capita—more than three times larger than the

Table 4-1 Allocation of U.S. Foreign Assistance by Country Groups, 2002–04

Median dollars per person in recipient country

Country category	Aid amount
By income	
Low income	3.50
Lower-middle income	5.43
Upper-middle income[a]	10.56
By quality of governance and policy	
(low-income countries only)	
Passed 11 or more MCC indicators	4.36
Passed 6–10 MCC indicators	2.04
Passed 5 or fewer MCC indicators	3.45

Source: Author's calculations based on World Bank country classifications and foreign assistance data from the OECD's online database.

a. Fifteen recipient countries that receive $5 million or more in total assistance.

median for low-income countries. The United States provided Jordan with assistance amounting to $100 per capita between 2002 and 2004, and Israel received $90 per capita. No single low-income country other than Iraq received as much as $30 per person, and only a handful received more than $15 per person. U.S. bilateral assistance to sub-Saharan Africa averaged just $6 per person in 2004.[11]

Consider the eighty-one low-income countries with regard to their governance and economic policies. There are many ways to judge the quality of these two factors, but the sixteen indicators used by the Millennium Challenge Corporation to select countries constitute a reasonable standard. The eighty-one countries were divided into three groups according to the number of MCC hurdles the country passed. For the top group (which passed eleven or more MCC indicators) the median amount of aid received was $4.36. For the middle group (which passed from 6 through 10 indicators), the median amount was $2.04. For the bottom group, which passed 5 or fewer hurdles, the median amount received was $3.45. Thus there was only a small per capita difference in aid between the group with the strongest governance and best policies, and the group with the weakest.

Of course, to a great extent these patterns result from the United States' allocating much of its aid to security and diplomatic partners such as Iraq, Jordan, Pakistan, Israel, and Egypt. It is completely legitimate and desirable for the United States to do so. However, these funds should be allocated from accounts separate from those provided primarily for development purposes and should be evaluated for their effectiveness by different standards, since they are aimed at achieving different goals. A key reason for widespread pessimism on aid effectiveness is that aid allocated for political reasons is judged by its impact on economic objectives, even though that is not its primary purpose.

Options for Refining Allocation Rules

In their research Collier and Dollar show how a reallocation of official development assistance to countries with the most severe poverty and better policies and institutions could approximately double aid effectiveness.[12] They arrive at a "poverty-efficient" allocation of aid—aimed at maximizing the extent of poverty reduction that could be realized with a given amount of aid—by first deriving a relationship between policy governance scores and economic growth, and then determining the relationship between economic growth and poverty reduction. They find that an optimal allocation of global aid flows would almost double the number of people lifted out of poverty, an outcome that they estimate would require a tripling of aid budgets under current arrangements.

In addition to the Collier-Dollar mathematical formula, there are other approaches for allocating aid in as "poverty-efficient" a manner as possible. The World Bank's performance-based allocation system provides similar formal rules for aid allocation, although the two differ in some ways (and thus arrive at somewhat different allocation rules). The World Bank's system is based on a combination of income levels and on its country policy and institutional assessment scores, which are based on the bank staff's assessments of sixteen policy and institutional components. The Millennium Challenge Corporation evaluates the quality of policies and governance through sixteen indicators, which overlap with but are not identical to those of the World Bank's country policy and institutional assessment.

One could imagine a range of formal models that would achieve similar ends, each with slightly different allocation rules, depending on which policies and governance measures were included, which were given the most weight, and the precise income categories and poverty measures chosen. Long hours have been spent in donor meetings arguing the finer points of these performance-based allocation systems, with different analysts arguing for slightly different formulations. The purpose here is not to argue in favor of a particular approach but rather for the concept of thinking more systematically about identifying the countries with the greatest needs and best policies and institutions. Almost any one of these approaches is far superior to the current way that aid is allocated. As Collier and Dollar have pointed out, the idea is not to set aid allocations by a rigid, mechanistic formula that must be precisely adhered to like a straitjacket.[13] Rather, the idea is to establish a system that provides some analytical guidance for donor agencies interested in allocating their aid more effectively and to provide some defenses against the overt manipulation of aid for political or commercial purposes. Of course, a large amount of assistance will continue to be directed for nondevelopment purposes, many of which are legitimate national security goals of donor countries, but these should be accounted for separately, as discussed later. But if donor agencies start with a transparent, objective formula aimed at maximizing the poverty effectiveness of aid, it will be harder for other parts of the bureaucracy to change aid allocations since the costs of a reallocation will become more transparent.

In the United States, it makes most sense to start with the MCC framework, as it has been widely debated and generally accepted as a legitimate, albeit not perfect, method of evaluating countries. One possibility would be for all U.S. agencies to adopt the MCC framework as a way of evaluating recipients and extend it to select not just the top performers, but different groups of performers based on their overall scores. This framework could be used as the basis for not only delivering different amounts of aid to recipient countries but delivering it differently, depending on their characteristics, as discussed below.

Expand the Toolkit: Differentiate Approaches Based on Recipient Capabilities and Needs

Making aid more effective requires more than just reallocation. Changes are required in how the U.S. delivers aid. To a large extent, most development assistance is provided in the same way to countries with weak governance and poor policies as it is to countries with a much stronger demonstrated commitment to and capacity for development initiatives. But providing aid the same way across all countries makes little sense, given the differing circumstances on the ground. Some recipient countries suffer intense and ongoing political instability whereas others are much more stable. Some governments have a strong commitment to good development policies whereas others give only lip service to poverty reduction and development. Some have stronger institutions that are more able to implement their development strategies whereas others have weaker capacity. The quality and ability of agencies outside the government—NGOs, the private sector, charitable organizations—to help implement development programs also vary widely.

The U.S. government should recognize more fully these differing characteristics across recipient countries and alter accordingly the methods it uses to deliver assistance. Specifically, the government should better formulate a set of distinctive strategies to deliver and manage aid in different kinds of low-income countries, depending primarily on the quality of the recipient country's demonstrated commitment to good policies and strong institutions.

The Millennium Challenge Corporation is a key first step in this direction. It is noticeably different in two ways. First, it operates with the clear underlying assumption that more aid should be delivered to countries with a demonstrable commitment to good policies and strong governance. Second, it designs assistance packages differently by accepting the principle of strong national ownership and broader participation for those countries where this makes the most sense. Beyond these two characteristics, it is still too early to tell exactly how the MCC will differ in the way its aid will be managed and monitored, and whether in fact it will turn out to be as innovative as its early promise.

So far the MCC is providing its funds through quasi-independent project management units established in each country to receive funding and implement projects. While this differs from current USAID practices, it is similar to some approaches used by USAID in the 1970s and 1980s and by some multilateral development banks today. This approach has a mixed record and may do little to help build long-term financial, institutional, and procurement capacity. It is also not yet clear how well coordinated and harmonized MCC procedures will be with other donors, or whether it will become one more set of reporting requirements. And although there has been much discussion of its being performance based, it is not yet clear whether this will in fact be the case.

This idea of distinctive strategies for different countries should be carried over to other U.S. assistance agencies. USAID has used a variety of financing and implementation models over the years, including direct loans and grants to governments as budget support, host-country contracts, commodity assistance programs, fixed-amount reimbursable arrangements, contracts and cooperative agreements with third parties to implement programs (the current predominant model), and other mechanisms. While there are many reasons why USAID's practices have evolved, it may have moved too far in some directions. Moreover, it has not developed different approaches for different countries. For almost all its recipients, USAID staff design the projects, and while there is consultation with the host governments, USAID takes the lead in project design, regardless of the quality of governance in the host country. Projects are contracted out to third parties for implementation, usually for a three-year period, with little or no money provided directly through the host government. Projects are evaluated, but feedback loops are weak, so the information generated through evaluation provides little guidance for results-based management.

Moving forward, U.S. agencies should use three different strategies to deliver assistance, depending on recipient country characteristics. To better illustrate the point, table 4-2 shows a first cut that sorts the eighty-one low-income countries into three basic groups according to their MCC scores. The top group corresponds (roughly) to the top quartile of the MCC countries (assessed by the number of hurdles they pass), which in turn is similar to the group of MCC-eligible countries. The second group corresponds (roughly) to the middle half of MCC countries, and the third group, to the bottom quartile. Obviously, these groupings could be modified and improved. The main point here is not to decide on the precise method for grouping or the precise list of countries but rather to introduce the idea of different strategies for different countries.

Well-Governed Countries

This group of countries has shown the strongest commitment to sustained development by implementing reasonable policies, strengthening key institutions, and improving governance more generally. Given sufficient support, these are the countries that are most likely to achieve long-term development, similar to what USAID called "transformational development" in its 2004 white paper.[14] The U.S. government should provide the largest amounts of funding on a per capita basis to these countries. Moreover, since these nations are relatively well governed and have shown the greatest commitment to development, they should be given much more responsibility to set priorities and design aid-financed activities consistent with their own development strategies. In the long run, it is critical that these countries expand their capacity to conceptualize and implement development programs; yet too often the U.S. and other official donors undermine that capacity by designing programs themselves. And while the recipient government should play a strong lead role, the U.S. and other

Table 4-2 Country Grouping, Based on Number of MCC Hurdles Passed

Top performers	Number	Medium performers	Number	Poor performers	Number
Lesotho	14	Burkina Faso	11	Cameroon	5
Moldova	14	The Gambia	11	Guinea-Bissau	5
Mongolia	14	India	11	Tajikistan	5
Vanuatu	14	Mozambique	11	Zimbabwe	5
Armenia	13	Senegal	11	Afghanistan	4
Bolivia	13	China	10	Cambodia	4
Honduras	13	Guyana	10	Comoros	4
Madagascar	13	São Tomé and Príncipe	10	Congo	4
				Côte d'Ivoire	4
Nicaragua	13	Timor-Leste	10	Eritrea	4
Ukraine	13	Zambia	10	Ethiopia	4
Benin	12	Bangladesh	9	Sudan	4
Georgia	12	Bhutan	9	Turkmenistan	4
Ghana	12	Egypt	9	Central African	3
Kiribati	12	Indonesia	9	Republic	
				Haiti	3
Malawi	12	Kyrgyz Republic	9	Lao People's	3
Mali	12	Papua New Guinea	9	Democratic Republic	
				Togo	3
Morocco	12	Paraguay	9	Burundi	2
Philippines	12	Rwanda	9	Chad	2
Sri Lanka	12	Solomon Islands	9	Iraq	2
Tanzania	12	Uzbekistan	9	Korea, North	2
Uganda	12	Vietnam	9	Liberia	2
		Azerbaijan	8	Myanmar	2
		Kenya	8	Yemen,	2
		Syria	8	Republic of	
				Angola	1
		Cuba	7	Guinea	1
		Nepal	7	Congo,	0
		Niger	7	Democratic Republic of	
				Somalia	0
		Nigeria	7		
		Sierra Leone	7		
		Djibouti	6		
		Mauritania	6		
		Pakistan	6		

Source: Author's calculations based on data from the MCC website.

donors should ensure that there is broad-based participation from other sectors in establishing some of the key priorities. The MCC has set a strong example in this area, and other agencies should follow suit.

Funding for activities in these countries can either come from general development assistance accounts or from specific vertical programs, such as those for HIV/AIDS, depending on the particular mix of activities. On the recipient side, in some countries a portion of funds could go directly to national governments, not just to contractors. Under certain circumstances, some U.S. development assistance should be provided as direct budget support in countries that have adequate financial and procurement systems in place, as discussed below. In this way U.S. assistance can support broad development strategies, not just individual initiatives, reducing transaction costs and increasing aid efficiency. In addition, some funding could support activities of NGOs.

Moreover, the United States should be willing to make longer-term commitments in these countries—for five years (or more)—subject to the requirement that the recipient show continued good governance and achieve reasonable results. Longer commitments allow well-governed countries to improve planning and manage their finances better, especially for multiyear investment projects. Shorter time horizons create uncertainty and risk, and undermine the ability to hire good staff and make sound long-term decisions. Finally, as in all countries, there should be a more serious effort at managing for results (a topic discussed in more detail later). Programs should be monitored and evaluated carefully: those that show results should be funded generously while those that do not should receive less funding or be shut down.

Countries with Average Governance

These countries should receive less funding than the well-governed ones. Recipients should play an active role in setting priorities and designing projects but should not be given as much flexibility, and the United States and other donors should be actively involved in ensuring broad-based participation and technical rigor. Although country ownership is important, it is less feasible and desirable where weaker governance and less demonstrable commitment to strong development policies prevail. Still, there is clearly room for the U.S. government to allow for greater involvement and ownership by these countries.

Under these circumstances budget and program support should be limited, if used at all. Most funding should go toward projects that meet standards of technical rigor and are consistent with the country's overall development strategy. These projects should be designed in cooperation with the government but not fully by the government or with funds provided through the government budget. A larger share of funding should go to support local NGOs. Also, the range of activities supported should be narrower than in well-governed countries, with a focus on key activities where achieving results seems most likely and where the government has shown the strongest commitment. As a result, although funds could come from both broad development assistance accounts and vertical funds, a larger share is likely to come from the latter since the activities are more narrowly defined.

The length of financial commitments should be shorter than for well-governed countries, perhaps around three years, contingent on progress and results. Project performance should be monitored carefully, with strong performance supported by increased financial support and longer commitments, and weak results leading to less aid. In some ways this is similar to how USAID operates now, although there should be a greater focus on results management, fewer earmarks, less aid "tied" exclusively to purchases from contractors and suppliers in the U.S., more predictable flow of assistance (contingent on results), and perhaps some limited funding going directly to the budget.[15]

Low-Income, Poorly Governed Countries

This group of countries roughly corresponds to what the World Bank calls low-income countries under stress and to what the Organization for Economic Cooperation and Development (OECD) refers to as "difficult partnerships." They include failed, failing, weak, and fragile states. The cost of weak states is high: Chauvet and Collier found that the average fragile state experienced economic losses of $100 billion, exceeding total annual global expenditures for official development assistance.[16] Instability in these countries also significantly hurts their neighbors: having a fragile state as a neighbor typically decreases a country's annual economic growth rate by 1.6 percent. Since the attacks of September 11, there has been significant discussion within the U.S. government about fragile and failing states; however, until recently, there has been little fundamental action, a point underscored by the bipartisan Commission on Weak States and National Security.[17] The creation of the State Department's Office of the Coordinator for Reconstruction and Stabilization was an important step in the right direction, as was USAID's recent publication of its strategy document for Fragile States.[18]

In some of these fragile states, U.S. assistance is likely to be heavily influenced by strategic and security considerations.[19] There is a clear need for a much stronger emphasis on conflict prevention rather than reaction. (In recent years the United States was clearly in reactive mode to events in Haiti, Liberia, and other countries.) Close donor coordination and adoption of consistent, joint approaches is critical in these countries.

In the weakest states, aid should be tightly focused on humanitarian relief, establishing security, and providing basic services to the poor. The United States and other donors should focus on a very limited set of very high priority activities, at least some of which should have the potential for quick results that can be demonstrated to policymakers and the general public to help consolidate the process of further reform. Donors should play the main role in setting priorities and designing activities, usually in close consultation with the security entities in the donor countries. In some cases, financial assistance must be closely coordinated with security goals and with military involvement, particularly in immediate postconflict situations where UN troops are on the ground. Program aid and budget support is out of the question. Planning horizons and length of commitment should be shorter than in other countries, typically one to three years.

In some countries where governance is weak and deteriorating, no aid should be provided at all. In many others, the assistance that is provided should be directed through civil society groups and NGOs rather than the government. Although it is important to try to build government institutions where possible, in some countries with the most recalcitrant governments, this is not possible, and so the bulk of assistance should be directed through NGOs. The World Bank and Collier and Dollar have suggested establishing independent service providers, similar to an expenditure-side version of an independent revenue board, to oversee the delivery of basic services.[20] These independent service providers would be autonomous from the government and directly accountable to the donors, acting as "wholesalers" through which donors would provide funds to "retail" providers of services. The goal is to help support delivery of basic services without necessarily working with or through a corrupt or highly bureaucratic and ineffective government.

Operating in these countries is much riskier than other places. As a result, programs in poorly governed states require very careful monitoring, regular reappraisal, flexible responses as initiatives begin to work or fail, and a higher tolerance for failure than those working in other countries. One of the most difficult questions for donors dealing with poorly governed countries is when to continue providing some aid and when to stop. Since aid tends to be least effective in poorly governed countries, continuing with disbursements may have high opportunity costs since the same aid could be used more productively elsewhere. Moreover, aid flows, if not directed carefully, can help sustain bad governments or further weaken the quality of governance. However, there may be significant costs from entirely disengaging—such as a greater risk of further destabilization and violence, or a deterioration of health and education systems—and possibly high payoffs for remaining engaged. It is probably true that it is important for the international community—not all donors, but perhaps some—to maintain dialogue even with the most difficult governments. But the risks are considerable, and policymakers (and congressional funders) need to recognize that there will be many failures alongside some successes. Like a venture capitalist for whom perhaps 10 percent of investments are big winners, 25 percent break even, and the majority lose money, policymakers need patience and the willingness to withstand some losses in order to achieve some big payoffs, in at least some countries.

Should the U.S. Government Ever Provide Budget and Program Support?

The United States delivers very little of its aid as direct budget or program support. However, this was not always the case. During the 1970s and 1980s, a significant share of U.S. aid was provided in this way. The United States moved away from this approach because of valid concerns that recipient governments were managing the money poorly, with poor accounting standards, weak or nonexistent auditing, widespread corruption, and other problems. This was especially the case during the period of widespread macroeconomic imbalances, large budget deficits, and runaway inflation that characterized most developing countries in the 1980s, when fiscal discipline was very weak.

Generally speaking, the move away from broad-based budget support made sense at the time for the vast majority of countries. But it came at a cost. U.S. contractors and representatives of other donors typically establish separate offices and accounts for the funds and then hire the most talented government officials to manage the accounts. The MCC requires that countries establish separate entities with separate staff and budget to oversee funds. Since many donors take this approach, funds are divided in numerous separate accounts, making the allocation of resources and macroeconomic management much more difficult. This process significantly weakens government capacity and undermines the establishment of strong and accountable institutions. In other words, instead of helping to strengthen one of the most critical institutions in developing countries— the budget process—donor practices tend to weaken it, with long-term detrimental consequences.

Some analysts suggest that the key criterion for providing budget support is that the objectives of the donor and the recipient country be aligned.[21] At one level this makes sense: if both donors and recipients place a high priority on roads, schools, and clinics, then providing donor funds through the budget is likely to achieve those goals. But if donors and recipients have quite different objectives, then donors will be unsatisfied with the results of budget support. However, the biggest concern of most donors, including the United States, is not differing objectives but lack of strong financial oversight and controls.

How can this tension between the donor's need for effective oversight and accounting be balanced with the imperative to strengthen local institutions? Discussions that focus on either complete budget support or project support are not particularly helpful. A better approach would be to use budget and program support in limited circumstances in a small number of countries that have adequate financial and procurement systems in place. This is a subset of countries that not only has good governance generally but specifically has minimally effective financial oversight and standards in place. Initially the amount of budget support should be limited, but it should grow as financial systems improve. Thus, in countries that meet minimal standards for accounting, auditing, and transparency in their fiscal activities, an initially small share of funding could go through the budget—perhaps 10 percent. Benchmarks and targets should be established to guide continued improvement in financial management. A larger share of funding could go through the budget, up to 25 or 50 percent, or even more, as the quality of financial oversight improves. This criterion would not necessarily affect the total amount of assistance the United States gives to a country, but it would determine the share provided through the host government's budget.

Properly designed, this approach would help strengthen the budget as an institution (rather than weaken it as with current practices) and help establish it as the key mechanism to determine national priorities and allocate scarce resources among competing goals. It also would, over time, help build transparency, accountability, and strong fiduciary practices, and strengthen complementary parliamentary and civil society mechanisms for oversight. Furthermore, this approach would create internal incentives for countries to improve their financial arrangements in order to qualify for increased budget support. Recipients want to receive funding through their budget, and therefore they would be motivated to improve auditing and accounting standards so as to make that happen. In this way budget assistance would help strengthen public financial institutions rather than weaken them. The goals would have a multiyear horizon, such that five or seven years down the road, the country would have strong financial oversight systems in place.

Although it is more difficult to measure results when assistance is provided in this way, tangible goals can still be met. If the United States donates $10 million to the Tanzanian budget to construct roads, then, at the end of the day, it can still measure whether or not those roads were built, just as well as if the money had been allocated through a separate account. The outcomes of MCC projects in Madagascar or Nicaragua can be observed and measured just as easily if the funds go through their budgets as through a separate accounting entity. But by providing a portion of the funds as budget support to a limited number of countries according to their financial oversight capabilities, U.S. aid could help institutions strengthen over time rather than weaken.

Improve Monitoring and Evaluation and Manage for Results

In many U.S. assistance programs, monitoring and evaluation (ME) systems are weak, and aid disbursements bear little correlation to performance. Although projects are regularly evaluated, this information often is not easily available to the public, and there are few feedback loops so that these assessments can inform policymakers' decisions about future programs. There is little systematic, historical information about what works and what does not. For example, no solid evidence is available about whether education projects tend to work better than infrastructure projects, or about the circumstances under which certain education projects work better than others. This lack of information makes it harder to allocate new funds efficiently and increases the perception that aid is ineffective. In addition, ME activities are carried out by the donor with only limited input from recipients, so a potentially important set of links is missed between local ownership in establishing key goals, participation in ME activities to gauge progress, and accountability to both the donor and target beneficiaries for results.

There are four core reasons why stronger ME capacity is needed. First, it will create incentives to achieve better results. Projects should have clearly specified benchmarks that correspond to desired outcomes. Some of these should be intermediate targets (such as building a certain number of schools, purchasing so many textbooks) and some should be longer-term goals (such as increasing the primary school completion rate or the immunization rate by a certain amount). Although creating measurable benchmarks is not always easy, there is much room for improvement over current practices. Countries that reach specified benchmarks should continue to receive funding—even an increase in funding—while those that do not should see a reduction. Too often both donors and recipients know that ultimately they will not be held accountable for achieving specified results, which dilutes the incentives for strong performance.

A second reason for strengthening ME is to generate the information necessary to achieve better results. ME systems and results-based management are not intended just to be punitive. Rather, the idea is to produce the data needed to keep programs on track toward achieving their intended outcomes. An effective ME system is required to detect problems at an early stage and to enable the midcourse corrections necessary to achieve specified goals and targets.

Third, an ME system would improve allocation of funds to get the most out of each dollar spent. Well-designed ME systems should provide the aggregate information that policymakers need to direct more funds toward activities that are effective and less toward those that are not. If most programs aimed at strengthening stock exchanges do not work, then those programs should be discontinued, with the funds going toward more successful agricultural programs (if that is what the data suggest). But in the absence of that information, policymakers cannot make these kinds of informed choices.

Finally, ME systems can refine the design of new projects in the future. Such projects should incorporate the lessons learned from previous ones if performance is to continue to improve. It is not enough to generate useful and accurate information: mechanisms are needed to ensure that such information reaches those who are designing new activities.

How can ME efforts be strengthened in U.S. assistance programs? Several steps would help.

Collect Better Data

To monitor progress, it is essential that implementers gather relevant baseline data at the outset of every project and program, and continue to collect such data throughout the project. In other words, monitoring and evaluation must be built into projects and programs from the beginning, not added on as an afterthought halfway through the process. In too many aid projects, monitoring and evaluation only begin after two years have elapsed (for a "midterm" review) and utilize consultants who have not been involved in the project and parachute in for a short review. These evaluations rarely achieve much good.

Use Randomized Trials for Some Projects

Evaluating results is a tricky business. If a health project ends with the village showing a 10 percent decline in infant mortality after five years, how much of this is due to the project and how much is due to other factors? One way to untangle this problem for at least a small number of projects is to introduce a more rigorous evaluation process involving randomized trials or comparison with a treatment and control group, as is done with most medical and other scientific experiments.[22] A small amount of funds—say, 3 to 5 percent—could be designated for projects that incorporate evaluations with control and treatment groups. Project design would include specifying a control group and establishing systems for monitoring that group in tandem with the treatment group throughout the life of the project. For example, if an NGO wanted to offer breakfast to schoolchildren to improve attendance and learning capacity, the proposal would include the designation of a control village that did not introduce the program. Project monitors would track attendance, body weight, school achievement, and a range of other indicators in both villages throughout the life of the project.

Introducing control and treatment groups is time consuming and somewhat expensive, and there is no need for this approach in all projects. It also can raise certain ethical issues, especially for health care interventions, although this technique is both common and essential for testing medications throughout the world. Ultimately, it is the surest way to evaluate what works and what does not, and the results would be invaluable for designing subsequent projects and making aid more effective.

Introduce a New Independent ME Body for All U.S. Government Aid Agencies

No agency can ever fully evaluate its own efforts. Conflicts of interest will always arise, and no agency wants to criticize itself. Moreover, monitoring and evaluation constitute a specialized set of work, and some standard practices should be followed across agencies. One solution would be to establish a small U.S. government agency, in some ways similar to the Government Accountability Office, with the responsibility of monitoring and evaluating foreign assistance projects across all U.S. government agencies. Representatives from this agency would be involved in the project design phase from the outset, ensuring that baseline data are being collected and appropriate benchmarks are set. It would perform midterm reviews and final evaluations, and make its findings public. It would carry out randomized trials, as described earlier, where appropriate. This would ensure fair, independent, and consistent evaluation of projects, and would provide a wealth of information to policymakers, members of Congress, and the general public about what is working and what is not. Each agency would transfer a share of its funds to finance the new agency.

Reorganize Budgetary Accounts to Align Them with Specific Goals

Aid that is intended to meet diplomatic and strategic goals should be accounted for separately from aid to achieve development objectives, which in turn should be separated from humanitarian assistance. USAID's recent white paper identifies five key areas: transformational development, fragile states, humanitarian responses, strategic states, and transnational issues.[23] Each of these areas has different goals and different metrics for success, so they should be evaluated on different grounds and funded separately. Recently there has been some talk about reorganizing the budget accounts in this way. This is a good starting point and should help policymakers better manage for results and improve performance. But just reorganizing budget accounts without deeper changes will not be sufficient to significantly improve the outcome of U.S. foreign assistance.

Does the United States Provide Enough Development Assistance?

The United States provides more foreign assistance than any other country. U.S. nonmilitary aid for economic development in the poorest countries of the world—termed official development assistance by the Development Assistance Committee of the OECD—reached $19 billion in 2004. Aid to richer countries such as Israel pushes the figure higher.[24] However, the United States provides less than almost any other donor nation as a share of national income. Official development assistance from the United States is the equivalent of 0.16 percent of U.S. GNP—just one-sixth of 1 percent of total income—placing it twenty-first among donor countries. Aid as a share of U.S. national income is also very small by historical standards. In the 1960s aid averaged 0.51 percent of U.S. GNP—more than three times the current level—and much closer to the international goal of 0.7 percent established at that time. Between 1970 and the end of the cold war, aid averaged 0.24 percent of U.S. GNP, about 50 percent more than current levels. Including private assistance, even adding in upper range estimates of private contributions through foundations and charitable organizations, total U.S. foreign aid—public and private—is the equivalent of only about 0.32 percent of U.S. income, which would place the United States perhaps fifteenth among the twenty-two major donors in terms of total foreign aid.[25]

U.S. assistance to low-income countries is especially small, as noted earlier. U.S. bilateral assistance to low-income countries averages just $3.50 per person in those countries, and U.S. bilateral assistance to sub-Saharan Africa averages just $6 per person.

The total quantity of U.S. foreign aid, of course, is not really the point, nor is where the United States ranks relative to other countries. This is not a beauty contest. The real problem that these figures highlight is that the current quantities of U.S. foreign aid are too small for the United States to meet its key foreign policy objectives. Consider the following examples.

First, while important progress has been made in the war on terrorism, we have not turned the tide. The administration has provided significant funding for certain frontline and weak states, but these amounts will have to continue and likely increase. For example, Afghanistan is only receiving one-twentieth of the funding that Iraq receives, despite its similar size and much greater development needs, and its future prospects remain murky. Pakistan, Indonesia, Turkey, and other countries will require significant support going forward.

Second, increasingly and unfortunately, people around the world look to the United States with resentment and distrust rather than as a beacon of hope for prosperity and peace. All indications suggest that the tide of global opinion has turned against the United States in the last three years. Simultaneously, in many countries public opinion is also turning against more open trade and globalization. Regardless of whether these views are justified or not, the key point is that in many developing nations, the United States is not winning the war for hearts and minds to believe in the American vision for the world.

Third, the gap between the richest and poorest countries has widened considerably during the last twenty years, breeding bitterness and anger among people who believe—rightly or wrongly—that the rich have rigged the international system against them. As many people enjoy greater prosperity, some 1.2 billion people are left behind to live on $1 a day or less.[26] Unfortunately, many citizens of poor countries see economic opportunity, escape from poverty, and political freedom as distant dreams. Approximately 113 million primary-school-age children are not in school, a fact that does not bode well for future generations, and more than 27,000 children die every day from preventable diseases.[27] We are not winning the fight to reduce global poverty and build a more inclusive world in which poor countries can prosper. If the United States is to win the war on terrorism, it needs poor countries as well as rich ones to support the values it champions and to believe that they, too, can climb out of poverty and achieve economic and political freedom. But they need help to do it, and the assistance the United States provides is not enough to make a real difference.

Finally, HIV/AIDS, tuberculosis, malaria, and diarrheal diseases continue to ravage poor countries and threaten to expand to create major social and economic disintegration in key countries such as South Africa, Nigeria, Ethiopia, India, China, and Russia. Public health spending in sub-Saharan Africa (outside of South Africa) averages just $6 per person per year, and with incomes averaging less than $350 per year, these countries simply do not have the resources to fight these diseases on their own.[28] Even with the President's Emergency Plan for AIDS Relief, we are losing a war that we possess the technology to prevent.

The good news is that the United States has the resources and the ability to step up to the challenge. However, it must significantly expand the size of its foreign assistance programs beyond that of the MCC.

Conclusions

U.S. foreign assistance has contributed to achieving important goals in security, poverty reduction, and humanitarian relief. Nevertheless, there is much potential to significantly improve these programs. In particular, U.S. foreign assistance can dramatically improve the allocation of aid and provide more to countries with the greatest needs—the poorest ones—and to countries with relatively strong governance and economic policies. It can change the way it delivers aid by introducing a wider array of approaches that are consistent with the strengths and weaknesses of different recipient countries. Aid for poor countries with stronger governance and policies should be given more flexibly, allowing greater local input and longer time horizons; in those countries with poorer governance and policies, aid should be more narrowly focused, with much stronger oversight and shorter commitments. Aid quality and outcomes can be improved through a greater emphasis on results-based management and stronger monitoring and evaluation procedures. With these steps U.S. foreign assistance can more effectively support economic growth and poverty reduction, with each dollar going further to achieve these goals.

Notes

1. Lael Brainard and others, *The Other War: Global Poverty and the Millennium Challenge Account* (Brookings and Center for Global Development, 2003); U.S. Agency for International Development (USAID), *Fragile States Strategy* (www.usaid.gov/policy/2005_fragile_states_strategy.pdf [January 2005]); William Easterly, "The Cartel of Good Intentions: The Problem of Bureaucracy in Foreign Aid," *Journal of Policy Reform* 5, no. 4 (2002): 223–50.

2. See Michael Clemens, Steven Radelet and Rikhil Bhavnani, "Counting Chickens When They Hatch: The Short-Term Effect of Aid on Growth," Working Paper 44 (Washington: Center for Global Development, November 2004); Craig Burnside and David Dollar, "Aid, Policies, and Growth," *American Economic Review* 90, no. 4 (2000): 847–68. For a recent, short, nontechnical review of the research on aid and development, see Steven Radelet, Michael Clemens, and Rikhil Bhavnani, "Aid and Growth," *Finance and Development* 42 (September 2005): 16–20.

3. Ruth Levine and the What Works Working Group with Molly Kinder, *Millions Saved: Proven Successes in Global Health* (Washington: Center for Global Development, 2004).

4. Paul Collier and David Dollar, "Aid Allocation and Poverty Reduction," *European Economic Review* 46, no. 8 (2002): 1475–1500.

5. See Lael Brainard, chapter 1 in this volume.

6. Birdsall, however, points out that country ownership and broader participation are not the same thing. Nancy Birdsall, "Seven Deadly Sins: Reflections on Donor Failings," Working Paper 50 (Washington: Center for Global Development, December 2004).

7. For earlier discussions of some of these ideas, see House International Relations Committee, *U.S. Foreign Assistance after September 11th: Major Changes, Competing Purposes, and Different Strategies,* testimony of Steven Radelet, 108 Cong. 2 sess. (February 26, 2004); Steven Radelet, "Aid Effectiveness and the Millennium Development Goals," Working Paper 39 (Washington: Center for Global Development, April 2004).

8. Author's calculations based on the foreign assistance database of the Development Assistance Committee, Organization for Economic Development (Paris).

9. Ibid.

10. Measuring aid per person in the recipient country is the clearest way to compare across countries because it avoids confusion that can arise from different population sizes and different income levels. Looking at total amounts of aid can be misleading because of population size. The United States gave an average of $83 million per year

between 2002 and 2004 to both Tanzania and El Salvador. But Tanzania has 37 million people whereas El Salvador has 6.7 million, so the United States gave about $12 per person in El Salvador and just $2 per person in Tanzania. Aid measured as a share of gross domestic GDP can be misconstrued because of differences in GDP. U.S. assistance to Israel was just 0.5 percent of Israel's GDP between 2002 and 2004, but this low ratio simply reflects Israel's large GDP. The assistance amounted to almost $90 per Israeli, about three times more than the U.S. gave to *any* of the eighty-one low-income countries in the world between 2002 and 2004, except Iraq.

11. Steven Radelet and Bilal Siddiqi, "U.S. Pledges of Aid to Africa: Let's Do the Numbers," *CGD Notes*, July 2005.

12. Collier and Dollar, "Aid Allocation."

13. Ibid.

14. USAID, Bureau for Policy and Program Coordination, *U.S. Foreign Aid: Meeting the Challenges of the Twenty-First Century* (January 2004).

15. By some estimates, as much as three quarters of U.S. assistance is "tied," so that contracts must be awarded to U.S. shipping companies, consulting firms, and suppliers. This practice can significantly increase costs and slow delivery, for example, in the provision of food assistance.

16. Lisa Chauvet and Paul Collier, "Development Effectiveness in Fragile States: Spillovers and Turnarounds" (www.oecd.org/dataoecd/32/59/34255628.pdf [January 2004]).

17. See Jeremy M. Weinstein, John Edward Porter, and Stuart E. Eizenstat, *On the Brink: Weak States and U.S. National Security: A Report of the Commission for Weak States and U.S. National Security* (Washington: Center for Global Development, 2004).

18. USAID, *Fragile States Strategy*.

19. For a more detailed discussion, see Cronin in chapter 6 of this volume.

20. World Bank, *World Bank Group Work in Low Income Countries under Stress: A Task Force Report* (www1.worldbank.org/operations/licus/documents/licus.pdf [September 2002]); Collier and Dollar, "Aid Allocation."

21. Tito Cordella and Giovanni Dell'Ariccia, "Budget Support versus Project Aid," Working Paper 03/88 (Washington: International Monetary Fund, April 2003).

22. For more information on randomized trials, see the work of Abhijit Banerjee, Esther Duflo, and Sendhil Mullainathan at the Abdul Latif Jameel Poverty Action Lab, Massachusetts Institute of Technology (www.povertyactionlab.com).

23. USAID, *U.S. Foreign Aid*.

24. Note that these figures are lower than the total amounts in the foreign operations budget since some of those funds do not count as official development assistance by the standard international definitions.

25. See the OECD Development Assistance Committee foreign assistance database.

26. See World Bank Group, "'05 World Development Indicators" (devdata. worldbank.org/wdi2005/Section1_1_1.htm [February 2006]).

27. UNESCO Institute for Statistics, *Children Out of School: Measuring Exclusion from Primary Education* (Montreal, Quebec, 2006).

28. Radelet and Siddiqi, "Pledges of Aid to Africa."

CHAPTER 5

Humanitarian Assistance Expands in Scale and Scope

Steven Hansch

Arguably, no action is more reflective of the American spirit, or more likely to win friends and allies, than is America's proven leadership in responding quickly and proficiently to disasters that poor countries are unable to manage on their own.

Given its remarkable professionalization in the last twenty years, U.S. humanitarian aid is likely to continue to improve in efficiency and effectiveness. Better timeliness of delivery, accuracy of targeting, and evidence-based project design count among the key improvements that have allowed the United States to be a world leader in humanitarian aid. Despite progress in these areas, several factors indicate that the demand for humanitarian aid will continue to increase:

—Growing threats from natural disasters attributable to population growth in poor parts of the world, increasingly concentrated in quake and flood prone areas;

—More awareness of disasters from distant corners of the world, once ignored by the news media, but increasingly on the radar of the press, public, and Congress;

—Mounting pressure to reorient foreign aid from development to emergencies and epidemics, as hundreds of millions of people escape poverty in such countries as India and China; and,

—The expanding scope of the concept of humanitarian aid.

This chapter surveys the architecture and recent evolution of U.S. government humanitarian aid and identifies the bottlenecks constraining the better use of U.S. taxpayer dollars to reduce excess deaths and suffering in poorer nations.

The United States is by far the biggest single humanitarian donor in the world and among the most effective and technically well equipped. Humanitarian aid is one area of official assistance where the United States truly shines—in large measure because of strong public and congressional support for significant and relatively flexible funding. The credible record on humanitarian relief has emerged despite the poor internal organization of the federal government, one that is characterized by multiple, overlapping jurisdictions and the absence of a single locus of control.[1]

Beginning with Herbert Hoover's efforts during World War I, the U.S. government has led the world in providing the most technically informed, politically neutral, and effective emergency assistance. And yet, there are clearly evident ways to improve U.S. government aid.

The United States could realize even greater returns on investment in humanitarian relief if it were to leverage foreign donations and press for rationalization of the sprawling and confused United Nations (UN) apparatus that is involved in relief operations and disaster risk reduction. More generally, humanitarian assistance would benefit greatly if more resources were devoted to prevention; the economic and governance deficiencies underlying complex emergencies were addressed; certain gaps in humanitarian capabilities were beefed up, such as water supply and protection; and resources were channeled toward countries on the basis of measured needs, rather than according to the news cycle.

In recent years the term "humanitarian assistance" has come to refer to aid for problems that previously had been treated as separate categories: refugees, natural disasters, famine, collapsed states, genocide, war, economic emergency, and so on. Beginning in the early 1990s, aid professionals came to lump each of these areas of work into the category: humanitarian aid or humanitarian action.[2] Still today, the category *humanitarian aid* continues to expand in its usage. In many discussions, the boundary line between humanitarian and development assistance is undefined. The U.S. military employs the term humanitarian to refer to any military action meant to help a civilian population overseas, which effectively subsumes all forms of development assistance, as well as security, and even active combat operations under the humanitarian rubric. Most civilian aid workers do not apply this very broad humanitarian application to military-related action; rather they limit the definition of humanitarian aid to responses to refugee crises, famine, and other catastrophic disasters.

In this chapter, *humanitarian assistance* is defined as any aid intended for the reduction of suffering and death resulting from large hazards that threaten large loss of life above normal levels. Those hazards may be brief in duration, such as earthquakes, or recurrent, as what happens during protracted civil conflict. In recent years, the humanitarian label has been applied ever more broadly to include disaster risk mitigation and post-crisis recovery in instances where the intention of the aid is to reduce vulnerability to specific, abnormal hazards, even for nonimmediate threats.

Humanitarian aid by civilian agencies, therefore, tends to address peoples affected by war, refugee flight and settlement, disease epidemics, civil strife, mass persecution, natural disaster, famine, and failed government institutions. Large amounts of humanitarian aid tend to be given in the aftermath of a large loss of life, as happened after the tsunami in the Indian Ocean in 2004, where the intention of the aid was to reduce suffering and facilitate recovery. A significant amount of humanitarian aid also goes to prevent any surge in deaths, which can occur in large-scale camps of displaced persons, for example, in Darfur. Humanitarian aid has traditionally been targeted to displaced persons, such as refugees, as a top priority because this population tends to have the highest death rates over protracted time periods.

Threats

Although the incidence and timing of humanitarian disasters is difficult to predict with precision—hence their manifestation as emergencies—nonetheless a great deal is known about the most likely causes and the vulnerable countries. Moreover, important strides have been made in recent years in the efficiency and timeliness of relief operations in preventing the worst outcomes of disasters and in reducing some of the main causes of emergencies.

An analysis of trendlines shows that natural disasters, violent conflict (for example, war), pandemics, and famine will continue to place tens of millions of people at risk and in need of international aid each year but will cause fewer and fewer deaths.[3]

The United States benefits much more than it has in the past from multilateral assessments of needs in foreign lands. Since the late 1990s, the United Nations, World Bank, and key donors have increasingly agreed on what to look for in emergencies and postconflict recovery.[4]

Historical records point to famines and interstate wars as the types of emergencies that killed the greatest numbers of persons.[5] But the roles of both in causing large numbers of deaths have diminished. Interstate wars have declined in number, and the numbers of people killed have declined as well. The probability of being killed in a war or invasion is smaller now than at any time in history.[6] Similarly, the annual total of deaths worldwide due to starvation during famines and related emergencies has declined continuously since World War II and the Great Leap Forward.[7] Just in the last generation, the threat of famine has been largely conquered, in significant part because of the early warning systems and global food-aid pipelines created by the United States.[8] The Famine Early Warning System Network (FEWS NET) was designed by the U.S. Agency for International Development (USAID) and has an annual budget of $12 million a year.[9] FEWS NET has played an important role in preventing deaths during large food crises in the Sahel, the Horn of Africa, and southern Africa. Despite its humble profile, FEWS NET may have saved more lives per dollar invested than has any other federal effort. Global commercial food markets also play a role, as they provide automatic buffers to food shortfalls wherever they occur.

Global refugee numbers have been declining since 1991, when they had reached a post–World War II peak of 21 million.[10] During the 1990s, more existing refugees were repatriated than new refugees were created. Moreover, high death rates, which had been registered in refugee camps in the 1970s and 1980s, have diminished because of measures funded by the Department of State to address the preventable causes of death in these camps. The science of refugee relief made enormous strides from epidemiologic studies spearheaded by the Centers for Disease Control and Prevention (CDC).[11]

As a broad generality, the total number of deaths due to natural disasters has declined worldwide despite the growing numbers of people who each year are affected by these hazards. This decline reflects income growth, improved local disaster warning systems, and better housing codes. With a few notable exceptions, such as the tsunami in Southeast Asia in 2004, flood and quake disasters kill fewer people today than they did in the past. Because of growing economic development and improved standards for disaster mitigation, this trend should continue if bolstered by expanded efforts for mitigation aid, early warning systems for various hazards, and economic development. Accordingly, despite obvious needs to respond to large natural disasters such as the 2004 tsunami or the 2003 earthquake in Bam, Iran, most USAID funding for humanitarian assistance has shifted from natural disasters since the late 1980s and toward complex emergencies that involve violence, forced and protracted displacement, and fragile states.

Violent Conflict Will Continue to Displace Millions of People

In the twenty-first century, most humanitarian assistance will be delivered into fragile states and war zones, where access and staff safety will be complicated by local conditions. Complex humanitarian emergencies—that is, those that involve violent conflict—will likely concentrate around three distinct areas: the poorest areas of sub-Saharan Africa, where about half of U.S. humanitarian aid is already focused; front-line states where Muslims have recently been engaged in violent conflict (Chechnya, Kashmir, Indonesia, Iraq, and Afghanistan); and large coastal populations that are vulnerable to flood disasters. In particular, small island states such as the Maldives or the Caribbean states will face heightened risk as ocean levels rise.

On the basis of long-term trends, fewer people will be killed in wars between states.[12] In addition, internal wars of rebellion have declined since 1992, most notably in Latin America and in South and Southeast Asia.[13] As the frequency of war declines, the extent of associated risk to large populations is also likely to decline between now and 2015. Yet, numerous low-intensity conflicts within states persist, and the lethality of combat grows.[14] In all likelihood, the United States will continue to be challenged to find ways to fund the protection of civilians in remote areas such as Darfur, Burundi, Kashmir, Burma, Somalia, the Democratic Republic of the Congo, Colombia, Sri Lanka, and Chechnya.

Because of better data collection, coupled with more extensive penetration by aid professionals and journalists into far-flung parts of the world, the perception exists that complex emergencies—in particular, civil wars—are getting worse. In reality they are not; we are just getting better at reporting them. Another myth is that civilians are targeted more frequently in today's wars than they were in past conflicts. Unfortunately, modern warfare does involve the frequent targeting of civilians, which leads to substantial civilian casualties. But civilians have represented a large share of casualties in every historical period.[15]

Humanitarian aid has saved the most lives in cases of protracted crises. During the last twenty years, Burundi, Rwanda, Somalia, northern Uganda, Sierra Leone, Liberia, Mozambique, Angola, and the Democratic Republic of the Congo have proven vulnerable to ongoing, predictable complex emergencies. Because of weak governance and poor economic conditions, it is likely that conflict and displacement will continue to occur in these same countries in the years ahead. Many of these countries have been left behind by the forces of democratization and globalization. In the absence of economic diversification and growth in manufacturing jobs, populations depend on peasant farming or livestock herding. At the household, district, and regional levels, there is little resilience to protect families during times of shortage or disaster. The lack of economic opportunity locks families into competition with their neighbors, instead of gainful complementarity, and turns land-use disagreements into a source of local grievance and war. The lack of economic diversity also limits their ability to call on their governments for protection, since their governments focus their efforts on tax collection on raw commodities (such as oil, diamonds, or timber).

Food Insecurity

While much of Asia has successfully progressed beyond a state of food insecurity, which the region experienced during the 1980s and 1990s, most of sub-Saharan Africa continues to struggle with food insecurity. Many sub-Saharan countries have worse malnutrition rates now than they did in the 1970s and have seen little progress in improving agricultural yields. The three main problems entrenching food insecurity in Africa are:

—An inadequate (although gradually growing) road network linking farmers to markets;

—An extreme reliance on only rainfall to supply crops, with a very small percentage of agricultural lands fed by irrigated water;

—The repeated economic shocks from recurrent war: eighteen different sub-Saharan nations have been set back by protracted conflicts and mass population displacements during the last twenty years.[16]

Ethiopia represents an extreme case of persistent and therefore predictable dependence on outside help to stave off famine. Famine conditions arise roughly every third year, resulting in long-term dependence on external food assistance by more than 6 million persons every year.[17] The famines in 1999 and 2001 led to excess deaths from measles, repeating the same causes of death in the 1984–85 famine, even though the onset of the famine was slow and well predicted and measles is easily preventable through immunization. Two-thirds of the country faces inadequate water supply as an underlying dilemma. Overall, Ethiopia's ability to become food secure is impaired by inadequate irrigation, too little economic diversification, and too few roads connecting surplus-producing parts of the country to areas in need.

Southern Africa, in aggregate, also faces challenges of food insecurity. Too many producers in Zambia and Malawi are unable to diversify beyond subsistence cultivation. Much of Zimbabwe has recently become dependent on U.S. and other foreign food aid. Two factors will render Southern Africa increasingly prone to famine in the years ahead. First, in every country, the proportion of farmers who grow only maize for consumption or sale continues to increase,[18] which in many regions represents the only major commercial crop. This leaves the region vulnerable to poor harvests during which times trade within the region will probably be inadequate to staunch a famine. Secondly, most agricultural production remains rain fed, without the option of irrigation, which exacerbates the risk of maize crop failures.[19]

Natural Disasters Will Not Abate

Humankind's technology has thus far been unable to reduce the frequency of short-onset natural hazards, such as floods, severe weather, volcanic eruptions, earthquakes, or tornadoes. Meanwhile, as populations and property swell in scale, these natural hazards will appear to be ever more threatening. In the future, every two or three years, graphs will be produced to show that the latest large natural disaster led to more property damage than any preceding it in history.

Yet while tens of millions of persons are exposed to these hazards, poverty-reduction programs and better building standards will continue to reduce the numbers of people who die because of the hazard.

Almost all the deaths from these short-onset natural disasters occur immediately. Floods kill people through drowning, and quakes kill through hypothermia, crushing, secondary wound infections, subsequent organ failure, and the like.[20] International relief aid plays little or no role in reducing death rates. International aid makes a difference in the prevention of death through thoughtful programs in high-risk areas that reduce the vulnerability of populations and by improving local preparedness for instant response. In the case of the tsunami in 2004, most of the 250,000 lives that were lost could have been spared had four programs been in place: teaching populations to swim; an early warning system to alert villages (for example, through public speakers); building of raised, fortified structures (with pylons deep into the ground) to which people in each village could flee; and relocation of people living on beachfronts to higher ground.[21]

Long-Onset Hazards

Another factor driving new threats is long-term climate change. Because disaster prevention seeks to predict future hazards and mitigate their harm, the humanitarian aid community is tied to the debates about climate change, though in a manner different from the scientific and political debate. Disaster experts recognize that climate is always changing through long- and medium-term cycles. Prominent climatologists now predict that sea levels will rise continuously in the decades ahead, which will displace coastal industries and populations and could render entire small island nations uninhabitable (for example, in the south Pacific and Caribbean and Indian Ocean).[22] Future shifts in climate patterns may expose new countries to heat stress, droughts, and greater variability in rainfall patterns. Rising sea levels will not only inundate coastal communities and small islands, but they will increase coastal erosion and affect groundwater, eventually affecting irrigated agriculture.

The U.S. Role in International Humanitarian Relief

In sharp contrast to its image as a "stingy" superpower, the United States government provides a disproportionate amount of international humanitarian assistance. Americans are actively supportive of humanitarian relief, which is evidenced by sizable private giving and is mirrored in strong congressional support for generous and quite flexible funding. Current trends suggest that U.S. humanitarian assistance will continue to grow, regardless of declines in development needs and assistance. This strong support for humanitarian aid shows both the best of America's generous and can-do spirit and the downside of the public's limited and media-directed attention span.

Humanitarian Funding Has Increased

Humanitarian assistance has seen strong, consistent growth over the past few decades, although it still remains smaller than the development (non-emergency) share of U.S. assistance, and small as well in relationship to funding for security and peacekeeping. The annual budget of USAID's Office of U.S. Foreign Disaster Assistance (OFDA)—the lead organization of the federal government for overseas emergencies—has grown from $25 million in the mid-1980s (1/200th of USAID's budget) to $300 million today. On the basis of the long-term trends, humanitarian aid will continue to grow both in sheer volume and as a proportion of total U.S. foreign assistance. Indeed, given the trends, humanitarian aid may represent half of overall U.S. foreign aid within ten or twenty years.

Congress has given OFDA valuable "notwithstanding" authority, (which is an exception from the normal procedures that slow down governmental decisionmaking and prohibit aid from going through certain channels or to certain areas) to spend its money on a moment's notice, free of the entanglements that are the result of the earmarks that limit much of the rest of foreign aid. Since Congress has a long-standing habit of tacking on extra money for the latest emergency in its supplemental appropriations at mid–fiscal year, OFDA's actual funding can fluctuate from year to year with the occurrence of new emergencies and their subsequent publicity. In the 1990s, OFDA received an average of $153 million a year, excluding 1999, when it received $250 million in response to the Kosovo conflict.[23]

In 1989, the incoming head of OFDA, Andrew Natsios, made a pivotal decision to reorient OFDA attention away from responding to short-onset natural disasters and instead toward protracted emergencies, where the opportunity to save lives would be much greater. In fact, until that point, OFDA had achieved much of its success in saving lives not through relief but through mitigation programs that reduced the risk from recurrent hazards. For example, OFDA improved the design of houses in earthquake-prone zones of the Andes to prevent large numbers of deaths from collapsing buildings during a quake. The expansion of OFDA's budget has, therefore, coincided with OFDA's growing engagement in relief to displaced populations and long-term complex emergencies. The downside has been that OFDA remains hobbled in its ability to spend its own funds for disaster risk reduction, so that it can more efficiently save lives in advance of the hazard.

Will Emergencies Garner a Larger Share of the U.S. Aid Pie?

As reflected in outpourings of public sentiment and private donations, emergencies capture the public's interest, even if mostly during the associated media cycle. Large emergencies also routinely garner political support from Congress, which has driven dramatic and sustained increases in official U.S. spending on humanitarian aid over the past twenty years, during a time when the levels of long-term (nonemergency) development assistance waned. This trend is likely to continue. Historically, public support for problems overseas draws from current examples of extreme need. As more and more developing countries grow their way out of poverty, the public no longer equates places like South America or Southeast Asia with poignant human deprivation. Increasingly, the perception of "need" is equated with humanitarian need.

Many Americans see humanitarian action as being more compelling, kind, and ethical than other forms of international activity.[24] In addition to roughly $2 billion a year provided for humanitarian aid by the federal government, Americans privately gave another $1.8 billion through private voluntary agencies for the 2004 south Asian tsunami disaster alone.[25]

An instructive and pertinent example is the shift in the use of U.S. food aid during the past twenty years. For most of the history of the U.S. Food for Peace (FFP) program (funded through Public Law [P.L.] 480), the largest share of U.S. food aid in any given year was for development programs, not for humanitarian purposes. But by the late 1990s, most of U.S. food aid was directed toward such humanitarian purposes as famine relief and aid to refugees. This trend in food aid is evident not only for U.S. assistance, but also for other donors and especially for the United Nation's World Food Program (WFP), which prided itself on being a development agency for most of its history, but which today proclaims itself to be "the world's largest humanitarian relief agency." These changes in food aid in recent years were not by happenstance but were due to a strategic shift made by USAID to reorient aid toward humanitarian emergencies.[26]

Much of the persistent support for humanitarian assistance draws its strength from ethics and emotion. Humanitarian advocates agree with Dr. Fiona Terry, founder of the Australian section of Médecins Sans Frontières, who writes, "Humanitarian action is more than a technical exercise at nourishing or healing a population defined as in need; it is a moral endeavor based on solidarity with other members of humanity. . . . The sole determinant in the allocation of humanitarian assistance should be the level of need of the target population, with priority accorded to the most vulnerable."[27]

Increasingly, humanitarian aid appears to enjoy core support from politicians and the public that is lacking for other foreign assistance programs because of raw emotions and a sense of a moral obligation. As a result, programming for humanitarian aid is typically under less pressure to articulate a strategic rationale. But the Bush administration has increasingly made the case for using humanitarian aid as part of an overall strategy to influence large-scale changes in countries affected by complex emergencies, such as Afghanistan, with the concept of fragile states and the need to focus aid on those areas most likely to breed alienation. The importance of the security dimensions of humanitarian assistance has increased since the tragedy of September 11, affecting the safety of humanitarian aid staff (Americans in particular) in places like Afghanistan and the intensity of U.S. official engagement with fragile states.

Common Myths Inhibiting Humanitarian Aid

Paradoxically, humanitarian aid enjoys broad support from the American public, yet at the same time, the public views it as being largely a Band-Aid gesture of sympathy. Media coverage reinforces the idea that although emergency aid is important for ethical reasons, its efficiency and impact are slight. In reality, however, cost-benefit studies show that properly targeted U.S. humanitarian aid gives the best return on investment relative to both development and security assistance.[28] This is true whether humanitarian aid is measured by the number of lives saved, the more technical disability-adjusted life years spared, or the long-term human potential for economic growth by the targeted aid recipients (especially children).[29] Humanitarian assistance uses inexpensive, rapidly effective approaches that produce incredibly high payoffs.

The technical design and targeting of U.S. humanitarian aid has improved greatly since the 1970s, in parallel with improvements in medical science, public health, and allied industries. Indeed, the entire approach to the field has become more professional. USAID's humanitarian aid is increasingly evidence based and fine tuned to the needs reported in each separate disaster. Nevertheless, superficial thinking, mythology, and misconception persist about which types of aid are most needed in different emergencies. The American public generally believes that disasters call for the massive airlift of all sorts of commodities, from clothing (for example, sending sweaters to people living in the tropics) to household amenities and heavy equipment and field hospitals, most of which are rarely useful, let alone critical. Invariably, what is needed most is the import of ideas, experience, and certain simple items to be used in community-based settings, such as vitamin A, oral rehydration salts, vaccines, plastic sheeting, and water pumps.

Another misconception is that disasters breed fearsome epidemics of strange new diseases. Tropical diseases such as cholera, malaria, and dysentery are important, but they are not introduced to new areas in emergencies. Meanwhile, rare tropical diseases play little role in threatening large numbers of lives during emergencies

Whether a disaster involves refugees, famine, or complex emergencies, the main causes of death are inevitably the same primary health care problems that are the main daily killers throughout the developing world: diarrhea and dysentery, respiratory infection, malnutrition, measles, and malaria. With help from the Centers for Disease Control and Prevention, USAID and nongovernmental organizations (NGOs) have learned that a successful response requires a public health and primary care approach to control these problems at the population level, not with a focus on high-quality but low-volume clinics. Thus, although the public instinctively seeks to donate surplus supplies, the most pivotal good transported by aid agencies in response to disasters in developing countries is knowledge about primary health care, community outreach, and project management, delivered in the form of aid professionals.

The United States provides a large portion of global funding for multilateral humanitarian assistance, when one includes the various contributions made through a range of offices and agencies. In the division of responsibilities among donor nations, the United States has demonstrated a comparative talent in humanitarian challenges. Contrary to much of the bad publicity surrounding America's perceived stingy official development assistance record, a greater proportion of U.S. aid is for humanitarian aid that gives a high return on investment, while much of European and Japanese aid is for development assistance, often tied to business arrangements or given without accountability through government budgets of former colonies.[30] The quality of U.S. humanitarian aid is enhanced by intangibles including strategic ideas, management skills, and technological and scientific advances—such as vaccines—that are developed in the United States and then shared around the world.

U.S. Government Management of Foreign Emergencies

At present, humanitarian aid is managed by disparate parts of the U.S. government, fragmented across different agencies, and lacks coherence. As a result, on many issues of humanitarian coordination, the Department of State and USAID have taken competing positions and approaches. Nowhere in the federal system is there one locus responsible for policy, planning, and coordination of the multitude of U.S. assets available for the range of emergencies reviewed above. Instead, most decisionmaking and analysis of U.S. humanitarian assistance is ad hoc and reactive, and much of the government's preparedness for emergencies is overly oriented toward assuming the last crisis is a good predictor of what lies ahead.

USAID

Overall, the bulk of technical expertise, related to the challenges of working in developing countries, rests within USAID. Indeed, many of the government's best efforts in the developing world have been due to the creation, management, and dissemination of a body of technical knowledge. Health, agriculture, nutrition, microeconomic, and shelter programs at USAID have pushed key envelopes in helping dozens of the poorest countries to better understand their options. One of USAID's great triumphs has been its country-by-country demographic health survey, which provides scientifically robust snapshots of a nation's health status and practices, focusing on women and children. Although it has been successfully applied in many countries, it should be adopted and applied within countries in crises and especially in postconflict countries.[31]

The Office of U.S. Foreign Disaster Assistance provides the bulk of funding for emergency relief but avoids funding transitional activities related to reconstruction, governance, demining, and such soft sectors as basic education or capacity building of social safety nets. Although it is the lead entity for providing aid to avert disaster impact, OFDA spends relatively little on early warning or mitigation of disasters, in part because it is not as popular with Congress or the public as is relief that comes after a disaster.[32] OFDA's scope of action is limited to funding implementing partners, including UN agencies, the Red Cross, foreign governments, consulting firms, and firms that sell relief supplies. Two-thirds of OFDA's funding is for field work by operational NGOs, mostly based in the United States.[33]

OFDA is the most important U.S. humanitarian account by far, as it is used for such a wide range of crises, hazards, and modalities of response. It is fortunate that OFDA's budget has grown as much as it has, vis-à-vis other accounts. OFDA has tried unsuccessfully to expand on the Famine Early Warning System to create some sort of early warning for complex emergencies. Early warning can be a sensitive issue, as no state likes to see official diagnoses that its government is about to be overthrown.

Another part of USAID, the Office of Transition Initiatives (OTI) was created to help lead the transition from relief operations to longer-term recovery. However, left to its own management, OTI has instead gravitated toward promoting the growth of activist civil society, mass media, and grassroots democracy and governance, leaving a U.S. vacuum on the transition from emergency response to reconstruction and development. Instead of serving primarily as a funder for physical reconstruction or transitional health care, for instance, OTI has focused much of its work on influencing governance (such as removing autocrats like Milosevic in Yugoslavia) and funding democratic elections.[34] Unlike OFDA, OTI has developed a comparative advantage in working with local civil societies overseas, the media, and other atypical partners.

Since 1999, OTI has also migrated into the funding of livelihoods, such as short term employment for low paid workers in the public works sector, which overlaps with a traditional sector of OFDA. In this way, OTI is working more closely in tandem with OFDA. Both share congressional notwithstanding authority and the ability to pick and choose where to go.

While OFDA manages field-level assessments and monitors the overall USAID response to emergencies, the Office of Food for Peace, which sits in the same bureau as OFDA and OTI, administers a huge portion of net resources for emergencies.[35,36] Considering the added aid from FFP and the Department of Agriculture, roughly half of all funds and expenditures in most emergencies are for food, food transport, and nutrition programs.[37] Food for Peace maintains a symbiotic relationship with its food-aid NGO partners who, through their advocacy on Capitol Hill, have opposed initiatives from other parts of USAID for the appropriation of funds for the purchase of local foods, which is the appropriate and efficient response in some emergencies.[38]

In many ways, FFP has led the rest of USAID in testing approaches to developmental relief that specifically promote transition by helping people reestablish assets, wealth, livelihood, and self-reliance. Food aid programmed by FFP has gone through distinct phases in recent decades. In the 1980s it was largely for maternal and child health. In recent years, NGOs have increasingly proposed to FFP to use food aid for livelihood strengthening through asset building. In the years ahead, FFP is likely to turn more attention to applications related to whichever UN Millennium Development Goals (global benchmarks for achieving minimal human needs, established over many years in different international conventions and treaties) remain unmet, for example, hunger, job creation, reducing maternal mortality, and the postcrisis return and relocation of populations.

FFP also manages one of the most cost-efficient investments USAID has ever made: the Famine Early Warning System Network. FEWS NET collects, analyzes, and disseminates remotely sensed and ground-based early warning data on a regular basis. FEWS NET has quietly empowered the aid community to avert famines and save millions of lives during the past twenty years. This prevention of famine crises remains one of America's great unsung achievements abroad.

Department of State and Multilateral Organizations

The State Department manages several accounts for multilateral organizations, including some of the emergency operations of UNICEF and the United Nations Office for the Coordination of Humanitarian Affairs (OCHA). The State Department's Bureau of Population, Refugees, and Migration (PRM) specifically manages the funds provided by the United States to the United Nations High Commissioner for Refugees (UNHCR) and to the International Organization for Migration (IOM) and the International Committee of the Red Cross (ICRC), neither of which is part of the United Nations.

Through this close relationship with the UN, and UNHCR in particular, the United States has achieved much of its humanitarian impact abroad. UNHCR depends on the United States for roughly one-third of its global budget for refugee care.[39] Because of its flexibility and accountability, UNHCR is among the most effective UN agencies in responding to the worst refugee crises, coordinating the whole array of aid agencies, and subcontracting or subgranting technical work to "fast-response" NGOs, which can jet in on only a few days' notice to set up a refugee camp and mount relief. More than half of the NGO response that UNHCR depends on is from American aid agencies. In many of the world's largest crises, such as border relief operations in Afghanistan, Cambodia, Chad, Sudan, Ethiopia, Kenya, Mozambique, Honduras, and Mexico, thousands of Americans have worked through private NGOs under the funding and legal umbrella of UNHCR, using U.S. funds appropriated by Congress. UNHCR, although widely regarded as effective and efficient, should not be given greater levels of funds by the United States unless and until other donors expand UNHCR's gross income, so that the agency does not appear to be merely an arm of the U.S. government. UNHCR's effectiveness would decline if it were not seen as neutral. The United States probably would contribute more in absolute terms to UNHCR if other donors would raise their contributions to increase the overall budget of UNHCR. However, a number of European countries, most notably France and Germany, have failed to show interest in supporting UNHCR, despite its global front-line work (see figures 5-1 and 5-2).[40]

The International Committee of the Red Cross provides unique capabilities. Established out of the intergovernmental agreement known as the Geneva Conventions, ICRC works to protect prisoners and civilians through the application of internationally forged laws of war. The ICRC is often the biggest and most operational agency assisting war-affected populations, such as internally displaced persons (IDPs) in many complex emergencies. U.S. government officials have long viewed the caliber of ICRC's fieldwork to be among the most professional and efficient. Unlike other international bodies, the ICRC is rarely criticized in terms of the management or efficiency of its field work. The United States recognizes that ICRC's mandate requires it to reliably respond to the worst needs in the worst war zones regardless of how dangerous the undertaking is.

Figure 5-1 U.S. Government Funding of Multilateral Humanitarian Assistance, 2003

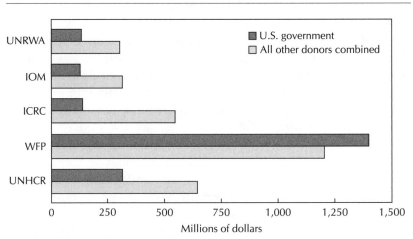

Source: Annual reports of UNRWA, IOM, ICRC, WFP, UNHCR.
UNRWA: United Nations Relief and Works Administration; IOM: International Organization for Migration; ICRC: International Committee of the Red Cross; WFP: World Food Program; UNHCR: United Nations High Commissioner for Refugees.

Other Federal Agencies

Other federal agencies also play salient roles in overseas relief, albeit in a haphazard pattern. For instance, during the Afghanistan humanitarian aid effort in 2002, seven different stand-alone bureaus or agencies were involved in the health sector, from the Indian Health Service to the Office of Global Health Affairs in the Department of Health and Human Services (HHS).[41]

The Centers for Disease Control and Prevention has played a pivotal role in turning humanitarian aid from art to science. Although unrecorded and unsung, the CDC's influence on the policies and practices of the major UN agencies, of USAID, and of many NGOs has been responsible for much of the improvement and impact of the aid industry. Unfortunately, the extraordinary influence of CDC on international aid, which has not been actively publicized, has been restricted in recent years, as current HHS leadership has clamped extra layers of bureaucracy on top of CDC, driving many of CDC's most talented staff to leave the organization or, at least, to abandon involvement in international efforts.

The Department of Agriculture provides substantial aid in two distinct areas. First, it purchases and provides all the food that is used by

Figure 5-2 Comparison of Contributions to Multilateral Humanitarian Assistance, 2003

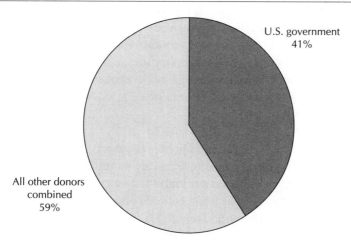

U.S. government
41%

All other donors
combined
59%

Source: Annual reports of UNRWA, IOM, ICRC, WFP, UNHCR.

USAID and NGOs. Less well known is the support by the U.S. Forest Service to USAID for the creation, training, and staffing of incident-command teams for disaster response overseas. Applying the staffing models used in the response to domestic fires, the Forest Service is responsible for most of the models applied by USAID for intervening, communicating, and coordinating players in larger overseas emergencies.

The Federal Emergency Management Agency (FEMA) has bilateral aid programs of its own, with hardly any meaningful coordination with USAID. FEMA's value is due to the sharing of technical information with other governments, typically related to disaster mitigation that is relevant to middle- or high-income countries, but not the poorest.

Competition versus Coordination

Though intertwined in their work, these distinct parts of the U.S. government manage significant chunks of humanitarian activities by themselves, with minimal communication or coordination across agencies. Confusion surrounds the overarching authority for planning and harmonizing these individual efforts. There is no desk in the U.S. government that tracks all U.S. humanitarian donations, all humanitarian donations just to the UN system, nor donations just to NGOs.

The Humanitarian Information Unit (HIU) was created in 2002 at the initiative of the Bureau of Intelligence and Research at the Department of State to provide a central source of data for the U.S. government. In practice, the HIU serves as a partial bridge between the State Department and USAID. Although the HIU has grown and enjoys buy-in and cooperation from various federal agencies, it has confined its attention to the real-time analysis of specific crises. It has not, in contrast, focused on the response by the U.S. government to crises, the tracking of resources in the United States, emerging trends, or the patterns of response to smaller neglected or remote disasters.

In 1994 the White House assigned to the USAID administrator (through a Presidential Decision Directive) the responsibility for coordinating disaster response across the departments and agencies of the federal government. However, this coordination has largely been an exercise of information gathering, and no attendant controls or budget authorities came with this designation. Thus, USAID, FEMA (now a part of the Department of Homeland Security), and the Departments of State, Defense, Agriculture, Labor, Justice, and Health and Human Services all have their own individual policies and plans with regard to the sharing of resources, science, and seconded personnel overseas. Neither USAID nor the State Department nor the National Security Council has had the capability to keep abreast of the many far-flung and often creative humanitarian aid activities of these different branches of the government, let alone those of foreign states, U.S. companies, or foundations.

With regard to multilateral relations, the strongest point of the United States for coordination on humanitarian aid may be the State Department's Bureau of Population, Refugees, and Migration. It has the advantage of having the most ongoing contact with and understanding of other donors, the UN system, and the politics associated with complex emergencies. But PRM lacks the field-based technical knowledge of USAID in the design and implementation of programs for shelter, nutrition, health, drugs, vaccine, family planning, and logistics. OFDA also could more readily draw on the considerable expertise in the various functional branches of USAID in these sectors.

Persistent Deficiencies in the U.S. Approach

Systemwide, the network of funders and implementing agencies for U.S. humanitarian aid fails to provide aid that is balanced or proportionate across sectors or geographic areas. There is no methodology for balancing and prioritizing humanitarian needs. The humanitarian problem of internally displaced persons is the most important case representing this lack of coordination and prioritization.

U.S. Confusion over Internally Displaced Persons

The disjuncture between USAID and the State Department is most apparent concerning the needs of IDPs. Whereas the State Department has the lead role for addressing the needs of cross-border problems including refugees (through UNHCR), USAID has in turn always had the natural lead role for addressing crises within a country, whether the problem is famine, conflict, or complex combinations of hazards. In simple terms, the State Department's PRM has been the focus of funding for monitoring refugee camp operations, while USAID's OFDA has historically been the primary source of funding for programs helping IDPs.

But this model sounds cleaner in principle than it is in practice. One complication for OFDA's lead role is that the agency that has been the most involved with conflict-affected IDPs is the ICRC, which is overseen by PRM, not OFDA. Another wrinkle is that OCHA, a multilateral agency with a close relationship with the State Department, is increasingly the lead UN agency for organizing information and setting priorities for internal crises. OFDA and the State Department share funding support for OCHA.

Although the State Department has a claim on the lead role for multilateral solutions, in dollar terms much of the volume of aid for IDPs still comes from OFDA and Food for Peace, and much of the in-country presence by Americans is through USAID. Because the UN does not have any lead agency for implementing a humanitarian response within a country (comparable to the role that UNHCR performs when refugees cross a border), most IDP operations have been run by grants from donors to NGOs. There is a need for some UN agency (perhaps UNHCR with an expanded mandate) to coordinate aid multilaterally for in-country responses to IDPs, including subgranting aid to NGOs.

Since the 1991 Gulf War, UNHCR has at times been asked by the UN General Assembly to play a lead role among UN agencies in coordinating aid for IDPs. However, UNHCR has not sought this responsibility because the substantial costs go well beyond UNHCR's current budget. In 2005, the State Department and USAID agreed that USAID might fund UNHCR to meet the field needs of IDPs. This arrangement makes sense to address the specific problem of IDPs; however, it reduces the clarity of the division of labor between the State Department and USAID and increases the complexity of cross-cutting agreements, mandates, and memoranda-of-understanding that currently constitute the architecture of humanitarian response.

Life-Saving Interventions Are Unbalanced across Sectors

In an emergency response, the U.S. government is limited by the capabilities of its implementing partners, namely NGOs and the UN. Overall, NGOs have improved their efficiency and competence, particularly with the codification of consistent guidelines for humanitarian aid, published in the Sphere Project's handbook: *Humanitarian Charter and Minimum Standards in Disaster Response.* Supported by U.S. schools of public health and the CDC, NGOs have turned humanitarian aid into more of a science than the makeshift art it once was.

However, as a group, NGOs do not offer a balanced portfolio of services. Hundreds of operational NGOs (that is, NGOs that work in the field, as opposed to NGOs that advocate or write reports only) position themselves to provide medical care and food aid, with the result that other sectors, such as water supply, hygiene, and protection from violent attack, receive too little attention. In their work and in the image they advertise to the public, nongovernmental relief organizations tend to emphasize and thereby reinforce the same images that sell for the sake of fundraising. The classic image of an expatriate doctor doling out food to malnourished orphans drives donations. And, in turn, it drives how NGOs choose what to do. Given how little the news media and the public understand emergency relief, the range of needs in emergencies are reduced to these two categories: medical care and nutrition. Secondarily, a few NGOs advertise their transport capabilities, for airlift of medical supplies, medical equipment, surgeons, clothing, and household items, without regard to whether or not these goods are needed in the emergency in question.

Although U.S. funding offices, such as OFDA, make efforts to lure and compel NGOs to work in neglected sectors, their scope is limited. Meanwhile, the U.S. government plays virtually no role in shaping how the public views emergencies or targets their donations—whether donations are given on the basis of actual needs or because of the public's age-old misperceptions.

In emergencies, people die because of the weakest link, whatever the neglected sector may be. For instance, providing enough food but no water (a common occurrence) results in almost as many deaths as if no aid were provided at all. Unfortunately, while hundreds of NGOs like to give food and medical care, few U.S. NGOs focus on water supply, sanitation, or engineering. This gap in water supply is mirrored at the UN level, where no UN agency has reliably volunteered to lead water-supply solutions from one emergency to the next. UNICEF is viewed by many agencies, including the U.S. government, as the best prospect for deploying water experts and coordinating water projects. However, the UN views UNICEF as an agency defined by advocacy for children rather than by sectors or even operations. Regardless of how well UNICEF may provide water in select emergencies, it remains an unreliable leader on water supply for most emergencies.

Similarly, too few NGOs focus on public health campaigns to preemptively control communicable diseases, such as measles, shigellosis, tuberculosis, meningitis, cholera, or intestinal parasites. The Measles Initiative for sub-Saharan Africa represents a rare model for how a critical need can be successfully met through creative partnering and buy-in by key agencies. Pioneered by the American Red Cross, with the United Nations Foundation as financial intermediary, the Measles Initiative blends the field tactics of UNICEF with the scientific contributions of the World Health Organization (WHO) and the volunteer staff of the Red Cross movement in the field to achieve vertical immunization of huge populations in Africa. The goal of the Initiative is to reduce measles deaths globally, not specifically in response to an emergency, during which many children would die.[42]

In addition, too few NGOs take seriously shelter construction or camp management. Expertise on appropriate shelter programs tends to reside within the donor community, particularly OFDA, and other foreign aid agencies including the European Commission for Humanitarian Aid and Germany's technical assistance agency, GTZ.[43]

One of the weakest areas for donor governments such as the United States is in support for programs that directly protect civilians in conflict zones from being killed, attacked, or raped. Even when NGOs provide "practical" protection from these harms, they receive little donor funding for this. The United States in particular has demonstrated an inability to fund the protection work of civilian counterparts. Since NGOs, and not the military, are spread through front-line villages and zones of conflict in every poor nation, the missed opportunity of the U.S. government to work with civil society to save lives in emergencies is a glaring gap.[44]

Despite recent efforts, USAID has not yet been able to introduce "practical protection," which adapts tactics at the local level to avert massacres, into field programming.[45] For example, while the administrator of USAID in 2004 complained about the government of Sudan's brutality in villages of Darfur, 100 percent of USAID's funding in Darfur ended up being used for the traditional Band-Aid sectors of food, nutrition, and water supply in IDP camps, However, no funding was awarded to NGOs attempting to introduce protection in the villages of Darfur to avert massacres, where the killings were allegedly occurring.[46] A recent innovative project funded by PRM established a unique "protection-surge" unit within the IRC, which provides a cadre of professionals who can be deployed into the field to intervene to save lives from intentional harm. This successful model should be replicated or adopted by other NGOs.

The Deployment of Aid among Competing Crises

Within the community of humanitarian aid monitors, it has long been understood that there are enormous discrepancies in the levels of aid received among emergencies. These discrepancies do not correlate with the severity or urgency of the crisis or the scale of need. Inevitably, every year the deployment of humanitarian funds follows a power curve: one crisis gathers more funds by far than do other crises. Typically, the most publicized three or four crises in any one year attract more funds than the next twenty or more combined, regardless of their relative needs. Most UN appeals for emergencies, even the relatively more highly visible emergencies, generate on average 30 percent of the funding sought.[47]

The problem can be stated as the following: the funds that are donated between emergencies have little correlation to where the needs are greatest, that is, where the funding could save the most lives. In any given season, American private donations are concentrated on funding the most sensationalized crisis reported on television. Meanwhile, the vast majority of disasters receive little or no news coverage. As a rule of thumb, humanitarian donations follow news coverage, and news coverage follows the military.

News editors understand that their reading public cannot absorb much variety, and instead they look for a continuing story line. In 1992 that story line became Somalia; in 1994, Rwanda; in 1995, Bosnia; in 1999, Kosovo; in 2004, Darfur; in 2005, the tsunami. Aid for Afghanistan, for example, generated vastly more news coverage in 2002, because of the news cycle that concentrated on U.S. intervention, than it did during the twenty-four years of crisis before the U.S. intervention, despite the greater needs during the preceding period.

The driving force is familiarity. The vast majority of the American people had never heard of Somalia, Rwanda, Kosovo, Cambodia, Darfur, or Aceh until each took its momentary turn at the top of headlines as "the world's worst emergency." Nor, still today, have most Americans ever read or heard about Baluchistan, Manipur, Guinea, Burundi, Eritrea, Tajikistan, the Ferghana Valley, or the Spratley Islands.

Other donor governments also decide how to apportion their humanitarian funds on the basis of interests other than where is the greatest need. Most European nations and Japan donate to regions of the world where they have stakes and investments, particularly where they had former colonial outposts. The United Kingdom for example devotes a disproportionate amount of attention and aid to Sudan and India, whereas France gives to West Africa, Italy to Ethiopia, Spain to Latin America, and Japan to Southeast Asia.

Because so much donor funding is unbalanced, a counterbalance would be useful. To an important degree, the U.S. government performs this balancing role. The two key loci for humanitarian aid in the federal government—OFDA and PRM—provide aid that is based on hard humanitarian need more than what any other donor does. It is not strictly humanitarian, as at times funding from OFDA and PRM is targeted to a particular area because of political pressure, either from the White House or from earmarks by Congress. Still, most of the work of OFDA and PRM aims to ensure that aid is deployed to where lives are at greatest risk. This is one of the best, yet least heralded, of America's legacies in foreign assistance and one that should be preserved.

Recommendations: Toward a New Approach

Enhance U.S. Leadership vis-à-vis Other Donor Nations

Because it has a more comprehensive and complete set of aid capabilities than has any other donor, the United States is in a position to play a pivotal role in demonstrating how best to donate to achieve humanitarian impact. The United States should better coordinate other donors, all of which are smaller, to give also according to humanitarian need. The Good Humanitarian Donorship initiative, to which USAID and the Department of State have been parties since its inception in 2003, proposes that donors increase their adherence to certain principles, including:

—Respect and promote the implementation of international humanitarian law, refugee law, and human rights;

—While reaffirming the primary responsibility of states for the victims of humanitarian emergencies within their own borders, strive to ensure flexible and timely funding, on the basis of the collective obligation of striving to meet humanitarian needs; and

—Allocate humanitarian funding in proportion to needs and on the basis of needs assessments.

The United States should propose methods within the Good Humanitarian Donorship initiative by which donor agencies can restructure the way that the hundreds of different donor offices can come together in a more coherent approach to funding time-sensitive UN programs.

Use International Organizations More Strategically by Harmonizing U.S. Influence in the United Nations

The international structures for humanitarian response are increasingly revolving around the UN system. Progress is inhibited by vested interests, lack of creativity, and the institutional inertia within each agency that resists any change or loss of visibility. The United States can use the UN better to leverage more and more-appropriate contributions from other governments. In essence, UN relief agencies serve as a joint pool into which each government is coaxed to give its share. In this way, the United States can goad other countries into providing their fair share to important initiatives. For too long, the U.S. government has shouldered an unreasonable proportion of the budgets of key humanitarian programs, including UNHCR's, WFP's, IOM's, and UNICEF's. Newer industrializing countries should be encouraged to come to the table and contribute.

But to achieve better burden sharing, the United States needs to speak with a clear and coherent voice on humanitarian issues, in dealings with other donors, and in dealings in the governing bodies of the UN. To accomplish this, Congress should clarify that the Department of State is the lead agency within the federal system for humanitarian policy, planning, and relations with UN bodies. This requires that other federal agencies follow the Department of State's lead in their own bilateral funding arrangements (which carry clout) with each of the UN specialized agencies. Clearly, USAID has substantially more knowledge and capacity for the many technical components of humanitarian aid. USAID should do a better job of providing technical briefs to the State Department so that policy can be crafted that better takes into account USAID's experiences with and needs of the UN. Within the State Department, a new Humanitarian Policy and Planning Bureau should be created out of PRM and encouraged to take a lead role in working with the UN system in planning a more coherent, integrated, proactive response to disasters, forced migration, and the consequences of war overseas.

The United States therefore should lead in pushing for large, structural changes because they will not occur otherwise. The U.S. government should push as soon as possible for consideration of how UN agencies can be reshaped and re-formed to get more timely, efficient, and balanced responses to humanitarian needs. Right now, too many agencies respond to emergencies through a vested interest in selling their product (for example, food for WFP and the Food and Agriculture Organization [FAO]).

Far too much time and expense is lost now to complex and continuous debates between agencies over which is responsible for what, when, and where. This drain on resources would be reduced, and responsibility and accountability improved, through a consolidation among agencies. The United States should therefore examine prospects for drawing together the various humanitarian offices and initiatives spread across a dozen UN agencies into one, specialized, operational UN humanitarian assistance agency. Its mandate would be to take whatever actions are necessary to reduce excess deaths from any disasters, wherever they occur, rather than debating where they should work and how, as every UN agency currently does. This may best be achieved through an expansion of UNHCR's mandate, scope, and budget.

Repair Gaps in Field Implementation

Failures of humanitarian aid, which result in deaths, disability, and suffering, need to receive expanded attention by focusing on gaps in specific sectors, such as water supply, hygiene, field communications, early warning networks, practical protection, child survival related to diarrhea and respiratory infections, and threats from cold weather. Through control of the purse strings, the U.S. government can force corrective action in terms of bolstering the skills and orientation of UN agencies and NGOs toward these sectors.

In particular, the U.S. government should find new solutions for achieving the provision of water supply in emergencies. Because UNICEF has been unreliable in this sector, it should not be relied upon as the only multilateral lead agency. The United Nations Office for Project Services (UNOPS) could be given support to develop contracts with engineering networks to provide more tactical support for water supply in emergencies.[48] UNHCR could establish memoranda of understanding with more implementing agencies. A long-term indefinite quantity contract could be used to build capacity among NGOs willing to commit to water supply with their privately funded programs as well.

Expand the Use of Market-Based Relief Interventions

Congress should support USAID's interest in gradually expanding the funding available for the local purchase of food for aid. In a triumph of politics over good policy, Congress rejected the administration's fiscal 2006 budget request for $300 million to procure food within the area of an emergency (if food is available and at a low price), because of entrenched opposition from U.S. agricultural interests. This ignored important lessons learned by USAID about saving lives when time is short: when and where feasible, local purchases of food tend to save months of time in responding to a food crisis compared with traditional food aid, in which food is procured, packaged, and shipped by ocean freighter from the United States.

Bridge the Gulf between Crisis Response and Preventive Economic Solutions

Two other weakest links in humanitarian assistance are in addressing the economic causes of grievance, conflict, and displacement and in putting in place sizable economic and governance programs that facilitate the transition from emergency response to reconstruction and ultimately development. Programs such as transition, governance development, and poverty alleviation are critical preventatives to break the oft-repeated cycling back into violence (these issues are addressed in more detail in chapter 6 of this book). Collectively, humanitarian aid agencies have avoided examining how to improve economic diversity and job creation. The U.S. government, in partnership with the World Bank, should initiate an extensive inquiry into what kinds of gainful employment can be introduced into areas of protracted emergencies for the purpose of creating jobs for refugees and internally displaced people. Economic tools, which are routinely applied in other parts of the world, should be introduced to identify economic opportunities in perpetually failing states such as Somalia, Haiti, Cambodia, Afghanistan, Liberia, or at-risk states such as Azerbaijan, Nigeria, the Democratic Republic of the Congo, Rwanda, Burundi, Peru, and Nicaragua.

USAID has already begun to analyze how to account for the dynamics of local markets when responding to disasters. Yet even in as well-funded and well-watched an operation as the $14 billion response to the December 2004 tsunami, humanitarian aid agencies have failed to recognize the implications of their massive aid programs on village life and on livelihoods based on construction, on regional economic development, or on how these effects relate to the long-term civil wars in Sri Lanka or Aceh.[49]

Double the Portion of Aid for Risk Mitigation, Prevention, and Preparedness

Congress should earmark more aid toward the upstream risk factors that can save lives, which are myriad, including relocation of populations from live volcanoes, better building standards in quake-prone zones, stockpiles of critical medical supplies in war-torn societies, and seed provision in famine-affected areas. Too much funding currently trails natural disasters, when lives have already been lost by the time the crisis makes the news. The most effective measures for reducing the impact of disasters on people are prevention, reduction of vulnerability, preparedness, early warning systems, local-level rapid relief response capacity, and developmental relief. Thus, the overarching priority must be to mitigate disasters, not simply to react to them. Mitigation is a more effective and more efficient approach to disasters, particularly when disasters are frequent and extensive. Because of continued global population growth, more people today than ever before are exposed to explosive disease epidemics such as measles and cholera, emerging diseases such as HIV/AIDS, reemerging diseases such as tuberculosis and malaria, and armed conflict.[50] Developmental relief can also mitigate regional (cross-border) crises that involve regular population movements and trade, such as between Ethiopia, Kenya, and Somalia.

The US should lead new movements to expand disaster-risk insurance and health insurance to the poorer communities of the world, which currently have less than 5 percent of any insurance. USAID has begun testing new measures that use the insurance industry to support disaster safety nets.[51]

The United States should also move away from its focus on international mechanisms, and target aid toward local-level networks of disaster prevention and response agencies, including community-based organizations and community volunteers.[52]

The Office of U.S. Foreign Disaster Assistance at USAID has world-leading expertise in how to channel this type of funding. A sizable increase of OFDA's budget, specifically earmarked for disaster risk mitigation, should lead a UN-wide effort to establish a minimum level of 20 percent of total humanitarian assistance funding aimed at disaster mitigation. At present, no single UN agency does a competent or sufficient job in promoting risk mitigation, although the office of the International Strategy for Disaster Reduction (ISDR), within the UN Secretariat, does an indispensable job of promoting the strategy of risk mitigation and helping to share knowledge about how to achieve it.[53] The budget of ISDR should be expanded, and OFDA and the UN system should have a firm mandate to dedicate 20 percent of its annual budget toward risk reduction.

Aid agencies remain much better at responding to rather than preventing civil strife, in large part because their predictive ability remains weak. The focus of the aid community's analysis of the precursors to strife is placed too heavily on political trends and too little on economics, geography, the rule of law, and the looting of natural resources.[54]

Government Has a Unique Bully Pulpit to Educate the Public

The U.S. government has the trust of the American public and a voice, interest, and stake in humanitarian issues, all of which are underutilized. The White House, secretary of State, and USAID administrator can dramatically change the terms of how Americans think about disasters, which in turn affects the pressures that the public can apply on Congress and local NGOs or faith-based humanitarian organizations. The network of U.S. private agencies involved in humanitarian relief is very active in lobbying Congress and the administration. But the reverse has been neglected. By better educating the public, the U.S. government has the opportunity to channel private contributions, which are individually small but large in aggregate, to better support government-established priorities.

The Office of U.S. Foreign Disaster Assistance should improve its public communications to specifically inform the public, through a network of journalists, about what donated items are needed from one highly visible emergency to the next. The White House should then take a priority subset of these messages and convey them to the public, in particular about the major gaps in humanitarian aid such as those countries and weak sectors (water supply, shelter, disease prevention, and so on) that are not in the headlines.

Instill Coherence within the U.S. Executive Branch

The relationship among relevant U.S. government offices and bureaus should be reorganized to allow coherent, timely, visionary leadership for humanitarian aid. Previous studies have looked at the need to de-conflict the respective roles of the embassies, regional military commands, Department of State, and OFDA in the real-time response to emergencies.[55] Another persistent bureaucratic problem is the handover from the relief side of USAID and State to any parts of USAID that can fill in for the medium term.[56] One option is to reshape the Bureau for Population, Refugees, and Migration into a new Humanitarian Policy and Planning Bureau of the Department of State, with the responsibility to provide policy coherence for U.S. government humanitarian policy and planning (refugees, IDPs, disaster- and conflict-related activities, and so on) and to set broad goals for USAID's programming, while leaving the details for implementation to USAID. This would rectify the gap in long-term analysis of humanitarian aid trends and neglected threats.[57] Within this set of policies and strategies, USAID would continue to take the lead in implementation, drawing on its technical expertise, and be responsible for tactical decisions.

A second option would be to merge OFDA with PRM, placing all humanitarian funding, planning, and response into one office. This super-OFDA would have the following dimensions:

—It would largely exist as a stand-alone office within USAID, with its own planning, evaluation, and procurement functions;

—It would include the current livelihood and protection components of OTI;

—It would have the lead authority for responses to food crises, thus, have authority for planning the use of FFP emergency resources (while not otherwise drawing on FFP personnel); this may include funds for the local purchase of food aid sought unsuccessfully by USAID in its recent congressional budget presentations;

—It would be organized to include a suboffice for multilateral affairs to liaise with OCHA and to fund UNHCR, ICRC, and other such international agencies;

—It would be assigned lead authority to establish and staff the field-based Disaster Assistance Response Teams (DART), which historically had been the call of OFDA but in recent years became politicized at the higher levels of USAID;

—It would be given an expanded budget to support programs for disaster risk reduction (mitigation and preparedness);

—It would be given the opportunity to look in depth at trends in disaster threats and project the possibilities for novel, atypical, or unexpected disasters;

—It would be allowed to invest greater resources into livelihood restoration, in which the United States has taken a lead role among donors in addressing the household economy of peoples affected by disasters;

—It would be encouraged by Congress to generate public education materials and to work with the media, the Government Accountability Office, and InterAction to better focus donations by the U.S. public;

—It would be required to work in closer association with the sector of U.S. private foundations that collectively control more potential humanitarian aid funding than does the federal government; and

—It would be given authorization by Congress to establish the type of "firewall protection" originally and currently afforded to the Peace Corps to ensure that its mission remains focused purely on its humanitarian mission and that it is not subject to the micromanagement and jealousies of other parts of USAID and the State Department, which in recent years have had the effect of politicizing U.S. aid.

With the merging and expanding of PRM and OFDA budgets, along with components of OTI and FFP, the budget of this new entity would exceed $1.5 billion, which would allow for a vastly improved capability to plan from year to year to meet the range of crisis needs that currently go underfunded.

A larger, more stable, and more coherent authority for U.S. humanitarian aid would have a much greater capability to talk with and make complementary plans with the large European Commission Humanitarian Office. It would also find different comparative advantages with the UN than the existing U.S. structure currently sees. As it is now structured, the U.S. government uses the network of UN humanitarian agencies instrumentally but not strategically. The United States undermines many of them, while neglecting the rest. And, in fact, the humanitarian aid capabilities of the UN provide much greater added value to other smaller donor nations (for example, Canada, Norway, Denmark, Spain, and Italy) than they do to the United States. With a greater coherence, the U.S. humanitarian aid authority would be able to play a leadership role internationally, informing other donors, in a way that now the UN alone fulfills.

Just as USAID's humanitarian aid bureau already includes the food aid office, a new humanitarian aid entity should also include much of USAID's health expertise. The arguments for giving priority to health threats are not different from those concerning humanitarian threats in ways that matter. In both cases, the benefits are visible and dramatic. In both cases, the effect is to engender goodwill while at the same time track and contain immediate transnational threats to the United States.[58] And in both cases, the bulk of the work is on delivering affordable health care, surveillance, and scalable delivery mechanisms to the poor and vulnerable, mostly children. Most humanitarian aid is about health, in one way or another.[59]

Improve Congressional Oversight

As humanitarian aid is gradually becoming the primary mission of USAID, Congress needs to better understand the objectives and intentions of U.S. humanitarian aid programming. Currently, too much aid is perceived as reacting to haphazard and seemingly disconnected crises in random points around the world. Too much of the reporting by aid agencies to USAID and to Congress about U.S. humanitarian action is buried in incidental details of dates, exotic names, and particular activities. Reporting is disproportionately about how many metric tons of supplies were transported, displacing reporting about what was achieved. This approach inhibits transparency and effective oversight. It prevents Congress from assuming more of a stake in humanitarian aid and standing tall in how it reports to the public.

Congress should request a biannual "Humanitarian Strategy" report from the administration and an annual "Humanitarian State of Affairs" report that allows Congress to learn what works, what does not, what are the results of humanitarian interventions, and what is the return on investment. These reports should emphasize the measurement of results, not merely actions. They should compare and contrast the costs and benefits (all benefits, short term and long term) of relief, mitigation, and planning and assess how the United States can more effectively leverage the work of multilaterals and NGOs.

Draw on the U.S. Military's Comparative Advantage, Not on Its Stereotype

The U.S. military itself barely understands which among all its extensive assets can be of greatest value in filling gaps in humanitarian aid. The U.S. military starts too often by asking what it has available to give rather than asking what is needed and unavailable from other civilian aid groups. Meanwhile, civilian aid groups are often so hostile to any potential military role that they stereotype the military as only being good at using weapons (for security) or airlifting supplies.

There are some myths about what are the military's unique capabilities. One myth is that only the military has "lift" capability to move large volumes of supplies. In fact, NGOs and the WFP have comparable capability to transport goods across countries and continents, and at much less cost to the public. During the highly visible airlift of food into Afghanistan during the winter of 2001–02, the U.S. military delivered only a tiny fraction of the total brought in through conventional operations by WFP and NGOs like IRC. The truth is that the U.S. military does have a unique capability in two areas of transport: rapidly deployed airlift and maritime operations. The UN and NGOs can lease C-130s and helicopters more efficiently than the military can in the long term, but in the short term (counted in hours or days), the U.S. military has an advantage. Therefore the Department of

Defense can respond much faster in those emergencies in which response cannot wait a few days. Second, civilian agencies have not demonstrated any capability in real-time assistance at sea or for small islands. The U.S. Navy alone has provided critical access for search-and-rescue of boat people (such as Southeast Asians, Haitians, and Cubans) and for reaching coastlines of affected areas such as Aceh, Indonesia.

The Defense Department controls a network of laboratory facilities that far exceeds the collective lab capabilities of all NGOs combined, another neglected potential humanitarian asset. Thus, the military can play a complementary role to humanitarian operational agencies in identifying the type and characteristics of drug susceptibility of pathogens encountered in emergencies, just as the Naval Medical Research Unit did in setting up a field laboratory to assist WHO in Banda Aceh in late December 2004, within days after the tsunami hit.

Resist World Trade Organization Purview over Humanitarian Aid

In recent Doha rounds of debate within the World Trade Organization, specific items of aid (such as food aid and monetization) have become bargaining chips, as if they were in some way related or relevant to trade negotiations. In 2006, one proposal floated by the WTO working group specified that humanitarian food aid could only be provided internationally through the United Nations.[60] In other words, USAID would be prohibited from delivering food during a famine through its most effective and professional partners like Catholic Relief Services, World Vision, and CARE.

The U.S. government should take a firm stand that humanitarian aid is not a subsidiary issue of trade talks. Private, voluntary aid and humanitarian aid should not be hemmed in but should be expanded. Humanitarian aid—whether food, drugs, volunteer labor, or technology—should not be a topic of consideration under the World Trade Organization.

Establish Best Practices in Enhancing Fragile State Capacities

On a more formal basis, the United States as an aid donor to fragile states needs to improve the capacity of those governments to in turn use resources to work with technical agencies. In states struggling from recent crises, such as Afghanistan, Iraq, and East Timor, there is too little experience or competence within the target governments to know how to work with the appropriate United States–based NGOs, or UN agencies, or engineering firms. As a result, unnecessary tension grows between the governments and these aid agencies that receive donor funds directly.

Require Impact Measurement

Humanitarian aid has coasted for too long on the excuse that it is too busy saving lives to be bothered with collecting evidence about its effectiveness or cost efficiency. The effectiveness of humanitarian programs can be measured. And measurement will surely find that the impacts of humanitarian aid programs range from the very large (that is, a positive impact that is very cost-efficient) to the negative. Just as Congress and the U.S. commercial sector have learned that management requires some measures of results, so too, does humanitarian aid need to catch up with a world that is increasingly evidence based.

Conclusion

American humanitarian aid donations often have greater impact than Americans realize. Most Americans would be gratified to learn about the incredibly positive track record of their donations for saving the lives of refugees and famine-affected and other disaster-threatened populations. Congress, too, would benefit from being informed about the results of humanitarian aid, for which no good reviews have yet been written.

A refocused attention on humanitarian aid should attempt to correct two persistent problems in global humanitarian aid. First, too little aid is dedicated to risk reduction programs that save lives through activities before the onset of a disaster. There are many reasons why this sector is perpetually underfunded, but USAID has been a long-time leader in spending money wisely in mitigation programs.

Second, most of the deaths that occur needlessly in emergencies occur during crises in areas of the world that do not generate the big headlines, such as Angola and the Democratic Republic of the Congo in the 1990s. The Office of U.S. Foreign Disaster Assistance has for many years been the "best foot forward" of America in responding to a wide array of less-known disasters. It has been limited, however, in the extent to which its resources and attention have been politically managed, thus devoting resources to countries such as Kosovo and Iraq where the United States has had large stakes, but where OFDA's expertise has had little benefit to add.

A revamped U.S. humanitarian architecture would merge together the resources currently spread thinly across OFDA, OTI, PRM, FFP, and other offices. It would allow for a greater share of resources to go to neglected crises, to IDPs, and to disaster risk reduction. And it should be given the scope and liberty to do so—to reclaim its "best-foot-forward" status by being given more independence to pursue its mission according to humanitarian needs and not according to political aims.

Notes

1. See chapter 2 in this volume.

2. There is no single agreed upon definition or usage for humanitarian assistance. For some groups, such as Médicins Sans Frontières, what makes aid humanitarian or not is whether the aid is given without politics, without partiality, and without any affiliation with military action. For other agencies, humanitarian refers more to the nature of the need, that is, urgent, life-or-death circumstances. For other agencies, humanitarian has to do with the spirit of the aid: altruistic, across borders, asking nothing in return. In this chapter, the term refers to the problems being addressed: significant and abnormal increases in risks to human lives.

3. International Federation of Red Cross and Red Crescent Societies, *World Disasters Report, 2002* (Geneva, Switzerland) (www.ifrc.org/publicat/wdr2002/ [July 26, 2006]).

4. See Uwe Kievelitz and others for the United Nations Development Group. *Practical Guide to Multilateral Needs Assessments in Post-Conflict Situations: A Joint Project of the United Nations Development Programme, World Bank, and United Nations Development Group, 2004.*

5. The recent Ethiopia-Eritrea war, during which 100,000 were killed, demonstrates how lethal a war can still be. Centers for Disease Control and Prevention, "Famine-Affected, Refugee and Displaced Populations: Recommendations for Public Health Issues," *Morbidity and Mortality Weekly Report* 41, no. RR13, 1992 (Atlanta, Ga.: CDC, U.S. Health and Human Services) (www.cdc.gov/mmwr/preview/mmwrhtml/00019261.htm [July 26, 2006]).

6. Howard LaFranchi, "A Welcome Surprise: War Waning Globally," *Christian Science Monitor,* October 18, 2005.

7. Steven Hansch, "How Many People Die of Starvation in Humanitarian Emergencies?" Report 29 (Washington: Refugee Policy Group, 1995).

8. Ibid.

9. FEWS has received between $12 and $13 million each fiscal year since it added 8 offices since 2004. FEWS has requested $13.2 million for fiscal year 2007. Personal communication with Gary Eilerts, FEWS program manager, USAID, May 17, 2006.

10. Over 2 million refugees fled the aftermath of the first Gulf War. As they returned home in late 1991, the long upward trend in refugee numbers turned around. While there was a slight upward blip in 1999 and 2000 during the new downward trend, the overall decline in refugee numbers has continued. For statistics on refugee flows and

populations, see the Statistics website of the UN Refugee Agency (http://www. unhcr.org/cgi-bin/texis/vtx/statistics [May 17, 2006]).

11. See the various publications by CDC doctors Phil Nieburg, Michael Toole, and Ron Waldman, such as "The Association between Inadequate Rations, Undernutrition Prevalence, and Mortality in Refugee Camps: Case Studies of Refugee Populations in Eastern Thailand 1979–1980 and Eastern Sudan 1984–1985," *Journal of Tropical Pediatrics* 34 (1988): 218–20.

12. Because our accounting for deaths within states has been historically incomplete, it is difficult to compare the better-documented death rates in wars between states with civil unrest within states. The largest interstate wars of recent years—Iran-Iraq and Ethiopia-Eritrea—had massive casualties but not as large as the world wars of decades before.

13. Civil wars continue to recur in Burma, Sri Lanka, Pakistan, Nepal, Afghanistan, the Philippines, and the Ferghana Valley, Kyrgyzstan, but they are declining in severity and frequency.

14. See the war mortality data sets maintained by SIPRI (Sweden), as well as Charles B. Keely, Holly E. Reed, and Ronald J. Waldman, "Understanding Mortality Patterns in Complex Humanitarian Emergencies," in *Forced Migration and Mortality,* edited by Holly E. Reed and Charles B. Keely (National Academy of Sciences, 2001), pp. 1–37. Two recent mortality surveys capture the civilian deaths in conflict: Les Roberts, Richard Garfield, and Gilbert Burnham, "Mortality Before and After the 2003 Invasion of Iraq: Cluster Sample Survey," *Lancet* (October 2004); Les Roberts, "The Iraq War: Do Civilian Casualties Matter" (Cambridge, Mass.: MIT Center for International Studies, July 2005); Centers for Disease Control and Prevention, "Elevated Mortality Associated with Armed Conflict: Democratic Republic of Congo, 2002," *Morbidity and Mortality Weekly Report* 52 (2003): 469–71.

15. The forcible displacement of populations, besieging of cities, and mass execution of civilians were strategies of war in ancient Central America, of Genghis Khan, and during the Middle Ages. When Rome conquered Carthage, it destroyed the city, displaced the entire population, and destroyed its agricultural productivity. The primary cause of death during the American Civil War, World War II, and other protracted crises was largely due to the coeffects of malnutrition, diarrhea, malnutrition, and other primary diseases.

16. Angola, Burundi, DRC (formerly Zaïre), Central African Republic, Chad, Côte d'Ivoire, Ethiopia, Eritrea, Guinea, Liberia, Mozambique, Rwanda, Sierra Leone, Somalia, Sudan, Uganda, and Zimbabwe, not to mention other African countries such as Mauritania and Algeria. See Princeton N. Lyman and J. Stephen Morrison, "More than Humanitarianism: A Strategic U.S. Approach toward Africa" (Washington: Council on Foreign Relations, 2005), pp. 104–05.

17. See Margie Ferris Morris, "Planning for the Next Drought—Ethiopia Case Study: An Assessment of the Drought Response 1999–2001 and Current Preparedness," under contract number HRN-I-00-99-00002-00 (Washington: USAID, March 2003), p. 5.

18. See Steve Hansch and colleagues, "Genetically Modified Food in the Southern Africa Food Crisis of 2002–2003" (Washington: Institute for the Study of International Migration, Georgetown University School of Foreign Service, 2004), p. 61, endnote.

19. A series of USAID policy papers about maize production in southern Africa are available from Michigan State University, for example, Pedro Arlindo and David Tschirley, "Regional Trade in Maize in Southern Africa: Examining the Experience of Northern Mozambique and Malawi" (2003).

20. See Eric K. Noji, "Earthquakes," in *The Public Health Consequences of Disasters,* edited by Eric K. Noji (Oxford University Press, 1997), chapter 8.

21. Research has demonstrated that the ability to swim was a significant risk factor determining who survived from the 2004 tsunami. See Debarati Guha-Sapir and colleagues, "Risk Factors for Mortality and Injury: Post-Tsunami Epidemiological Findings from Tamil Nadu" (Brussels: Center for Research on the Epidemiology of Disasters, Université Catholique de Louvain, April 2006) (www.em-dat.net/documents/Publication/RiskFactorsMortalityInjury.pdf). For a statistical overview of the human toll of the tsunami, see UN Office of the Special Envoy for Tsunami Recovery, "The Human Toll" (www.tsunamispecialenvoy.org/country/humantoll.asp [May 24, 2006]).

22. See Robert J. Nicholls and Nobuo Mimura. "Regional Issues Raised by Sea-Level Rise and Their Policy Implications," *Climate Research* 11 (December 17, 1998): 5–18.

23. Calculation made by Abby Stoddard: "The US and the 'Bilaterlisation' of Humanitarian Response," background research prepared for Overseas Development Institute HPG Report 12 (London: ODI Humanitarian Policy Group, December 2002) (www.odi.org.uk/hpg/papers/background12US.pdf).

24. More Americans are writing about how humanitarian intervention is embedded in ethical principles that are more fundamental than are international laws and treaties. See Brian D. Lepard, *Rethinking Humanitarian Intervention: A Fresh Legal Approach Based on Fundamental Ethical Principles in International Law and World Religions* (Pennsylvania State University Press, 2002).

25. Data about private giving are notoriously difficult to interpret because of the lack of consistently used categories. The main recipients of private donations, nongovernmental organizations (NGOs), do not apply any one agreed-upon category for "humanitarian" action, or emergency relief, or some other comparable situation. Money is often tracked by named campaigns (such as "the tsunami" or "Rwandan genocide"), but much of the private giving for aid in the poorest and most afflicted areas, whether Burma or Mozambique, is difficult to categorize. Depending on the semantic choice used for humanitarian relief, private giving for humanitarian aid could be argued to be as low as $300 million a year or as high as $4 billion. For a good discussion of the range of estimates in private giving, see Steven Radelet, "Think Again: U.S. Foreign Aid," web exclusive of *Foreign Policy* (February 2005) (www.cgdev.org/doc/commentary/FP_Radelet_2_05.pdf), p. 2. Also see "U.S. Assistance Exceeds $480 Million One Year after Tsunami" (Washington: USAID, Department of State, December 2005) (usinfo.state.gov/gi/Archive/2005/Dec/22-175699.html [August 2, 2006]).

26. Much of the decisionmaking that has led to these changes has been made by the Office of Food for Peace (FFP) in USAID. The director of that office has considerable latitude in influencing how nongovernmental organizations (NGOs) and the World Food Program (WFP) will use this food aid. In the early 1990s, the director, Robert Kramer, began questioning the long-term focus on development aid and pushed WFP

to begin a more-balanced use of its food aid to give more attention to the areas of greatest food insecurity, which inevitably tend to be areas of crisis.

27. Fiona Terry, *Condemned to Repeat? The Paradox of Humanitarian Action* (Cornell University Press, 2002), p 244.

28. Bjørn Lomborg, ed., *Global Crisis, Global Solutions* (Cambridge University Press, 2004), p. 149.

29. The high benefits per cost of humanitarian aid operations, where they are high, are demonstrable from the sector-specific efficiencies in the sectors of primary health, immunization, prevention of malnutrition, water supply, and sanitation. A series of cost-benefit comparisons were undertaken by the *Economist,* working with the Copenhagen Business School, finding that primary health care interventions in the worst hit parts of the world demonstrated much higher impacts per dollar than other foreign aid initiatives. Bjørn Lomborg, *Global Crisis, Global Solutions,* p. 128.

30. The appearance that Americans give less than Europeans is compounded by the arbitrary choice, in many statistical presentations of the Organization for Economic Cooperation Development (OECD), to divide total aid by GNP. As a result, the fact that Americans work longer hours and more creatively and produce more counts against Americans. The French, while giving substantially less foreign aid than Americans, appear to give more because of their choice to work shorter hours and take more holidays, which, as a consequence, generates less GNP. Their consumption of greater leisure time is not counted in OECD comparisons of levels of donation giving.

31. A similar recommendation was made by the World Health Organization (WHO) for Afghanistan. See WHO, "Reconstruction of the Afghanistan Health Sector: A Preliminary Assessment of Needs and Opportunities," Document WHO-EM/EHA/003/E/G/01.02 (Cairo: WHO, Regional Office for the Eastern Mediterranean, January 2002).

32. In 2005 OFDA allocated only $32 million out of a total budget of $604 million to disaster preparedness activities, or a little more than 5 percent, which is indicative of its long-term level, as well as the level of preparedness and prevention funding that other donors also give. See *Annual Report for Fiscal Year 2005, Office of U.S. Foreign Disaster Assistance* (Washington: USAID Office of U.S. Foreign Disaster Assistance, 2006) (www.usaid.gov/our_work/humanitarian_assistance/disaster_ assistance/publications/annual_reports/pdf/AR2005.pdf [July 26, 2006]), p. 99.

33. *Annual Report for Fiscal Year 2004, Office of U.S. Foreign Disaster Assistance* (USAID, 2005).

34. USAID, Office of Transition Initiatives, "USAID/OTI Serbia and Montenegro Field Report, March 2001" (www.usaid.gov/our_work/cross-cutting_programs/transition_initiatives/country/serb/rpt0301.html [May 18, 2006]).

35. USAID is organized into large bureaus. Although OFDA and FFP used to be stand-alone offices, they were reorganized into the same new bureau, created in 1991, Bureau for Humanitarian Response. Ironically, the person who created and first headed that bureau, Andrew Natsios, also took the lead nine years later in reorganizing it again and renaming it the Bureau for Democracy, Conflict, and Humanitarian Assistance (DCHA), its current title. See also Anita Menghetti and Jeff Drumtra, "Improving the U.S. Government's Humanitarian Response," *Ethics & International Affairs* 18, no. 2 (2004): 45.

36. In fiscal year 2006, Food for Peace received 77 percent of the total budget of the Bureau for Democracy, Conflict, and Humanitarian Assistance (www.usaid.gov/policy/budget/cbj2006/cent_progs/central_dcha.html [May 18, 2006]).

37. A review of the UN's Consolidated Appeals Process (CAP) Financial Tracking System (FTS) shows that roughly half the total funds requested for large emergencies are for food aid, and food aid requests tend to be well-met relative to other needs (ocha.unog.ch/fts/globsum.asp?year=2006 [August 2, 2006]).

38. Celia Dugger, "Food Aid for Africa Languishes in Congress," *New York Times,* October 13, 2005.

39. As of May 1, 2006, the United States contributed $216,796,577, 34 percent of the total for 2006. UNHCR, "Contributions to UNHCR Programmes" (www.unhcr.org/cgi-bin/texis/vtx/partners/opendoc.pdf?tbl=PARTNERS&id=443654fb2 [May 18, 2006]).

40. France and Germany contribute less than half what the United Kingdom donates to UNHCR; the United States alone gives a donation ten times that of France and Germany combined. UNHCR, "Contributions to UNHCR Programmes."

41. Author's personal interview with staff at the Department of Health and Human Services.

42. See the Measles Initiatives website (www.measlesinitiative.org).

43. GTZ, Deutsche Gesellschaft für Technische Zusammenarbeit, is a quasi-governmental organization implementing much of the German government's emergency assistance, including shelter construction and environmental protection.

44. There is a growing literature about the failure of protection. See Stephanie T. Kleine-Ahlbrandt, "The Protection Gap in the International Protection of Internally Displaced Persons: The Case of Rwanda" (Geneva: Graduate Institute of International Studies, 2004).

45. Ibid.

46. Full disclosure: the author of this chapter was involved in interagency meetings in Darfur, Khartoum, and in Washington, D.C., about protection and in the development and proposing to donors of projects by several NGOs to introduce protection into villages of Darfur. The author met, as well, with UN representatives who also because of concerns about liability, like USAID, felt uneasy about sponsoring efforts that would place Americans in harm's way.

47. Oxfam International, "Predictable Funding for Humanitarian Emergencies: A Challenge to Donors," Policy Position Paper (Oxford, Great Britain, 2005).

48. One such network is the nongovernmental aid association of engineers coordinated by RedR (Registered Engineers for Disaster Relief), which is based in the United Kingdom.

49. See Rebecca Jones, "Breaking of Structures: The Impact of Recovery Efforts after the Tsunami on Long-Term Development and Poverty Reduction in Sri Lanka," Thesis and substantial research project, American University, 2006.

50. Theresa Braine, Mexico City, "Was 2005 the Year of Natural Disasters?" *Bulletin of the World Health Organization* 84, no. 1 (2006): 1–80 (www.who.int/bulletin/volumes/84/1/news10106/en/ [July 28, 2006]).

51. The World Food Program has experimented with a hedge against insufficient rainfall, in Ethiopia, by purchasing a policy with Axa Re, the French reinsurance company, that would pay out early disaster relief, faster than would the UN's food response.

See Mark Tuner, "UN Takes Out First Drought Insurance Policy," *Financial Times,* March 6, 2006.

52. Patricia Weiss Fagen and Susan Martin, "Disaster Management and Response: Capacity Building for Developing Country Institutions" (Washington: Georgetown University, Institute for the Study of International Migration, 2005).

53. The International Strategy for Disaster Reduction (ISDR) is a remnant of what had been the International Decade for Natural Disaster Reduction (IDNDR) in the 1990s and is a part of the Office for the Coordination of Humanitarian Assistance (OCHA). Unlike other offices of OCHA that manage budgets of field offices and programs, the ISDR is primarily about the management and promotion of knowledge and has no operational components.

54. Enormous strides have been made in recent years because of the work of Paul Collier, whose network of analysts has produced two volumes; see Paul Collier and Nicolas Sambanis, *Understanding Civil War: Evidence and Analysis,* vol. 1: Africa, and vol. 2: Europe, Central Asia, and Other Regions (Washington: World Bank, 2003).

55. Presentation by James Kunder, 2001, "Federal Foreign Disaster Response Plan."

56. Presentation by Michael Hess, assistant administrator, USAID, November 2005, "USAID's First Responder to a Crisis: Bureau of Democracy, Conflict, and Humanitarian Assistance."

57. Numerous evaluations find that the humanitarian aid community is country-focused and reactive and does not examine new disruptive events in history. See "Ambiguity and Change, Humanitarian NGOs Prepare for the Future," a report prepared for World Vision, CARE, Save US, Mercy Corps, Oxfam USA, Oxfam UK, and Catholic Relief Services (Medford, Mass.: Alan Shawn Feinstein International Famine Center, Tufts University, August 2004).

58. So argues Jordan S. Kassalow in "Why Health Is Important to U.S. Foreign Policy" (New York: Council on Foreign Relations and Milbank Memorial Fund, May 2001).

59. Which is one reason why the majority of delivery agencies are primarily staffed by health professionals (for example, International Rescue Committee, International Medical Corps, Médicins Sans Frontières, among others.) and why the major knowledge banking and training organizations for humanitarian aid are schools of public health (Johns Hopkins University, Columbia University, London School of Tropical Medicine and Hygiene, Tulane University).

60. See the letter by Richard Stearns, president of World Vision, to U.S. Trade Representative Robert J. Portman, "Trade Negotiators Could Starve the Hungry," October 17, 2005 (www.worldvision.org [July 26, 2006]).

CHAPTER 6

Development in the Shadow of Conflict

Patrick Cronin

F oreign assistance programs broadly conceived must be bolstered as an integral part of the national security strategy of the United States government. A serious—but realistic—capacity to turn swords into plowshares and prevent conflict before it begins must be a core mission of the U.S. government in the twenty-first century. In addition, when conflict does arise, the U.S. government must be prepared to conduct effective stabilization and reconstruction operations with international allies. Since the end of the cold war, the United States has continuously found itself involved in postconflict rebuilding, whether on a grand or small scale and whether in the lead or in support. Civil and local wars, genocide, protracted political violence, and fragile state institutions have fostered terrorism and other security threats, undermined U.S. foreign policy objectives, undermined development investments, deepened poverty and human insecurity, violated U.S. core values and interests, and created recurring humanitarian hazards. Amidst this disorder affecting large parts of the developing world, agreement has gradually coalesced around the critical need to establish better capacity for conflict prevention, peacemaking, and state building. Despite the scale of the problem and the absence of greater coherence inside the U.S. government, modest yet incremental steps have been taken to address the broad subject of development in the shadow of conflict.

Three major gaps in U.S. capacity have become apparent in recent years in U.S. rebuilding efforts from the Balkans to Afghanistan and Iraq. First, the United States requires much more joint civilian-military cooperation

The author wishes to acknowledge the tremendous support, advice, and assistance received from a variety of colleagues and friends, with special thanks to Lael Brainard, Carlos Pascual, Benjamin Landy, Scott Kofmehl, and especially Katherine Smyth.

if it is to undertake successful rebuilding operations, both because development in the midst of conflict is a hazardous and resource-intensive task and because success requires equal amounts of military, political, and economic development expertise. Civil-military cooperation has improved significantly in recent years; however, a wider and deeper commitment to interagency planning and policy execution will be needed. As the 2006 Quadrennial Defense Review (QDR) noted, interagency coordination is essential to achieving the national security strategies of the United States government.[1] Second, the United States should significantly expand its civilian capacity for supporting such contingencies. Presently, the Department of Defense dwarfs the planning, resource, and operational capabilities of the State Department and the United States Agency for International Development (USAID). As it designates the secretary of state as the lead actor in coordinating stabilization and reconstruction operations, the National Security Presidential Directive 44 (NSPD 44) provides political support for enacting necessary reforms.[2] However, increased budgetary resources, further political will, and continued improvement of interagency cooperation will be critical to enacting the mission of NSPD 44. Third, the United States needs to assign far greater priority to the tougher development challenge of providing for the security, political participation, and economic livelihood of people in countries afflicted by nonexistent to poor governance and state institutions. This challenge must be viewed with a long-term perspective; however, there are short-, medium-, and long-term measures required to achieve this transformational vision.

The events of September 11, 2001, which were preceded by terrorism spawned in the failed state of Afghanistan, grew into a threat against the U.S. homeland and served to refocus foreign policy on the connection between failed states and security in the developing world. Belatedly recognizing the importance of the relationship between development and security, Washington reclaimed from Tokyo the top donor ranking with respect to absolute official development assistance for the first time in more than a decade.[3]

Much of the attention on foreign assistance has been focused on the HIV/AIDS pandemic and on "good performers" and more stable parts of the developing world. Certainly successful development is more assured when recipient countries are committed to effective and transparent policies, and the Millennium Challenge Account promises to provide incentives for good governance and sound policies. Similarly, the HIV/AIDS pandemic and other major diseases demand massively improved assistance, and U.S. initiatives are providing global leadership in stemming HIV/AIDS and malaria, in particular.

However, dealing with good performers and transnational health problems without addressing countries on the verge of or already immersed in conflict and instability is a recipe for disaster, especially in a world in which lawlessness, ideology, and lethality can project unconventional firepower through terrorist acts. Thus the United States must increase its ability to grapple with countries in which there is great fragility and the seeds of conflict. Yet, with the notable exception of effort in Afghanistan and Iraq, the United States has not established an enduring and deep capacity for conflict prevention, peacemaking, stabilization, and reconstruction. In the exceptional cases of Afghanistan and Iraq, massive postconflict rebuilding efforts have not resulted in a corresponding degree of success, in large part because of acute problems in strategy, planning, capacity, implementation, and assessment. There are still too few resources, too many decisionmaking centers, too little capacity on the civilian side, too little integration of effort among interagency and international actors, too much ad hoc crisis response, and too little long-term prevention. (For an example of what happens when such factors are not adequately addressed, see box 6-1.) There are, however, opportunities for improvement. In a November 2005 directive, the Defense Department states that "stability operations are a core U.S. military mission that the Department of Defense shall be prepared to conduct and support."[4] The 2006 QDR reflects this policy change.[5] The key policy challenge now will be to assign adequate priority to this mission and devote the necessary budgetary resources and personnel to the civilian agencies and departments involved, particularly in the State Department and its Office of the Coordinator for Reconstruction and Stabilization.

This chapter briefly examines the U.S. context for development and reconstruction in the face of conflict and state weakness. It considers the relationship between conflict and security, a brief overview of the U.S. historical experience with operations of this kind and the terminology used to describe them, an assessment of U.S. government initiatives to date, lessons identified if not learned, and recommendations for future policy.

Rationale

Although no one should be satisfied with the current level of U.S. capacity for postconflict reconstruction and stabilization operations, there is little denying the growing chorus of voices in the past five years that seeks to expand U.S.

BOX 6-1 From War to Peace: The Case of Liberia

Liberia is a country in the midst of a political transition.[1] Although democratically elected President Ellen Johnson Sirleaf took office in January 2006, there is a continuing potential that Liberia will return to civil war. United Nations Mission in Liberia (UNMIL) peacekeeping forces have momentarily halted the blood feuds between the minority with ancestry rooted in freed American slaves and the majority indigenous Liberians, and between former president Charles Taylor's supporters and two competing rebel movements who now share in the transition electoral process. However, destabilizing forces remain nearby: Taylor is in Nigeria, and UNMIL lacks authority to seize Taylor's former estate.

Meanwhile, 1.5 million of Liberia's 3 million people are huddled in makeshift urban slums, and many more remain uprooted and desperate in refugee camps. Remote, vacant villages without schools or health clinics await an influx of returnees before the rainy season again severs the lines of communication. Although this is a resource-rich nation, with diamonds, iron ore, fisheries, and highly arable land that for years provided the world's best rubber and valuable timber, it lacks working institutions. With 85 percent of Liberians unemployed, it is a state on life support. Monrovia is one of the last capitals in the world without an electric grid.

The UN presence is large though meagerly funded. Although the humanitarian and development missions have been subordinated to and somewhat hampered by the primary tasks of keeping the peace and conducting a national election, more than fifteen UN agencies are on the ground assisting in the myriad tasks of holding up a nation. This strong UN presence contrasts sharply with a skeletal American embassy staff.

The UN has brought peace, the sine qua non of development. But the strength of the peacekeeping mission has not been matched by a smooth transition toward recovery and sustainable development. Moreover, after the early departure of the Office for the Coordination of Humanitarian Affairs and the arrival of a special representative of the secretary general, as is the practice in peace operations, the UN has given short shrift to the continuing need to coordinate a diverse humanitarian relief effort. On the ground, it is not difficult to find criticism of the UN for leaving some thirty nongovernmental organizations to fend for themselves. Partly because of poor and unpredictable funding, the UN is also criticized for a slow, halting, and incomplete job of disarmament, demobilization, and reintegration (DDR) of combatants. With respect to the internally displaced and refugee population hunkered down in neighboring Côte d'Ivoire and elsewhere, the UN is planning to return hundreds of thousands of Liberians to their rural homes for an election in the middle of the rainy season; many experts assume that these people are likely to stay a short while and then make their way back to Monrovia in search of jobs, schools, and medical care. Interviews with some of the leaders of the more than 40,000 Liberians settled in Buduburam

BOX 6-1 From War to Peace: The Case of Liberia (*continued*)

Refugee Camp in Ghana suggest they have no intention of going home soon, raising the difficult question of forced return. Without external peacekeepers ex-combatants surely would bring their guns out of hiding, and the slightest grievance could be seized to create mayhem and grab power, just as an incident in the fall of 2004 led to a swift but thankfully short-lived violent outburst.

The chief charge against UNMIL and its special representative to the secretary general, who is British and whose deputy is American, is that little action has been taken to implement what was a surprisingly successful joint United Nations–World Bank needs assessment. A "successful" peacekeeping mission and even one "free and fair" election will hardly set this failed state on a path toward economic development; the state-building process is much more complex and long term. Rebuilding (or building) government institutions, promoting civil society, and enacting durable reform processes are part of the long-term state-building agenda. But then again, which development agency around the world would be successful at animating what the American ambassador has called "a dead state"?

Direct U.S. leadership in stabilization and reconstruction operations has remained minimal. Leaving aside the assessed contribution for peacekeeping operations and UN core funding (27 and 22 percent, respectively), the United States has a small amount of emergency monies to help with the election or the DDR of ex-combatants. It also has a one-time $200 million appropriation from Congress to create jobs and a small-infrastructure program, even though the prospect of the private sector returning to Liberia in the next year remains slim at best.

One testament to America's abandonment of Liberia is the decrepit John F. Kennedy Hospital, a sprawling complex on the outskirts of Monrovia, built thirty-five years ago with funding from USAID. Imagine a 1960s-era American hospital, and then remove all the equipment and put it through a war and years of neglect, and there you have the JFK Hospital in Monrovia. In a nation with few doctors, possibly less than forty in the entire country, the hospital carries on despite its almost complete lack of resources and personnel. A young child, abandoned by his mother days before, squirms all day on the filthy floor of the hospital entrance, not far from the faded "ambulance" sign that still hangs outside in hope that the hospital may one day again have one. Another boy who arrived at 7 a.m. is still sitting with his family at nightfall in the hot waiting area of this forgotten monument to American development assistance from the 1960s. Hundreds more are like this boy, left waiting, many suffering from diarrhea, malaria, and other treatable diseases.

Beyond the devastating humanitarian crisis, there are questions to consider and lessons to be drawn regarding U.S. policy for stabilization and reconstruction operations. Among the many lessons, one is the

(*continued*)

BOX 6-1 From War to Peace: The Case of Liberia (*continued*)

importance of local partnership. Long-term development assistance, such as JFK Hospital in Monrovia, is not possible without local government cooperation and support. While USAID might be able to rebuild the hospital, the Liberian government will need to provide resources to employ doctors, provide medical equipment and medicines, and maintain the facility. If there is no such capacity within the Liberian government, then the hospital—and many other projects—will not be successful.

There would appear to be no real hope in sight for a country that is ostensibly governed by a transitional government but in reality functions only through the United Nations special representative of the secretary-general and his 17,000 peacekeepers and police. Who will determine the fate of Liberia? Who will create the security and political and economic framework to enable a new generation of Liberian leaders to gradually emerge? Perhaps they will come from the Buduburam Refugee Camp in Ghana. Which UN presence will be remembered: the one represented by two Nepalese police officers, here as part of the UN police force, who sodomized a thirteen-year-old Liberian girl, or the incredibly compassionate and seasoned assistance of some of the humanitarian and development professionals from various UN agencies working in the country? While the United States is a junior partner in this stabilization and reconstruction operation, its support is critical. Without it there is a much higher likelihood of an ever-worsening conflict and deepening hopelessness.

---

1. This analysis is based on an intensive fact-finding trip to West Africa, including Liberia, during March 2005.

---

capabilities. Indeed, in some ways the political debate in Washington on state building has come full circle since the early days in the aftermath of the cold war when then-National Security Adviser Brent Scowcroft told President George Herbert Walker Bush that a "new world order" was emerging. The resulting peace dividend, we now know, proved short lived, underscoring the insight imparted by the Danish philosopher Søren Kierkegaard that life is understood looking backward but must be lived forward.

The reluctant humanitarian relief effort in Somalia, which grew into an ill-fated peace-enforcement mission, subsequently spilled over into America's greater support for international efforts centered on the United Nations or, in the case of the Balkans, on the North Atlantic Treaty Organization. Under the George W. Bush administration, an initial disdain for nation building was replaced by the need to create a viable state out of one country barely governed by religious zealots, who gave free rein to terrorists, and out of another that had remained stable only by dint of its dictator's ruthlessness. The range of stability, security, transition, and reconstruction (SSTR) operations in which the United States participated in the 1990s and its varied level of success in these missions underscore the importance of reassessing the objectives, goals, capabilities, and areas of improvement for U.S. engagement in future SSTR operations. As Afghanistan and Iraq are different missions with different goals, U.S. participation in SSTR operations in the post–September 11 environment—and in the 1990s—highlights the varied U.S. goals and capabilities.

The events of September 11, 2001, were a watershed experience for the American body politic: across the political spectrum, they broadened the recognition that the developing world in general—and certain failed and failing states in particular—directly affected U.S. national security. Although the United States was engaged in SSTR operations in the 1990s (and before), the September 11 terrorist attacks reframed the debate and inextricably linked SSTR to U.S. national security. This nascent consensus found expression in parts of the Bush administration's 2002 National Security Strategy, which declares that "weak states . . . can pose as great a danger to our national interests as strong states" and goes on to identify the main characteristics of weak states as "poverty, weak institutions, and corruption."[6] The strategy also articulates a national goal for Americans to champion human dignity aspirations, whether by fostering democratic and free institutions or relieving human misery. Such human rights–oriented idealism combined with pragmatic, national security–oriented realism have also found expression in studies and documents from a range of viewpoints, including the reports for the United Nations conducted by a high-level panel on emerging threats and the secretary general's proposal for sweeping reform.[7]

In an era in which the world's wealthiest 225 people are worth more than the poorest 2.5 billion, weak and failing states matter to the United States on several levels.[8] There is often a combination of a compelling national security imperative, a foreign policy consideration, a humanitarian calling, a cost-effective preventive benefit, and a foreign and public diplomacy benefit. (See box 6-2.)

These reasons for dealing with weak and failing states appear to command growing bipartisan support in principle; however, there must be the political will to dedicate resources to address these humanitarian crises. Moreover, Canada, Japan, European allies, and other countries have

BOX 6-2 Why Weak States Matter

National Security

States too weak to police their own territory sometimes pose direct threats to U.S. national security interests. They can become sanctuaries for terrorism since their poor or absent internal security mechanisms allow terrorists room to flourish and expand their reach internationally. In the failed state of Afghanistan, for example, terrorists operating from a core of radical Islamic ideology were able to acquire increased means and expand their operations beyond that country's borders—as far as the United States. Illicit transnational networks, including terrorist and trafficking groups, exploit the lax security, border controls, and law enforcement that facilitate the illegal movement of people, finances, drugs, and weapons. Notable examples are Somalia (admittedly one of the truly ungoverned states), used as a haven for al Qaeda in the 1990s, and the former Soviet states of Central Asia, which serve as an international nerve center for trafficking in weapons and drugs. And despite the heavy U.S. troop presence, Afghanistan still remains a base for terrorists and produces a massive proportion of the world's heroin.

Foreign Policy Predicaments

Weak and failed states also create indirect foreign policy and security problems. In particular, a failing or failed state generates spillover effects, which potentially include the ability to project and support violence in other conflicts that may more directly affect U.S. interests. For example, state weakness in West Africa has undermined the stability and prosperity of much of the subregion. Lawless states can also provide sanctuary to transnational actors who export extremist ideologies, trained fighters, and weapons and resources to raging local conflicts, such as those occurring around Israel and in Iraq, Chechnya, or Kashmir.

Economic Costs

Weak and failed states create mounting financial burdens for the United States and other developed countries who repeatedly find themselves forced to respond to deadly violence, rogue regimes, and humanitarian crises. Although early prevention and effective intervention would be more cost effective in many cases, the practice has been to react to crises, treat the symptoms rather than the underlying causes of conflict, and to repeat this pattern on a periodic basis. As Paul Collier has argued, more than 50 percent of developing world conflicts relapse within five years, with the concomitant costs rising with each subsequent episode.[1] In a related point on economic costs, the United States can reduce its economic costs—and potentially increase its effectiveness—through multilateral cooperation. U.S. contributions to UN peacekeeping mis-

BOX 6-2 Why Weak States Matter (*continued*)

sions in the Democratic Republic of the Congo and Liberia for fiscal year
2006 are $302 million and $198 million, respectively.[2] To provide some
perspective, if one U.S. military division were able to withdraw its troops
one month early, the cost savings would be $1.2 billion.[3]

Humanitarian Crises

Weak and failed states create humanitarian imperatives for action, especially from a country such as the United States that prides itself on helping those in need and believes in promoting universal values. In cases
of extreme humanitarian crisis, the United States is compelled to act;
however, there are crises that can be averted with planning that
addresses both short-term and long-term conflict prevention.

1. For more on the internal costs of civil conflict, see Paul Collier, "On the Economic Consequences of Civil War," *Oxford Economic Papers* 51 (1999): 168–83; Paul Collier, Anke
Hoeffler, and Mans Soderbom, "On the Duration of Civil War," Working Paper 2681 (Washington: World Bank, May 2001).

2. Department of State, "FY 2007 International Affairs (Function 150) Budget Request:
Account Tables—Contributions for International Peacekeeping Activities," February 6, 2006
(www.state.gov/s/d/rm/rls/iab/2007/html/60203.htm [April 2006]).

3. Carlos Pascual, "Societies Transitioning from Conflict," lecture at the Kennedy School of
Government, Harvard University, Boston, October 26, 2005.

expressed broad support for these imperatives for intervention, although
there is no shortage of disagreement about which institutions should be
strengthened and the role of American power in such operations.

From the perspective of U.S. decisionmakers, it may be useful to distin-
guish among three different objectives when contemplating improving the
ability to conduct development in the shadow of conflict. The first priority
should be to incorporate state-building capabilities into an intervention led
by U.S. armed forces. As recognized in the QDR, the "long war" against terrorists cannot be won by military means alone. Effective intervention requires
military and civilian resources to address security, governance, and civil society. As seen recently in Afghanistan and Iraq, whether of choice or necessity,
there will be times when the world's supreme military power leads a military
intervention and incurs or accepts a responsibility to help establish a new
government and state. Although such cases may be rare, especially on the
scale of the past two interventions, lack of such a capability poses a threat to
U.S. national security on a par with the original threat that engendered the

intervention. For instance, failure in Iraq is often seen as tantamount to crushing attempts at a stable, peaceful, reforming Middle East and inviting increased levels of international terrorism. A particular shortcoming appears to be conducting development in the midst of conflict, as the tortuous evolution of provincial reconstruction teams in Afghanistan attests.

A subordinate priority should be a general U.S. capability to support state building and peace operations led by the United Nations or other international or regional actors. Obviously, America's unparalleled military capabilities—for example, in executing airlifts and gathering intelligence—provide a comparative advantage in some situations. However, the United States would do well to pursue its national security interests in a strategic, cost-effective manner by providing greater assistance to multilateral peacekeeping and state-building missions. A February 2006 Government Accountability Office study estimated that it would cost the United States twice as much to lead a peacekeeping mission similar to the current UN-led Stabilization Mission in Haiti.[9]

Another ancillary point is that cost-effective capabilities should center on providing greater planning, resources, and agility for preventive action and development in countries that could slip into conflict. While this third objective threatens to become an open-ended call for resources to devote toward conflict prevention, targeted short- and long-term policies and strategies with commensurate resources are a critical component of stabilization and reconstruction operations.

At the risk of repetition, let me restate some of the basic premises on which this expanded area of foreign assistance ought to be based. First, the growing body of evidence since the end of the cold war, in general, and the events of September 11, 2001, in particular, indicates an irrefutable relationship between U.S. national security and weak and failed states in the developing world. Simply reducing foreign assistance to friends, "feel good" humanitarianism, or "cherry-picking" among the best performers will not negate the threats emanating from these failing or failed states. Moreover, the limited peace-building capabilities will restrict U.S. interventions to a unidimensional instrument of military power. Second, the United States will continue to face problems relating to stabilization and reconstruction during and immediately after conflict. While the United States might not engage in operations on the scale of Afghanistan and Iraq in the near term, there is the potential for smaller-scale interventions and SSTR operations that will require improved capabilities and clearer priorities. Third, an integral part of the matrix is preventative measures, a separate consideration from the operational aspects of postconflict missions but one that entails alleviating poverty and promoting economic and political development in some of the toughest reaches of the planet. All of these goals require U.S. government departments and agencies, international allies, and international organizations to better coordinate resources and increase the priority of these issues. However, for this cooperative process to work, all of these external actors must coordinate their programs effectively with domestic actors in order to build local ownership and capacity.

Evolution of U.S. Policy on Development and Security

Lacking the colonial experience of the European powers, the United States received some of its most important lessons in state building in the aftermath of the Second World War, although some scholars have argued that the U.S. government's first state-building operation was the reconstruction of the South in the 1860s.[10] While some critics would chastise U.S. planners for looking to these "outdated" examples for guidance in the midst of the recent challenge of rebuilding Iraq, the seemingly distant reconstruction missions in Germany and Japan sixty years ago remain the most successful, large-scale state-building experience of the United States. This is not to say that the United States has not contributed to the peace, prosperity, and often governance of many other states around the world subsequent to World War II. However, it is one thing to encourage a functioning foreign state apparatus to nurture democracy and free markets over time, and it is another matter to step into a vacuum of official authority left by conflict and try to quickly establish a framework for security, self-governance, livelihoods, and justice. On a budgetary level, U.S. investments in postconflict state building in Germany were $11.7 billion during 1946 and 1947, the first two years after World War II.[11] This level of financial commitment has not been, and arguably will not be, attained by the current or any future administration.

The experience in Germany and Japan would not be replicated throughout the cold war. The United States certainly fostered successful development in the Republic of Korea and the Republic of China in the aftermath of conflict, but the programs were far more at arm's length and reliant on local authorities than during the postwar occupation of Germany and Japan. In the Vietnam War, the United States undermined the capability of the indigenous government and its institutions. By the time it tried to focus more effort on nurturing those capabilities at both national and local levels, the American people had tired of conflict, which led to a U.S.

withdrawal. Other U.S. military interventions were not followed by occupation, nor did they incorporate ambitious plans for rebuilding nations or states. In Panama and Grenada, the United States had a singular focus on regime change, neglecting the broader state-building mission.

The conclusion of the cold war engendered a rash of low-level conflicts in regions not widely regarded as vital to U.S. interests. America's involvement in such conflicts, though relatively more frequent, was inconsistent and subject to changing political tides in the United States, as suggested by the abrupt volte-face in Somalia and the unpopular decision to get more involved in Bosnia and Kosovo in the 1990s. Today, in Somalia, which lacks the high-level political support behind operations in Iraq and Afghanistan, the U.S. intervention has concentrated on military means without significant state-building assistance.

Gradually, however, the international community and the United States have come to a greater consensus on the importance of being able to restore order and initiate state building in the wake of conflict. Conflict prevention, too, has gained in currency, if engendering somewhat less of a consensus because of the difficulty of knowing how to achieve it and the lack of broader public concern, which often coalesces only after a humanitarian tragedy penetrates public consciousness.

Candidate George W. Bush's dismissal of traditional "nation-building" activities, a central point of his campaign in 2000, was rapidly transformed by the events of September 11.[12] Indeed, the administration swung from a disdain for state-building work to a staunch conviction that the U.S. government had the wherewithal to erect democratic institutions and make them stick in the inhospitable lands in and near the Persian Gulf. The administration's response to the postconflict challenges in Afghanistan would prove relatively modest in comparison to the scope of the transformation proposed for Iraq: the latter campaign is comparable in scope only to efforts still under way in Kosovo, and in scale, only to post–World War II Japan and Germany.

The impediments to effective stabilization and reconstruction operations are widely catalogued, and the answers would seem to be before us all. As stated by Robert Orr, the creation of additional U.S. capacities to rebuild countries after conflict is necessary but insufficient by itself. (See box 6-3.) The challenges faced by the United States at the present time and for the foreseeable future require not only a capacity but also a strategy and an appropriate level of political will to enact changes to increase U.S. government capacity in SSTR operations.[13]

BOX 6-3 Essential Elements of Strategy for
Postconflict Reconstruction

Prioritize

Define the national interest and triage cases accordingly: focusing first on countries with WMD [weapons of mass destruction]; followed by countries that are used by terrorists as a base for international operations; followed by states that affect the prospects of achieving top U.S. foreign policy objectives (such as peace in the Middle East); followed by countries whose collapse could flood the United States with refugees; concluding with states whose energy supplies might render them of particular interest to the United States. Stabilization and reconstruction is a matter of national security and must be framed within this perspective. While none of these factors alone would automatically compel U.S. involvement, recent history and emerging trends in these countries strongly tip the balance toward the likelihood of U.S. involvement in some cases in the short- to medium-term future. Planning must be carried out accordingly.

Support Allies

Be prepared to assist allies and provide high-priority international public goods. The United States will need to deploy on occasions when allies' vital interests are primarily at stake. However, there is a fine balance to be treaded between supporting allies' needs and becoming a global enforcer. Moreover, there should be a different threshold for becoming involved in such cases. This statement also mandates the balancing of capabilities with the range of U.S. interests, including readiness to assume the role of junior partner as necessary.

Build Agreement

Ensure basic interagency agreement on interests and goals from the outset of operations, building and maintaining bipartisan consensus. As the QDR emphasized, interagency coordination will be essential to addressing the national security challenges related to SSTR operations. [Adding to Orr's analysis, interagency and congressional support is necessary on strategic and resource levels.]

Be Flexible

Foster flexibility of goals, strategies, resources, and level of participation. U.S. assistance in SSTR operations should exhibit flexibility in the speed and type of response.

Stay the Course

Ensure sustainability of interventions. While initial goals of stabilization may be achieved relatively rapidly, lasting stability is generally achieved

(continued)

> ### BOX 6-3 Essential Elements of Strategy for
> ###   Postconflict Reconstruction (*continued*)
>
> over a period of five to ten years. This time frame is completely at odds with both our military planning and our political landscape.
>
> **Multilateralize**
>
> Prioritize multilateralism. Multilateral involvement brings additional capacity, legitimacy, and burden sharing as well as additional international support at the time of completing a mission (even if the transition is to an internal government).
>
> ---
> Taken from Robert C. Orr, "An American Strategy for Post-Conflict Reconstruction," in *Winning the Peace,* edited by Robert C. Orr (Washington: Center for Strategic and International Studies, 2004), pp. 289–304.

Terminology

It is important be as clear as possible about what is being called for and, if possible, to link those objectives and prescriptions to other prevailing debates and decisions inside and outside the United States. Furthermore, the intent here is not to get tripped up over the neuralgia that some feel for terms such as "nation building" but rather to use common sense and objectivity to find solutions to what appear to be real policy problems.

As such, I am comfortable with the official definitions that grew into the United Nations' lexicon regarding peace operations: peacekeeping, peacemaking, peace enforcement, and peace building. I am similarly in accord with the general tenets of what is required in postconflict reconstruction operations.

At the same time, I am willing to employ the terminology of the moment in Washington, which has come to label the heart of the solution as "stabilization and reconstruction" activities, even though other governments find these terms too suggestive of military-led interventions. Within the Defense Department, the terms "SSTR operations," "stability operations," and "stabilization and reconstruction operations" are used almost interchangeably. These terms still suggest reactive efforts, but there is no reason that they must do so. Conflict prevention is and should continue to be integrated into this lexicon. Preventive, proactive strategies are critical to the overall stabilization and reconstruction framework. Common sense suggests that this broader stabilization and reconstruction framework can well incorporate elements of early warning, long-range planning, and other aspects of prevention. In fact, recent initiatives within the State Department, USAID, and the broader U.S. government have clearly integrated prevention into the overall rubric, including NSPD 44—a long-overdue successor to the Clinton administration's Presidential Decision Directive 56.

As for the terminology with respect to weak and failing states, again one needs to recognize the range of terms used by academics and government officials alike. "Fragile states" seems too broad a term given that so many states in the developing world are almost by definition fragile and subject to sudden change. As the recent report of the Commission for Weak States and U.S. National Security suggests, the core functions of the state amount to providing for the security, economic welfare, and political participation of its people.[14] A serious default in any one of these functions constitutes state weakness; defaults in all three areas suggest a failing or failed state. Weak states are those that are unable or unwilling to ensure provision of security and basic services; Zimbabwe would be one example. Failed states are those in which the central government does not exert effective control over its territory and population and is unable or unwilling to ensure provision of vital services to significant parts of its own territory; Somalia exemplifies this condition. Under these criteria some thirty states in conflict at present or in the past five years might be joined by another two dozen weak states that threaten to slip into greater political violence or civil war.

Recent Innovations

There is no program or set of programs that can cure the world of weak and failed states or adequately respond to the challenge of state building in Iraq or conflict prevention in the Democratic Republic of the Congo, for example. Nonetheless, such sober, complex realities should not weaken the case for effective, coherent programs to help establish peace out of war or avert conflict via conflict prevention measures. And there is no substitute for top-level leadership in both the executive and legislative branches of government when it comes to defining what U.S. interests are, what U.S. government capabilities are and should be, and what are the possible array of strategies to address the diverse range of potential scenarios.

One of the earliest policy innovations inside the U.S. government after the end of the cold war was the recognition in the Clinton administration's

Defense Department that it should seek to support human rights, democracy, and peace operations. Whatever the merits of the mounting interest in peace and stability operations, however, the notion of shifting the U.S. armed forces away from their principal mission of fighting wars was such a contentious proposal that it became a major election issue in the 2000 presidential campaign. Despite this, the Defense Department's 2005 directive officially placed stabilization and reconstruction operations on a par with traditional military combat operations.[15]

Less contentious and further removed from public scrutiny was a modest but effective innovation inside USAID: namely, the creation of the Office of Transition Initiatives (OTI). The Clinton administration established this office to help "advance peace and democracy in priority countries in crisis" by working "on the ground to provide fast, flexible, short-term assistance targeted at key political transition and stabilization needs."[16] The OTI budget authorities enable it to disburse funds without the conventional USAID oversight process, which typically requires six to twelve months for funding approval and allocation. However, OTI funding and capacities are limited—certainly not up to tackling a major state-building effort like the recent attempts in Afghanistan and Iraq. The fiscal year 2006 OTI budget was $40 million, a much smaller scale than the more than $18 billion in stabilization and reconstruction funds allocated for Iraq and the more than $56 billion cost for Iraq reconstruction from 2004 through 2007, as estimated by the World Bank, UN, and the Coalition Provisional Authority (an amount recently regarded as a low-end estimate).[17] Moreover, OTI country involvement is short term, usually two to three years, spent working closely with USAID missions and other donors to effect the transition from immediate humanitarian need or to capitalize on short windows of opportunity for aid to make a positive, longer-term, sustainable impact. This duration of involvement is only half or one quarter of the time most experts believe is required to set up a nascent government after a conflict (that is, five to ten years).[18] Thus, though quick and agile, OTI is too small to lead a major stabilization and reconstruction operation.

Unfortunately, the asymmetry in resources between the Defense Department and the rest of the U.S. government creates numerous challenges in finding the right way to balance interagency capabilities and leads to misgivings within the Defense Department over whether civilian agencies have the capacity to manage state building. Although NSPD 44 gives the State Department the lead role in planning for stabilization and reconstruction operations, more funding and personnel will be needed if it and associated agencies are to build the capacity they need to carry out this mission.[19] Even so, there are questions about the effectiveness of State Department leadership in a crisis, especially given the Defense Department's understandable penchant for wanting to control operations in the midst of a conflict. There are also questions about whether the State Department's Office of the Coordinator for Reconstruction and Stabilization will gain traction and become a sort of Joint Chiefs of Staff for the State Department, or whether its mission, culture, and resources will be integrated into preexisting regional bureaus.

As an outgrowth of the experiences in Iraq and Afghanistan, the U.S. government has focused on integrating interagency resources to plan and execute stabilization and reconstruction operations. This effort finally became official in August 2004, when the Office of the Coordinator for Reconstruction and Stabilization (S/CRS) was created within the State Department to help lead and coordinate joint operations across agencies, with a focus on prevention, preparation, and response for stabilization and reconstruction operations. Its establishment was intended to address long-standing concerns regarding the lack of the appropriate capabilities and processes to deal with transitions from conflict. However, Congress's commitment to the project is divided, as evidenced by the Senate's approval of $74 million for S/CRS in fiscal 2006 appropriations while the House in essence allocated nothing.[20]

National Security Presidential Directive 44, issued in December 2005, solidifies the State Department's role as the coordinator and lead actor in both the planning and execution of stabilization and reconstruction operations; however, NSPD 44 also provides for consultation and close coordination with the Defense Department.[21] NSPD 44 clarifies interagency lines of authority, and Defense Department Directive 3000 outlines the operational responsibilities and realignment of resources within the Defense Department.

However, further action is needed to more clearly assess and align the interests, goals, and priorities of stabilization and reconstruction with the resources, personnel, and execution capability of these agencies. Capabilities and procedures include adequate planning for stabilization and reconstruction operations, efficient interagency coordination structures and procedures in performing such tasks, and appropriate civilian personnel for many of the nonmilitary tasks required. Other critical issues include the distribution of resources among the various executive branch actors, maintaining clear lines of authority and jurisdiction, and balancing short- and long-term objectives for designing, planning, and conducting postconflict operations.[22] The fiscal year 2007 budget for S/CRS requests $20.1 million for operating costs and personnel and $75 million for a conflict response fund, which will begin to improve the office's operational capacity and ability to plan.[23]

Although the State Department is designated as the coordinator and leader of stabilization and reconstruction operations across agencies, NSPD 44 and Directive 3000 highlight one fundamental point: the participation and leadership of the Defense Department remain vital to stabilization and reconstruction scenarios—without them, no operation has legs.[24] State Department efforts alone cannot be sufficient: S/CRS already has a capacity gap, and how much real capacity it would have to deal with the next conflict is not clear. Although the White House provides guidance through NSPD 44 regarding the leadership and coordination of stabilization and reconstruction operations, and although new, related positions are being added to the National Security Council, questions remain. While the leadership for planning and prevention is critical, there are further complexities of interagency coordination in the execution of policies, plans, and strategies. Who will lead stabilization and reconstruction efforts on the ground in conflict and postconflict situations? Does the State Department have the capacity (and possibly, the ability) to lead all necessary planning? Will resources be shifted toward the State Department to compensate for its additional responsibilities?

Beyond logistical and operational matters, there are larger questions of political will. There is no apparent consensus in our body politic regarding the operational side of development. Are Congress and, more abstractly, the American people willing to support these operations—willing to invest the resources, both human and financial, to address the national security interests related to stabilization and reconstruction operations? It will take between ten and twenty years to build a "culture of development" in the United States. Steps are being taken, but like the state-building process, developing a political culture within the U.S. government to support these operations will be a long-term process.

Lessons Learned

The requirements of state building are complex and will vary from case to case. Nonetheless, several lessons are prominent from recent experiences. If they are lessons identified but not yet learned, they seem to demand adaptation and innovation on the part of the U.S. government. Those lessons center on six requirements:

—realistic and comprehensive planning for postwar operations;

—establishment of capable indigenous security and police forces;

—capability to provide rural development and assistance, such as food and medical aid, in the middle of intermittent insurgency, terrorism, and low-level political violence;

—authority and means to rapidly move money on the ground in a way that creates livelihoods and has an immediate impact on the lives of those most affected by the conflict;

—unity of U.S. and international command of a temporary government and a coherent plan for a transition to self-government; and

—leveraging international support for the costly and long-haul requirements of state-building and peacemaking operations.

The following case studies illustrate these lessons.

Postconflict (Phase IV) Planning: The Case of Iraq

There is now consensus that the intensive planning for the 2003 war in Iraq failed miserably with respect to the state building needed after major combat operations ended. Eisenhower said that a plan is nothing, the planning everything. Moreover, no plan survives unchanged after the beginning of a war, and this is perhaps particularly true of postwar plans. However, there was *no* postwar plan for an insurgent Iraq before the war began. Moreover, the first team tasked with postwar operation, led by former Lieutenant General Jay Garner, was expected to be in and out in three months.[25] This lack of realistic planning for so-called Phase IV (postconflict) operations—now recognized as a less-than-accurate term since it is difficult (and possibly, futile) to delineate the difference between conflict and postconflict operations—in Iraq proved to be a costly mistake. The possibility of an insurgency and the reality of a failed state without government institutions, capacity, or administration were not accounted for. The failure to secure the country and mobilize more people to the cause of the post-Saddam order provided a breeding ground for insurgents and former Baathists determined to use deadly force to get their way.

One planning mistake was making best-case assumptions about the tranquility and capacity of post-Saddam Iraq. Another egregious problem was the failure to integrate the best ideas from the State Department into Defense Department planning, despite the fact that the State Department had conducted comprehensive working groups among experts to review likely Iraqi future scenarios and needs. While the Future of Iraq Project would not have been *the* answer to postwar operations, the Defense Department's marginalization of the State Department's postconflict planning effort and the minimal State Department role in the initial stabilization and reconstruction period did not encourage interagency cooperation and did not mobilize all available U.S. government resources to address the situation.[26] A third and related problem was the White House failure to more effectively unify the fiercely fragmented bureaucracy. Rather than mediate the internecine battles among agencies, the National Security Council (NSC) gave the Defense Department the lead in stabilization and reconstruction because of the conflict-related dimension of operations and the huge operational capacity the armed forces possessed. However, the failure to foster a unified, interagency approach led to the quick demise of the Office of Reconstruction and Humanitarian Assistance (ORHA), which was soon replaced by the Coalition Provisional Authority (CPA) in April 2003. Despite the presence of personnel from other agencies, ORHA and CPA were largely the Defense Department's show, and it soon recruited willing members to staff ORHA and CPA's swelling ranks, regardless of their qualifications to fill the positions at hand.

Given that military planning for the Iraq war began over a year before the invasion, failure to plan for the postwar situation has rightly been roundly criticized. And when planning for stabilization and reconstruction finally did occur, a multitude of errors in judgment were made, including

—thorough preparation for a large-scale humanitarian emergency that never materialized but far less thorough preparation for rapid development and job creation;

—the assumption that coalition troops would be welcomed as liberators and the corresponding failure to anticipate the insurgency;

—the belief that Iraq's security forces would remain intact and could be put into action for reconstruction and stabilization operations;

—underestimation of the damage to the basic service infrastructure and government institutions of Iraq; and

—an unrealistic estimation that stabilization and reconstruction efforts could be achieved in a short time frame (less than one year).

Once ORHA had been established, its planning process should have included input from other agencies and nongovernmental organizations. More extensive intelligence on the state of the Iraqi infrastructure and military would have strengthened the planning process, especially regarding security. In the absence of a standing capacity in the U.S. military to assume policing duties, allies with policing experience should have been approached. While it was reasonable to expect Iraqi forces to assume some responsibility for policing duties as a long-term solution, it was unreasonable to anticipate that they could be relied upon without significant, medium- to long-term training and support. In addition, the lack of a plan for the DDR of Iraqi forces, both politically and technically, is symptomatic of a general unwillingness in the U.S. government to formalize and institutionalize such programs.

As of July 2005, the good news was that the training of large numbers of Iraqi military, security, and police forces finally appeared on track. Moreover, a political process with a hope of securing greater Sunni participation in the new government was beginning. Less optimistically, reconstruction money was being diverted to security due to the unstable security environment, other funds remained unspent, and many of the allocated funds were not addressing the basic needs of Iraqis. As a February 2006 GAO report states, "The U.S. reconstruction program has encountered difficulties with Iraq's inability to sustain new and rehabilitated infrastructure projects and to address maintenance needs in the water, sanitation, and electricity sectors."[27] In February 2006 the average amount of electricity generated was below estimated prewar levels.[28] According to a recent International Republican Institute poll, "inadequate electricity" was the biggest problem "requiring a political or governmental solution," 10 percentage points ahead of any other problem, including security.[29] In short, essential services are not being provided.

Security Sector Reform: The Case of Afghanistan

As most recently seen in Kosovo, Afghanistan, and Iraq, U.S. and international reconstruction and stabilization operations suffer from a profound lack of constabulary and policing capacity. Indeed, Ireland outranks the U.S. in its civilian policing contribution to current UN missions by almost 100 personnel, including police, military observers, and troops.[30] This problem extends into a number of areas, including the lack of mechanisms for calling up international constabulary forces, the shortage of qualified civilian police available for swift deployment, and the lack of rapidly deployable legal experts to provide support in setting up an interim legal code and courts. While the security demands in post–September 11 America have somewhat diminished the pool of personnel qualified for such operations, the United States can address this need by increasing funding for initiatives such as training police officers from allied countries, leading an international diplomatic effort to increase the availability of national constabulary forces (including support for existing efforts on the part of the European Union), and providing equipment on request.

Development in Harm's Way: The Case of Afghanistan

In order to establish stabilization and reconstruction operations in Afghanistan after major combat operations were completed, the U.S. government in late 2002 deployed Provincial Reconstruction Teams (PRTs) to several important cities and provinces. These units consisted principally of U.S. troops, usually 50 to 100, complemented by civilian specialists from other U.S. government agencies. The teams were a Defense Department response to the failure of earlier attempts to attract civilian agencies to these efforts in Afghanistan and to a continuing deterioration of the tenuous links between the provinces and the capital. Initial problems aside, they generated important benefits: they began to bolster stabilization efforts, helping broaden the influence of the Kabul government; and they monitored and assessed the situation in the provinces. However, the reconstruction component was not as effective because the PRTs needed more personnel from civilian agencies.

The PRTs were not explicitly mandated to provide security; rather, they were established in areas where security was better than average.[31] While they should not be viewed as a substitute for peacekeeping forces, the PRTs may be judged as an overall success, notably in fields not easily quantified such as public outreach, monitoring, and assessment. The U.S. ambassador to Iraq, Zalmay Khalilzad, is beginning to apply lessons learned from his tenure as ambassador to Afghanistan by supporting the use of PRTs in Iraq. Even so, it must be said there are competing and different models for PRTs even in Afghanistan, and just because one can field a civil-military team does not necessarily guarantee its effectiveness in accomplishing an overly ambitious mission. It does, however, hold some hope for avoiding being a "garrison development team," holed up in a Green Zone or capital and unable to reach critical regions of a war-torn country.

Moving the Money to Where It Is Most Needed

Standards for accountability can make spending public money difficult. However, there are times when accountability becomes secondary to addressing acute demands, such as the needs and expectations of a dislocated, postwar population wondering where their livelihood will be coming from or whether they have a stake in the fledgling government and order. Modifying standard accountability mechanisms begins with a clear-eyed assessment of the priorities by senior decisionmakers, who at times must sacrifice standard operating procedures in order to meet the unique demands of a situation. Only the White House, particularly through the NSC and the Office of Management and Budget, can hope to overcome the bureaucratic imperatives and cultures of the government's many separate silos. The Office of Management and Budget plays a critical role in adjudicating priorities—which oftentimes are best determined on the ground in the country where action is being taken. In the 2006 QDR, the Defense Department recommends expanded Commander's Emergency Response Program (CERP) funds and authority.[32] Expanding CERP and other similar provisions for funding certain stabilization and reconstruction projects will give military and civilian leaders on the ground the ability to meet urgent humanitarian needs and implement other short-term, lost-cost, high-impact plans. In effect, CERP provisions are part of the "hearts and minds" campaign, providing for the immediate needs of people in the postwar period. But there is the unintended hazard that a military-funded effort could lead to military "mission creep" further into the work that is more properly left to development specialists.

In addition, there is a need for a comprehensive review and dialogue between USAID and Congress over procurement and contracting practices in foreign assistance. The USAID contracting system is stymied by a lack of personnel and a restrictive procurement system that ties up contracts of all sums in byzantine, time-consuming approval processes not appropriate for postconflict and near-conflict emergencies. In addition, monitoring and assessment of procurement activity is inefficient. One consequence of these inadequacies is a tendency to award huge contracts to U.S. companies, regardless of their ability to address urgent needs in foreign locales in a manner that attracts greater local ownership and buy-in.

Transitional Governance: The Case of Iraq

The United States faces a trade-off between power sharing and burden sharing when establishing a de facto temporary protectorate over a postconflict country. This trade-off is hardly unique to stabilization and reconstruction operations. Nonetheless, the experience of the past fifteen years does not point to a single model for transitional governance, and probably one does not exist. UN trusteeships under a UN special representative to the secretary general may work for peace operations in which the U.S. has not deployed major conventional forces, as described in the cases of Liberia (see box 6-1) and East Timor (see discussion below). However, recent experiences in Afghanistan and Iraq hint that major U.S.-led interventions are likely to prove difficult to hand off to the international community en route to establishing self-governance. Bosnia and Kosovo illustrate another model of transitional governance, where international cooperation was strong and burdens were shared widely among allies. Issues ranging from the size of the intervened country to the political will of international allies affect the transitional governance model and the level of international participation.

Although the postwar environment was complex, the deleterious decisions made by the CPA in Iraq—such as the marginalization of the Sunni population, lack of outreach to provincial governments, and micromanaging and sidelining the Iraqi Governing Council—were not inherent in the chosen model of transitional governance. One could imagine a U.S.-led approach better attuned to the realities on the ground that would not necessarily have made these mistakes. However, it is evident from the example of Iraq that in the short to medium term, the United States will not be able to manage a transition without improvements in the interagency process and stronger international cooperation. The 2006 QDR astutely emphasizes that these are the two critical areas to improve.

There is, moreover, the simple reality that a U.S. vice consul model, akin to that of MacArthur in Japan, lacks the international legitimacy that UN involvement bestows. Regardless of how well the CPA is governed, there is greater perceived lawfulness in multilateral efforts. The use of a vice consul model to govern postwar Iraq without UN involvement until spring 2004 meant that the U.S. occupation was denied both the benefit of extensive experience in managing postconflict transitions and the aura of international legitimacy that the UN alone could confer. Finally, so much depends on this single transitional authority, the viceroy, that it is inherently difficult to find someone with the necessary skills and breadth of knowledge in the U.S. government to effectively do the job. It calls to mind the axiom of Clausewitz that the best generals understand statecraft and the best politicians understand military affairs. One wonders whether the United States could not do better by grooming potential vice consuls, within either the U.S. or the UN framework.

In the final analysis, different models will be used in different situations. However, the U.S. government and international community, principally through the UN and European allies, will need to improve cooperation and work to establish a range of strategies, capabilities, and resources that can enact plans that are collectively designed.

Leveraging the International Community: The Case of East Timor

Whatever the problems of maintaining stability in Timor Leste, the case does point to a successful model for forging serious coalitions. America's role in East Timor provides a successful model of junior partnership. The United States participated in the reconstruction of East Timor as an active junior partner but did not lead international efforts or pay the majority of the costs. Continuous international pressure—led by the Clinton administration—and a change in the Indonesian government led Jakarta to allow a referendum on independence for East Timor in 1999. Residents voted overwhelmingly in favor of separation, and the situation exploded. Pro-Indonesia militias terrorized the island and killed thousands of East Timorese. American efforts led to passage of a UN Security Council resolution in support of international intervention in East Timor. In September 1999 Australia led a thirty-one-nation intervention force that drove out the violent pro-Indonesia militias, stabilized the border with West Timor, and restored law and order in East Timor.

Many challenges faced the international community seeking to stabilize East Timor. East Timorese refugees, pro-Indonesian militiamen, and ex-combatants living in squalid refugee camps in West Timor had to be repatriated. In addition, there were no government institutions, a legal system did not exist, and almost no East Timorese possessed administrative experience. In addition, 75 percent of the physical infrastructure had been destroyed in the fighting.[33] Finally, East Timor was plagued by extreme poverty, illiteracy, and high infant mortality.

Numerous countries and international institutions participated in the reconstruction effort. While the international force maintained order, particularly through the deployment of Australian constabulary that created a secure environment, the international community, led by a retired U.S. general, trained a domestic police force to eventually take over security responsibilities. The UN International Organization for Migration demilitarized and reintegrated some pro-Indonesia forces back into East Timorese society, and the UN Transitional Administration in East Timor (UNTAET) served as the transitional government. East Timorese held numerous administration positions in UNTAET, preparing them to take over government functions after formal independence in 2002. Currently, a democratically elected government is in power, and prospects for economic development are promising thanks to the oil and gas sector, assistance to rebuild infrastructure, and an internationally supported emphasis on tourism and agriculture.

The U.S. role was secondary, but crucial, consisting of military (logistics, intelligence, and support), diplomatic, and economic assistance. American soldiers efficiently rebuilt schools and health posts, winning the praise of the local populace and deterring pro-Indonesia militia elements that could have destabilized the situation. U.S. diplomatic involvement was significant leading up to and after the conflict. The Clinton administration led the push for a UN Security Council resolution and pressured the Indonesian government for a referendum on independence. During the stabilization process, a hard-nosed American ambassador negotiated with Australia for East Timor's rights to the Timor Gap oil and gas deposits, leading to the Timor Sea Treaty. Economically, USAID's Office of Transition Initiatives provided flexible, fast assistance that other donors could not. Moreover, USAID's experience and comparative advantage supported the development of democracy, governance, and civic education.

The stabilization and reconstruction operations in East Timor contain important lessons that, unfortunately, have not been applied to Liberia. Ultimately, successfully filling the role of junior partner does not mean indiscriminately scaling down all involvement but rather focusing with full commitment on a limited range of tasks. Selective U.S. involvement can be used to leverage greater involvement and leadership on the part of regionally based allies, establishing a more legitimate, effective operation. Whether this was sufficient to leave East Timor with a viable economy and stability in the longer run will only be answered in time.

A New Approach: Recommendations for Strategic Planning, Interagency Coordination, and Effective Implementation

Conflict and the developing world are inseparable and cannot be "solved" in the usual time frame in which Washington makes policy and budgetary decisions. The events of September 11, 2001, make abundantly clear that the United States must create a more robust capability for preventing conflict, promoting peace, supporting international burden sharing, and assuming leadership of major stabilization and reconstruction operations, particularly where U.S. strategic interests are at stake.

The fact that there are no quick or easy solutions to the problems of stabilization and reconstruction should not prevent the development of strategies, resources, and capabilities to handle such operations. Perhaps the first and most important recommendation is that the next time the commander in chief gives the order to develop plans for restoring order and launching a country on a path toward sustainable self-government, senior officials need to inform the president frankly about the severe limitations the U.S. government faces in undertaking such an enterprise on a grand scale. Resources are being developed, cooperation and coordination are being promoted, and policy documents reveal a shift in recognizing stabilization and reconstruction as key missions; however, these processes must continue if the U.S. government is to meet the ongoing challenges of its overseas operations. Few senior officials responsible for such activities made the limits of our stabilization and reconstruction and state-building capabilities clear to President George W. Bush before the war in Iraq was launched. Instead optimistic scenarios were presented about the level of conflict after the deposition of Saddam Hussein and the viability of the Iraqi state. In fact, some assessments appeared to suggest that after undertaking the immediate task of delivering humanitarian assistance, the United States could leave most of the reconstruction to a relatively prosperous and technically skilled Iraqi citizenry. The recent experience in Iraq could lead one to conclude that America can plan a military intervention in secret very well, but it cannot plan a lasting political victory in the aftermath of successful military operations. Stabilization and reconstruction planning must be part of the comprehensive military and civilian plan that is established for any intervention.

Although the United States has the ability to conduct effective stabilization and reconstruction operations to some degree and the potential to effect the reforms necessary to improve these capabilities, there are some inherent limits to the U.S. role—and any external actor's role—in stabilization and reconstruction operations. The United States has three strikes against it when contemplating leading major postwar reconstruction efforts. First, the imperative of military secrecy that surrounds a major U.S. intervention as well as bureaucratic infighting exclude many people with country knowledge and expertise, particularly civilians in and outside of government, from participating in stabilization and reconstruction planning. A related problem is a lack of resources and personnel in civilian agencies to undertake the amount of planning that could be conducted by the military. Second, the very act of intervention, however noble the cause, almost always provides incentives for insurgency against the world's hegemonic power, an insurgency that is likely to raise the costs of state-building considerably. Third and finally, the United States government routinely operates on a basis of short-term crisis management, an approach incompatible with the long-term (at least five- to ten-year) process of stabilization and reconstruction. The U.S. involvement in Iraq and Afghanistan could prove the exception to this attention-deficit disorder—but the exception that proves the rule. Other instances of state building, such as in East Timor, were successful largely because they were smaller operations and undertaken through international and regional structures that provided greater legitimacy and staying power.

Among the many extant recommendations or steps urged within the U.S. government, the following ten recommendations would seem to highlight key areas of reform that could generate the greatest capability at the least cost in the shortest period of time.

Support the Further Evolution of the New Directorate of Stabilization and Reconstruction Activities within the National Security Council

This office oversees the development of interagency contingency plans, addresses operational and budgetary requirements in such cases, and coordinates interagency actions during operations. This NSC directorate should be given a stronger role in reviewing stabilization and reconstruction plans, but it should not be given the responsibility of constructing them since this process is extremely labor and time intensive. As it does with many foreign policy issues, the NSC should promote interagency coordination, resolve interdepartmental disputes, and coordinate information from many different perspectives. By supporting the implementation of NSPD 44, the NSC can help establish lines of authority between the Defense Department, State Department, USAID, and other relevant departments and agencies to promote better cooperation and coordination on a range of issues, such as the budget. In addition, the NSC can act as an "impartial" facilitator to promote and lead civilian-military cooperation and coordination. While NSPD 44 designates the State Department as the lead actor in stabilization and reconstruction operations, a strong yet limited coordination role for the NSC is necessary.

Clarify the Division of Labor between the State Department and USAID

The State Department should, in close consultation with the USAID administrator and his staff, make the policy decisions and lead the planning effort; USAID should be delegated broad authority to implement the programs and activities in the field. The nature of the relationship, especially since the reforms of the late 1990s, makes the administrator of USAID subordinate to the secretary of state but keeps the rest of USAID independent; and yet the secretary of state does have overall oversight of USAID budget and plans. Beyond the legal questions this arrangement engenders, there is the huge chasm in culture between a development agency and a diplomatic department. However, complex contingencies, state building, and stabilization and reconstruction operations in failed and recovering states demand that these two entities be positioned to provide their utmost in the service of U.S. national interests. Secretary Rice's recent changes, such as making the USAID administrator simultaneously the State Department's director of U.S. foreign assistance, are the beginning of further coordination and cooperation. Additional reforms to budget accounts and authorities will be necessary to make State Department–USAID coordination in stabilization and reconstruction operations even more effective.

Provide the State Department and USAID with Adequate Resources to Undertake Stabilization and Reconstruction Operations

The core mission of the State Department's Office of the Coordinator for Reconstruction and Stabilization is "to lead, coordinate and institutionalize U.S. Government civilian capacity to prevent or prepare for postconflict situations, and to help stabilize and reconstruct societies in transition from conflict or civil strife."[34] Resources for the three components of the S/CRS mission—prevention, preparation, and response—will need to be increased. The military component of stabilization and reconstruction must continue to receive crucial funding, but as the 2006 QDR recognizes, U.S. national security strategies will not be achieved by military means alone. Civilian staff, resources, and skills must be substantially increased. If the State Department is expected to fulfill its duties within NSPD 44, it must receive the commensurate increases in funding and personnel. Furthermore, the growing relationship, cooperation, and coordination between the Defense and State Departments must continue to be fostered by senior officials throughout the government. According to Assistant Secretary of State John Hillen, the relationship between the State and Defense Departments must be reinvigorated in order to promote coordination and cooperation on all levels, including planning, training, and actual operations.[35]

Lessons Must Be Learned from Afghanistan and Iraq

While the U.S. government might not expect to devote the resources, capabilities, and political will to interventions of the scale and scope occurring in Afghanistan and Iraq, there are important lessons from these operations that must be integrated into the overall government response. One lesson, regarding national security, is that a country does not get to choose its battles in all cases; therefore, the U.S. government must be prepared to respond adequately to any stabilization and reconstruction mission. Another lesson is that improved interagency coordination is key to the success of an operation. In addition, multilateral state-building efforts, which increase burden sharing and legitimacy (international and domestic), appear to be more cost effective and have a higher likelihood of success. A further lesson is that PRTs are a useful, decentralized tool for carrying out stabilization and reconstruction operations. However, to be more effective, they require greater civilian participation.

Increase the Emphasis on Multilateral Approaches

International partnerships for stabilization and reconstruction operations will be more cost effective, increase burden sharing, bolster legitimacy, and increase the likelihood of success. International cooperation could include creation of an independent assessment arm, perhaps in the World Bank, to measure what is effective and required in terms of financial resources and overall capabilities to succeed in different conflict and post-conflict environments. This last recommendation underscores the larger point of improving international partnerships but also highlights the importance of understanding the resources needed to conduct an effective state-building operation.

Prepare Civilian Agencies to Lead Transitional Governance, Whether under U.S. or International Auspices

Within the U.S. government, the military has the most capacity to operate in conflict situations and conduct stabilization and reconstruction operations. However, the State Department and other civilian agencies must be given the funds and the mandate to plan and execute stabilization and reconstruction operations. However, increased leadership requires increased capacity, and this sector of the government must receive the funding and staffing that will allow it to achieve optimal capacity.

Increase Efforts on Prevention

While the major focus of these recommendations (and the entire chapter) has been on stabilization and reconstruction operations, the prevention component of the S/CRS mission should not be neglected. Regional bureaus within the State and Defense Departments, USAID, and the intelligence sector must collaborate with S/CRS, the NSC, and other relevant offices in order to identify potential conflicts, create conflict prevention strategies, and execute plans before conflict prevention is superseded by conflict reaction.

Establish a Larger Reserve Constabulary and Policing Force

The U.S. government must explore strategies that would increase potential policing units for stabilization and reconstruction operations. These strategies should include both domestic and international options. International partnerships are essential; however, the United States must also develop a coherent strategy to recruit domestic police to participate in stabilization and reconstruction operations.

Support Proposed Legislation, Budgets, and Plans to Create a Reserve Civilian Corps for Rapid Response

While "active duty" civilian capacity must be increased, when stabilization and reconstruction operations occur, there will be a need to recruit personnel from a reserve civilian corps that is capable of providing key expertise, skills, and knowledge to a particular operation. Overall, the detailed plans and policies promoting civilian-military cooperation must receive the necessary funding and support in order to become operational.

Establish Clear Guidelines for Rapid Disbursement of Funds to Local Populations

It is essential that resources be moved into the hands of the local people, who must be invested in the stabilization and reconstruction process if it is to succeed. Commander's Emergency Response Program funds and other short-term, high-impact programs that provide "walking around money" are key elements in the campaign to win "hearts and minds," a campaign that must succeed if stabilization and reconstruction operations are to fulfill their mission.

Notes

1. Department of Defense, *Quadrennial Defense Review Report* (February 6, 2006).

2. White House, "National Security Presidential Directive/NSPD-44: Management of Interagency Efforts Concerning Reconstruction and Stabilization," Washington, December 7, 2005 (www.fas.org/irp/offdocs/nspd/nspd-44.html [April 2006]).

3. Organisation for Economic Co-operation and Development, "Net ODA from DAC Countries from 1950 to 2004," updated December 15, 2005 (www.oecd.org/dac/stats/dac/reftables [April 2006]).

4. Department of Defense, "Directive 3000.05: Military Support for Stability, Security, Transition, and Reconstruction (SSTR) Operations" (www.dtic.mil/whs/directives/corres/pdf/d300005_112805/d300005p.pdf [April 2006]), p. 2.

5. Department of Defense, *Quadrennial Defense.*

6. White House, *The National Security Strategy of the United States of America* (September 2002).

7. See High-Level Panel on Threats, Challenges and Change, *A More Secure World: Our Shared Responsibility* (New York: United Nations, January 2005); Secretary General, *In Larger Freedom: Towards Security, Development and Human Rights for All* (New York: United Nations, September 2005).

8. A 1998 estimate from the United Nations Development Program cited in Jeff Gates, "Statistics on Poverty and Inequality," May 1999 (www.globalpolicy.org/socecon/inequal/gates99.htm).

9. Government Accountability Office, *Peacekeeping: Cost Comparison of Actual UN and Hypothetical U.S. Operations in Haiti*, GAO06-331 (February 2006).

10. See Tony Smith, *America's Mission: The United States and the Worldwide Struggle for Democracy in the Twentieth Century* (Princeton University Press, 1994).

11. James F. Dobbins, "America's Role in Nation-Building: From Germany to Iraq," *Survival* 45, no. 4 (2003): 87–110.

12. Regarding candidate Bush's stance on nation building, see CNN, "Vice President Gore and Governor Bush Participate in Presidential Debate," October 3, 2000 (www.cnn.com/ELECTION/2000/debates/transcripts/u221003.html [April 2006]).

13. Through the State Department's Office of the Coordinator for Reconstruction and Stabilization, a U.S. government interagency planning matrix was developed for sta-

bilization and reconstruction operations, which was based on Orr's study for the Center for Strategic and International Studies (CSIS). See Robert Orr, ed., *Winning the Peace* (Washington: CSIS, 2004). The fifty-four-page stabilization and reconstruction planning matrix outlines key issues in five areas: security, governance and participation, humanitarian assistance and social well-being, economic stabilization and infrastructure, and justice and reconciliation. See Office of the Coordinator for Reconstruction and Stabilization, "Fact Sheet: Post Conflict Reconstruction: Essential Tasks Matrix" (www.state.gov/s/crs/rls/52959.htm [April 1, 2005]). The Office has since produced a general planning framework that could be the basis for an all-of-government approach in the future, although it remains uncertain how the Defense and State Departments will share leadership and decisionmaking in practice and how well it will help coalition members pull together.

14. See Jeremy M. Weinstein, John Edward Porter, and Stuart E. Eizenstat, *On the Brink: Weak States and U.S. National Security: A Report of the Commission for Weak States and U.S. National Security* (Washington: Center for Global Development, 2004).

15. Department of Defense, "Directive 3000.05."

16. USAID, "Transition Initiatives" (www.usaid.gov/our_work/cross-cutting_programs/transition_initiatives/ [June 2005]).

17. For OTI funding, see Department of State, "FY 2007 International Affairs Summary" (www.state.gov/documents/organization/60299.pdf [April 2006]). For U.S. government funding of Iraq's reconstruction costs, see Congressional Budget Office, *Paying for Iraq's Reconstruction* (January 2004). The estimate for 2004 through 2007 comes from Government Accountability Office, *Rebuilding Iraq: Stabilization, Reconstruction, and Financing Challenges,* GAO-06-428T (February 8, 2006), p. 2.

18. James Dobbins and others, *America's Role in Nation-Building: From Germany to Iraq* (Santa Monica, Calif.: RAND, 2003).

19. See Department of State, Office of the Spokesman, "President Issues Directive to Improve the United States' Capacity to Manage Reconstruction and Stabilization Efforts" (www.state.gov/r/pa/prs/ps/2005/58067.htm [December 14, 2005]).

20. Office for the Coordinator of Reconstruction and Stabilization, "S/CRS Budget and Legislative Issues Update," December 2005 (www.crs.state.gov/index.cfm?fuseaction=public.display&id=7A66909B-8158-4EDA-837B-D5A455E7871E [August 2006]).

21. White House, "National Security Presidential Directive/NSPD-44."

22. Nina M. Serafino and Martin A. Weiss, *Peacekeeping and Conflict Transitions: Background and Congressional Action on Civilian Capabilities* (Congressional Research Service, Library of Congress, April 13, 2005).

23. Department of State, Office of the Coordinator for Reconstruction and Stabilization, "S/CRS Reference Guide to President Bush's FY 2007 Budget Request" (www.crs.state.gov/index.cfm?fuseaction=layout.LayoutDisplay&layoutid=180ccabf-9d8d-441f-b72e-2127a1cd9b1d&CFID=156021&CFTOKEN=53606997 [April 2006]).

24. White House, "National Security Presidential Directive"; Department of Defense, "Directive 3000.05," p. 2.

25. CNN, "Garner, Bodine Set to Leave Iraq," *CNN Sunday Morning,* May 11, 2003 (transcripts.cnn.com/TRANSCRIPTS/0305/11/sm.21.html).

26. See Bathsheba Crocker, "Iraq: Going It Alone, Gone Wrong," in *Winning the Peace,* edited by Robert Orr (Washington: CSIS, 2004), pp. 193–209.

27. Government Accountability Office, *Rebuilding Iraq,* p. 2.

28. Michael O'Hanlon and Nina Kamp, "Iraq Index: Tracking Variables of Reconstruction and Stabilization in Post-Saddam Iraq" (www.brookings.edu/fp/saban/iraq/index.pdf [February 2006]).

29. Glenn Zorpette, "Re-engineering Iraq," Spectrum Online, February 2006 (www.spectrum.ieee.org/feb06/2831).

30. UN, "Contributions to United Nations Peacekeeping Operations: Monthly Summary of Contributions," March 31, 2006 (www.un.org/Depts/dpko/dpko/contributors/2006/march_1.pdf).

31. Milan Vaishnav, "Afghanistan: The Chimera of 'The Light Footprint'," in *Winning the Peace,* edited by Robert Orr (Washington: CSIS, 2004), pp. 241–62.

32. Department of Defense, *Quadrennial Defense.*

33. World Bank, "County Brief: Timor-Leste" (web.worldbank.org/WBSITE/EXTERNAL/COUNTRIES/0,,pagePK:180619~theSitePK:136917,00.html).

34. Department of State, Office of the Coordinator for Reconstruction and Stabilization, "About S/CRS" (www.state.gov/s/crs/c12936.htm [April 2006]).

35. John Hillen, "The Changing Nature of the Political-Military Interface," presented at the Joint Worldwide Planning Conference, Garmisch, Germany, November 30, 2005 (www.state.gov/t/pm/rls/rm/58189.htm [April 2006]).

CHAPTER 7

The Changing Complexion of Security and Strategic Assistance in the Twenty-First Century

Patrick Cronin and Tarek Ghani

One of the oldest and most enduring purposes of U.S. foreign assistance has been to counter security threats to the nation. Throughout the cold war, the United States provided security assistance—in the form of money and military training and hardware—to contain Soviet power. During that time the boundaries of so-called security assistance were broadly consistent with the 1961 Foreign Assistance Act definition of U.S. government programs that provide "defense articles, military training, and other defense related services by grant, loan, credit, or cash sales in furtherance of national policies and objectives."[1] Increasingly, however, a much broader category of assistance, motivated primarily by the objectives of countering security threats, extends to economic development programs, humanitarian assistance, and debt relief. For this reason security and strategic assistance is more readily identified by the immediate purpose that it is intended to advance and the criteria by which it was allocated than by the ultimate end use to which it is directed.

In the aftermath of the cold war and the watershed of September 11, 2001, the United States needs to do more to move away from this narrow security assistance model to a new model that is suited to multiple strategic objectives as opposed to the singular strategy of containment. It must move from the one C of containment to the five Cs of counterterrorism, counterproliferation, counternarcotics, coalition building, and conflict management. As set out in the overarching conceptual framework for this book, we separate the analysis of countering security threats into those that require working with foreign partners and those that emanate from the poor performance of foreign states.[2] The challenge of poor performers, dealing with both pre- and postconflict situations, was addressed in the previous chapter.[3] This chapter examines the challenges of providing assistance to states to meet the other four security goals: countering terrorism, countering the proliferation of nuclear and other mass-destruction weapons, countering illegal narcotics and transnational crime, and coalition building.

Despite a spike in funding for new initiatives over the past several years, there has been no major reform of U.S. security assistance programs since the sea change in security wrought by the events of September 11, 2001. To be sure, there are some signs that the State Department under the leadership of Dr. Condoleezza Rice is interested in reform; for instance, Dr. John Hillen, the assistant secretary of state for Politico-Military Affairs, has attempted to redirect security assistance and other programs away from narrow, limited ends and toward larger, strategic goals, namely those that help to foment a "transformation" of international affairs. Whether this new direction leads to effective policy, legislative, and programmatic reforms, however, remains to be seen. Generally governments are not very amenable to rapid reform. Meanwhile, independent reviews have suggested genuine opportunities to improve planning, management, and reporting structures.[4] Ineffective bureaucratic structures and outdated laws make it difficult for the federal government to cope with unprecedented security threats from global terrorism, transnational criminal networks, and failed states. When assessed in terms of threats to national security and the lives of the American people, improving the coherence and effectiveness of international strategic and security assistance programs is a neglected yet pressing national priority.

This chapter examines the context for security assistance programs, evaluates their record of performance, and recommends starting points for improvement. It begins with a brief review of security assistance trends over the last fifteen years, starting with the end of the cold war and continuing into the post–September 11 environment. This is followed by an assessment of U.S. programs in counterterrorism, counterproliferation, counternarcotics, and coalition building. The discussion concludes with recommendations for strengthening the performance of U.S. security assistance programs.

U.S. Security Assistance: From the Cold War to Iraq

With the end of the cold war, the single-minded clarity engendered by high-stakes, superpower rivalry was replaced with the ambiguity of a complex landscape of competing international threats, including terrorism, failed states, transnational threats, and rising powers such as China. As Lieutenant General Ernest Graves, former director of the Defense Security Cooperation Agency, presciently observed in 1991, "Without a unifying threat from the Soviet Union, policy differences are likely to be harder to resolve."[5] However, after the September 11 terrorist attacks and the subsequent interventions in Afghanistan and Iraq, terrorism abruptly emerged as a new unifying threat.

The post–September 11 security environment is radically different from that of the cold war and has required officials to focus more on transnational and nonstate threats to the national security of the United States and its allies. Describing the current security environment and its threats, Assistant Secretary of State John Hillen asserted,

> We contemplate the brewing threats of "Perfect Storms" of failed governments, ethnic stratification, religious violence, humanitarian disasters, stateless militants, apocalyptic terrorists, cataclysmic regional crises, and the proliferation of dangerous weapons. While we keep our eyes on possible peer or near peer competitors, our security attentions are more frequently drawn to the dynamics of threats produced by lagging economies, unintegrated and disenfranchised populations, transnational crimes, illicit sub-national power structures, poorly or ungoverned spaces, and destabilizing bulges of uneducated and unemployed youths.[6]

With the end of the cold war, the composition of U.S. security assistance shifted partly to meet the needs of the new security landscape. In general, funds for coalition building slowly declined, and new nonproliferation initiatives, primarily the Nunn-Lugar Cooperative Threat Reduction Program, began to make up part but not all of the difference. The big exception to this decline has been the coalition-building programs to promote stability in the Middle East, which have occupied a prominent spot on the strategic radar screen since the Camp David Accords of 1979 and continued to absorb the majority of security assistance. In 1998, in response to prodding from Congress, Israel agreed to a decade-long reduction in its customary economic support program, worth $1.2 billion a year, in exchange for a hefty increase in support from the Foreign Military Financing (FMF) program. At the same time, Egypt continued to be the second largest beneficiary of foreign military financing and to consume a lion's share of Economic Support Funds (ESF)—the funding stream over which the secretary of state theoretically retains the most flexibility to employ economic assistance in support of foreign policy goals.[7] By 2003 inclusion of additional

Table 7-1 Top Five Recipients of Foreign Military Financing

Billions of current dollars

1983		1993		2003	
Recipient	*Funding*	*Recipient*	*Funding*	*Recipient*	*Funding*
Israel	1.70	Israel	1.8	Israel	3.1
Egypt	1.30	Egypt	1.3	Egypt	1.3
Spain	0.40	Portugal	0.9	Jordan	0.60
Turkey	0.29	Turkey	0.45	Pakistan	0.22
Greece	0.28	Greece	0.32	Afghanistan	0.19

Sources: Defense Security Cooperation Agency, *Fact Book 2003, Fact Book 1999,* and *Fact Book 1989.*

countries from the Middle East and South Asia in the FMF program came at the expense of "southern tier" NATO allies, as table 7-1 shows.

Security assistance began to rise in the late 1990s, primarily due to an aggressive counternarcotics effort in the Andean region and renewed attention to coalition-building programs aimed at providing hardware, training, and support for potential regional allies. Security assistance experienced a further surge after the September 11 terrorist attacks, with FMF appropriations increasing dramatically to $6 billion in 2003—roughly 20 percent of the overall International Affairs budget.[8] This surge in military aid was spurred by three related factors: relaxed legal strictures regarding arms transfers, military assistance to states involved in the campaign to oust the Taliban and al Qaeda from Afghanistan, and increased counterterrorism assistance around the globe.[9] In addition, several new assistance programs were subsequently launched, most notably the Middle East Partnership Initiative, designed to promote political reform in a region where poor governance was deemed a contributory cause to terrorism and threats, and a major counternarcotics program in Afghanistan.

Counterterrorism

Immediately following the September 11, 2001, terrorist attacks, the Bush administration proposed a new unifying security paradigm in its "global war on terror." The phrase was far from felicitous: while it certainly emphasized American resolve—in particular not to sit idly by while terrorists gained access to weapons of mass destruction—it conflated many troubles into a single cause, overemphasized military means relative to other policy tools, including economic assistance, and was open to misinterpretation by many, especially in predominantly Muslim countries, as a struggle against Islam. The 2002 National Security Strategy, which defined this paradigm, stressed the national security threat posed by weapons of mass destruction under the control of actors with radical ideologies.[10] The 2002 strategy, and its successor published in early 2006, assumed that security and development were closely linked and stressed the need to resolve pressing foreign policy issues with a comprehensive, balanced approach. Among other steps, the administration has sought to redirect and expand strategic assistance in response to the reality that the broader Middle East is the primary source of radical terrorism driven by extremist anti-American and anti-Western ideologues.[11] The defeat of these terrorists is a central priority for U.S. policymakers; the process and strategy to achieve this goal is a central question for U.S. foreign policymakers today.

However, reducing U.S. foreign and security policy objectives to countering a tactic may create too narrow a focus. Indeed, even if Iraq has become a locus of terrorist activity, the security challenges and goals there, such as the promotion of democracy, are not all fundamentally related to terrorism. Ultimately, it may be more useful to move from counter-terrorism to a broader concept of countering military and security threats, irrespective of the adversaries' tactics.

Nonetheless, given its current importance, counterterrorism seems like the best category under which to organize some foreign assistance priorities and programs. The intervention to oust the Taliban was part of a larger strategic response to clamp down on radical Islamists and their sponsoring states. This broader strategy will require bolstering U.S. and allies' capabilities (such as intelligence, financial controls, and security forces) for counter-terrorism cooperation, economic development, and democratic reform. It will require providing alternatives to some of the underlying causes of support for terrorism and terrorists, including through programs targeting economic development to create jobs in at-risk countries. In addition, a broader strategy might encompass encouraging democratic reform among "strategic allies" in predominantly Islamic countries where the absence of good governance could bring about dangerous revolutions (Pakistan and Egypt, for instance).

In devising a comprehensive strategy to defeat terrorism in the Middle East and elsewhere, U.S. policymakers cannot afford too narrow a view of the challenges posed by the terror threat.[12] The broader Middle East comprises highly differentiated political, economic, and social environments. The United States has unique relations with individual countries in the region, ranging from close strategic ally to diplomatically frozen. There is no single model for promoting security and development in the Middle East and the majority-Islamic nations of South and Southeast Asia.

In addition to stanching the growing sectarian strife in Iraq and the resurgence of the Taliban in Afghanistan, U.S. strategies for security in the Middle East should focus on promoting cooperation in the war on extremism, general force transformation, and alliance building for pursuing terrorists. Within this last category, the United States must seek to bolster the military and security (including police) capacity in the Middle East as well as the civil society and governance capacity.

U.S. policymakers have an assortment of nonmilitary assistance tools to secure strategic goals in the Middle East and other nations targeted by international terrorists. They include economic support, democracy assistance, antiterrorism programs, "threat reduction" and nonproliferation assistance, and stabilization and reconstruction activities.

Tensions between Stability and Reform

Since the Camp David Accords, the vast majority of security assistance has been directed at a handful of countries in the Middle East. In addition to military assistance, the United States has provided tens of billions of dollars in economic assistance, which has served to build strategic relationships with governments and security forces in the region, especially Egypt, Israel, and Jordan. Significant budget support, major infrastructure projects, and effective expert advice on reform in key sectors have been provided on largely a grant basis by the State Department's Economic Support Fund. Many observers agree that this security assistance has encouraged certain states to adopt a more peaceful posture toward Israel and has sustained a democracy in Israel and moderate, stable regimes in Egypt and Jordan. These are no small achievements, to be sure.

Moreover, in Egypt and Jordan, millions benefit daily from clean water and modern wastewater infrastructure provided by U.S. government-funded programs. However, these economic assistance programs do not neatly translate into spreading American values and promoting democratic, market-oriented reforms. Egypt and Jordan, as well as other allies in the region including Saudi Arabia, are frequently cited for human rights abuses and political repression.[13] In both Egypt and Jordan, Islamic parties unsympathetic to the United States are poised to take power if the traditionally tough internal security regimes are relaxed and free elections occur. The Middle East is home to a growing population of anti-American extremists who threaten to challenge local governments and also spread terrorist violence and unrest. Why have U.S. security, economic, and other assistance programs not translated into more sweeping reforms in the Middle East? Is the U.S. goal political and economic modernization or simply stability? The balance (and paradox) of these two priorities drives U.S. foreign policy.

President George W. Bush offered one explanation for his administration's shift toward what many would call a more idealistic and ambitious goal of democratization in the Middle East:

> Sixty years of Western nations excusing and accommodating the lack of freedom in the Middle East did nothing to make us safe—because in the long run, stability cannot be purchased at the expense of liberty. As long as the Middle East remains a place where freedom does not flourish, it will remain a place of stagnation, resentment, and violence ready for export. . . . Therefore, the United States has adopted a new policy, a forward strategy of freedom in the Middle East.[14]

In many countries in the Middle East and South Asia, poor governance—manifested in repressive regimes, human rights abuses, and corruption—has contributed to the rise of anti-Western ideologies. Weak and poorly governed states are more susceptible to terrorism, organized crime, and civil war.[15] Without accountable and more transparent governance in each country, U.S. efforts are likely to be unproductive or at least only address short-term needs (stability) at the cost of long-term goals (political and economic modernization). But achieving better governance, which in turn is predicated on sound institutions and a pervasive culture of a rule of law, is particularly challenging and apt to be a long, drawn-out struggle.

There is bipartisan consensus among policymakers that improved governance and broader political, economic, and social freedom could alter the conditions that give rise to radical extremism in the Middle East. *The 9/11 Commission Report* stated that "a comprehensive U.S. strategy to counter terrorism should include economic policies that encourage development, more open societies, and opportunities for people to improve the lives of their families and to enhance prospects for their children's future."[16] The 2002 Arab Human Development Report published by the United Nations Development Program highlighted three major deficits that have held back human development in the region: "governance, women's empowerment, and access to knowledge."[17]

The Middle East Partnership Initiative

The Middle East Partnership Initiative (MEPI) is the Bush administration's central program in the region. MEPI, along with ESF appropriations, provides grants aimed at four different but related challenges or "deficits" that prevent greater openness and growth in the region: economic reform, political reform, women's empowerment, and education. MEPI represents an attempt to shift the strategic goals and centralize the management of U.S. security assistance to the Middle East. This policy change has had a major impact on the management of Economic Support Funds, which are the largest component of the initiative and the account from which specific MEPI projects are funded.

The basic rationale was that previous ESF to the region in general and Egypt in particular had yielded too little in the way of good governance. (If that were not the case, then why was there still so much concern over succession in Egypt and over the potential sudden rise to power of religious extremists?) Thus even as Congress mandated a steady reduction in ESF flowing to Israel and Egypt to support the historic Camp David Accords, the administration sought to add new security assistance funds through a separate line item for MEPI. Unfortunately, earmarking U.S. assistance money for controversial and necessarily somewhat intrusive programs in a region where the United States was especially unpopular was always going to be problematic. That is why some leaders inside and outside Congress sought to deliver the assistance through multilateral channels, whether the UN Development Program or a new regional or international fund not unlike the Global Fund for AIDS, Malaria, and Tuberculosis. Until the end of the 1990s, the State Department made country allocations of ESF and allowed the U.S. Agency for International Development (USAID) autonomy in programming and managing the implementation of these support fund appropriations. Currently, Congress makes country and regional program allocations in the annual Foreign Assistance Appropriation acts, while the State Department and the Office of Management and Budget dominate the selection of projects and cash payment terms. USAID continues in most instances to manage the implementation of U.S.-funded grants and contracts with private companies, nongovernmental organizations, and recipient governments.

Democratic reform and more accountable governance have not been a priority of U.S. strategic assistance to the region. Congressional attempts to link Middle East ESF to other human rights or economic issues had always been opposed and defeated by successive administrations. Nonetheless, lawmakers have sought to ensure that U.S. assistance supports a range of reforms. For Egypt only, Congress required that any portion provided as cash transfer "shall be provided with the understanding that Egypt will undertake economic reforms which are additional to those which were undertaken in previous fiscal years."[18] And indeed, cash payments as a percentage of ESF have declined, in part because this form of government-to-government assistance does not offer benchmarks for measuring results.

Today, MEPI provides smaller grants to American and Arab non-governmental organizations in hopes of strengthening Arab civil society and democratic governance. MEPI has provided parliamentary and municipal election support in Bahrain and women's legal rights training in Morocco (the political pillar), provided technical assistance for commercial law development in Algeria and trade technical assistance to Bahrain (the economic pillar), helped to set up the Internet in schools in Yemen and created an Arabic-language early reading program across the region (the education pillar), and created a family protection program in Jordan and entrepreneurship training for women across the region (the women's empowerment pillar).[19]

However, despite laudable intentions, overall U.S. assistance to the region does not offer measurable incentives to promote governance reform or disincentives to thwart it. Citing funding constraints and a lack of detail submitted in budgetary requests, Congress has appropriated less to MEPI than the president has requested. MEPI received $29 million in appropriations for fiscal year 2002, $90 million for fiscal year 2003, $89.5 million for fiscal year 2004, and $74.4 million for fiscal year 2005.[20] The administration is spending $120 million for fiscal year 2006 and has requested the same amount for fiscal year 2007.

The sheer difference between MEPI and FMF funding is staggering. In 2003, for instance, MEPI funds remained a minuscule 5.4 percent of the U.S. economic assistance package to the Middle East. Thus any strategically important government resisting reform can nonetheless count on receiving the great majority of its aid package intact. If democracy promotion is a primary goal, the budget does not reflect the rhetorical priorities. Middle Eastern leaders are far more apt to feel a cutoff of military assistance than they are the impact of small reform programs.

While rhetoric supporting good governance and democratic reform is attractive to U.S. policymakers, MEPI has failed to institute reliable, systematic criteria for measuring and evaluating results. This opens democracy and governance projects to charges that MEPI is not sufficiently committed to reform to support critical strategic goals. However, one must ask whether the partnership initiative is receiving sufficient funds for these efforts and whether the executive and legislative branches are prioritizing these budget items.

U.S. diplomacy toward its allies in the Middle East must continue to strike a delicate balance between focusing on governance assistance versus traditional project implementation support. In U.S. government-funded assistance to the Middle East, there is a tension between political and economic reform, on one hand, and stability, on the other. These two goals are not mutually exclusive; however, the transitions to political and economic reform can create instability. In addition, the United States has limited or no leverage in some countries, such as Saudi Arabia and Iran, for any reform. Trade, however, has become an increasingly important lever to promote reform and closer relationships within the region. The outcome of this complex balancing of interests, priorities, and relationships will determine the sustainability and success of assistance programs in the region in the long term.

Egypt: A Case Study in U.S. Ambivalence

The United States provides nearly $2 billion in security assistance to Egypt annually in the form of military and economic aid. U.S. aid to Egypt, which has flowed uninterrupted since 1974, has played a vital role in achieving American strategic objectives in the Middle East. It has been instrumental in establishing and sustaining peaceful relations between Israel and Egypt. U.S. economic aid has also led to improvements in Egyptian living standards, economic development, and U.S.-Egypt trade. Finally, U.S. assistance has helped strengthen the Egyptian central government, which has yielded a modicum of stability not just in Egypt but in the broader Middle East as well.

However, these achievements have come at a price. The Emergency Laws, which have extended since the assassination of President Anwar Sadat in 1981, continue to deny freedom of speech and freedom to organize, and ban political parties in Egypt. Loath to countenance democratic reforms, the Egyptian government has also been slow to enact economic reforms, which has contributed to economic stagnation and high unemployment rates. The recent parliamentary elections showed some signs of democratic liberalization, but the old phenomena of security force interference and low voter turnout remained.

Poor governance and the lack of economic and political freedom foment despair and unrest. Political repression, human rights abuses, and the grim economic outlook in Egypt propel radical Islamic extremists toward terrorism. Because the United States is linked to the government of Hosni Mubarak through its hefty assistance packages, many Egyptians view the United States as complicit in these crimes.

The Bush administration has expressed frustration with the pace of reform in Egypt and urged governance reform and improved human rights in the broader Middle East, including through a series of unprecedented public statements by Secretary of State Condoleezza Rice.[21] In addition, U.S. aid officials and lawmakers have fought to accelerate reform by shifting assistance resources to support nascent Egyptian civil society institutions. For instance, in June 2005 the House of Representatives for the first time mandated that $100 million of Egypt's $495 million ESF assistance package must be used for specific programs in education and democratic and economic reform.[22]

However, democracy assistance faces significant obstacles. The U.S.-Egypt bilateral aid agreement establishes the Egyptian government's right to veto any U.S.-funded assistance project or nongovernmental organization, which in the past has limited USAID in project selection and implementation.[23] Only in 2003 did Egypt begin to allow ESF funds to be disbursed directly to nongovernmental organizations providing technical assistance and training in support of governance reform rather than requiring these funds to go through the central government.[24]

Despite an increased emphasis on democracy promotion and economic reform in economic aid, traditional military assistance accounts for the bulk of U.S. assistance to Egypt. Since 1998 the United States provided Egypt with some $1.3 billion of military assistance each year—nearly 75 percent of total assistance to that country.[25] This aid plays a role in ensuring stability in the region, as Egypt's amplified force strength confers prestige upon its military establishment and commands respect from its Arab allies.[26]

As the United States started to draw down economic aid to Egypt in 1998, it began to elevate emphasis on trade. High-level cooperation during the Clinton administration resulted in a Trade and Investment Framework Agreement. Recently, the United States and Egypt established three Qualified Industrial Zones—in Alexandria, Cairo, and Port Said—to promote foreign investment.[27] A U.S.-Egypt free trade agreement could help to develop the Egyptian economy by as much as 3 percent, according to a study of the Institute for International Economics.[28] However, the Mubarak government has failed to implement fundamental economic reforms necessary to move forward on such an agreement.[29]

USAID programming has posted solid development gains but only modest reforms, especially in democratic governance. It has mainly disbursed congressionally appropriated ESF funds through cash transfers and technical assistance to the Egyptian government, which recommended or selected projects, institutions, and individuals for funding. USAID programs for physical infrastructure such as wastewater and to promote health have been successful. However, key economic and political reform programs, such as the $200 million in ESF funds paid annually to the Egyptian government by cash transfer "to improve economic policy," have created little impetus for reform.

The Bush administration is surely right that ending human rights abuses should be a priority in foreign affairs, not just because it is morally ethical but because it promotes a national security interest by supporting the long-term stability of states. However, resources and other instruments of persuasion do not appear to be applied according to these priorities.

The shift in U.S. economic assistance policy reflects a desire for reform. It is more than a cosmetic change but only a modest reorientation in terms of both dollars and content—in all likelihood too modest to affect governance in Egypt. Yet a dramatic shift in aid could undermine regime stability in Egypt, posing a high risk to U.S. security interests in the region. The effects on geopolitical stability in the Middle East and on Arab relations with Israel are hard to predict. Again, the balancing of reform and stability must be reconciled.

Counternarcotics

Moving foreign assistance away from cold war containment toward a more varied set of goals includes a second "C"—counternarcotics—which relates to ongoing efforts to combat the flow of illegal narcotics into the United States. The criminal networks responsible for the production and sale of illegal narcotics are a threat not only through their trade but also because their activities and funds can abet dangerous transnational threats such as radical terror groups and further weaken states that cannot enforce the rule of law. Indeed, production of hard narcotics is concentrated in states mired in conflict: 92 percent of the world's heroin is produced in Afghanistan, and 66 percent of the world's cocaine is produced from coca grown in Colombia.[30] While this is hardly a new threat, it is of heightened importance in the aftermath of September 11 and the Afghanistan campaign.

The ready, inexpensive supply of cocaine and heroin from the Andean region and Afghanistan, respectively, represents a major security challenge to the United States. In Colombia profits from the cocaine trade finance insurgent movements from both left-wing revolutionaries and right-wing paramilitaries. In Afghanistan a growing opium market is financing both fundamentalist insurgents and global terrorists, contributing both to the primary threat to the integrity and stability of the fledgling Afghan government and to the spread of global terrorism. The collapse of either state under pressure from destabilizing elements associated with the drug trade would imply serious consequences for the local, regional, and global security situation. U.S. counternarcotics policy must support states against collapse and cut off the funding flows to criminal and terrorist networks.

Both in the Andes and Afghanistan, the U.S. approach to counternarcotics has been organized into five core areas: eradication, interdiction, judicial reform, alternative development, and public information. Eradication, the most controversial of these policy tools, involves the destruction of crops either by aerial fumigation or by ground-based methods. Interdiction efforts target drug laboratories and major transit routes by deploying security forces to seize drug stocks, destroy processing facilities, and arrest traffickers. Judicial reforms are intended to strengthen weak legal institutions against the twin pressures of intimidation and corruption that prevent the enforcement of existing counternarcotics laws. Alternative development projects present local drug farmers with opportunities to develop legal economic livelihoods. Finally, public information efforts seek to undermine the perception of the drug trade as a legitimate activity.

In both Latin America and Central Asia, an effective counternarcotics policy will require an improved equilibrium between short-term tools of eradication and interdiction and long-term approaches such as alternative development and judicial reform. More emphasis on the latter tools would help build public support among poor farmers and ensure that wealthy traffickers are strongly deterred. The security and development aspects of counternarcotics efforts should be treated as complementary elements. For instance, the U.S. experience in Afghanistan indicates that alternative development and public information programs can make the difference when eradication efforts fail. From 2004 to 2005, poppy production actually decreased 48 percent even as the State Department reported that eradication programs for both years had been unsuccessful.[31]

Multiple agencies of the U.S. government share responsibility for developing, implementing, and coordinating counternarcotics policy, including specialized offices and bureaus within the White House, Department of Defense, Department of State, Department of Justice, and USAID. The White House Office of National Drug Control Policy, created in 1988, formally directs the policymaking process through the National Security Council. In addition to its leadership on domestic drug issues, the Office of National Drug Control Policy is charged with evaluating, coordinating, and overseeing the international antidrug efforts of all executive branch agencies.

The counternarcotics program is housed within Special Operations and Low-Intensity Conflict at the Department of Defense. The Defense Department is the lead federal agency for detecting and monitoring drug trafficking activities and plays a substantial role in drug enforcement training for U.S. and foreign authorities.[32] At the Department of State, the Bureau for International Narcotics and Law Enforcement Affairs (INL) is charged with supporting the U.S. government's priorities in reducing drug imports and minimizing the impact of international crime. The INL is involved in eradication and interdiction efforts alongside the Defense Department and also coordinates capacity-building programs aimed at reform and strengthening of law enforcement and judicial systems.

The INL relies heavily on the Department of Justice and USAID to implement its mandated functions. At the Department of Justice, the Drug Enforcement Agency takes the lead in working with its drug law enforcement counterparts in foreign countries. USAID is the primary agent for implementing alternative development programs, though such work is increasingly subcontracted out to nongovernmental organizations. As table 7-2 shows, the balance of counternarcotics resources between the

Table 7-2 National Drug Control Budget, 2005–07

Millions of dollars

Agency	Fiscal year		
	2005 (final)	2006 (enacted)	2007 (requested)
Department of Defense	1,147.8	936.1	926.9
Department of State	1,165.1	1,056.7	1,166.7

Source: Office of National Drug Control Policy, *National Drug Control Strategy: FY 2007 Budget Summary* (Executive Office of the President, February 2006).

Department of Defense and the Department of State, the two primary spending agencies, has been relatively even over the past several years.

Andean Counterdrug Initiative

The Andean Counterdrug Initiative (ACI), managed by the INL, is the primary U.S. counternarcotics program in Colombia, Bolivia, and Peru.[33] From 2000 through 2005, the ACI received approximately $4.3 billion. An additional $734 million was appropriated for fiscal year 2006, and the administration has requested $721.5 million for fiscal year 2007. With fully 90 percent of the U.S. cocaine supply passing through its borders, Colombia receives over 60 percent of ACI funding annually.[34] ACI supports Plan Colombia, a six-year national counternarcotics plan enacted by President Andres Pastrana (1998–2002) and continued by President Alvaro Uribe, which will soon come up for review.

ACI's objectives are "to eliminate the cultivation and production of cocaine and opium, build law enforcement infrastructure, arrest and prosecute traffickers, and seize their assets."[35] In addition to eradication and interdiction efforts, ACI also supports alternative development and "institution-building" programs, though independent reviews have been very critical of their progress.[36] Fiscal year 2006 appropriations for ACI in Colombia totaled $469.5 million, with roughly two-thirds of funding dedicated to interdiction—leaving only one-third of the total for alternative development, institution building, and promotion of the rule of law.[37] (See table 7-3.)

Table 7-3 Fiscal Year 2006 Andean Counterdrug Appropriations, Colombia

Millions of dollars

Programs	Funding
Interdiction	310.9
Alternative development and institution building	131.2
Rule of law promotion	27.4
Total	469.5

Source: Connie Veillette, "Andean Counterdrug Initiative (ACI) and Related Funding Programs: FY2006 Assistance," RL33253 (CRS, January 27, 2006).

Afghanistan Counternarcotics Program

Since the fall of the Taliban regime in late 2001, narcotics trafficking has become an increasing source of instability in Afghanistan, which now supplies about 87 percent of the world's illicit opium trade.[38] The Afghan government and international authorities launched eradication programs in spring 2002 and again in 2003, first with the promise of cash compensation and then with the promise of reconstruction projects. Both programs faced serious credibility issues with farmers as a result of irregular delivery of promised assistance, and thus poppy cultivation rapidly expanded both in total area and number of provinces.[39] CARE International and the Center on International Cooperation strongly criticized U.S. and U.K. officials for pledging development assistance to rural populations cultivating poppies and then failing to deliver on their promises after eradication efforts.[40] With the export value of opium valued at $2.8 billion—over half the size of the licit Afghan economy—such failures of public confidence could have serious political ramifications in undermining the Karzai administration in upcoming parliamentary elections.[41]

In November 2004 the State Department's International Narcotics and Law Enforcement Bureau launched a renewed interagency initiative to support counternarcotics programs in Afghanistan. Referred to as "Plan Afghanistan" by former INL assistant secretary Robert Charles, the initiative's efforts focused on the five pillars of eradication, interdiction, judicial reform, alternative development, and public information.[42] In fiscal year 2005, the U.S. government spent $966.19 million on counternarcotics activities in Afghanistan, much of it appropriated in the 2005 emergency supplemental for Iraq and Afghanistan.[43] The administration requested $433.7 million for fiscal 2006, and data are not yet available on budget allocations for the year.

Prospects and Constraints

The results of counternarcotics efforts in Afghanistan and the Andes are unclear. With counternarcotics assistance to Afghanistan becoming substantial only in the past few years, initial results are hard to judge. The fragile political situation also leaves much room for concern. In contrast, there are five years of operations to assess in Colombia, Bolivia, and Peru. Globally, the Office of National Drug Control Policy notes the achievement of "a 33 percent decline in coca cultivation over the past two years" and "since

2001, [prevention of] the production of over 500 metric tons of cocaine."[44] However, as figure 7-1 indicates, the street price of cocaine has fallen dramatically over the last decade, and press reports indicate that it has held steady over the past several years of sustained counternarcotics efforts.[45] While the price drop could reflect diminished demand, the availability of inexpensive cocaine casts doubt on the claim that counternarcotics efforts in the Andes have been successful.

Both the Council on Foreign Relations and the International Crisis Group, two respected independent foreign policy organizations, have released major reports recently highlighting the failures of global counternarcotics efforts.[46] As both reports note, security and development approaches offer complementary tools for combating the security threat posed by illicit narcotics. It is essential for policymakers to place greater emphasis on difficult questions of economic development and governance

Figure 7-1 Decline in Street Price of Cocaine, United States, 1990–2003

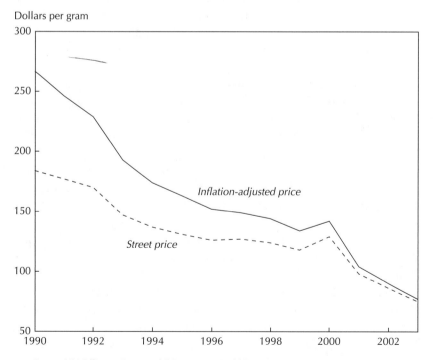

Source: UN Office on Drugs and Crime, *2005 World Drug Report (Vienna: 2005).*

when approaching the drug-trade problem. Without supporting the development of legal economies and political institutions that are both effective and accountable, efforts to stem the supply of illicit narcotics and choke off related financing for insurgent and terrorist groups will remain ultimately unsuccessful.

Coalition Building

Security assistance is a critical tool for building coalitions—whether ad hoc coalitions of the willing or extant or longer-term alliances—in support of U.S. national security goals. Economic and military assistance can build coalition support not only for interventions (as in Afghanistan and Iraq) but also for both general and specific efforts to combat Islamic extremism, promote peace processes, and implement peace agreements (as in the Middle East and Sudan), as well as for other major U.S. foreign policy initiatives as they arise (from United Nations Security Council votes to particular assistance with a national security priority). As with other forms of security assistance, an inherent tension often arises between the use of assistance to achieve immediate coalition-building goals versus sustained improvements in governance and human rights. In some cases the United States is concurrently providing support both to an allied government and to nongovernmental actors seeking that government's reform.

At the policy level, military assistance to some "allies" sparks regular criticism for bolstering political regimes with poor governance records in order to build a coalition. This tension between focused national security objectives and broader human rights and development goals will not be easily resolved, but it still deserves much greater public discussion. At the organizational level, critics have charged that the State Department has yielded significant ground to the Defense Department in the current military buildup, undermining a traditional check and balance in foreign assistance policymaking. Finally, typical implementation challenges have included the lack of flexibility that frontline operators confront due to the nature of congressional appropriations, which seek accountability by restricting the use of funds, often to specific sectoral projects.

As highlighted in the 2005 U.S. National Defense Strategy, government-to-government assistance to help train and equip allied national forces is "one of our military's most effective tools in prosecuting the Global War on Terrorism."[47] Until recently, military assistance programs were implemented by the Defense Department under State Department policy guidance, and training programs were the exclusive responsibility of the State Department. Critical delays in the training and effective deployment of the Iraqi and Afghan national armies and police forces have been widely acknowledged as key constraints to providing adequate security in both countries. Recently, Congress agreed to the president's request to provide all appropriations for training and supporting indigenous security forces in Iraq and Afghanistan directly to the Department of Defense. But as these cases and numerous others have shown, executing successful military assistance programs is extremely difficult work, complicated by policy disputes, organizational imbalances, and implementation challenges.

By congressional mandate responsibility for military assistance programs is shared by the Department of State and the Department of Defense. The secretary of state through the State Department Bureau of Political-Military Affairs supervises security assistance programs; this includes selecting the eligible countries and determining the scope and content of their assistance packages. The secretary of defense directs implementation of the programs, primarily the transfer of defense articles and services from government to government. Within the Defense Department, the Defense Security Cooperation Agency manages arms sales and military education programs.

There are two primary military assistance programs. The Foreign Military Financing program provides grants and loans to enable strategic allies and friendly nations to purchase U.S. weapons, equipment, and services. The International Military Education and Training program provides military training to allies and friendly nations on a grant basis. In addition, there are two additional programs for assisting global conflict resolution efforts: the Peacekeeping Operations account, which supports voluntary multinational peacekeeping efforts where no formal cost-sharing mechanism is in place, and the Contributions for International Peacekeeping Activities account, which is the main channel for support to UN-mandated peacekeeping activities. Finally, in 2005 President Bush established the Global Peace Operations Initiative, designed to increase the capacity of other nations in peacekeeping activities. This program receives funding from within the Peacekeeping Operations account. Table 7-4 lists funding trends for these four programs from 2005 through 2007 and shows that FMF has held steady at roughly three quarters of overall funding, even as the amount of U.S. military assistance has fluctuated over the past three years.

Table 7-4 U.S. Military Assistance Programs, including 2005 Emergency Supplemental Appropriations

Millions of dollars

	Fiscal year		
Program	2005 (actual)	2006 (estimated)	2007 (requested)
Foreign Military Financing	4,995	4,465	4,551
International Military Education and Training	89	86	89
Peacekeeping Operations	548	173	201
Contributions to International Peacekeeping Activities	1,219	1,277	1,329
Total military assistance	6,851	6,001	6,170

Source: Department of State, "FY 2007 Budget in Brief," February 6, 2006 (www.state.gov/s/d/rm/rls/bib/2007/).

The fiscal year 2005 Emergency Supplemental increased military assistance by augmenting both the FMF and the Peacekeeping Operations funds. These added expenditures paid for peacekeeping operations in Sudan and increased FMF for Jordan and Pakistan. The supplemental also included two new accounts: an Afghanistan Security Forces Fund ($1.3 billion) and an Iraq Security Forces Fund ($5.7 billion), which more than doubled the size of military assistance programs.[48] In both cases the funds are intended to finance the training, equipping, and deploying of national security forces (including military, protective services, border personnel, and, in the case of Iraq, police). In addition, these funds are intended to support the building of infrastructure and capabilities within the Afghan and Iraqi governments to take over the development of their own security forces.

Coalition Building: Prospects and Constraints

As exceptional cases of military assistance, Iraq and Afghanistan are considered too important to fail by the Bush administration. Despite this, both have faced serious challenges. At present the primary hope for a successful U.S. exit is a legitimate political transition and rapid scale-up of national security forces. In both countries progress on security sector reform has been slow and hampered by political, financial, and security obstacles. In Afghanistan early recruits for the new Afghan National Army drew heavily from the Tajik ethnic group that made up the Northern Alliance political leadership, causing Pashtun tribal leaders to complain of ethnic bias. In addition, salary scales put initial recruit pay at $70 a month, less than many private sector opportunities for able-bodied men.[49] In Iraq, where similar obstacles emerged, insurgents have aggressively targeted the Iraqi police and military, including their recruiting stations.

In late March 2005, Pakistan made headlines when the U.S. engaged in talks to sell F-16s to the country as an incentive for greater political and military cooperation. The announcement by Secretary Rice sparked public protest from India, which warned against disturbing the military balance with its regional rival, and opposition from congressional leaders concerned about proliferation of sophisticated military technology.[50] In the post–September 11 period, Washington has depended heavily on its strategic relationship with Islamabad to topple the Taliban regime it had helped bring to power in Afghanistan and to contribute to regional counterterrorist and counter-narcotics efforts. Still, the deal raised serious questions about the trade-offs inherent in military assistance, such as the value of creating a new strategic alliance at the risk of undermining a traditional relationship and increasing the military power of an unstable regime. Also, the implications remain unclear, both in strategic terms and with regard to America's global reputation, of the decision to provide assistance to a military regime on an uncertain path toward democracy, especially with the subsequent revelations of Abdul Qadeer Khan's role in the proliferation of nuclear technologies.

Given recent media coverage, Uzbekistan also presents a timely case study of the tension in security assistance between coalition-building objectives and America's commitment to human rights and development norms. In May 2005, in the city of Andijan, a crackdown by Uzbek security forces on a demonstration left at least 170 dead, although opposition groups claim the number of deaths was in the low thousands. Controversially, many of the military units apparently involved in the event had received U.S. security assistance over the past several years, primarily as support for Uzbekistan's role as an ally in the Afghanistan campaign and broader counterterrorism efforts.[51] Initially, State and Defense Department officials disagreed over the need to demand an independent investigation, with Secretary Rice supporting the proposal on human rights grounds and Secretary Rumsfeld demonstrating concern for the strength of the U.S. military alliance with Uzbekistan.[52] The Defense Department position has apparently prevailed but not without criticism from a bipartisan group of six senators who warned that "in the aftermath of the Andijan massacre, America's relationship with Uzbekistan cannot remain unchanged."[53] Ties between Uzbekistan and the United States have become increasingly strained, with the U.S. closing its military hub there later in 2005.

Similar to counterterrorism and counternarcotics efforts, the effectiveness of traditional military aid programs is difficult to judge. Is it sufficient, for example, to measure the number of troops trained, or the volume of arms delivered, when the primary objective is the creation and strengthening of alliances deemed essential to U.S. national security? How do you measure the strength of an alliance: in small and large favors over time? And with which countries, if any, are we unwilling to form alliances? Commitment to human rights norms is a defining characteristic of American values in the global arena, but how do we confront trade-offs between security cooperation and national values?

Military assistance programs have had a mixed record of success, including some of the most public failures of U.S. foreign policy such as the Vietnam War and the Iran-Contra scandal. Furthermore, interpretations of the strength of alliances built through military aid and the influence gained through assistance are deeply contested both within and outside government. The establishment of an independent monitoring task force or commission dedicated to reviewing the objectives and progress of U.S. military assistance programs might be a valuable first step in resolving this dilemma. Such an undertaking, directed by a board of retired eminent military and foreign service officers, could report regularly to Congress on the difficult evaluation issues raised here.

Counterproliferation

Many security strategists see the control of weapons of mass destruction (WMD) by terrorist organizations as the preeminent threat to U.S. and global security today and for some years ahead.[54] The Lugar Survey on Proliferation Threats and Responses estimated that the combined risk of a WMD attack over five years is as high as 50 percent; over the next ten years, however, the risk rises to as much as 70 percent.[55]

Meeting the proliferation threat is a two-part challenge, and foreign assistance can provide important support for solutions to each of these challenges. First, the United States must continue its efforts to dismantle weapons and restrict the movement of WMD across borders. This has been a major U.S. objective in the past fifteen years, since the launching of the Nunn-Lugar legislation that created new authorities for dismantling and controlling the massive stockpiles of weapons left over from the cold war.

This objective was given greater urgency after the terrorist attacks of September 11, 2001, and other attacks in cities worldwide raised the specter of nuclear weapons falling into terrorist hands. A second critical objective is dealing with new or nascent nuclear programs in states such as Iran, North Korea, India, and Pakistan. This section will consider foreign assistance as it applies to the first challenge.

Across different agencies the United States is estimated to spend over $1 billion on international nonproliferation programs in fiscal year 2007. In 2002 the United States committed to maintain this level of expenditure until 2012 as part of the G-8 Global Partnership against the Spread of Weapons and Materials of Mass Destruction, otherwise known as "10 plus 10 over 10." Under the program, the United States formally committed to spend $10 billion on nonproliferation projects in Russia over ten years. The U.S. funding is to be matched by the rest of the G-8 nations over the same period of time.

Counterproliferation security assistance is administered primarily by three different departments. The Department of Defense receives most of its counterproliferation appropriations as part of the Nunn-Lugar Cooperative Threat Reduction program, for which the department requested $372.2 million for 2007.[56] The Cooperative Threat Reduction program mainly focuses on the elimination of nuclear, biological, and chemical weapons and weapons infrastructure in Russia and the Ukraine, as well as improving security for the transport and storage of weapons in Russia. Since 1991 this program and others in different agencies have provided American technical expertise and over $9 billion for cooperative projects to safeguard and destroy WMD and related materials, technology, and infrastructure and to prevent the proliferation of WMD expertise. As of 2005 the program had destroyed or dismantled a total of 6,632 warheads and is expected to increase that number to 8,567 by 2012.[57]

The Department of Energy requested $834.4 million for nonproliferation programs in the 2007 budget.[58] Nearly one-third of the Energy Department's nonproliferation spending goes toward Russia and the former Soviet republics, supporting programs to protect WMD materials and expertise from terrorists and to dismantle nuclear reactors. These programs redirect 8,200 former WMD personnel to peaceful employment every year and are helping power plants transition to lower-enriched uranium or fossil fuels.[59] The rest of the department's nonproliferation funding is used domestically for fissile materials disposition and to secure sources of nuclear material for homeland security purposes.

The Department of State manages the Export Control and Related Border Security Assistance program for radiation detection and other assistance to interdict nuclear smuggling. It requested $45 million for this program in fiscal year 2007. The Export Control program has been credited for strengthened export control systems in countries such as the Czech Republic, Hungary, Bulgaria, Romania, Latvia, Poland, Estonia, and Lithuania.[60] The State Department also supports efforts to redirect WMD scientific expertise. It was responsible for completely dismantling Libya's uranium enrichment program in 2004 and has played a key role in redirecting Iraqi WMD experts to peaceful employment.

The Proliferation Security Initiative (PSI) was announced on May 31, 2003, as an international partnership of countries to coordinate efforts to interdict the transport of nuclear, biological, and chemical weapons. According to the State Department's Bureau of Nonproliferation, the PSI is neither a formal institution nor a treaty organization but a statement of purpose in support of interdiction of nuclear technologies based on countries' "ability and willingness to contribute."[61] The program is operated by the State Department, and it is unclear exactly how it is funded. So far participant countries have carried out several joint interdiction exercises and shared intelligence about proliferation threats. The State Department has credited cooperation between the United States and ten different participant countries with eleven successful interdiction efforts.[62] In addition, under the auspices of the PSI, the United States has signed ship-boarding agreements with Belize, Croatia, Cyprus, Liberia, Panama, and the Marshall Islands.

The PSI represents a shift in U.S. counterproliferation strategy to better address the possibility that terrorists could acquire WMD via international smuggling. Since the United States is unable to secure all borders and interdict all smuggling unilaterally, it is crucial that it encourage cooperation from other nations on interdiction efforts. Smuggling threats also no longer lie solely in the former Soviet Union, where most counterproliferation efforts have been focused. Intelligence sharing, training exercises, and ship boarding agreements all help bolster international interdiction capacity and are a step in the right direction. However, the State Department has been unclear about the details of PSI programs and which countries have participated. It would be difficult at this time to assess the effectiveness of the initiative without inside information.

Counterproliferation programs have produced quantifiable results and tremendous gains in Russia and the countries of the former Soviet Union. The impact of threat reduction and nonproliferation assistance undoubtedly extends far beyond the localized region of the former Soviet Union. There is growing awareness today of the threat posed by the possible acquisition of nuclear, chemical, and biological weapons by fragile states and terrorist groups. This threat has led to calls, including from President Bush, to expand threat reduction and counterproliferation assistance to regions outside the countries of the former Soviet Union.[63]

There has been some limited movement in that direction, with an increase in the fungibility of some funding for counterproliferation. The fiscal year 2004 National Defense Authorization Act allows the administration to use up to $50 million in unobligated funds from the Defense Department's Cooperative Threat Reduction program in nations outside the former Soviet Union. A similar provision permits the president to use up to $50 million in unobligated funds from the Depart of Energy's international nuclear materials protection and cooperation programs. The State Department's $40 million (in fiscal year 2005) Nonproliferation and Disarmament Fund functions as a contingency fund to enable rapid response to nonproliferation targets of opportunity and is not used to fund substantial, ongoing cooperative threat reduction programs.

A prevailing issue for managing counterproliferation assistance is the relative balance between focusing on emergency response and controlling the marketplace for weapons materials and expertise. Countries that have already acquired WMD or that are known to seek such weapons are often mentioned as potential recipients of nonproliferation assistance. These countries include India, Pakistan, and Iran. However, it is not likely that assistance would act as a credible incentive to reduce weapons programs. Counterproliferation assistance aimed at stopping the movement of nuclear scientists and materials over to illicit nuclear operations should continue to focus on the countries of the former Soviet Union. Threat reduction and nonproliferation assistance to support counterproliferation in these countries would be more likely to succeed if included in a broader package of military, economic, and political incentives focused on achieving specific goals.[64]

Conclusion and Recommendations

Looking to the future of security and strategic assistance programs, the central challenge for U.S. policymakers and implementers is to create a comprehensive strategy to strengthen the relationship between security and development of better governance. Military counterterrorism efforts cannot be successful without a full complement of judicial and law enforcement, nonproliferation, and stabilization and reconstruction initiatives to address the weak states that provide a launching pad for terrorist groups. Likewise, counternarcotics efforts in Afghanistan and the Andes will not be successful until alternative livelihoods and judicial reform programs are as effective as interdiction and eradication initiatives. Finally, in an ongoing climate of global insecurity, coalition building through traditional military aid and narrowly focused economic support will remain an important foreign policy priority, with tensions between U.S. national security objectives and U.S. commitment to human rights and development norms remaining an ongoing point of debate.

In the post–September 11 environment, the burden will fall to U.S. government officials to lead in bridging the security-development gap. Committed leadership and thoughtful, balanced decisionmaking throughout the interagency process as well as meaningful consultation between the executive and legislative branches of government are all essential to achieving U.S. foreign policy objectives. With a clear setting of goals and a relentless focus on providing the necessary resources and strategic planning to achieve those results, much more is possible.

With this in mind, we make the following policy recommendations. First, Congress should request a complete administration review of security assistance programs: objectives, priorities, management and oversight, accountability, and lessons learned from past programs. To the extent that the administration is serious about "transformational" diplomacy, it should demonstrate how economic aid programs can contribute to such strategic goals. The State Department may well need new authorities to help flexibly move funds to different programs, but the quid pro quo for increased flexibility should be more transparent accountability to Congress.

Second, the Middle East Partnership Initiative should be canceled if demonstrable successes cannot be documented after five years of spending. The administration should consider contributing to a multilateral international fund in which the United States is only a minority partner. At the same time, it may be that more rather than less foreign assistance is required to support democracy and governance programs.

Third, counternarcotics programs, particularly for Afghanistan, should focus on a far more creative range of solutions, ranging from eradication at one extreme to ideas such as legalizing opium to support a legal, international need for medicine. In a country like Afghanistan, where more than half of the nation's economy is driven by the trafficking in opium, there is a strong necessity to provide incentives and real alternatives for the many people whose livelihood depends on an illegal drug.

Notes

1. *Security assistance* is defined in the Department of Defense dictionary as a "group of programs authorized by the Foreign Assistance Act of 1961, as amended, and the Arms Export Control Act of 1976, as amended, or other related statutes by which the United States provides defense articles, military training, and other defense related services by grant, loan, credit, or cash sales in furtherance of national policies and objectives." See "Department of Defense Dictionary of Military and Associated Terms," as amended through April 14, 2006 (www.dtic.mil/doctrine/jel/doddict/data/s/04768.html).

2. See Lael Brainard, chapter 1 in this volume.

3. See Patrick Cronin, chapter 6 in this volume.

4. For example, see Government Accountability Office, *Reporting of Defense Articles and Services Provided through Drawdowns Needs to Be Improved,* GAO-02-1027 (September 2002), and *U.S. Efforts to Help Other Countries Combat Nuclear Smuggling Need Strengthened Coordination and Planning,* GAO-02-426 (May 2002).

5. For reviews of cold war security assistance history, see Ernest Graves, "Security Assistance and Arms Sales," *Washington Quarterly* 14, no. 3 (1991): 47; Stephanie Neuman, "Arms, Aid and the Superpowers," *Foreign Affairs* 66, no. 5 (1988): 1044.

6. John Hillen, "The Changing Nature of the Political-Military Interface," remarks presented at the Joint Worldwide Planning Conference, Garmisch, Germany, November 30, 2005 (www.state.gov/t/pm/rls/rm/58189.htm).

7. Carol Migdalovitz, "Israel: Background and Relations with the United States," Issue Brief 82008 (Congressional Research Service [CRS], U.S. Library of Congress, Issue Brief for Congress, updated March 16, 2006).

8. For a more detailed analysis of recent foreign military sales, see Richard F. Grimmett, "U.S. Arms Sales: Agreements with and Deliveries to Major Clients, 1996–2003," RL 32689 (CRS, December 8, 2004).

9. Human Rights Watch, "Dangerous Dealings: Changes to U.S. Military Assistance after September 11," February 2002 (hrw.org/reports/2002/usmil).

10. White House, *The National Security Strategy of the United States of America* (September 2002). These themes are also emphasized in the 2006 National Security Strategy.

11. The *broader Middle East* is a term that includes Pakistan, Afghanistan, and North Africa.

12. It is useful to think of the terrorist threat as consisting of three circles. The first circle consists of al Qaeda leadership, including Osama Bin Laden, members of which are being captured or killed. The second circle is made up of combatants who adhere to a transnational ideology of terror. This group has emerged in response to local conflict and political conditions and includes Hamas and Hezbollah. The third circle comprises a decentralized group of "freelancers" and roving jihadists whose size, operational capabilities, and influence are largely immeasurable. See Philippe Errera, "Three Circles of Threat," *Survival* 47, no. 1 (2005): 71–88.

13. For a review of human rights abuses, see Human Rights Watch, *World Report 2006* (February 2006).

14. White House, "President George W. Bush Discusses Freedom in Iraq and Middle East," remarks at the 20th Anniversary of the National Endowment for Democracy, U.S. Chamber of Commerce, Washington, November 6, 2003 (www.whitehouse.gov/news/releases/2003/11/20031106-2.html).

15. U.S. Agency for International Development, *Foreign Aid in the National Interest* (2002).

16. National Commission on Terrorist Attacks upon the United States, "What To Do? A Global Strategy," in *The 9/11 Commission Report* (Government Printing Office, 2004), section 12.3, p. 379.

17. United Nations Development Programme, *Arab Human Development Report: Creating Opportunities for Future Generations* (Geneva: 2002).

18. *Consolidated Appropriations Act, 2005*, H. Rept. 4818, 108 Cong. 2 sess. (December 8, 2004), p. 118, stat. 2976.

19. For more on specific programs funded by MEPI, see Office of the Spokesman, Department of State, "Department's Mideast Partnership Funds over 100 Programs: Fact Sheet," March 9, 2005 (usinfo.state.gov/mena/Archive/2005/Mar/09-625548.html [April 17, 2006]).

20. Jeremy Sharp, "The Middle East Partnership Initiative: An Overview," RS21457 (CRS, updated February 8, 2005). For information on the fiscal year 2007 budget request, see Department of State, "FY 2007 International Affairs (Function 150) Budget Request" (www.state.gov/s/d/rm/rls/iab [May 2006]). MEPI funds are listed under ESF.

21. David Rogers, "House Panel's Bill Requires Egypt to Spend Aid on Rights Promotion," *Wall Street Journal,* June 22, 2005, p. A4.

22. Ibid.

23. Ibid.

24. Neil King Jr., "Tentative Steps: Democracy Drive By. America Meets Reality in Egypt," *Wall Street Journal,* April 11, 2005, p. A1.

25. Jeremy Sharp, "Egypt-United States Relations," Issue Brief 93087 (CRS, updated: June 15, 2005).

26. Force quality and readiness issues limit Egypt's ability to make effective use of its modern weapons. See Anthony Cordesman, *The Arab-Israeli States Military Balance: National Force Development and Trends,* working draft (Washington: Center for Strategic and International Studies, 2005).

27. Egypt-U.S. Business Council, "Qualified Industrial Zone" (www.us-egypt.org/en/programs/qiz.asp [April 2006]).

28. Ahmed Galal and Robert Z. Lawrence, *Anchoring Reform with a US-Egypt Free Trade Agreement* (Washington: Institute for International Economics, May 2005).

29. Bessma Momani, "Promoting Economic Liberalization in Egypt: From U.S. Foreign Aid to Trade and Investment," *Middle East Review of International Affairs* 7, no. 3 (2003): 88–101.

30. National Drug Intelligence Center, "National Drug Threat Assessment 2006," Document 2006-Q0317-001 (Department of Justice, January, 2006).

31. Office of National Drug Control Policy, "Estimated Poppy Cultivation in Afghanistan," press release, November 23, 2005.

32. Department of Defense, "Counternarcotics Mission Statement" (www.defenselink. mil/policy/sections/policy_offices/solic/cn/mission.html [May 2006]).

33. ACI is complemented by an additional set of U.S. foreign assistance programs targeting the Andean region, including Foreign Military Financing, International Military Training and Education, Development Assistance, Child Survival and Health, and the Economic Support Fund. Other countries covered under ACI include Brazil, Ecuador, Panama, and Venezuela.

34. Connie Veillette, "Andean Counterdrug Initiative (ACI) and Related Funding Programs: FY2006 Assistance," RL33253 (CRS, January 27, 2006).

35. Ibid.

36. For example, see Government Accountability Office, "Drug Control: Efforts to Develop Alternatives to Cultivating Illicit Crops in Colombia Have Made Little Progress and Face Serious Obstacles," GAO-02-291 (February 8, 2002).

37. The requests for Peru and Bolivia were $112 million and $90 million, respectively.

38. Christopher M. Blanchard, "Afghanistan: Narcotics and U.S. Policy," RL32686 (CRS, updated May 26, 2005). In addition, congressional hearings have recently explored the likelihood that drug profits are financing terrorist group activities.

39. William Byrd and Christopher Ward, "Drugs and Development in Afghanistan," Social Development Papers, Conflict Prevention and Reconstruction, no. 18 (Washington: World Bank, December 2004).

40. CARE International and the Center on International Cooperation, "Counternarcotics Policy in Afghanistan: Too Early to Declare Success," Afghanistan Policy Brief (March 2005).

41. Larry Goodson, "Afghanistan in 2004: Electoral Progress and Opium Boom," *Asian Survey* 45, no. 1(2005): 93.

42. Robert B. Charles, "Counternarcotics Initiatives for Afghanistan," State Department On-the-Record Briefing, Washington, November 17, 2004 (www.state.gov/p/inl/rls/prsrl/spbr/38352.htm).

43. Blanchard, "Afghanistan: Narcotics and U.S. Policy."

44. Office of National Drug Control Policy, "John P. Waters, Director of the White House Office of National Drug Control Policy" (www.whitehousedrugpolicy.gov/about/director_bio.html [April 2006]).

45. "The Price of Powder," *Economist,* November 25, 2004, p. 65.

46. International Crisis Group, "War and Drugs in Colombia," Latin American Report no. 11 (Washington: January 27, 2005); Council on Foreign Relations, *Andes 2020: A New Strategy for the Challenges of Colombia and the Region* (Washington: January 2004).

47. Department of Defense, "The National Defense Strategy of the United States of America" (March 2005).

48. Both funds are to be managed by the Department of Defense.

49. Tom Coghlan, "Afghans Flee Army over Taliban and Low Morale," *Daily Telegraph,* June 9, 2005 (www.telegraph.co.uk/news/main.jhtml?xml=/news/2005/06/09/wtal09.xml&sSheet=/news/2005/06/09/ixworld.html [July 2006]).

50. Amy Klamper, "House Lawmakers Attempt to Block F-16 Sales to Pakistan," *CongressDaily,* April 15, 2005.

51. C. J. Chivers and Thom Shanker, "Uzbek Ministries in Crackdown Received U.S. Aid," *New York Times,* June 18, 2005, p. 1.

52. R. Jeffrey Smith and Glenn Kessler, "U.S. Opposed Calls at NATO for Probe of Uzbek Killings," *Washington Post,* June 14, 2005, p. A15.

53. Ibid.

54. For more on the scope of the threat, see Daniel Benjamin, "Terrorist Groups: The Quest for Apocalyptic Capabilities," in *The Challenge of Proliferation: A Report from the Aspen Strategy Group,* edited by Kurt M. Campbell (Washington: Aspen, 2005), pp. 43–52

55. Richard G. Lugar, "The Lugar Survey on Proliferation Threats and Responses," June 2005 (lugar.senate.gov/reports/NPSurvey.pdf [July 2006]).

56. William Hoehn, "Preliminary Analysis of the U.S. Department of Defense's Fiscal Year 2007 Cooperative Threat Reduction Budget Request," Policy update (Washington: Russian American Nuclear Security Advisory Council [RANSAC], March 2006).

57. Jeffrey Read, "Reported Accomplishments of Selected Threat Reduction and Nonproliferation Programs, by Agency, for Fiscal Year 2004," Policy update (Washington: RANSAC, July 2005).

58. Hoehn, "Preliminary Analysis."

59. Read, "Reported Accomplishments of Selected Threat Reduction."

60. Ibid.

61. Department of State, Bureau of Nonproliferation, "The Proliferation Security Initiative" (www.state.gov/t/isn/rls/other/34726.htm [July 2006]).

62. Stephen G. Rademaker, Assistant Secretary of State for Arms Control, "The Proliferation Security Initiative (PSI): A Record of Success," Testimony before the House International Relations Committee, Subcommittee on International Terrorism and Nonproliferation, Washington, June 9, 2005 (www.state.gov/t/ac/rls/rm/47715.htm [May 2006]).

63. White House, "President Announces New Measures to Counter the Threat of WMD," Remarks at Fort Lesley J. McNair–National Defense University, February 11, 2004 (www.whitehouse.gov/news/releases/2004/02/20040211-4.html).

64. Amy F. Woolf, "Expanding Threat Reduction and Nonproliferation Programs: Concepts and Definitions," RS21840 (CRS, October 5, 2004).

CHAPTER 8

Removing Impediments to an Effective Partnership with Congress

Charles Flickner

ontemporary congressional interest in foreign assistance is generally limited to areas of concern to one or more members, often manifested in the form of "hundreds of congressional directives and special budget measures," known as earmarks.[1] If a core problem in foreign aid is to "strike a balance between legitimate oversight of how tax dollars are spent and counterproductive overregulation," Congress is neglecting its lawmaking and oversight role and intruding into the realm of the executive through its attempts to manage aid implementation.[2]

There is no evidence that more than a handful of elected members of the U.S. federal legislature ponder the broad concepts discussed elsewhere in this volume. Dealing with child survival or girls' education is more concrete than struggling to fix failed states. To the extent that there is debate on aid broader in scope than earmarks, directives, and prohibitions, the issues typically are whether development assistance should focus on poverty alleviation or growth or whether aid should go to governments that systematically refuse to cooperate with the United States or systematically violate human rights.[3]

As a consensus emerges that foreign aid has reverted to the "haphazard and irrational structure" described by President Kennedy in 1961, few look to Congress to spearhead its rehabilitation.[4] Complaints by senior officials about the inflexibility they encounter, especially in utilizing assistance resources to respond to rapidly changing situations overseas, meet with an unsympathetic response in Congress.[5] Often efficient program implementation is impossible because of the reluctance of Congress and the Office of Management and Budget (OMB) to fund sufficient aid agency staff.

The intermittent oversight conducted by a few congressional committees and the Government Accountability Office examines failings of the executive branch, while generally ignoring outdated and ineffective hurdles to aid effectiveness cherished by the legislative branch.[6] Senior executive branch officials seek to shut out committees by working through the congressional leadership and prefer that funding be in the form of a near-blank check. Restoring a balance between the legislative powers vested in Congress, including its power of the purse, and the executive power vested in the president is key to an effective partnership.

Before seeking to restore a balance between Congress and the executive branch, it is useful to understand how the current imbroglio came about. Systematic review of existing assistance programs has been largely displaced by narrow legislation designed to impose on the executive the priorities of narrow constituencies. This shift is primarily the result of internal developments within Congress that are discussed below and has been exacerbated by three trends within recent administrations. First, decisionmaking has been increasingly concentrated in the Executive Office of the President, beyond the reach of congressional oversight.[7] Second, the executive has been disinclined to seek permanent legislation to validate major foreign assistance initiatives, preferring to work, if congressional approval is required, within the annual appropriations process. Finally, legislative initiatives on behalf of special interest or advocacy groups that restrict the provision of foreign assistance have been signed into law without due consideration of their cumulative impact by Congress or the president.

The case for a more effective partnership between the legislative and executive branches is founded on anticipation that the dynamics of the relationship will remain extremely fluid and that the recent level of support in the Capitol for foreign interventions and generous levels of foreign assistance is likely to diminish. Should the current level of concern about ballooning federal deficits diminish and the interventions in Afghanistan and Iraq both achieve success, support for other interventions abroad and more generous levels of foreign aid may materialize. Either way, the status quo is not viable. This chapter examines how the current situation came about and suggests how Congress could be constructively engaged in the rationalization of foreign assistance for the twenty-first century.

Ignoring the Big Picture:
Congress and Foreign Assistance Today

It is generally conceded by Congress that the president has the initiative in foreign and national security policy. Congress retains a potentially significant role through its power of the purse and through legislation such as the War Powers Act. But over the past three decades, with the notable exception of support for the armed opposition in Nicaragua, Congress has deferred to presidential decisions in foreign policy and international security.[8]

As Congress over the last six decades has declined to exercise its "Power . . . To declare War and make Rules concerning Captures on Land" in the face of increasing numbers of armed interventions abroad or to significantly redirect presidential foreign policy initiatives, it has moved away from setting broad policy for foreign aid to narrowly focused foreign assistance initiatives.[9] There is special legislation to promote assistance mechanisms, such as microcredit or clean water programs; to link assistance to varying performance criteria ranging from religious freedom to international trafficking in persons; and to limit assistance to nations that fail to adequately interdict illegal drugs being exported to the United States, accept criminal deportees from the United States, or exempt U.S. citizens from the jurisdiction of an international court.

The legislative hurdles that dismay executive officials responsible for foreign assistance are often located in provisions of appropriations acts that are usually valid for one or two years or in freestanding authorization acts that are valid until repealed. The appropriators are inundated by requests from lobbying firms on behalf of dozens of universities seeking a slice of the foreign aid pie. The Foreign Assistance Act of 1961, the law authorizing nonmilitary foreign assistance, has been amended more than 140 times and now exceeds 380 pages, but much of it is outdated, and it no longer serves as policy guidance for the executive branch.[10] Rather, the Foreign Assistance Act has become a menu, from which administration lawyers pick and choose provisions.

As more decisions about uses of foreign assistance are concentrated in the White House (and, since 2003, the Department of Defense), officials at the State Department and the U.S. Agency for International Development (USAID) are less able to brief authoritatively or negotiate effectively with Congress.[11] Recent presidential initiatives are handled by White House staff who by custom seldom talk to counterparts on Capitol Hill, especially those in the opposition party. Implementation is left to existing or new agencies that were not part of the initial planning. As a result, a small White House legislative staff that traditionally focuses on domestic affairs struggles to act as intermediaries between the cloistered staff in the Executive Office of the President and those members of the legislature who insist on a meaningful role for Congress in international affairs.

The Changing Role of Authorizations

Every survivor of a high school civics course should recall the basic distinction between the authorization and appropriations committees of the House and Senate. "Authorizations establish, continue, or modify programs or policies; appropriations fund authorized programs and policies."[12] This model bears little resemblance to actual practice with regard to foreign assistance programs.

The authorizers continue to play the key role in the *establishment* of programs. Every major new bilateral foreign assistance program since 1985 has passed through the authorization process, although sometimes departing from conventional procedures on the road to enactment.[13] The Foreign Relations Committee continues to command national attention during controversial nomination hearings, and its recent chairmen and senior members of both parties are national figures. The status accorded to committee members by diplomats, the media, and the foreign policy establishment remains high, but committee membership is less valued within the Senate.[14]

The gap between theory and practice appears in the authorizers' role to *continue or modify* foreign assistance programs. Between 1962 and 1985, the committees used comprehensive authorization acts as the primary vehicle to renew or modify existing programs. Such annual or biannual laws emerged because the authorizing committees "wanted greater control of and oversight over executive and presidential activities . . . [and to] put pressure on the appropriating committees . . . [for] what they believe to be the necessary level of appropriations for new and existing federal agencies, activities, and programs."[15]

As a result of the new congressional budget procedures of the 1970s and the authorizers' response to them, comprehensive foreign aid authorization bills lost their influence over appropriations levels.[16] The difficulty in resolving opposing Senate and House provisions on abortion exacerbated the situation after 1994, as the authorizers and appropriators each sought to move the volatile issue into the other committee's jurisdiction.[17] The ability of the contemporary chairmen to shepherd broad policy bills through the entire legislative process to enactment is reduced by conditions beyond their control. One alternative has been to use committee bills and hearings to influence the executive or international organizations. Two successful examples are Senate Foreign Relations Committee Chairman Richard Lugar's advocacy of improved postconflict stabilization and reconstruction efforts, and House International Relations Committee Chairman Henry Hyde's advocacy of United Nations reform. Legislation drafted by each chairman was not considered by the other house of Congress, but Lugar influenced the establishment of the State Department Office of Conflict, Reconstruction, and Stabilization, and Hyde's bill was used to boost reform efforts at the United Nations.[18] The Senate leadership failed to make time available to consider these bills.

There is no simple explanation for the atrophy of the periodic reauthorization process for foreign assistance. With fits and starts, the process continues for the diplomatic and citizen services activities of the State Department. Numerous foreign assistance reauthorization bills have been approved for floor consideration by the authorizers, and some have passed the House or the Senate, but none has been enacted during the past two decades.[19] The less comprehensive foreign assistance authorization bills that eventually became law since 1985, however, generally accomplished one of three objectives: validated new regional programs, particularly in postcommunist Europe; linked ongoing foreign assistance to new criteria related to violation of human rights and provided for suspension of aid if the criteria were met; or mandated certain types of aid delivery favored by public advocacy groups.

Clues for the eclipse of the broad, ongoing authorization process may be found in the original objectives for commencing periodic reauthorizations as part of the Foreign Assistance Act of 1961: control and oversight over the executive branch and influence on appropriations levels. Once influence over appropriations levels was lost, interest in comprehensive oversight over existing assistance declined and was replaced by the types of legislation described in the previous paragraph. And yet consistent and effective oversight by the authorizers can significantly influence the quality and quantity of foreign assistance. A case can be made that when key members of Congress have a stake in foreign assistance programs, particularly when they participated in their enactment, the subsequent oversight is both effective and constructive.

One possible explanation is the size, objectives, and culture of the respective staffs of the primary authorizing committees and appropriations subcommittees. The objectives of appropriations staff are to draft a bill that will have as much bipartisan support as possible, pass with minimum commotion, and be signed by the president, and, after enactment, to ensure that its provisions are implemented. An understanding of policy is essential to success, but policy is viewed through the lens of implementation.

Authorization staff who deal with international affairs have a broader range of objectives and are more often focused on policy rather than legislation. Committee markup and consideration by the House or the Senate can be unstructured and lengthy. For most staff, hearing preparation is a major concern, and in the Senate controversial nominations can trump routine tasks for some. Oversight associated with hearings seldom involves the nuts and bolts of policy implementation such as procurement. Some staff necessarily focus on the personal interests of a single committee member.

Personal contact with the chairman or ranking minority member is necessarily limited because of the large staff, which can cause tension or frustration. The discrepancy in staff size between authorizing and appropriating committees is startling. The Senate Foreign Relations Committee (authorizing) has fifty-seven staff members whereas the Foreign Operations Subcommittee (appropriating) has five.[20] In the House the International Relations Committee has fifty staff members whereas the appropriations subcommittee has six. The effectiveness of the professional staffs of these committees determines the extent and utility of congressional oversight over foreign assistance.[21] It is generally conceded that oversight conducted by the smaller appropriations staffs can have a more direct impact.

Under current conditions it is prudent to assume that broad oversight over foreign assistance by many authorizers will continue to take a back seat as long as their committees have minimal influence over resources, which are controlled by the appropriators. As current conditions change, new opportunities for the authorizers may emerge.

Impact of the Congressional Budget Process on Foreign Assistance

There once was a sustained partnership between Congress and the executive branch in support of foreign aid. Congressional leadership came from the authorizing committees, and executive leadership was provided by USAID. In seeking an explanation for the subsequent shifts in the balance of power among key U.S. government actors in foreign assistance, some history is in order.[22]

In the 1970s a reduction in the influence of congressional authorizing committees over foreign assistance commenced with the enactment of the Congressional Budget and Impoundment Control Act of 1974, commonly known as the Congressional Budget Act.[23] Before its initial implementation in fiscal year 1976, there was no dollar ceiling on foreign assistance appropriations. There was little fiscal discipline to constrain the authorizers or the appropriators. The only formal obstacle to fully appropriating foreign aid at the dollar levels set forth in periodic reauthorization acts was the ability of foreign aid's advocates to mobilize a majority of votes in the Senate and the House.

Under the Congressional Budget Act, purported ceilings on spending limits for the programmatic budget categories of the federal budget, including the international affairs budget (function 150), are set through annual congressional budget resolutions.[24] Beginning with the fiscal years 1975–76 bill to reauthorize foreign assistance, pressure emerged for the annual authorization levels to conform to the congressional budget resolution. When, in the first years of the new process, Senate Budget Committee Chairman Ed Muskie successfully invoked a Congressional Budget Act point of order to defeat a conference agreement on the annual Department of Defense authorization bill, causing it to be sent back to conference, a shock wave went through both houses of Congress. A difficult learning curve ensued for all participants as the congressional budget process evolved over the next decade.

Several new and technically challenging procedures required under the Congressional Budget Act generated employment and new skill sets on Capitol Hill and, to a lesser extent, within the executive branch. The most important of the new procedures were crosswalking and scorekeeping.

Crosswalking is a procedure in which the functional totals enacted in the budget resolution are allocated to each committee with budgetary jurisdiction under section 302(a) of the Congressional Budget Act. Each committee is then required to subdivide its share of the budget among its programs or subcommittees under section 302(b).[25] Since authorization committee and subcommittee jurisdictions have never fit neatly into federal budget categories, crosswalking required an unrealistic level of coordination among committees as well as complex assumptions about future appropriation levels. After initial attempts to engage, most authorizing committees found it was impossible to construct realistic scenarios for budget functions where they were only one of several key players. Although the formal crosswalking process had broken down among the authorizers by the end of the 1970s, it survives informally among many committees inasmuch as those committees no longer authorize programs at unrealistically high levels.[26] To the extent that foreign assistance authorizers have abandoned the annual authorization exercise, they have effectively ceded the power of the purse entirely to the appropriators—although of course the reverse causality may be at work.

Crosswalking today survives only in the appropriations committees where the process can be managed within a single committee. This so-called 302 allocation by the chairmen of the appropriations committees of the total amount of discretionary appropriations established by the congressional budget resolution among the twelve subcommittees eventually became recognized as the determining factor in the annual foreign aid budget process, leaving no role for the authorizers. As an appropriations committee begins to consider its regular bills in May or June of each year, its chairman circulates among the members a proposed dollar ceiling (or allocation) for each subcommittee. The sum of all subcommittee ceilings cannot exceed the discretionary ceiling in the most recent congressional budget resolution.[27] Recommendations are based on extensive prior consultations with other key appropriators and so are generally ratified without modification.

It is interesting to note that on several occasions during the 1990s, congressional budget agreements "fenced" the national defense and international affairs functions by making separate allocations, known as firewalls, to the appropriations committees for the two functional categories, greatly reducing the ability of the appropriators to transfer funds out of— or into—international affairs programs.[28] Once separate allocations for function 150 (international affairs) ended, appropriators came to recognize that the scorekeeping and 302 allocation provisions of the Congressional Budget Act strengthened their hold over foreign assistance.

Scorekeeping is the process of measuring the budgetary effects of pending and enacted legislation against a baseline, and is the responsibility of the budget committees, with assistance from the Congressional Budget Office (CBO).[29] In other words, scorekeeping is a CBO estimate of the outlay or deficit impact of an appropriation bill or amendment, or of an authorization bill *as if* it were fully appropriated. Scorekeeping, as mandated by the Congressional Budget Act, created a new emphasis on outlays—that is, funds actually expended—rather than appropriations—that is, budget authority, or the authority to incur binding obligations against the U.S. Treasury.[30] Scorekeeping required authorizers and appropriators to engage in a form of creative bookkeeping, as differing combinations of foreign assistance programs could result in complying with the function 150 level for appropriations while concurrently exceeding the total estimated deficit.[31] Scorekeeping decisions by a determinedly independent CBO staff occasionally caused the modification of presidential initiatives.[32]

Two long-standing provisions of law that prohibit obligation of appropriations for unauthorized activities have not proven effective in recent years.[33] When disagreement over abortion, lack of floor time, or intrusion of nongermane issues has derailed committee-reported reauthorization bills, there has been little appetite to invoke these provisions to shut down all or part of the State Department or USAID.

The Senate Foreign Relations Committee and the House International Relations Committee recognize their opportunity to reengage in the resource allocation process by authorizing assistance programs within realistic funding levels. This could, in turn, create an incentive to increase systematic oversight over foreign assistance programs. Other authorization committees, such as the House and Senate Armed Services Committees, continue to influence resource allocation through annual reauthorization bills, and a reengagement by both international authorization committees could make a positive contribution to the informed exercise of the congressional power of the purse.

Consolidation and Proliferation: Congress and the Executive since 1995

By 1990 a consolidated congressional "gang of four" appropriators made most congressional decisions affecting foreign assistance.[34] They faced a tsunami-like threat when Republicans took control of the House in 1995. Pressure from rank-and-file members, supported by much of the leadership, for massive reductions in foreign aid caused panic among foreign aid advocates. In the face of a House budget resolution slashing function 150, a Gulf Coast conservative became an unlikely champion of foreign aid. Reducing the totals for foreign assistance from $15 billion to $13 billion, instead of $9 billion as proposed initially by the Republican conference, House Foreign Operations Subcommittee Chairman Sonny Callahan took the lead in a series of substantial reforms of foreign assistance that continued and went beyond those previously undertaken by his predecessor as chairman, David Obey.[35] There were no similar pressures on foreign assistance in the Senate, but it went along with the House.

These reforms did not address broad conceptual or structural issues affecting foreign aid, nor did they attempt to respond to the challenges already offered by failing states such as the former Yugoslavia or Somalia. The reforms were attempts to get the administration to pay more attention to critical problems, to more attractively brand foreign aid, and to make room for new requirements by phasing out legacy programs. The changes after 1995 included

—creation of a distinct Child Survival and Disease Program Fund with a large component to fight HIV/AIDS, in response to long-standing concerns among appropriators in the Senate and the House;

—an agreement with Israel to phase out its post–Camp David $1.2 billion annual economic aid package over a ten-year period, freeing economic support funds for other strategic countries; and

—establishment of a linkage between multilateral debt relief and commitments by the beneficiaries to forgo new loans for a period, breaking the lend-and-forgive cycle among the poorest and most badly governed nations.

Callahan continued Obey's efforts to end foreign assistance earmarks but, like Obey, encountered strong resistance from the Senate and pro-Israel advocacy groups.

Between 1995 and 1998, as the appropriators were reviewing and restructuring individual foreign assistance programs, usually on a bipartisan basis, the authorizers were locked in a partisan struggle with the Clinton administration over plans by some Republican leaders to merge USAID, the U.S. Information Agency, and the Arms Control and Disarmament Agency with the State Department. After four years of bitter struggle, USAID was preserved as a nominally independent agency in return for an agreement with the executive branch to concur in the abolition of the U.S. Information Agency and the Arms Control and Disarmament Agency.[36] The prolonged struggle among the authorizers diverted their attention from reengagement in the annual reauthorization process. In recent years the committees have attempted, without success, to renew the process, as discussed above.

It is hoped that the January 2006 nomination of a new director of foreign assistance, with the rank of deputy secretary in the Department of State, will over time reduce unproductive tensions between the State Department, USAID, and the quasi-independent Millennium Challenge Corporation and the Office of the Global AIDS Coordinator. It is vital that this appointment not generate another layer of bureaucracy. Ironically, over the previous decade, the State Department's unceasing efforts to informally absorb USAID, to take control of country assistance allocations without accepting concurrent responsibility for implementation, weakened both agencies.[37] The secretary of state's decision to designate the administrator of USAID as the State Department director of foreign assistance could bring a semblance of command and control to U.S. foreign assistance. It is uncertain at this time whether the director or a subordinate will be the main liaison with Congress on foreign aid resource issues.

Many more federal actors other than USAID and the State Department are active in foreign assistance.[38] Former USAID administrator Andrew Natsios characterized the deployment of foreign assistance as " 'constipated' and splintered among too many federal agencies."[39] It appears that any effort to expand the authority of the director of foreign assistance over foreign assistance programs at the Treasury and Defense Departments and at other federal agencies will be deferred until aid programs managed by the State Department and USAID are effectively coordinated. Under Presidents Clinton and George W. Bush, Congress allowed an increasing percentage of foreign assistance to be undertaken by domestic and autonomous overseas agencies. The Treasury, Health and Human Services, and Labor Departments have become more actively engaged in foreign aid programs previously within the domain of the State Department or USAID.[40] President Bush has convinced Congress to establish independent federal agencies or autonomous programs created specifically to bypass the State Department and USAID. Funding of foreign assistance by the Department of Defense also has increased significantly during his term and now includes a massive police training program in Iraq.[41]

Before the appointment of a director of foreign assistance, a similar position of lower rank at the State Department helped facilitate the generally amicable relations among the House and Senate chairmen and ranking minority members of the Foreign Operations Committees and the executive branch. And since its establishment in 1982, the position of director of the Office of Resources, Plans and Policy at the Department of State also functioned as a key link with the appropriators.[42] With direct access to and the confidence of the secretary of state, OMB staff, and key Capitol Hill actors, most of the seven individuals who held this position over two decades were able to pull together timely and accurate information and, on occasion, to facilitate resolution of differences between congressional committees and the executive. Necessarily walking a fine line between advocacy and candor, this position offers a model for a more effective partnership. The role was critical as the number of public hearings was reduced in favor of closed briefings and overseas reviews of programs in the field, but the position has been left vacant by Secretary of State Condoleezza Rice for more than one year. It is uncertain whether the greatly expanded responsibilities of the director of foreign assistance will allow the appointee to assume this liaison role in addition to his or her other planning and management duties.

Facing New Challenges: Foreign Operations Appropriations

As one of the recurring bouts of scandal enveloped Capitol Hill in early 2006, the dominant role of the appropriators came under scrutiny from all quarters. Special appropriations provisions or earmarks were singled out as the prime vehicle for corruption, with appropriations subcommittee chairmen mocked as having "turned pork into haute cuisine of late."[43]

Foreign assistance appropriators freely use legislative earmarks and report directives, but they are relatively restrained purveyors of pork. According to the widely used *Pig Book* released by Citizens Against Government Waste, only 18 of the 13,997 pork-barrel projects in the federal budget are located in the 2005 Foreign Operations Appropriations Act.[44] Most of the foreign assistance earmarks that generate concern in the executive branch do not meet this watchdog organization's standards for pork, having been requested by the president, been the subject of hearings, or having not greatly exceeded the previous year's funding level.

However, the totality of earmarks and directives are a significant impediment to more effective foreign assistance. Between 1993 and 2006, three House Foreign Operations Subcommittee chairmen from both parties have fervently opposed binding earmarks but have had to compromise with Senate bills that included dozens of them. Most earmarks differ little from the president's request, but a few arguably intrude into the executive power of the president. Directives can be a valid expression of congressional intent: in both the House and Senate, directives in report language can serve to clarify bill language, warn the executive about management deficiencies, or increase flexibility for the executive. In reality, however, many are not written to promote good governance. It also should be noted that several of the most debated earmarks and directives that affect foreign assistance for HIV/AIDS were inserted in 2003 at the insistence of the White House staff. Regardless of the source, the overall impact is chaotic and disruptive to sound management in the public interest.

As budget deficits again become a major issue, relations between the Appropriations and Budget Committees will need to be strengthened, especially in the House, where there is less overlap in committee membership than in the Senate. The old issues associated with crosswalking will return with increased attention to budget resolutions. Some observers would be surprised to learn that there is no requirement that the appropriations total for international programs must conform to the amounts provided for function 150 in the current 2006 budget resolution.[45] It is a little known fact that since 1995, in the absence of separate budget resolution allocations for international affairs, appropriations for foreign assistance and other international programs in most years have *exceeded* budget resolution ceilings for function 150 by significant amounts. This has been the outcome of discreet shifts within the section 302 allocation process by the chairmen of the full appropriations committees.[46]

One outcome may be a return to a practice used on several occasions during the 1980s, when congressional budget resolutions "fenced" the national defense and international affairs functions by making separate allocations to the appropriations committees for each, greatly reducing the ability of the appropriators to transfer funds out of, or into, international affairs programs.[47] On one occasion influential Senator Robert C. Byrd explained that he had acquiesced in the provision of a separate allocation for function 150 in order to prevent transfers from domestic programs *into* international ones in the Middle East. If support for foreign assistance diminishes, a separate fenced allocation for function 150 may serve to prevent transfers *out of* international programs into domestic ones.

In fact, more often than not, unanticipated requirements for foreign aid have long evaded fiscal limits. Since September 2001, appropriations for military and reconstruction activities in Iraq, Afghanistan, and neighboring nations have been funded through supplemental appropriations that were unconstrained by budget limits. That deficit-driving practice has come under increasing criticism, and offsetting reductions from other foreign assistance or domestic appropriations may be required in order to fund future foreign policy initiatives.

The Foreign Operations Subcommittee's allocation effectively determines the annual level of foreign assistance, other than what is provided through emergency supplemental acts. All significant civilian foreign assistance programs other than food aid are funded under the Foreign Operations, Export Financing, and Related Programs Appropriations Act.[48] As allocations for domestic appropriations subcommittees are increasingly constrained by bipartisan concerns over high fiscal deficits, new foreign assistance programs that have emerged in other appropriations acts are likely to migrate to the Foreign Operations Subcommittee in future years.[49]

Foreign assistance appropriators face both resource and cultural challenges at the end of the first decade of the twenty-first century. With regard to resources, the President's Emergency Plan for AIDS Relief and the Millennium Challenge Corporation were funded initially by deficit spending and did not require reductions in existing foreign assistance accounts. Both new programs make huge claims on future foreign assistance budgets, especially the AIDS initiative, which is likely to require escalating funding for lifetime treatment of beneficiaries.[50] Successful enactment of both initiatives may have convinced some that peremptory restructuring of foreign assistance by the president is the path to success, but the ability to sustain them in the absence of deep congressional support is uncertain.[51] Initial congressional support for both presidential initiatives was based on assurances that their funding would be additional, relative to other aid accounts. Claims that both could be sustained without cutting other foreign aid will be hard to support as future funding requirements are disclosed.

With regard to committee culture, the unwelcome attention on "pork" and other earmarks is accompanied by demands for increased transparency. Both threaten elements of appropriations committee culture that have hitherto been assets: focus on results, working out of public view, and bipartisanship. A somewhat dated example of how these elements can operate is the case of the successful campaign by a single appropriator to provide Stinger missiles to the Afghan mujahideen.[52] Most of these elements are unusual by contemporary Capitol Hill standards, especially bipartisanship.

Annual appropriations bills are known as must-pass legislation. Deadlines may be stretched, but an enacted bill is the result sought every year. Closing down the government for lack of funding is out of the question since the debacle of the last attempt in 1995–96. Long-term continuing resolutions at the prior year's funding levels have gone out of fashion.[53] Thus the appropriators must secure sufficient support at every step of the legislative process to pass a bill each year. Indefinite delay or abandoning the effort are not options, as they are with many authorization bills.

Working out of public view is valued by the appropriators as facilitating the necessary compromises over deeply divisive issues such as abortion. It also facilitates accommodating the special concerns of influential members of both parties to secure their support. Most appropriations staff seek to minimize interaction with advocacy and special interest groups, whether by preference or because of time pressures, and necessary meetings are held within the Capitol complex. Preferred external contacts are agency and private field practitioners, without regard to rank or position. Interaction with the media is generally avoided, and arrogance associated with great power is a constant risk not always avoided. Assigned by the full committee to work with a subcommittee, the appropriations staffer is accustomed to accommodating multiple bosses.

All of these habits and internal procedures elicit suspicion from without, especially from an increasingly centralized congressional leadership. Whatever their shortcomings, the appropriators regularly deliver for presidential signature a full set of regular appropriation bills and one or more supplemental bills annually. Because of this ability to pass legislation on a regular basis, the appropriations process is often viewed by the leadership as the vehicle of choice for important initiatives, such as the Millennium Challenge Account and the Iraq Reconstruction Fund.

These are but the most predictable of the challenges that both authorizers and appropriators face as foreign assistance recedes from recent record funding levels. Continued support for foreign assistance at sustainable levels will require a broader coalition in Congress, less dependent on the favor of appropriators. In the absence of increased coherence and more effective U.S. foreign aid, the emergence of a broad coalition in support of foreign assistance is unlikely.

Hurdles or Barriers: Congressional Restrictions on Foreign Assistance

Despite the congressional deference to the president on foreign policy discussed earlier in this chapter, most recent presidents and secretaries of state have been outspoken in their complaints about congressional interference in foreign policy.[54] The key deficiency cited is Congress's failure to grant sufficient flexibility in the use of appropriations. Also cited are the numerous legislative restrictions that limit the provision of foreign assistance, prompted by concerns ranging from nuclear nonproliferation to religious freedom.[55]

This perceived lack of flexibility has placed a greater premium on securing additional appropriations that can be used "notwithstanding any other provision of law."[56] The fiscal year 2006 budget request included a proposal to shift $275 million for Afghanistan, Sudan, Haiti, and Ethiopia—

which in previous years would have been requested for the Development Assistance account—into the Transition Initiatives account, to allow the use of "notwithstanding" authority.[57]

Of course, taken literally, as a few officials are prone to do, such "notwithstanding" language can be viewed as the ultimate congressional abdication of its constitutional responsibility. Fortunately, career lawyers in the executive branch have managed until now to limit the potential abuse of "notwithstanding" provisions. They can cite the body of precedents that limit their use in practice to the waiver of legislative provisions that limit the use of foreign assistance.[58]

Before the 1990s virtually all foreign assistance was managed by USAID. Its bureaucratic culture ensures that its program managers comply with congressional restrictions on the uses of foreign assistance, but State Department program managers are less likely to be familiar with them. The primary reference for USAID remains the thirty-eight-page "Statutory Checklist" of key general and country-specific restrictions on foreign assistance.[59] The checklists are compiled and updated by USAID's legislative counsel to guide program managers through the thicket of *legislative* restrictions on foreign assistance.[60] At first glance the restrictions appear to be extremely burdensome.

The actual impact of the statutory restrictions on assistance is often less than purported. For example, the statutory checklists begin with ten examples of various "notwithstanding" authorities that USAID might use to provide assistance when it would otherwise be prohibited:

—disaster and famine assistance;

—transition initiatives;

—health and disease prevention, child survival, and HIV/AIDS;

—assistance for Eastern Europe and the Baltic states;

—assistance to the independent states of the former Soviet Union;

—assistance to Iraq;

—assistance to Afghanistan (only for loan defaults), Lebanon, Montenegro, Pakistan, victims of war, displaced children, displaced Burmese, victims of trafficking in persons and combating trafficking, and, with exceptions, for tropical forestry, biodiversity conservation, and energy programs aimed at reducing greenhouse gas emissions;

—assistance implemented by nongovernmental organizations;

—P.L. 83-480 Title II emergency food programs; and

—Economic Support Funds for democracy activities in the People's Republic of China and Hong Kong.[61]

If a legislative restriction threatens to impede a foreign assistance initiative proposed by the executive branch, it may not be necessary to shoehorn it into one of these programs or to entrust it to a nongovernmental organization. There are other options. Paradoxically, virtually all congressional restrictions on foreign assistance include authority for the president or the secretary of state to waive the restriction under certain conditions, ranging from a finding that the proposed assistance is in the national interest of the United States to a determination that the proposed assistance is *vital* to the national *security* interests of the United States. However, restrictions with regard to nuclear proliferation are generally not waived. These distinctions matter. The requirement for the president or the secretary of state to make such a determination does give rise to dialogue between Capitol Hill and the executive.

In the infrequent instances where specific waiver or "notwithstanding" authority has not been provided, the president may invoke section 614 of the Foreign Assistance Act. Under this provision (and limited to $50 million annually for any country), "The President may authorize the furnishing of assistance without regard to any provision of this Act . . . and any Act authorizing or appropriating funds for use under this Act . . . when the President determines and so notifies in writing the Speaker of the House . . . and the chairman of the Committee on Foreign Relations . . . that to do so is important to the security interests of the United States."[62] Although section 614 also requires that the president "consult with, and shall provide a written policy justification" to the authorizing and appropriations committees of both houses of Congress, the concurrence of the Speaker and the chairman of the Foreign Relations Committee is customarily deemed sufficient for the president to exercise this authority.[63]

In effect, almost all congressional restrictions of the president's use of foreign assistance are hurdles of varying heights, not barriers. In sensitive matters, such as aid to the Palestine Authority or North Korea, Congress reluctantly complies with presidential requests for funds, but in a convoluted manner that offers the pretense of congressional oversight and accountability while enabling the president to do what he wants.[64] In such examples, Congress includes an apparent blanket prohibition of assistance in one part of the legislation but also provides an obscurely drafted waiver provision elsewhere. Should the president utilize the waiver, Congress can assert that it opposed assistance to the Palestine Authority or North Korea. It is not pretty, but it works.

While it is not difficult to conclude that most congressional restrictions are less onerous than they appear at first glance, there are other challenges beyond earmarks and directives. Often the mostly informal process of notifying Congress of administration proposals to reprogram funds is a greater obstacle to executive flexibility than statutory prohibitions. Mid-level staff members have been known to use this process to delay the obligation of earmarked funds for six months.

The structure of appropriations accounts can become unintended restrictions that hobble the executive. An example is the separate account for USAID operating expenses. It resulted from futile appropriations committee attempts in the 1970s to obtain information about USAID human resource deployment. The information is now available, and the separate account no longer serves a useful purpose. The artificial distinction imposed on USAID by this legacy of long forgotten disagreements is burdensome. In its attempts to comply with new duties and obligate supplemental funds that dwarf its regular budget, the agency spends undue time and energy plotting ways to work around untenable funding levels requested by the OMB or appropriated by Congress. This and other legacy aid accounts should be reviewed for abolition or consolidation.

Another casualty of the 1970s was the small contingency fund for unanticipated opportunities. When President Richard Nixon on his 1974 visit to Egypt noticed President Anwar Sadat's admiration of an American helicopter, Nixon gave the helicopter to Sadat and used the contingency fund to pay for it. The appropriators drastically reduced the contingency fund at the next opportunity and eliminated it by 1980.[65] With proper conditions for its use, a small contingency fund should be restored so that the secretary of state does not have to scramble to find $1 million the next time Liberia needs U.S. aid to conduct elections.[66]

It would be a mistake to conclude that most congressional rules are made to be broken, as outright defiance may provoke severe consequences. An example is the adverse Capitol Hill reaction to administration announcements in late 2005 regarding expanded nuclear cooperation with India, without prior consultation with Congress about the necessary legislative changes.[67] Nonetheless, for the executive officials who must jump the hurdles of briefing skeptical members of Congress and their seemingly hostile staff, or engaging the president in what the White House staff may view as an insignificant waiver, it is understandable that many hold negative views of Congress.

One Capital, Two Cultures

In candid exchanges between career officials in the federal government and veteran Capitol Hill staff, it is frequently noted that they work in the same city but in two radically different cultures. For too many officials at the White House and the State Department, Congress is a foreign country, if not a rogue state. In a few Capitol Hill offices, American diplomats are dismissed as being more intent on defending foreign clients than defending the national interests of the United States. The cultures of Foggy Bottom and Capitol Hill have little in common, and individuals moving from one to the other often find it a difficult transition.[68]

Unequal Roles

Not surprisingly, a major impediment to an effective partnership between the executive and legislative branches of the United States government with regard to foreign assistance is a lack of understanding of the role of each by the other. The roles indicated by the Constitution have evolved over the past two centuries and provide ample precedents for cooperation or conflict, depending on the personal experience—or lack thereof—of key actors in both Capitol Hill and Foggy Bottom.

Of late there has been a proliferation of presidential initiatives in foreign assistance. These often originate within the executive branch with little congressional consultation until after the proposals are finalized. Indeed, the familiar pictures of White House meetings between the president and the congressional leadership are symptomatic of the failings of the partnership between Congress and the executive on foreign assistance in recent years. They offer clues to the frequent lack of results from these meetings, as well as clues to the mistrust evoked by failure to follow through on action that one principal believes the others have agreed to.

Unless they have a personal interest in the issue raised by the president, the congressional participants in such meetings are unlikely to comprehend immediately the full ramifications of the president's proposals regarding foreign assistance. Newly elevated members of the leadership are generally at a particular disadvantage, as most of them focus on domestic matters that influenced their climb to office. Some may give apparent assent to a request to support an international initiative, only to discover upon their return to the Capitol that they cannot or should not deliver what they indicated to the president. More experienced congressional participants in such meetings often decline to respond to such requests for support until they have had an opportunity to reflect and to consult with other senior members and aides. On the less frequent occasions when other leaders from the relevant committees are consulted, they are more likely to promptly evaluate the proposal, probe it for potential vulnerabilities, and offer the president sound, constructive advice.[69]

While warm personal relations between individual secretaries of state or national security advisers and individual members of the congressional leadership or committee chairmen and ranking minority members do occur, they have been the exception since 1993.[70] Some disturbing recent trends are a breakdown in routine communication and, on occasion, distrust between key actors in Congress and counterparts in the National Security Council and the Department of State. Such estrangement is not unique in American history, but it is a major departure from the collaboration that led to approval of the Marshall Plan, for example, or support for the formerly communist nations of Eastern and Central Europe after 1989.

Divergent Expectations

A second impediment to an effective partnership is the difference in expectations for foreign assistance. The possibilities and limitations of foreign assistance in the twenty-first century are not widely understood by key decisionmakers in either the executive or legislative branch. Serious efforts by the administrator of USAID over the past five years to develop a series of coherent and relevant policy papers on critical foreign assistance issues failed to elicit a response from the president or the secretary of state.[71] The persistent calls from Congress for new "Marshall plans" indicate that it fails to comprehend that the unique temporary circumstances of post–World War II Europe bear little resemblance to the long-term challenges facing current foreign assistance recipients in Africa or elsewhere. Inevitably, this leads to a recurring cycle of outsized hopes for foreign assistance followed by exaggerated disappointment—a cycle that could be broken if more American leaders carved out the time to better understand the dynamics of foreign assistance.

Recommendations

The January 2006 nomination of a single individual to the dual position of USAID administrator and State Department director of foreign assistance was an initial step toward aligning foreign assistance with changing national interests. By the time the president and the secretary of state take the next step of proposing ways to remove existing obstacles to a succinct set of objectives for effective foreign assistance, Congress should be prepared to engage. It will take a partnership to shape and implement the necessary changes in both Congress and executive agencies. To that end, the following new mechanisms are suggested to expand participation in resource decisionmaking beyond the appropriations committees.

Short-Term Mechanisms

Ban binding earmarks of foreign assistance funds for private or nongovernmental organizations and of amounts that exceed the president's request for countries or functional sectors. Relevant directives in report language would be deemed to be advisory only.

Require that wherever appropriators do not incorporate changes recommended by an authorizing committee to the conditions on assistance included in the most recent annual appropriations bill or to the president's request for a supplemental appropriation, the report accompanying an appropriations bill for foreign assistance must explain why a recommended change was not included.

Provide greater transparency regarding congressional intent in appropriations of foreign assistance. The level of detail in most appropriations accounts should be comparable to those for domestic and defense agencies. Expand the use of account text tables in Senate-House conference agreements that indicate the purposes for which funds are being appropriated. The conference agreement should also reconcile inconsistent and contradictory report language. This limits postenactment inter- and intraagency disputes over the allocation of funds and expedites the obligation of funds.

Abolish ineffective separate "operating expense" budget accounts, repeal outdated laws requiring annual authorization of appropriations levels, and restore a small presidential contingency fund solely for unanticipated policy requirements.

Limit the application of provisions allowing foreign assistance to be provided "notwithstanding any other provision of law" to cited laws that restrict foreign assistance. Limit the application of all country prohibitions to the central governments of such countries, allowing the continuation of assistance to private organizations or elected local or regional governments.

Restore a high-level resource management position in the State Department, in the office of the department's deputy secretary or director of foreign assistance, to concurrently serve as the primary contact with the appropriations and other relevant committees on resource issues.

Medium-Term Mechanisms

Establish a panel of independent experts to assess the current structure and operational efficacy of all federally funded foreign assistance. It would recommend changes within the executive and the legislature that would significantly increase aid's efficacy and better reflect the constitutional roles of the two branches. The panel's recommendations would be published in time for consideration by the 110th Congress.

Reengage the Foreign and International Relations Committees in the allocation of foreign assistance resources. Resume the process of drafting and passing annual or biannual bills authorizing realistic levels for foreign assistance accounts. Until it is possible to enact (through the House-Senate conference and the president's signature) authorizations for foreign assistance, the account levels reported by the committees or passed by each house should be deemed an authorization recommendation to be considered by the Appropriations Committees. Modify Senate and House rules to require that committee reports accompanying foreign operations appropriations bills include a detailed explanation of proposed funding levels in excess of those authorized by law or recommended by the authorizing committee.

Rationalize the reprogramming notification process by negotiating a more transparent and time-limited process for congressional consideration. Executive branch requests to reprogram funds, including presidential initiatives, for purposes different from those for which the funds were appropriated merit prompt acceptance or modification.

Notes

1. The quote is from a valedictory profile of Andrew Natsios's tenure as administrator of the U.S. Agency for International Development (USAID). See Celia W. Dugger, "Planning to Fight Poverty from Outside the System," *New York Times*, January 14, 2006, p. A4.

2. "Reforming Foreign Assistance," *Washington Post*, January 3, 2006, p. A16.

3. A notable exception to this generalization is Senator Richard Lugar's effective leadership in funding and deploying innovative foreign aid mechanisms to reduce threats from weapons of mass destruction in the former Soviet Union.

4. John F. Kennedy, "Special Message to the Congress on Foreign Aid," March 22, 1961, in *Public Papers of the Presidents of the United States: John F. Kennedy, 1961* (Government Printing Office, 1961).

5. A recent example is the exchange between a USAID administrator and members of the House Appropriations Committee on the subject of congressional earmarks and directives. See House Committee on Appropriations, Subcommittee on Foreign Operations, Export Financing, and Related Programs, testimony of Andrew S. Natsios, administrator, USAID, 109 Cong. 1 sess. (April 20, 2005).

6. In particular, these include staff abuse of the procedures after administration notification of proposed changes in the use of previously appropriated funds, the termination of a contingency fund for unanticipated emergencies (other than for disasters and refugees), and incoherent, contradictory, or poorly drafted directives in committee reports.

7. Examples include the bilateral commissions with Ukraine and Egypt, headed by former vice president Al Gore, and President George W. Bush's Iraq reconstruction program, especially the part funded by the UN Oil-for-Food Program.

8. No intervention by U.S. armed forces or accompanying "reconstruction" program has been delayed or terminated because of inadequate appropriations for the Defense or State Departments or the U.S. Agency for International Development, nor has any major foreign assistance initiative been blocked during this period. It is noted that U.S. ratification of the Nuclear Non-Proliferation Treaty and the Kyoto Protocol never took place because of the lack of consent by the Senate, but President Bill Clinton prudently declined to make Senate approval a priority, knowing that sufficient support was lacking.

9. See U.S. Constitution, Art. I, sec. 8. After authorizing the use of force against Iraq in late 2002, Congress failed to consider or pass broad policy legislation to direct the use of $20 billion in reconstruction funds for Iraq.

10. P.L. 87-195. For a complete list of public laws that amended the Foreign Assistance Act, see Senate Committee on Foreign Relations and House Committee on International Relations, *Legislation on Foreign Relations through 2004*, Joint Committee Print, vol. 1A (Government Printing Office, February 2005), pp. 15–19.

11. During 2003 negotiations with Congress regarding the $18 billion Iraq reconstruction supplemental appropriation, the proposed Millennium Challenge Corporation, and the President's Emergency Fund for AIDS Relief, the White House staff effectively shut out meaningful participation by the State Department or USAID. In the case of the last item, key provisions regarding the allocation of funds after September 30, 2005, for prevention and treatment of HIV/AIDS were inserted privately by the House leadership at the behest of the White House domestic policy staff *after* the legislation had been publicly reported by the International Relations Committee. The Senate agreed to the president's request to accept the House bill without amendment.

12. Walter J. Oleszek, *Congressional Procedures and the Policy Process* (Washington: CQ Press, 2004), p. 42.

13. *The Millennium Challenge Act of 2003* was enacted as Title VI of the fiscal year 2004 Foreign Operations Appropriation Act, Division E of P.L. 108-7, based on legislation reported from the House and Senate authorizing committees and subsequent consultations among authorizing staff and the appropriators. The separately enacted *U.S. Leadership against HIV/AIDS, Tuberculosis, and Malaria Act of 2003* (P.L. 108-25)

included contentious provisions inserted at the insistence of the White House and the House leadership, without being considered by any authorizing committee. The Senate then concurred without a conference, with the result that the Foreign Relations Committee had no voice in the final legislation.

14. This assessment is based on the number of junior members who exchange seats on the Foreign Relations Committee in order to join the Finance or Appropriations Committee. Chairman Lugar sought a change in Senate rules to permit members to remain on the Foreign Relations Committee while serving on one of the other committees.

15. Oleszek, *Congressional Procedures,* pp. 44 and 47. The phrase *authorizing committees* primarily refers to the Senate Committee on Foreign Relations and the House Committees on International Relations and Financial Services (international financial institutions and the Export-Import Bank). Other committees are becoming more involved in foreign assistance matters, including the House and Senate Armed Services Committees (cooperative threat reduction and certain security assistance); Senate Committee on Banking, Housing, and Urban Affairs (the Export-Import Bank and international financial institutions); the House Committee on Government Reform and the Senate Committee on Homeland Security and Governmental Affairs (procurement and reorganization); and the Senate Committee on Health, Education, Labor, and Pensions (global health).

16. The impact of the congressional budget process on foreign assistance is discussed in detail in the next section of this chapter.

17. Although restrictions on foreign organizations providing abortion services with nonfederal funds (the Mexico City Policy) had been addressed by executive orders since 1981, the new House majority in 1995 insisted on addressing it legislatively. As differences between the House and the Senate precluded disposing of the policy issue in permanent law, the Speaker held up and almost derailed the conference agreement on the fiscal 1996 appropriations for Foreign Operations for three months between November 1995 and February 1996 in an attempt to force the issue. For the next decade, the Mexico City Policy issue was addressed in annual appropriations acts but also served to inhibit enactment of comprehensive authorization legislation.

18. Chairman Lugar's bill (S. 2127, cosponsored by Senators Joseph Biden and Charles Hagel), was unanimously reported from the Foreign Relations Committee on March 18, 2004; the bill was reintroduced as S. 209 on January 31, 2005. See *Stabilization and Reconstruction Civilian Management Act,* S. 209, 109 Cong. 1 sess. (Government Printing Office, 2005). Chairman Hyde's bill to reform the United Nations passed the House and has been awaiting Senate action since June 21, 2005. See *Henry J. Hyde United Nations Reform Act of 2005,* H.R. 2745, 109 Cong. 1 sess. (Government Printing Office, 2005).

19. It should be noted that in 2003, 2004, and 2005, for the first time in many years, the Foreign Relations Committee unanimously cleared for Senate consideration several comprehensive foreign assistance authorization bills. The Senate merged the first bill, S. 1161, with an authorization for other State Department programs, S. 925, and considered it on July 9 and 10, 2003, but proceedings halted when amendments emerged pertaining to hate crimes and the minimum wage, threatening to delay three pending appropriations bills. The second bill, S. 2144, was never taken up by the Senate during 2004. On April 6, 2005, the Senate suspended debate on S. 600, a bill to authorize FY

2006 and 2007 appropriations for the Department of State and international broad-casting activities, for the Peace Corps, and for foreign assistance, in order for senators to attend the funeral of Pope John Paul II; the Senate leadership never found time to complete consideration.

20. Not all of the fifty-seven work for the chairman. Senior minority members of the committee are allowed to appoint a number of professional staff.

21. Oversight can be described as continuous review of how well programs are man-aged and meet their objectives, with attention to effectiveness and efficiency. For foreign assistance programs, oversight requires visits to field locations abroad and interaction with individuals actually carrying out the programs, as well as with purported benefici-aries of the assistance.

22. For a recent and useful summary of the evolution of U.S. international assistance and the role of Congress in previous attempts at reorganization, see Carol Lancaster and Ann Van Dusen, *Organizing U.S. Foreign Aid* (Brookings, 2005).

23. P.L. 93-344.

24. Until 1974 budget function 150 was a tool used solely by the OMB to assemble the president's budget request. It was a new term, then, for the members and staff of the authorizing committees and the foreign aid community. Now no longer particularly relevant, the term "function 150" is often used by advocacy groups as shorthand for for-eign assistance and diplomatic funding.

25. *Organization of the Congress: Final Report of the Joint Committee on the Organi-zation of the Congress,* December 1993 (www.rules.house.gov/archives/jcoc2.htm [Feb-ruary 2006]).

26. Authorization levels in recent years are generally consistent with the president's request or the most recent budget resolution passed by the relevant house. Chairman Lugar, especially, has advocated Senate budget resolution levels for function 150 as close as possible to the request.

27. Normally this would occur in late May, immediately after the approval by both houses of Congress of a concurrent resolution negotiated between the two budget com-mittees. If a budget conference has failed to reach agreement, the House and Senate may assign different interim allocations to the two appropriations committees, subject to later modification. Whatever device is employed, a procedural point of order will be upheld against a floor amendment that causes an appropriations bill to exceed its cur-rent allocation.

28. Several congressional budget agreements during the 1990s included separate fire-walls for function 150. See *Omnibus Budget Reconciliation Act of 1990,* P.L. 101-508, sec. 1311.

29. Bill Heniff Jr., *Baselines and Scorekeeping in the Federal Budget Process,* Report 98-560 (Congressional Research Service, Library of Congress, September 5, 2003).

30. Budget resolutions contain ceilings for both budget authority and outlays for the overall budget and for each function, such as function 150 (international affairs). For for-eign assistance, *appropriations* is generally interchangeable with the term *budget authority* used in budget resolutions. Any estimated discrepancy between outlays and revenues would be shown as the estimated deficit or surplus on September 30, the end of the fiscal year.

31. Most foreign assistance activities occur a year or more after the appropriation is provided; thus the actual disbursements or outlays occur over six years, primarily in

the second and third years. In years when overall foreign assistance levels are constant or declining, total outlays from prior years plus the current year may exceed the appropriations level.

32. Some notable examples were proposals to forgive international debt, provide loan guarantees for Israel, and provide contingent or callable capital for the World Bank.

33. See *Foreign Military Sales Act of 1971*, P.L. 91-672, sec. 10, and *State Department Basic Authorities Act of 1956*, P.L. 84-885, sec. 15.

34. This group was made up of the chairmen and ranking minority members of the House and Senate Appropriations Subcommittees on Foreign Operations.

35. As chairman of the Foreign Operations Committee between 1985 and 1994, Obey initiated debt relief for Poland in conjunction with debt relief for Egypt during the first Gulf War; moved bilateral foreign assistance to an all-grant basis, supported Secretary of State George Shultz in his tough-love support for Israel during its 1985 economic crisis; and in 1993 began the process of eliminating earmarks from the House foreign assistance bill.

36. See the *Foreign Affairs Reform and Restructuring Act of 1998*, enacted as division G of the *Omnibus Appropriations Act 1999* (P.L. 105-277). Contending House and Senate authorization committee staff presented divergent versions of the restructuring bill to the appropriators for inclusion in the Omnibus Appropriations Act in the final hours before the conference agreement was filed in the House; the version enacted into law is believed to have been drafted in the Senate.

37. The full story remains to be told about the yielding of much of USAID's operational autonomy to the State Department during President Clinton's second term. Ironically, the then-secretary of state led the opposition to congressional Republican efforts to merge USAID into the State Department. During President George W. Bush's first term, the State Department continued to oppose congressional efforts to clarify USAID's status as an independent agency under the policy direction of the secretary of state.

38. In 1993 the OMB did a review (Presidential Review Directive no. 20) of foreign assistance undertaken by domestic agencies. At that time the total amount of assistance-like overseas activities from the Departments of Health and Human Services, Housing and Urban Development, and Education, as well as the National Aeronautics and Space Administration and the Smithsonian Institution, exceeded $1 billion. In the intervening years, expanded overseas civilian activities by the Defense and Justice Departments and the Drug Enforcement Agency likely bring the total to more than $2.5 billion.

39. Dugger, "Planning to Fight Poverty."

40. The Department of Defense now directly funds training of security forces, including police in Iraq, and most of the Nunn-Lugar Cooperative Threat Reduction Program and controls most Iraq reconstruction funds. The Treasury Department now receives direct funding for an expanding international technical assistance program and debt relief. Health and Human Services funds a share of the Global Fund to Fight AIDS, Tuberculosis, and Malaria and part of the President's Emergency Plan for AIDS Relief. And the Labor Department funds international programs to combat child labor.

41. See Lael Brainard, chapter 2 in this volume, for an analysis of the operational consequences of this organizational sprawl.

42. This was the formal title of the position in 2002, before it was placed under the nominal authority of a new assistant secretary. During Deputy Secretary of State Richard

Armitage's term of office, the director continued to have direct access to the deputy secretary and, when necessary, to the secretary of state. The status of this vital position is uncertain; the most recent incumbent now occupies a senior staff position at the OMB, under the title of associate director for national security programs.

43. Stephen Moore, "Commentary," *Wall Street Journal,* January 16, 2006, p. A14.

44. Citizens against Government Waste, *The Congressional Pig Book 2005* (Washington, 2005).

45. For this reason the continuing focus on function 150 by foreign aid advocacy groups is puzzling.

46. Former House Appropriations Committee chairmen Bob Livingston and C. W. Bill Young, and former Senate Appropriations Committee chairmen Mark Hatfield and Ted Stevens were active members of their respective Foreign Operations Subcommittee for many years. Perhaps this experience accounted for their special consideration for foreign assistance in the 302 allocation process.

47. Such separate allocations are popularly known as *firewalls.*

48. Traditional food aid authorized under P.L. 83-480 (*Agricultural Trade Development Assistance Act of 1954*), purchased in the United States, is funded through annual Agriculture, Rural Development, Food and Drug Administration, and Related Agencies Appropriations acts.

49. Many "regular" domestic appropriations acts fund international programs, ranging from African and Asian elephant protection by the Department of the Interior to the anti–child labor programs of the Department of Labor. The new foreign assistance programs referred to above are ones that most clearly fall under the jurisdiction of the Foreign Operations Subcommittee, such as a contribution to the Global Fund to Fight AIDS, Tuberculosis, and Malaria from the last three Labor, Health and Human Services, and Education, and Related Agencies Appropriations Acts, 2003–05.

50. This issue is discussed in more detail by J. Stephen Morrison, chapter 3 in this volume.

51. Although the Millennium Challenge Account was developed within the Executive Office of the President with minimal congressional consultation, its structure and objectives were modified as the result of hearings in the House and the Senate and during committee markup and floor consideration in the House.

52. Expected to be a major movie, a book by George Crile, *Charlie Wilson's War* (Atlantic Monthly Press, 2003), is an excellent account of how the House Appropriations Committee actually functioned behind the scenes.

53. However, short-term resolutions to continue government operations during October and November for agencies whose appropriations have not been enacted are commonplace.

54. And recently a vice president has joined the ranks. On December 19, 2005, Vice President Dick Cheney told the Associated Press that the Budget and Anti-Impoundment Act had eroded the authority the president "needs to be effective, especially in the national security area." See Nedra Pickler, "Cheney Defends Presidential Powers" (apnews.myway.com/article/20051220/D8EK28B82.html [December 20, 2005]).

55. These limits to foreign assistance are usually contained in restrictive provisions in annual appropriations acts, as well as in permanent, narrowly focused laws that originate in the authorizing committees.

56. The use of the phrase "notwithstanding any other provision of law" or similar language is pervasive in legislation affecting foreign assistance. In this discussion, the relevant reference is to the *Foreign Assistance Act of 1961,* as amended, P.L. 87-195, sec. 491(b). The unauthorized Transition Initiatives account utilizes this authority to evade statutory restrictions on foreign assistance.

57. Department of State, *Congressional Budget Justification for Foreign Operations, Fiscal Year 2006* (February 15, 2005) pp. 30–31. The request was denied with the following explanation: "The potent authorities of this account were granted for use in limited and carefully targeted situations where flexibility and nimbleness were vital to successful transition. They were not intended to cover all USAID assistance to a given country." See *Report Accompanying H.R. 3057, Foreign Operations, Export Financing, and Related Programs Appropriations Act, 2006,* 109 Cong. 1 sess. (Government Printing Office, 2005), p. 29.

58. There is a consensus that the "notwithstanding" language does not apply to criminal statutes. Until recently, it was assumed not to negate small business provisions or procurement contracting provisions of law

59. USAID, *FY 2005 Statutory Checklists* (December 2004).

60. There is no analogous checklist of requirements imposed by executive orders or other presidential or cabinet-level directives. With the well-known exception of the Mexico City Policy on family planning and reproductive health, reinstated under a January 22, 2001, presidential memorandum for the administrator of USAID, few executive orders are restrictive.

61. See P.L. 87-195, secs. 116, 491(b), 498B(j), 502B, and 620A; P.L. 83-480, sec. 202(a); *Emergency Supplemental Appropriations Act for the Defense and for the Reconstruction of Iraq and Afghanistan, 2004,* P.L. 108-106, sec. 2209; and *Foreign Operations, Export Financing, and Related Programs Appropriations Act, 2005,* P.L 108-447, division D, title II and secs. 522, 526, 534, and 536; and P.L. 83-480, sec. 202(a).

62. P.L. 87-195, sec. 614.

63. It is generally recognized that excessive use of section 614, or using it in the face of bipartisan opposition, would lead to its repeal.

64. Technically, funds were provided for several years under Presidents Clinton and George W. Bush to the multilateral Korean Energy Development Organization, not directly to North Korea.

65. The Contingency Fund was reduced from its 1973 level of $25 million to $1.8 million in 1975. See *Continuing Appropriations Act, 1973,* P.L. 92-571, and *Foreign Assistance and Related Programs Appropriations Act, 1975,* P.L. 94-11.

66. The reference to the difficulty of finding a source of funds to support the 2005 Liberian elections is based on comments to House members responsible for international affairs by the secretary of state in late 2005.

67. See the opening statement of Chairman Lugar, *U.S.-Indian Nuclear Energy Cooperation: Security and Nonproliferation Implications,* Hearing before the Senate Committee on Foreign Relations, 109 Cong. 1 sess. (November 2, 2005). See also *U.S.-India Global Partnership: How Significant for American Interests?* Hearing before the House Committee on International Relations, 109 Cong. 1 sess. (November 16, 2005), and *U.S.-India Global Partnership: The Impact on Nonproliferation,* Hearing before the House Committee on International Relations, 109 Cong. 1 sess. (October 26, 2005).

68. This issue has been discussed in the *Foreign Service Journal* and addressed by Congress in the establishment of the Pearson Fellowships, which give career foreign service officers an opportunity to work in Senate and House offices for one year. Numerous former Capitol Hill staff members subsequently served on the National Security Council (NSC) staff, but few have returned from senior NSC positions to comparable positions in the House or the Senate.

69. In the aftermath of the 1994 election, when the margins between the majority and minority in each house were historically close, the congressional leadership expanded its authority over party members, and the role of committee chairmen was reduced. When a single party controlled both houses of Congress and the White House, as was the case after 2002, some observers noted the emergence of a semiparliamentary system. See Oleszek, *Congressional Procedures,* pp. 318–22. For a recent analysis of the "inalterable changes in the way power is amassed and used on Capitol Hill," see Jeffrey Birnbaum and Jim VandeHei, "DeLay's Influence Transcends His Title," *Washington Post,* October 3, 2005, p. A1.

70. During the 1990s the House Foreign Operations Subcommittee chairmen hosted dinner parties for the secretary of state and subcommittee members. The practice was initiated by Chairman David Obey and continued for a year by his successor.

71. See USAID, *Foreign Aid in the National Interest: Promoting Freedom, Security, and Opportunity* (January 2003); *U.S. Foreign Aid: Meeting the Challenges of the Twenty-First Century* (January 2004); *Fragile States Strategy* (January 2005); and *Policy Framework for Bilateral Foreign Aid* (January 2006). The disconnect between the agency's efforts and the White House is exemplified by what happened with the USAID budget justification for fiscal year 2005: it was delayed for six weeks because of concerns by the OMB that its approval of the administrator's draft introductory remarks could be construed as presidential endorsement of USAID's January 2003 policy paper

Foreign Aid Reform Commissions, Task Forces, and Initiatives: From Kennedy to the Present

Larry Nowels

U.S. foreign assistance policy, programs, and organization have been the subject of extensive—some would say excruciating—examination by policymakers, academics, the broad international development community, and American lawmakers throughout the post–World War II period. Yet the formal channels for these efforts—the presidentially appointed commissions, legislative branch task forces, and lawmaking attempts—often floundered, failing to develop the consensus necessary to implement their policy recommendations. At best, some of these structured efforts yielded ideas that individually may have caught the attention of new administrations and may have formed the basis for selective reforms. But as comprehensive, integrated packages, the results have been modest. Only two such reform efforts—the early initiatives of the Kennedy administration and passage of the New Directions legislation in 1973—could be considered successful.

Presently, there has not been a broad foreign aid reform effort launched since early in the Clinton administration, and Congress has not enacted annual foreign assistance authorizations in two decades. Although the policy and program compositions have changed significantly during this period, they have not been the direct result of recommendations emerging from a formally constituted body or legislative review effort. This record is not necessarily surprising or unique within the circles of policy commissions and task forces focusing on any number of subjects: they are formed with great fanfare, disbanded after well-publicized events setting out the results of their deliberations, and in many cases forgotten.[1]

Since 1960 there have been at least seven major foreign aid reform efforts:

—Kennedy administration initiative and enactment of the Foreign Assistance Act of 1961;

—Peterson Commission, 1969–70;

—New Directions legislation, 1973;

—Humphrey initiative and the creation of the International Development Cooperation Agency, 1977–79;

—Carlucci Commission, 1983–84;

—Hamilton-Gilman Task Force, 1988–89; and

—Wharton Report and the Peace, Prosperity, and Democracy Act, 1993–94.[2]

This chapter looks at the history and rationale of each of these undertakings and examines the variety of characteristics that were common or different among the various groups. This is followed by a series of observations, based on the historical record, regarding the challenges confronting foreign aid reform initiatives. It then concludes with some thoughts as to what is necessary to maximize the potential for policy relevance and results.

Major Executive and Legislative Foreign Aid Reform Initiatives

The following are thumbnail sketches of the intent of the commission or project.

Kennedy Administration and the Foreign Assistance Act of 1961

During the earliest days of the Kennedy administration, top White House and State Department officials launched a strategy to legislate changes in U.S. foreign assistance policy and structure. They were guided in their effort by a belief that foreign aid funding was inadequate, bureaucratic organization was unnecessarily diffused, legislation providing authority and direction took a piecemeal approach, and there was too great a focus on short-term strategic matters and insufficient attention to the longer view of international development.[3] Within eight months after taking office, President Kennedy signed into law the Foreign Assistance Act of 1961 and a new organization, the Agency for International Development (now referred to as the U.S. Agency for International Development, or USAID) was established.[4] Both entities remain in effect today.

Peterson Commission

Formed in September 1969, the first year of the Nixon administration, the Task Force on International Development was chaired by Rudolph A. Peterson, president of the Bank of America. Known as the Peterson Commission, this group of exclusively private individuals examined the full breadth of U.S. foreign assistance and issued in March 1970 a series of recommendations for change.[5] A year later, the administration included a number of the Peterson Commission proposals in legislation to Congress. Lawmakers, however, did not embrace the group's major recommendations, as congressional committees were already at work drafting ideas for significant reshaping of U.S. development assistance policy that diverged from executive branch thinking.

New Directions Legislation

With growing dissatisfaction that American development assistance did not directly address the problems and needs of the poorest populations in the developing world, coupled with multiple defeats of foreign aid authorizing legislation in the 92nd Congress (1971–72), a group of House and Senate lawmakers, backed by private think tanks, drafted bills in 1973 focusing on the basic human needs of the rural poor.[6] The legislation, which passed Congress in that year and became known as the "New Directions" legislation, restructured American economic aid around several "sectoral" activities, including agriculture, population, education, and selected development elements such as the environment and energy. The New Directions bill amended the Foreign Assistance Act of 1961 and remains the core structure, although with important subsequent modifications, of current authorizing law. This sectoral approach began to change during the Reagan administration, with a greater emphasis on the role of the private sector in development and on increased aid conditionality. After 1987 these specific program activities no longer received annual authorizations of funds, and by the early 1990s, appropriations legislation had largely shifted away from the sectoral categories, providing instead resources for broader development aid accounts.

Humphrey Initiative and the International Development Cooperation Agency

Four years after passage of the New Directions legislation, Senator Hubert Humphrey mounted an effort to elevate the importance of development assistance in U.S. foreign policy decisionmaking and to better coordinate the various government departments involved in economic aid policy formulation and delivery. After Senator Humphrey's death, the Carter administration embraced the idea and developed a reorganization plan in 1979, establishing a "super" aid coordinating body—the International Development Cooperation Agency (IDCA). But with intense bureaucratic infighting throughout the process, the IDCA never functioned as envisioned. Several agencies, most notably the Treasury Department, operated outside the IDCA, and a series of USAID administrators served as acting IDCA directors until the organization was officially abolished in 1999.

Carlucci Commission

Two years into the first Reagan administration, the president appointed former ambassador and then-deputy defense secretary Frank Carlucci to head the Commission on Security and Economic Assistance, which had a mandate to better define the role of security aid vis-à-vis development assistance in U.S. foreign policy. There was a growing perception within the administration that foreign aid was "broken," that the program's unpopularity in Congress was growing, and that there was an increasing level of distrust between the two branches on aid matters. The commission issued a long series of recommendations in late 1983.[7] However, when attention shifted to Central America, the Kissinger Commission, and associated disputes, the Carlucci Commission effort received little attention.[8]

Hamilton-Gilman Congressional Task Force

With the end of the cold war only a few years away and an increasing recognition of changing global conditions, the chairman of the House Foreign Affairs Committee in 1987 appointed two senior members—Lee Hamilton and Ben Gilman—to shepherd a bipartisan effort to rewrite basic foreign aid laws. The initiative was intended to restructure legislation that was now over twenty-five years old to reflect the new realities of U.S. foreign policy, to narrow and clearly define the core objectives of American foreign aid, to streamline congressional restrictions placed on administration management of the program, and to repair the unpopularity in Congress and the divisiveness in executive-legislative relations over foreign assistance. Although the House Foreign Affairs Committee endorsed legislation reflecting much of the Hamilton-Gilman Task Force's recommendations, key members, including Representative Gilman, dissented from some of the major proposals.[9] Without executive and Senate support, the initiative died.

Wharton Report and the Peace, Prosperity, and Democracy Act

In the early months of the Clinton administration, Deputy Secretary of State Clifford Wharton was named to lead a review of U.S. foreign aid policy that would design a post–cold war policy framework and reform USAID.[10] After giving assurances to a Democrat-controlled Congress that a plan would be presented shortly, Deputy Secretary of State Wharton fell out of favor within the administration and resigned before releasing his report. The executive branch subsequently sent Congress draft legislation that flowed from the Wharton effort—the Peace, Prosperity, and Democracy Act—in late 1993. But the bill stalled in the Senate, and after the 1994 elections in which Republicans took control of the House, the Clinton administration did not resubmit the act for legislative consideration.

Characteristics of Foreign Aid Commissions and Reform Groups

While these seven foreign aid reform efforts all shared one common goal—to modify and improve to one extent or another some aspect of American foreign assistance—they diverged in several other important ways. Collectively, they followed the same path but took different approaches, some of which contributed to their efforts while others worked against the groups' objectives.

Rationale

In general, the various commissions or legislative initiatives were motivated by three primary purposes:

—*Dissatisfaction with current foreign aid policy.* The Kennedy administration effort, the New Directions legislation, and the Carlucci Commission each formed largely around the premise that the structure and focus of

American foreign assistance policy was flawed and needed a comprehensive remake.

— *Lack of public or congressional support.* Foreign assistance, since its inception, has suffered from the absence of a constituency—or at least a *vocal* constituency—that promotes and encourages spending on foreign aid. More often, foreign aid, especially economic assistance, has been viewed as taking resources away from domestic programs that provide direct benefits to Americans. In the drafting of the Foreign Assistance Act of 1961, the creation of the Carlucci Commission, and the launch of the Hamilton-Gilman Task Force, this concern was one of utmost importance.

— *Changing global realities demanded change.* Especially with the end of the cold war, the shape and legislative foundation of American foreign assistance, still grounded in the rhetoric of the East-West confrontation, was one of the principal rationales for undertaking a reform initiative. The Hamilton-Gilman Task Force and the Wharton Report were both launched with this consideration in mind.

Primary Initiator

Both the executive and legislative branches of government have taken the lead in forming foreign aid reform groups. The Peterson Commission and the Wharton initiative each originated within the administration, whereas Congress launched the New Directions legislation and the Hamilton-Gilman Task Force. The Kennedy administration began the process of writing the Foreign Assistance Act of 1961 but later gained considerable help in Congress as the legislation wound its way to passage in 1961. Conversely, the idea of an overarching coordinating agency began with Senator Humphrey but was eventually put in place through an executive order.

Scope

Perhaps because of the inherent difficulties, few foreign aid reform initiatives have attempted to address the issue in the most comprehensive manner possible. Only the Peterson Commission issued recommendations that applied not only to the major economic and security elements of foreign assistance but also linked their proposals with changes in U.S. trade policy and ways to promote private investment in developing nations. Most efforts—the Kennedy administration initiative, the Carlucci Commission, the Hamilton-Gilman Task Force, and the Wharton Report—focused strictly on the more traditional humanitarian, development, and military assistance policies. Two other initiatives—the New Directions legislation and the creation of the IDCA—excluded consideration of changes in security assistance and addressed only economic and development aid reforms.

Membership

The makeup of the various foreign aid reform groups diverged widely. By far the largest and most diverse was the Carlucci Commission, composed of forty-two members, with a mix from the private sector (fifteen), Congress (nine), and congressional and executive ex-officio participants (eighteen). The Kennedy administration effort began as largely a White House–State Department initiative, but it turned into a broader effort after the president named Henry Labouisse, administrator of the International Cooperation Agency, to head a task force and issue recommendations. The Labouisse Task Force included private citizens, representatives from the Ford Foundation, and staff from the International Cooperation Agency. Congress ultimately became extensively involved during debate and passage of the 1961 act.

Other efforts, however, were more exclusive. The key participants in the New Directions legislation and the Hamilton-Gilman Task Force were largely members of Congress, although both initiatives reached out to private international development organizations and the executive branch for input and advice. The Wharton attempt evolved as a closely held State Department activity that faced obstacles at the White House, where a similar review was under way. Congress was brought into the discussion only after Wharton had left his post and State Department lawyers had drafted legislation to implement the findings and recommendations of the somewhat aborted Wharton Report. The Peterson Commission included only private citizens (sixteen), drawn mainly from the financial and legal sectors, the academic community, and corporations. Several had served in senior government or military positions, but none currently held public positions.

Agency Realignment Issues

Abolishing or restructuring existing government agencies is one of the most difficult and contentious activities to undertake by any administration or Congress. These foreign aid reform groups approached this matter in various ways, ranging from a comprehensive reorganization plan to more modest changes at the margins to no recommendations for change. The Peterson Commission set out what was perhaps the most ambitious agenda, calling for the creation of three entities: a U.S. International Development Bank, Institute, and Council, the last of which would operate out of the White House as a coordinating mechanism. The Kennedy administration initiative proposed to consolidate the two existing economic aid operatives—the International Cooperation Agency and the Development Loan Fund—into a single entity: the U.S. Agency for International Development. The Carlucci Commission, with an eye on integrating economic and security aid policies, suggested the creation of a new Mutual Development and Security Administration that would manage both aspects of foreign assistance.

Less ambitious were the IDCA, New Directions, and Hamilton-Gilman efforts. In its final form, the IDCA was created as an entirely new structure to coordinate USAID and a few smaller aid components, but this was a significant departure from its earlier version, which planned to incorporate the Treasury Department's aid responsibilities, the Peace Corps, and the Department of Agriculture's food aid programs under the new coordinating body. The New Directions legislation retained USAID as the primary economic assistance agency, adding only a new Development Coordinating Council to advise the president. The Hamilton-Gilman Task Force recommended the replacement of USAID with an Economic Cooperation Agency, but the responsibilities of the new entity would remain virtually the same.

The Wharton effort proposed no bureaucratic overhaul other than to strengthen USAID, an agency many perceived as severely weakened during the previous administration. Within two years, however, Congress and the administration embarked on a bitter debate, settled only late in the Clinton administration, over whether to abolish USAID and consolidate its responsibilities in the State Department.

Funding Issues

The question of how much to spend on foreign assistance is another thorny matter, especially at times of large budget deficits. Most foreign aid reform efforts either avoided the issue or made it a low-profile aspect of the overall package of recommendations or legislation. Only the Carlucci Commission proposed an increase in all types of American foreign assistance, including an increase in grant military aid that became a controversial subject among the commissioners. The Kennedy administration proposed an increase in economic assistance but with a corresponding reduction in military aid that would result in no change in the net size of the foreign aid budget. Despite the significant cuts to foreign assistance spending between

1985 and 1997, neither of the two reform initiatives undertaken during this period made funding a central topic.

Congressional Oversight Issues

The matter of executive-legislative relations and congressional oversight of foreign aid policies and implementation became prominent in recommendations made by both the Hamilton-Gilman Task Force and the Wharton Report and its associated draft legislation. Each proposed a reduction in congressional earmarking and the elimination and streamlining of a range of foreign aid restrictions and conditions that had been imposed over the years in legislation. The Carlucci Commission also proposed the creation of a formal executive-legislative consultation group. With the degree of partisanship and distrust between the two branches increasing after the Vietnam War and the policies in Central America during the early 1980s, leaders in both branches sought to create a better climate for cooperation and for more constructive oversight of foreign assistance by Congress. Achieving broad consensus, however, has proved extraordinarily difficult.

Legislation

All of the reform groups recommended new legislation to implement their proposals, although with varying degrees of action and success. The Peterson and Carlucci Commissions suggested statutory changes but did not include specific language in their reports. Each of the other efforts made legislation a significant part of the reform package. Draft bills that emerged from the Hamilton-Gilman Task Force and the Wharton Report were debated but not enacted. The Foreign Assistance Act of 1961, the New Directions legislation in 1973, and the IDCA bill and reorganization plan were examples of successful efforts to significantly rewrite existing laws, although the last initiative was never implemented as envisioned.

Key Challenges Confronting Foreign Aid Reform Efforts

With a nearly forty-five-year record of relatively modest success in foreign aid reform initiatives, several lessons can be drawn from the experience that may help future groups translate their recommendations into new policies that demonstrate impact and achieve the intended results. Nine specific themes are offered here that explain why some initiatives succeeded while others failed.

Gaining Direct Presidential–White House Participation

Having the president, or at least the senior White House staff, play a high-profile, actively engaged role in a foreign aid reform effort is highly desirable and perhaps crucial to its success. The most direct involvement of a president and White House occurred during the Kennedy administration. In the early weeks of the new presidency, communications from the National Security Council and Secretary of State Dean Rusk appealed for the highest level of presidential leadership in developing a strategy to alter U.S. foreign aid policy.[11] Within sixty days of his inauguration, President Kennedy sent Congress a special message on foreign aid and made the creation of the Labouisse Task Force the lead announcement of an April 1961 press conference.[12] Passage of the new Foreign Assistance Act was an important element in the administration's legislative agenda, and continuing constructive engagement among White House staff, State Department officials, and key members of Congress paid off with passage of the act on September 4, 1961.

None of the other foreign aid reform efforts had such direct White House, presidential, and State Department involvement. The Wharton group promised at least high-level participation by the State Department. But a separate White House review of funding for all U.S. foreign policy programs stalled completion of the Wharton Report. Subsequently, the deputy secretary fell out of the department's inner circle and resigned before his study was complete.

Congressional initiatives have never received strong administration support, let alone direct involvement of the president or secretary of state. In fact, it is more common for efforts directed by the legislative branch to encounter negative interventions by the executive branch. As the Hamilton-Gilman legislation advanced, for example, White House officials threatened a presidential veto when congressional support waned for earlier task force recommendations regarding fewer earmarks and program restrictions.[13]

Maintaining a Cohesive Message among the Primary Advocates

While all commissions, review groups, and other types of entities established to recommend policy change must go through a period of debate and airing of different opinions, once proposals are issued, it is critical for the participants to speak in a supportive and consistent voice while the matter is under consideration by the broader community. This was a particularly strong characteristic of the New Directions legislation and the Kennedy administration reform efforts. The principal architects of the New Directions process were a group of twenty-six House Foreign Affairs Committee members, representing a strong bipartisan core from which to advance the legislation. Equally important, the members of this "rump" group remained together in the following years to monitor how the executive branch implemented the New Directions policy changes.[14] In the case of the Kennedy administration efforts, not only did officials maintain an unusual degree of cohesion between the White House and State Department throughout the process, but an added level of credibility was achieved when the administrator of the International Cooperation Agency, Henry Labouisse, as chairman of the reform task force, recommended the abolition of his own agency.

Other efforts did not enjoy such cohesion. The creation of the International Development Cooperation Agency was heatedly debated within the executive branch, with the Departments of State and Treasury in opposition and USAID in favor. As the original Humphrey bill became watered down through executive in-fighting, USAID Administrator John Gilligan resigned a month before the president's submission to Congress of the reorganization plan that would create a significantly weakened IDCA. Fourteen years later, the White House drew attention away from the Wharton effort by launching its own separate review of foreign policy programs and budgets. This had the effect of blurring the purpose and status of the Wharton Report. Likewise, the Hamilton-Gilman Task Force project was brought into question and its bipartisan nature eroded when Congressman Gilman withdrew support from two of the key recommendations: a five-year phase-out of military base rights assistance and a reduction in congressional earmarking.

Marshaling the Involvement of All Stakeholders

It is essential to solicit the active participation of the broadest array of those who will play a role in implementing a foreign aid reform proposal. Such stakeholders would include the White House and appropriate executive agencies, Congress, foreign policy activists, private sector interests, and nongovernmental and international organizations. The Carlucci Commission was perhaps the best example of being inclusive in its makeup and review process. At the other end of the spectrum was the Wharton project, which was very much an "inside" effort with little outreach to Congress or the broader foreign aid community until the later stages.

For congressional initiatives, it is especially important to gain support and active participation across houses to improve the chances of legislative success. Although the New Directions effort evolved around a concept developed by the House Foreign Affairs Committee, its Senate counterpart had launched a similar initiative after the Senate defeated a foreign aid bill in 1971. Consequently, the Senate Foreign Relations Committee was ready to follow the House's lead in considering the New Directions legislation. The Hamilton-Gilman Task Force is given high marks for soliciting the views of the broad foreign aid community, meeting frequently over a one-year period with key players within and outside the government.[15] However, the task force did not reach across Congress to engage the Senate Foreign Relations Committee until well after the House had begun to consider the task force's bill. The legislation received no action in the Senate.

Generating Early Congressional Involvement and Ownership if Legislation Is Planned

If legislation is necessary to implement reform measures, Congress is the critical institution. Recognition of this is one of the important factors that made the Kennedy administration effort succeed. Consultations with key committee members began immediately after Kennedy took office. The March 22, 1961, special foreign aid message, which came before the Labouisse Task Force had formed, signaled Congress that a proposal would be forthcoming. Thus supportive members of Congress were prepared to act once draft legislation arrived.

The Carlucci Commission tried to address this issue by including among the commissioners a number of members of Congress that could later help shepherd the recommendations from concept to law. But the bipartisan nature of the commission members began to erode as the Democrats raised concerns over a perceived bias in favor of security assistance. Ultimately, Representative Matt McHugh, a senior member of the Appropriations Committee, dissented on this issue in the commission's final report.

The Wharton effort evolved into a quagmire of raised congressional expectations, delayed delivery, and shunned legislative branch input until near the end. Deputy Secretary Wharton had told congressional committees in early 1993 that his work would be completed in ninety days, allowing

Congress ample time for consideration that year.[16] By the time a draft bill appeared in November 1993, congressional frustration was high and the Democrat-controlled Congress held no ownership of the proposal.

The same principle applies if it is the Congress that initiates: an invitation to the administration to participate should be extended and actively pursued. But the record indicates that the challenge may lie with executive officials who are reluctant to follow the congressional lead. Both the New Directions initiative and the Hamilton-Gilman Task Force sought out administration involvement. Following the defeat of foreign aid authorizing bills in the early 1970s, congressional leaders asked the executive branch to submit a proposal to overhaul development assistance objectives and policy. When a "business-as-usual" draft foreign aid bill arrived on Capitol Hill in early 1973, House and Senate committees abandoned efforts to work with the executive branch and moved to produce their own legislation. Years later the Hamilton-Gilman Task Force actively invited administration input throughout the year-long review period. But executive involvement did not reach a sufficiently high level. And when the task force's proposals to reduce earmarks and soften restrictions came under question by members of Congress, the administration moved away from endorsing the initiative.[17]

Comprehensive Reform Maximizes Impact but Faces Greater Challenges

A broad, comprehensive foreign aid restructuring effort that extends at least across all elements of assistance—and perhaps into trade and overseas investment policy as well—holds the promise of both achieving significant results and bringing greater policy coherence to this important foreign policy instrument. But with a wider scope, the prospects for more resistance and possible failure grow. The two most successful efforts took on a more targeted approach, tackling only a portion of the vast array of foreign assistance programs. The Kennedy administration initiative began with a broad examination of both economic and security assistance but ultimately only focused on economic matters. New Directions legislation, from the outset, sought to affect American policies and programs dealing with development assistance, especially those matters that most directly affected the poorest developing countries.

Moving beyond these targeted initiatives, those that attempted to address the broader framework of military and economic aid issues confronted resistance that undermined the bipartisan spirit of the effort. Both the Carlucci Commission and legislation that emerged from the Wharton Report encountered serious problems over the matter of balancing economic and military programs and over the degree of flexibility to afford the administration in managing security assistance. Seeking greater integration between aid and trade policy has not been part of most review efforts. Only the Peterson Commission, which drew its members exclusively from the private sector, issued recommendations that touched on trade and investment concerns.

Articulating a Clear Policy Message and a Plan for Implementation

Fashioning a foreign aid reform proposal that clearly states the problems, issues recommendations for fixing those problems, and sets out a path for implementation that is well understood by the targeted audience are important ingredients for success. Three of the reform efforts, in particular, were widely criticized for issuing less-than-clear alternative policy frameworks. The Peterson and Carlucci Commissions produced a lengthy list of individual recommendations but fell short on providing a sense of prioritization and how the separate proposals intersected into a coherent, comprehensive structure. Moreover, neither offered a "road map" for executive and legislative action to translate recommendations into reality.

In a similar way, critics of the Wharton effort argued that the proposal lacked a clear "vision" and a unified structure that would lead to a logical strategy framework. The new central objective of economic assistance—sustainable development—was not well defined and led to questions regarding exactly what types of activities would be supported under this overarching goal. Efforts to convince Congress to abandon appropriations tied to functional accounts and to base resource allocations on policy goals did not succeed during the first Clinton budget, even before the Wharton Report emerged. Submission of the Peace, Prosperity, and Democracy Act in late 1993 and a new budget proposal in early 1994 failed to satisfy congressional members who were skeptical of shifting to a more amorphous resource allocation scheme.[18]

Reorganizing Bureaucratic Structures

Not since the Foreign Assistance Act of 1961 and the creation of the Agency for International Development has a foreign aid reform commission or legislative initiative been responsible for restructuring how the government administers foreign assistance. Most groups proposed some action on this front but without results. Proposals to abolish agencies or diminish the authority of departments to exercise control over programs encounter serious resistance, usually from those most directly affected and perceived as the "losers" in the reorganization efforts. The difficulty in creating new agencies and alternative points of influence and control can be seen most clearly in some of the recent debates over establishing the Department of Homeland Security and implementing the intelligence reform structural recommendations of the September 11 commission. Events that spark a national crisis, such as the attacks of September 11, may be necessary ingredients for generating support for major bureaucratic reorientation. And even then, as witnessed in the debates over homeland security and intelligence reform, the path is difficult.

While most foreign aid reform groups proposed some sort of reorganization, the recommendations were either not taken seriously, represented marginal change of little substance, or were watered down during interagency discussions. The IDCA is a case in point. The original concept of the Humphrey proposal was to establish a new "super-coordination" body that would help integrate international development policy and programs across the entire U.S. government. But resistance immediately emerged from the Peace Corps, which operated with a large degree of independence, and from the Treasury Department, where continued oversight of U.S. participation in international financial institutions without "interference" of a coordinating unit was aggressively defended. Ultimately, the IDCA formed late in the Carter administration without a mandate to oversee these elements of U.S. development policy. With no interest in strengthening the IDCA evinced by President Reagan and subsequent administrations, the organization never functioned and was abolished in 1999.

Despite the lack of success by foreign aid reform groups in altering the governmental landscape, several foreign assistance agencies have been created in recent decades. The Overseas Private Investment Corporation, the Inter-American and African Development Foundations, the Trade and Development Agency, and the Millennium Challenge Corporation are examples of new structural actors in American foreign assistance. But to some degree the creation of these institutions is symptomatic of the absence of a successful comprehensive reform effort. Like new aid policy goals that have emerged over the years, these new structures have been added but not necessarily *integrated* into a coherent organizational framework, a situation that only compounds the problems of efficient coordination, duplication of effort, and bureaucratic rivalries.

Indeed, growing organizational incoherence is the central critique of foreign aid in chapter 2 of this book. In that chapter Lael Brainard surveys four potential organizational models, assessing their strengths and weaknesses in solving the major problems facing U.S. foreign assistance today. As she notes, the reform that holds the greatest promise for material improvements in the effectiveness of foreign assistance also faces the greatest political hurdles.

Forging a Congressional-Executive Partnership in Foreign Aid Policymaking

One of the most contentious foreign aid issues between these two branches of government has been the degree of congressional oversight—or the extent of congressional "intervention," as executive officials frequently characterize it. Little progress has been made in agreeing on an appropriate balance or the proper threshold for congressional involvement in foreign assistance program management.

Three of the reform groups proposed a reduced congressional role, especially in those areas the executive found most troublesome. The Carlucci Commission recommended that development and military assistance restrictions and conditions be modeled after the authorities that governed the Economic Support Fund. This fund is a highly flexible aid instrument, unencumbered by more rigorous program conditionality and congressional reporting, that provides economic support for security purposes or to countries of strategic importance to the United States. The major goal of the Hamilton-Gilman Task Force was to improve congressional-executive relations in foreign aid policymaking, which led to it to recommend reducing funding earmarks, relaxing some restrictions, and eliminating unnecessary reporting requirements. The Wharton Report and the Peace, Prosperity, and Democracy Act also sought broader executive flexibility and enhanced program authority, coupled with the consolidation of existing restrictions into a series of generic provisions that were not regional or country specific.

Each of these proposals faced stiff opposition in some congressional quarters. Representative McHugh dissented from the majority on the Carlucci Commission on the matter of enhanced military aid authority. Congressman Gilman withdrew support of his task force's recommendation to reduce earmarks. And the Wharton effort and the follow-on legislation upset key congressional allies by proposing more flexible security assistance authorities and the elimination of the Development Fund for Africa, an initiative that Democrats had enacted in the late 1980s in order to protect funding for development assistance in sub-Saharan Africa.

In chapter 8 Charles Flickner discusses the current impediments to an effective partnership between Congress and the executive branch. His recommendations recognize the limitations on Congress tying its own hands, and instead focus on reinvigorating the oversight role of authorizers; improving the effectiveness of communication among authorizers, appropriators, and executive branch officials; and narrowing the scope for certain types of binding earmarks and presidential initiatives to similar degrees.

Timing Foreign Aid Reform Recommendations to Maximize Success

Formulating a reform agenda that fits best within the executive schedule and the congressional calendar is a factor that should be given serious attention. Most observers will agree that new policy initiatives formulated early in a new administration and submitted to Congress before the summer-dominated season of appropriations bills is optimum.

The Kennedy administration effort is the best example that followed this conventional wisdom. The president first publicly announced plans to offer a foreign aid reform proposal on March 10, 1961, six weeks after taking office; submitted a draft bill to Congress on May 26; and signed the legislation on September 4. The New Directions initiative and the Hamilton-Gilman Task Force were also well timed. House and Senate authorizing committees produced bills in the spring of 1973, the first year of a new Congress, thereby avoiding debate on a major foreign aid issue during the following election year of 1974. The Hamilton-Gilman effort used the second session of the 100th Congress to conduct its review and formulate recommendations before circulating a draft bill early in the new legislative session after the inauguration of President George H. W. Bush.

Other initiatives were not as well timed, a factor that worked against their ultimate goal. The Peterson Commission did not issue its final report until March 4, 1970, too late for the Nixon administration to translate the recommendations into legislation that nonelection year. Even so, the White House took an additional thirteen months to submit a draft bill to a waiting Congress, a point at which the House Foreign Affairs Committee believed it was too late to consider. The Carlucci Commission produced its list of findings and policy proposals in November 1983, which would have forced administration attention during the final year of the first Reagan term and congressional debate during a period leading up to national elections. The Wharton effort promised a plan early in the Clinton administration but delivered it nearly a year later, another instance of an untimely debut in an election year.

While timing is important, unforeseen events can emerge to challenge and possibly derail movement on reform initiatives. Although it would be difficult to imagine any circumstances that might have transformed the IDCA into a functioning entity, the election of President Reagan in 1980, the transfer of Senate control to Republicans, and the emergence of Senator Charles Percy, an IDCA opponent, as chairman of the Senate Foreign Relations Committee sealed its status as an orphan organization. At the time the Carlucci Commission issued its report, the administration and Congress became increasingly distracted by events in Central America and the high-profile recommendations of the Kissinger Commission for U.S. policy in the region. Similarly, despite the delay of the Wharton Report, it may have been possible to refine the draft bill and resubmit it to Congress in 1995. However, the surprise loss of the House majority by Democrats in the 1994 election fundamentally altered the political landscape and ended any chance for reviving the Peace, Prosperity, and Democracy Act. Perhaps one lesson for policy review groups is to minimize the length of time between the conclusion of work and the implementation decision point.

Conclusion

The record of foreign aid reform commissions and comprehensive legislative rewrite efforts over the past forty-five years has been modest at best. Few achieved their intended results or will be remembered as a "model" process for future endeavors. Nevertheless, this is not to say that the findings and recommendations that emerged from the various reform groups had no policy impact. In fact, some proposals appear to have formed the basis for subsequent discussions and debates. The Hamilton-Gilman Task Force recommendations for reshaping U.S. development goals resemble to a large extent the structure proposed in the Wharton Report and are similar to development assistance strategic objectives adopted by USAID during the Clinton and Bush administrations. The task force's view that Congress should reduce the practice of earmarking initiated a debate that continues today. In the intervening period, foreign aid appropriations bills have eliminated a number of earmarks in the legislation itself and substituted a growing body of "soft" or nonmandatory provisions in committee reports that offer some degree of flexibility to the administration. The Wharton group debated the topic of abolishing USAID and merging its functions into the State Department but abandoned the idea. The issue returned a year later and continued as a contentious matter within and between the executive and legislative branches. Although not abolished, USAID has seen its responsibilities narrow as new foreign aid initiatives have emerged during the current Bush administration.

At the same time, it is clear that substantial changes in foreign aid goals, policies, and practices can occur without the backing of a formal commission, task force, or other similar effort. Incrementally, the shape of U.S. foreign assistance since the end of the cold war has undergone significant alterations. Separate aid programs emerged to help the states of Eastern Europe and the former Soviet Union transition to democratic societies and market economies. Relief for the most heavily indebted poor countries expanded during the 1990s, culminating in a multilateral framework within which the U.S. is a major participant.

There have been many more recent piecemeal developments as well. As detailed in chapter 3 by J. Stephen Morrison, promoting global health has become a dominant feature of American development aid policy, with a significant increase in emphasis and resources on combating HIV/AIDS, malaria, and tuberculosis. As shown by Steven Hansch in chapter 5, humanitarian assistance has expanded. A highly selective, performance-based program—the Millennium Challenge Account—has been established, as described by Steve Radelet in chapter 4. In the post-September 11 era, the war on terrorism, as discussed by Patrick Cronin and Tarek Ghani in chapter 7, has become an increasingly important foreign aid priority. Moreover, significant transitions in agency authority and policy guidance over foreign aid have occurred, with the Defense Department and domestic agencies assuming responsibilities that traditionally have been under the direction of the State Department and USAID. All of this has occurred separately from any broad reform process.

The very nature of this incremental approach, however, is what leads a number of analysts—including the contributors to this volume—to conclude that some type of overarching, comprehensive effort is needed to bring policy coherency and strategic relevance to American foreign assistance in the twenty-first century. Perhaps the record of previous efforts can help guide those responsible for the next attempt at a broad-based foreign aid reform initiative.

Notes

1. See, for example, Edward C. Luck, "U.N. Reform Commissions: Is Anyone Listening," keynote speech for the Conference on "The Ideas Institutional Nexus," University of Waterloo, Ontario, Canada, May 16, 2002 (www.sipa.columbia.edu/cio/cio/projects/waterloo.pdf [February 2006]).

2. Some will note that many other foreign aid reform recommendations have emerged during this period, including those sponsored by private groups or international organizations and financial institutions. Since this chapter focuses on efforts initiated by the executive and the legislature, these other equally thoughtful—and in some cases influential—projects are not discussed. The Ferris Commission, mandated by Congress in 1991, is also not examined due to its relatively specific focus on administrative issues at the U.S. Agency for International Development.

3. This analysis of the foreign aid program was submitted to President Kennedy by Walt Rostow, Deputy Special Assistant for National Security Affairs, in a memorandum dated February 28, 1961. See U.S. Department of State, *Foreign Relations of the United States, 1961–1963*, vol. IX: *Foreign Economic Policy* (Government Printing Office, 1997), sec. 6, no. 94, "Crucial Issues in Foreign Aid."

4. P.L. 87-195.

5. *U.S. Foreign Assistance in the 1970s: A New Approach. Report to the President from the Task Force on International Development* (Government Printing Office, March 4, 1970).

6. For an overview of several proposals, see Congressional Research Service, *The Reorganization of U.S. Development Aid* (Library of Congress, May 1973). This report was prepared for the House Committee on Foreign Affairs.

7. See Commission on Security and Economic Assistance, *A Report to the Secretary of State* (Department of State, 1983).

8. In July 1983, at a time of growing criticism over U.S. policy in Central America, President Reagan created the National Bipartisan Commission on Central America, chaired by former secretary of state Henry Kissinger. Amidst increasing American military involvement in the region, the commission recommended a doubling of U.S. economic assistance to $8 billion over five years and additional, but unspecified, amounts of military aid for El Salvador. The administration submitted legislation to implement many commission proposals, and the ensuing debate dominated contentious congressional foreign aid deliberations throughout 1984. Ultimately, Congress rejected a multiyear aid package for the region but approved $1.1 billion for fiscal year 1985.

9. House Committee on Foreign Affairs, *Report of the Task Force on Foreign Assistance*, H. Rept. 101-32 (Government Printing Office, February 1989).

10. Although no final report was publicly issued by the State Department, Deputy Secretary Wharton testified before the Senate Committee on Foreign Relations on July 14, 1993, where he discussed several preliminary observations and possible recommendations. See Senate Committee on Foreign Relations, *Fiscal Year 1994 Foreign Assistance Authorization*, Senate Hearing 103-322, 103 Cong. 1 sess. (July 14, 1993).

11. Memorandum from Secretary of State Rusk to President Kennedy, March 10, 1961. See U.S. Department of State, *Foreign Relations of the United States, 1961–1963*, vol. IX: *Foreign Economic Policy* (Government Printing Office, 1997), sec. 6, no. 95, "New Proposals for the Foreign Aid Program."

12. John F. Kennedy, "Special Message to the Congress on Foreign Aid," March 22, 1961, in *Public Papers of the Presidents of the United States: John F. Kennedy,* 1961 (Government Printing Office, 1961), pp. 203–12.

13. Rochelle Stanfield, "Built without a Blueprint," *National Journal,* no. 14, April 8, 1989, pp. 846–50.

14. Congressional Research Service, *The New Directions Mandate and the Agency for International Development* (Library of Congress, July 13, 1981).

15. For a complete record of the Hamilton-Gilman Task Force activities in 1988, see House Committee on Foreign Affairs, *Background Materials on Foreign Assistance,* 101 Cong. 1 sess. (Government Printing Office, February 1989).

16. Senate Committee on Foreign Relations, testimony of Clifton R. Wharton Jr., at his confirmation hearing to become deputy secretary of state, 103 Cong. 1 sess. (January 25, 1993).

17. John Felton, "Earmark Tradition Shows Staying Power on Hill," *Congressional Quarterly Weekly* 47, no. 17 (1989): 903.

18. Larry Nowels, *Foreign Aid Reform Legislation: Background, Contents, and Issues,* Report 94-23 (Congressional Research Service, Library of Congress, February 9, 1994).

Reforming Development Assistance: Lessons from the U.K. Experience

Owen Barder

It is one of the proudest achievements of the government that we have not merely introduced the International Development Bill, but have increased aid and development money as a proportion of our national income. . . . I believe that our obligations do not stop at these shores. Indeed, it is not merely right, but is in our long-term interest to offer a helping hand out of poverty to the poorest regions of the world.

—TONY BLAIR
House of Commons, March 7, 2001[1]

I n 1997 the incoming Labour government established the new Department for International Development (DFID), with responsibility for the $6 billion aid budget and other aspects of U.K. development policy, led by its own cabinet minister.[2] In the subsequent eight years, the new department established a reputation for itself, and for the U.K. government, as a leader in development thinking and practice. A 2005 study for the Canadian government found that "ten years ago, the DFID was considered a middle-of-the-pack development agency. Today it is generally considered to be the best in the world."[3] DFID was described by *The Economist* as "a model for other rich countries."[4] More new recruits to the management track of the civil service now apply to join DFID than to the traditional

The views expressed and all errors and omissions are the author's; this chapter does not necessarily reflect the views of the Center for Global Development or those of the Department for International Development. Thanks to Sir Brian Barder, Rex Browning, Sally Ethelston, Tony German, John Hicklin, Ruth Levine, Mark Lowcock, Lawrence Macdonald, Richard Manning, Simon Maxwell, David Mepham, Todd Moss, Grethe Petersen, Judith Randel, and Sir John Vereker for comments on an earlier draft.

first choices, the Foreign Office and Her Majesty's Treasury (the Treasury), combined. The overhaul of foreign assistance institutions and policies has been described by Tony Blair as one of the Labour government's proudest achievements and may be seen in time as one of its greatest legacies.

This chapter summarizes the institutional changes and policies that led to the establishment of the Department for International Development and its reputation as a global leader in development since 1997. It considers the objectives of policymakers in establishing the new structure, the extent to which these have been met, and the challenges in the years ahead. It draws lessons for other countries considering similar reforms.

Development Assistance and the Colonies, 1929–61

The British aid program evolved from relationships that began during the British Empire.

Before World War II

Until the 1920s the British government took the view that colonial administrations were responsible for maintaining law and order and that they should meet the costs of administration and such social services as were provided from any revenues that could be raised locally. Colonies were not encouraged to look to the U.K. government for financial or economic aid, and there were no programs for colonial development. Any aid to colonies was voted by Parliament annually and was generally limited to temporary emergencies.

It was not until 1929 that the British government accepted any legal responsibility for providing financial assistance to the colonies. The Colonial Development Act 1929 was intended mainly to reduce unemployment in the United Kingdom by promoting industry and trade.[5] It established a Colonial Development Fund that was not to exceed £1 million (about $70 million in 2004 prices) in any one year to support agriculture and industry in the colonies and in so doing promote "commerce with or industry in the United Kingdom." Funds were allocated by the Colonial Development Advisory Committee after a systematic examination of all schemes and projects put forward by colonial governments. The committee generally felt that the act did not permit aid for social services, recurrent expenditures, or projects that would not result in any gains for the United Kingdom.

Between 1935 and 1938, social unrest plagued the colonies. The Colonial Office became convinced that the rapid succession of disturbances in Trinidad, Barbados, and Jamaica were the result of low wages, high unemployment, and poor housing and sanitary conditions, and feared similar disturbances in other colonies that had similar problems. It became clear that the restrictions in the Colonial Development Act 1929 were not sustainable. The result was the Colonial Development and Welfare Act 1940, passed in wartime by a coalition government, which increased funds to £5 million a year (about $300 million in 2004 prices) and extended the purposes of the Colonial Development Act to include the welfare of the subjects of the colonies.

Postwar Development Policy

The postwar Labour government took the view that the U.K. government should play a substantial role in assisting the development of the colonies. The Colonial Development and Welfare Act 1945 replaced the two previous acts and increased aid to £120 million (about $6 billion in 2004 prices) over ten years.[6] This longer commitment was intended to allow colonial governments to plan long-term schemes of public works, social services, and agriculture.[7] Each colonial government was required to prepare a ten-year plan, in consultation with representatives of the local population. A large proportion of the money that went into each ten-year program was provided out of local revenues and loans: the British government sought to minimize the amount funded by aid "so as to prevent even a suggestion of political pressure from the United Kingdom."[8] The Colonial Development and Welfare Act established the United Kingdom's first systematic aid programs to be operated not mainly in the interests of the donor.

Two development corporations were established in 1947: the Colonial Development Corporation, to operate in the colonies, and the Overseas Food Corporation, to function anywhere in the world. The objectives of the corporations were to bring about a "speedier and more widespread development of our territories overseas for the benefit of the Colonial peoples, whose low standard of living can only be raised by greater use of their natural resources."[9]

Evolution of Policy, 1960–97

After World War II, there was a significant change in thinking in the United Kingdom and abroad about the role of foreign aid, driven by the success of

the Marshall Plan and by the changing relationships between the United
Kingdom and its colonies.

Changed Thinking about the Role of Aid

The success of the European Recovery Program (the Marshall Plan) generated optimism that the combination of capital and technical assistance could
transform economies in a very short time.[10] Though it is popular today, it is
worth recalling that it took some time and a considerable effort by President Truman and his colleagues to secure U.S. public support for the Marshall Plan. The State Department organized a large-scale and well-funded
public education program, including providing trips to Europe for many
members of Congress to see for themselves the need for U.S.-sponsored
reconstruction. In the end it was increasing Soviet intransigence and the
communist takeover of Czechoslovakia in February 1948 that eventually
persuaded Congress to approve the original Marshall Plan appropriation.[11]

The breakup of the British, French and other European empires created
a number of poor, independent countries, and it became increasingly
unsustainable for them to restrict development aid only to the remaining
colonies. The U.K. government declared in 1958 that aid would be extended
to former colonies that were members of the Commonwealth and to some
non-Commonwealth countries. The British began to offer a combination of
budgetary and technical assistance grants, concessionary loans, and loans
under the Export Guarantee Act. The Colonial Office, which was responsible for managing the colonies and the process of decolonization, worked
under a guiding principle of the "paramountcy of interests of the colonial
peoples," under which it had a duty to press for these interests within government even against Britain's other interests. Many officials who joined
the Colonial Office were idealistic, supportive of aid, and in favor of multilateral institutions.[12]

As well as increasing support for the idea of foreign aid, the Marshall
Plan also led directly to the establishment of an important international
development institution. The Organization for European Economic Cooperation (OEEC) had been formed in 1948 by the recipients of aid from the
Marshall Plan, and in 1960 the Development Assistance Group was established within OEEC as a forum for consultations among aid donors on
assistance to less developed countries. In March 1961 the Development
Assistance Group agreed to the Resolution of the Common Aid Effort (see
box 10-1). Later that year, the OEEC became the Organization for Eco-

---

BOX 10-1 Resolution of the Common Aid Effort

The Development Assistance Group:

—*Conscious* of the aspirations of the less-developed countries to achieve improving standards of life for their peoples;

—*Convinced* of the need to help the less-developed countries help themselves by increasing economic, financial, and technical assistance and by adapting this assistance to the requirements of the recipient countries;

—*Agree* to recommend to Members that they should make it their common objective to secure an expansion of the aggregate volume of resources made available to the less-developed countries and to improve their effectiveness;

—*Agree* that assistance provided on an assured and continuing basis would make the greatest contribution to sound economic growth in the less-developed countries;

—*Agree* that, while private and public finance extended on commercial terms is valuable and should be encouraged, the needs of some of the less-developed countries at the present time are such that the common aid effort should provide for expanded assistance in the form of grants or loans on favourable terms, including long maturities where this is justified in order to prevent the burden of external debt from becoming too heavy;

—*Agree* that they will periodically review together both the amount and the nature of their contributions to aid programmes, bilateral and multilateral, keeping in mind all the economic and other factors that may assist or impede each of them in helping to achieve the common objective;

—*Agree* to recommend that a study should be made of the principles on which Governments might most equitably determine their respective contributions to the common aid effort having regard to the circumstances of each country, including its economic capacity and all other relevant factors;

—*Agree* that the Chairman, assisted by the Secretariat, shall be invited to give leadership and guidance to the Group in connection with the proposed reviews and study.[1]

---

1. Adopted by the Development Assistance Group, March 29, 1961, London. See Helmut Führer, *The Story of Official Development Assistance. A History of the Development Assistance Committee and the Development Cooperation Directorate in Dates, Names and Figures* (Paris: Organisation for Economic Co-operation and Development, 1996).

---

nomic Cooperation and Development (OECD); its new emphasis on promoting development was epitomized by the rapid establishment within its structure of the Development Assistance Committee (DAC), which grew out of the Development Assistance Group.

The Marshall Plan therefore had a strong influence not only because it promoted the idea of economic cooperation and illustrated its possible effectiveness but also because it left an important organizational legacy in the DAC. The U.S. government played a leadership role continuously from the Marshall Plan to the establishment of the Development Assistance Committee, which was chaired by U.S. ambassadors from its creation until 1999.

Against this background in the early 1960s, a more coherent aid policy was beginning to develop within the United Kingdom. In 1960 a Treasury white paper argued that the best way to lift poorer nations out of poverty was through economic development.[13] It argued that the provision of private capital would be the main catalyst for this, but money from the United Kingdom exchequer would continue to provide aid. A 1963 white paper took an optimistic view of the prospects for developing countries and described aid as a transitory concept. It supported aid both as a good in itself but also because it encouraged trade.[14] In 1961 the Conservative government established the Department for Technical Cooperation to consolidate in one place the technical expertise for the colonies that had been spread across several government departments. The Colonial Office was being reduced in size as a result of decolonization, and many of its staff transferred to the Department for Technical Cooperation, helping to preserve the expertise that had been acquired during the colonial period.

Ministry of Overseas Development, 1964–70

In 1964 the incoming Labour government kept a manifesto promise to establish a Ministry of Overseas Development (ODM). Thus began a tradition of successive governments changing the organizational structure for administering development assistance, as shown in table 10-1:

Table 10-1 Evolution of British Foreign Assistance Structure, 1961 to Present

Structure	In cabinet	Outside cabinet
Separate government department	1964–67	**1961–64**[a]
	1997–present	1967–70
		1974–75
Answerable to the Foreign Office	1975–76	**1970–74**
		1977–79
		1979–97

a. Boldface indicates Conservative governments; the remainder are Labour governments.

The ODM combined the functions of the Department of Technical Cooperation and the overseas aid policy functions of the Foreign, Commonwealth Relations, and Colonial Offices and of other government departments. The intention was that this new ministry should develop and execute all aspects of development policy (not just aid), be separate from the Foreign Office (so that development policies were not subordinated to other foreign policy interests), and have a planning staff of economists (at a time when economists were rare within government).[15] The first three ministers of overseas development were members of the cabinet.[16]

A new white paper in 1965 made a case for aid based both on moral duty and on the long-term interest of the United Kingdom.[17] Aid was not to be given as a response to requests from developing countries but rather as a result of a joint effort to identify the needs of recipients. The goal of the new policy was to get the most development effect from aid, and so the 1965 white paper shifted policy toward project-tied aid, with financial terms linked to economic conditions in the recipient country.

The ODM did not live up to the high expectations that had been created. Aid spending rose only slightly during the Labour government's term of office, partly because of balance of payments and fiscal constraints. From August 1967 the ministerial office was demoted out of the cabinet, which greatly reduced its leverage within the government. Though the ODM remained a separate government department, it was no longer represented in the cabinet. The ODM was always an aid ministry rather than a development ministry—it did not have any impact on trade policy or political relationships with overseas governments, and even on aid the most important decisions were made by an interdepartmental committee. It was not able to define a coherent policy agenda: a further white paper in 1967 was largely a progress report, consisting mainly of a detailed account of the complexities of the British aid program.[18]

Ministry of Overseas Development, 1970–74

After the reelection of a Conservative government in October 1970, the Ministry of Overseas Development was incorporated into the Foreign Office and renamed the Overseas Development Administration (ODA). The ODA was overseen by a minister of state in the Foreign Office who was accountable to the foreign secretary.[19] In practice, there was little change as a result of this institutional shift. Though it was now a section of the Foreign Office, the ODA was relatively self-contained with its own min-ister, and the policies, procedures, and staff remained largely intact.

Reestablishment of the Ministry of Overseas Development, 1974–79

When it was returned to office in 1974, the Labour government announced that there would once again be a separate Ministry of Overseas Develop-ment with its own minister. However, as in the period from 1967 to 1970, the minister would not be a member of the cabinet.

The new government proposed a significant change in aid policy, set out in the 1975 white paper *The Changing Emphasis of British Aid Policies: More Help for the Poorest*.[20] British aid was to be focused on the poorest countries, many of whom had been hard hit by the rise in oil prices, the food crisis, and a deterioration in their terms of trade. Aid was to be allo-cated to have "the most effect in alleviating the worst poverty over the long term." The priorities would be

(a) to give an increasing emphasis in our bilateral aid to the poorest countries, especially those in the group most seriously affected by the rise in the price of oil and other commodities;

(b) to give special emphasis to programmes oriented towards the poorest groups within these countries, and especially to rural development;

(c) to promote situations in which British concessional aid funds can best serve to stimulate matching contributions from other governments, and to encourage the deployment of such aid through both multilateral and bilateral channels towards the poorest countries."[21]

Though the white paper played down the extent of the change that this entailed, this was a genuinely new focus on poverty. It adopted a basic needs approach, identified the rural poor as the main group to be brought out of poverty, and committed the United Kingdom to increasing the resources devoted to the agricultural sector. The white paper also recog-nized the importance of international institutions, including a substantial section on Europe, and it discussed the importance of international trade policy decisions and investment as well as aid.

Once again, the evolution of the aid program did not live up to the pol-icy aspirations set out in the white paper. An important weakness of the 1975 white paper was that it did not lift the constraint that U.K. aid could not, in general, be spent on meeting local costs. Aid projects often had to be selected not for their development benefits but because they could be designed in such a way as to have a high proportion of U.K. content. For example, the Indonesia program had to concentrate on groundwater projects because these were the only identifiable rural development activities that would use U.K. goods and services (such as consultants, drilling equipment, and pumps.) The problem of local costs was not solved until exchange controls were abolished in 1979.

From June 1975 the powers of the minister for overseas development were formally transferred to the foreign secretary.[22] From December 1976, after the resignation of Reginald Prentice, the minister for overseas development was no longer a member of the cabinet. Though the Overseas Development Ministry remained technically a separate government department, administratively distinct from the Foreign Office, this meant that in practice development was not given a separate voice within the government. In 1977, partly to shore up its difficult relations with U.K. business, the government introduced the Aid and Trade Provision. This enabled aid to be linked to nonconcessionary export credits, with both aid and export credits tied to procurement of British goods and services. Pressure for this provision from U.K. businesses and the Department of Trade and Industry arose in part because of the introduction of French mixed credit programs, which had begun to offer French government support from aid funds for exports, including for projects in countries to which France had not previously given substantial aid.[23] Though the amounts were initially capped at 5 percent of aid spending, the effect of the Aid and Trade Provision was to bias aid toward higher-income countries and more capital-intensive projects, and the developmental impact criterion for project approval was only superficially applied.

During the 1974–79 Labour government, the ODA had institutional independence, an ambitious policy agenda, and high-level political support. There was a reasonably generous increase in aid resources during this time, from 0.37 to 0.51 percent of national income, despite the government's precarious fiscal position. Yet the department failed to establish itself firmly within government, could not protect the aid program from being distorted by commercial objectives, and was unable to influence broader government policies that had an impact on poor countries. To a large extent this was because the department was not working within a supportive Whitehall environment and was not able to create one.[24] At the same time, chronic pressure on the balance of payments prevented the adoption of policies that separated aid from the promotion of U.K. exports.

Development Policies under the Conservatives, 1979–97

After the election of the Conservatives under Margaret Thatcher in 1979, the ministry was transferred back to the Foreign Office, as a functional wing again named the Overseas Development Administration. The ODA continued to be represented in the cabinet by the foreign secretary while the minister for overseas development, who had day-to-day responsibility for development matters, held the rank of minister of state within the Foreign Office.

New legislation, the Overseas Development and Cooperation Act 1980, changed little, affirming the government's broad powers to use aid funds for a wide variety of purposes. While the new government did not publish a new white paper on overseas development, there was nonetheless a significant shift in aid policy under the Conservatives. According to one writer, "Few things so quickly symbolized Mrs. Thatcher's victory in the 1979 general election as the changes that were soon made to government overseas development policy and spending."[25] The new minister for overseas development, Neil Marten, announced in February 1980 that the government would "give greater weight in the allocation of our aid to political, industrial, and commercial objectives alongside our basic developmental objectives."[26] The result was a significant expansion of the Aid and Trade Provision and a number of bilateral aid projects designed to support British businesses, including steel mills, Leyland buses, Hawker-Siddeley aircraft, and Westland helicopters.[27]

The statement also set out the government's preference for bilateral aid over assistance provided through multilateral institutions such as the European Commission. In practice, however, the difficulty of renegotiating international commitments meant that multilateral contributions were harder to reduce in the short term than bilateral aid. This meant that as the aid budget fell, the burden of reduction actually fell on the bilateral portion rather than the multilateral portion, and so aid provided through multilateral institutions actually rose as a share of a declining total.

The new government was more candid about its willingness to promote such foreign policy objectives as maintaining the U.K.'s leadership role in the Commonwealth and its permanent seat on the UN Security Council.[28] Thus although developmental concerns were still accorded considerable weight and Conservative ministers responsible for aid were held in good regard within development circles, there was a real shift of emphasis in the conduct of development policy.

During the 1980s the balance of payments gradually lost its political significance, partly as a result of the abolition of exchange controls in 1979 and partly because of what became known as the "Lawson Doctrine," which held that a current account deficit was not a cause for concern if it was the counterpart of a private sector deficit.[29] This reduced the government's macroeconomic interest in using the aid program to promote British exports. Whereas during the 1980s nearly half the British aid program was restricted to goods and services originating in the United Kingdom, this was gradually reduced in the 1990s and applied to only about 15 percent of bilateral aid by 1996.

With the fall of the Berlin Wall and the end of the cold war, the British government felt able to reduce the weight of foreign and economic policy considerations in its aid allocations, and instead to link aid more directly to democracy and good governance. In June 1990 Foreign Secretary Douglas Hurd stated that "economic success depends to a large degree on effective and honest government, political pluralism and observance of the rule of law, as well as freer, more open economies." He called on donors to redirect aid toward better-governed countries: "While countries tending towards pluralism, public accountability, respect for the rule of law, human rights, and market principles should be encouraged, those which persisted with repressive policies, corrupt management, or with wasteful and discredited economic systems should not expect aid donors to support their folly with scarce aid resources which could be used better elsewhere."[30]

The pressure to break the link between aid and commercial considerations was further increased in 1994 by a High Court ruling, regarding the Pergau dam project in Malaysia, that asserted there was no legal basis for the government to use development funds for primarily commercial purposes. (The Pergau Dam affair is explained in detail in appendix 10A.) Douglas Hurd wrote afterwards, "The Pergau episode vexed me greatly at the time. It spoiled what was otherwise a creditable record which Lynda Chalker with my support had built up on aid."[31]

Throughout the whole of its existence, the Overseas Development Administration was staffed mainly by home civil servants, although some members of the diplomatic service have spent parts of their careers there. At its peak in 1979, it employed 2,300 staff, which fell to 1,500 in 1987 as aid budgets were progressively reduced during the Thatcher administration. The rundown of staff numbers was complemented by a reduction in overseas manpower. In the mid-1960s there were about 16,000 British staff working on contract to developing countries, receiving a salary supplement from the Overseas Development Ministry. By 1990 this had been reduced to almost none.

Establishment of the Department for International Development

The Department for International Development was established by the incoming Labour Government in 1997. The creation of a single department with broad responsibilities for development issues followed naturally from Labour's desire to "join up" government as well as from its approach to foreign affairs.

Policy Context

Labour had been out of office since 1979, losing four consecutive general elections. Tony Blair became leader of the opposition in 1994 and set about modernizing the Labour party's image and policies, under the banner of "New Labour." He removed the commitment to public ownership from the party's constitution. With Gordon Brown, who would become finance minister in the Labour government, he neutralized the party's reputation for "tax-and-spend" by promising to spend no more than the Conservatives planned to spend.

Under Tony Blair, New Labour described itself as being committed to a pragmatic, evidence-based agenda. The 1997 manifesto declared that "New Labour is a party of ideas and ideals but not of outdated ideology. What counts is what works. The objectives are radical. The means will be modern."[32] Labour presented itself as offering an end to ideological and class politics. Instead, modern policymaking would be driven by research evidence about what was effective in addressing social problems and achieving intended outcomes. In key policy areas such as crime, education, and welfare, Labour officials talked about their commitment to finding out "what works."

One feature of the modernizing agenda was "joined-up government." New Labour had concluded that seemingly intractable problems such as social exclusion, drug addiction, and crime could not be resolved by any single government department. Instead, such problems had to be made the object of a concerted attack using all the arms of government—central and local government and public agencies, as well as the private and voluntary sectors.[33]

New Labour had a less well developed foreign policy agenda (except on relations with the European Union). It did, however, have a distinctive foreign policy message that it would bring an end to what it called "sleaze," as it described a number of connections between businesses, especially arms exporters, and foreign policy. This line of attack was boosted by the Pergau Dam case, in which aid was linked to commercial contracts in a way which was subsequently found to be unlawful.[34] In February 1996 Sir Richard Scott published the results of his inquiry into the sale of arms to Saddam Hussein's government in Iraq, contrary to the UN sanctions regime then in force. Robin Cook, Labour foreign affairs spokesman, enhanced his parliamentary reputation—and nearly brought down the Conservative government—with his charge that the government had sought to cover up its involvement in the illegal arm sales.[35]

For three decades foreign assistance programs had been influenced by the cold war, during which strategic and security interests had affected the government's choice of which countries to support and how; and by the need to support the U.K.'s balance of payments, which had encouraged governments to link overseas aid to British exports. By the mid-1990s, these pressures had largely disappeared, creating an opportunity for Labour to say that it would pursue a foreign policy with an "ethical dimension."[36]

Labour Party's Policy on Development

The publication in 1980 of the Brandt Report had led to renewed thinking about the role of rich countries in international development. The report argued that aid budgets should be increased, focused on the poorest countries, and provided through multilateral institutions; it also asserted that poor countries should have more influence over the decisions of those institutions.[37] During the 1980s and 1990s, independent nongovernmental organizations and consortiums such as the Independent Group on British Aid argued that British aid should be more focused on poverty, de-linked from commercial contracts, and part of a broader government strategy for international poverty reduction.[38] The *Reality of Aid* reports, published from 1993 onwards, set an agenda for both improving and increasing aid.[39]

Internationally, a new consensus was forming on development policy. In May 1995 development ministers and heads of aid agencies adopted a statement, "Development Partnerships in the New Global Context," that identified poverty reduction as the central challenge and endorsed a comprehensive strategy for tackling it.[40] Furthermore, they asked Jim Michel, the American who chaired the Development Assistance Committee, to produce a forward-looking reflection on "strategies looking to the next century."[41] The result was a set of concrete, medium-term goals, all based on the recommendations of major United Nations conferences, to be pursued on the basis of agreed principles: people-centered development, local ownership, global integration, and international partnership. These goals were presented in the report *Shaping the 21st Century,* which was approved by development ministers at the DAC High Level Meeting in May 1996.[42] The objectives agreed upon in this report became known first as the International Development Targets and, after the UN Millennium Summit in September 2000, as the Millennium Development Goals.[43]

While the Labour party was in opposition during 1994 to 1996, it created the Britain in the World Policy Commission to review Labour's policies on a broad range of international issues, including foreign policy, security, and development. The commission, chaired by Robin Cook, recommended the creation of a separate government department responsible for the broad range of international development issues across government, a focus on the poorest countries, and giving less weight to commercial and strategic considerations in overseas aid.

These recommendations were a natural fit with the New Labour agenda of policymaking based on evidence of what works and with joining up policy responsibility for difficult problems across a number of government departments. They had the political benefit of illustrating how the conduct of foreign policy would change to reduce the influence of commercial considerations. They also responded to the agenda to reform overseas aid being advocated internationally by nongovernmental organizations, academics, and others. In practice, the policy commission did not consider the recommendations in detail, and there had been little discussion of the proposals by the time they were hardened into party policy. The recommendations passed into the Labour party policy statement on foreign affairs for the 1997 general election, *A Fresh Start for Britain,* and in summary form into the manifesto:

> Labour believes that we have a clear moral responsibility to help combat global poverty. In government we will strengthen and restructure the British aid programme and bring development issues back into the mainstream of government decisionmaking. A Cabinet minister will lead a new department of international development.
>
> We will shift aid resources towards programmes that help the poorest people in the poorest countries. We reaffirm the U.K.'s commitment to the 0.7 percent

UN aid target, and in government Labour will start to reverse the decline in U.K. aid spending.

We will work for greater consistency between the aid, trade, agriculture, and economic reform policies of the EU. We will use our leadership position in the EU to maintain and enhance the position of the poorest countries during the renegotiation of the Lomé Convention.

We will support further measures to reduce the debt burden borne by the world's poorest countries and to ensure that developing countries are given a fair deal in international trade. It is our aim to rejoin UNESCO. We will consider how this can be done most effectively and will ensure that the cost is met from savings elsewhere.[44]

In the months before the election in 1997, Foreign Office officials suggested to Robin Cook and senior Labour party officials that it would be a mistake to transfer control of the development budget and policy away from the Foreign Office.[45] But at the same time, Sir John Vereker, the most senior civil servant at the ODA, was in close contact with Clare Short, the Labour party shadow secretary of state for overseas development; they agreed to argue for the proposed structures and policies of the future department.[46]

Immediately after Labour's victory in the general election, the new prime minister, Tony Blair, offered the aid portfolio to Clare Short. She was clear that she would not accept the job unless she were given a cabinet post with overall responsibility for development policy generally and not just aid.[47] Short, as secretary of state for international development, was not only a member of the cabinet but also a member of several interdepartmental ministerial committees. As the scope of DFID's work was to cover development policy broadly, she became a member of government committees on the environment, drug abuse, women's issues, health, and export credits, including arms sales. One example of the department's expanded role was that it was consulted on the approval of arms export license applications before they were issued.

Principal Changes to Development Institutions and Policy in 1997

There were three related changes to the structure of U.K. aid institutions and policy in 1997. First, an independent ministry, the *Department for International Development,* was created, headed by a member of the cabinet, with responsibility for aid and development. Like its predecessors, the new department had responsibility for bilateral aid and the funding of multilateral development institutions, but it was also given responsibility for ensuring a joined-up development policy across the government as a whole.

Second, *poverty reduction*—broadly defined—was identified as the overarching objective of aid and development policy. Quantifiable and measurable global targets were identified by which to track progress toward this objective, based on the International Development Targets (which later became the Millennium Development Goals).[48]

Third, the concept of development *policy coherence* was introduced, which acknowledged that managing aid spending was only one (and arguably not the most important) part of development policy, and that the new department had a legitimate voice in the formulation of government policy in other areas (such as trade, conflict, and foreign relations) for which other government departments had primary responsibility.

The New Policies 1997–2005

DFID came into existence at a time of considerable change in international thinking about development. For example, the market economic reforms in Africa had been considered necessary, but it was also observed that they had been painful for the poor and had not always delivered economic growth. While macroeconomic adjustment continued to be an important part of the policy prescription, there was a growing focus on poverty reduction, governance reform, and debt relief.

Establishing Objectives: The White Papers of 1997 and 2000

Within six months of its establishment, DFID had drafted a new government white paper, *Eliminating World Poverty*, which (as the title suggests) set out an ambitious agenda for U.K. development policies.[49] In 2000 the department published a follow-up white paper, looking specifically at the relationship between globalization and development.[50] The paper argued that globalization provided an opportunity to reduce poverty by making poor people and poor countries more productive through better access to markets, imported inputs, finance, and new technologies; but this opportunity would not be realized without supporting actions: some from rich countries and international organizations, and some within developing countries.

These white papers were important not only because of what they said but also because they put on the public record clear statements of the government's approach to international development. This had considerable impact in an environment in which there had not been a white paper for twenty-two years. Both white papers were accompanied by a well-organized publicity and communications effort to explain the new policies, both within the United Kingdom and abroad.

Poverty Reduction as the Goal of Development Policy, with Output Targets

The mission for poverty reduction was clearly announced: "We shall refocus our international development efforts on the elimination of poverty and encouragement of economic growth which benefits the poor."[51] The 1997 white paper shifted the government's measure of success from spending targets (for example, official development aid as a share of national income) to the achievement of the International Development Targets (later known as the Millennium Development Goals).[52]

Explicit Focus on Social Sectors

The 1997 white paper put special emphasis on investment in social sectors as a means to poverty reduction. This seemed to shift the emphasis away from investment in productive sectors such as agriculture and infrastructure (although in practice this shift was already under way before 1997).

Economic Growth and Liberalization

The 2000 white paper proclaimed the importance of economic growth as a means to reduce poverty. This shifted the balance back a little from the focus on social sectors after the 1997 white paper. Coming as it did in the year after the 1999 Seattle protests, the 2000 white paper set out the government's commitment to support trade liberalization and to help poor countries benefit from, rather than resist, globalization.[53]

Development Policy, Not Aid Policy

The white papers announced that in addition to managing the aid program, DFID would develop capacity to analyze a broad range of policies affecting development. This would include policies concerning the environment, trade, agriculture, investment, good government and human rights, conflict prevention, debt relief, financial stability, drugs, migration, and cultural links.

Pursuing Long-Term Poverty Reduction Rather than Short-Term Commercial Interests

The government was clear that the aid program should *not* be used to pursue short-term commercial interests, as this was thought to have an adverse impact on the effectiveness of the development budget. The Aid and Trade Provision program was abolished in the 1997 white paper, albeit replaced by the possibility of continuing to use "mixed credits" that met development criteria but still allowed aid to be tied to British contracts. In practice, mixed credits were not used, and they were formally ended by the 2000 white paper, which announced that U.K. aid would be completely untied.

New Partnerships

The white papers heralded a new way of working with other U.K. government departments, other donors and development agencies, developing countries, and with the private and voluntary sectors. In particular, a new aid relationship between Britain and the governments of developing countries was envisaged, in which developing countries that committed themselves to poverty reduction and good government could in return expect a longer-term commitment from DFID, more money, and greater flexibility in the use of resources. Where possible, DFID would move away from supporting stand-alone projects and dictating exactly how resources were to be used: "Where we have confidence in the policies and budgetary allocation process and in the capacity for effective implementation in the partner government, we will consider moving away from supporting specific projects to providing resources more strategically in support of sector-wide programmes or the economy as a whole."[54]

More Realistic Assessment of Britain's Role

The white papers acknowledged that Britain could make only a modest difference on its own, but there was much that the international community could do by working together. This led to a much more positive view of the need to work closely with other donors. Together with a raft of policy papers on particular topics, embracing collaboration with others helped DFID become extremely influential throughout the development community after 1997.

New View of the Role of the State in Developing Countries

The 1997 white paper criticized previous models of the role of the developing country governments as being either too statist or wrongly believing in a "minimalist" state. It asserted that "there is now an opportunity to create a new synthesis which builds on the role of the state in facilitating economic growth and benefiting the poor. . . . The state is responsible not only for providing the right economic framework but also for ensuring social justice: which means access to services such as health and education and respect for human rights."[55]

Devolution of Aid Management

The new partnership relationship was supported by increased decentralization of DFID's management. Strong field offices, operating with significant delegation of authority, would promote dialogue with recipient countries.

Increased Interdepartmental Cooperation on Conflict Reduction

An example of effective joining-up across government, and DFID's growing role in development policies and not just aid, was the establishment in 2001 of the Global Conflict Prevention Pool and the Africa Conflict Prevention Pool.[56] The purpose of these pools was to bring together the resources of the Ministry of Defense, the Foreign Office, and the Department for International Development to permit a more strategic approach to conflict reduction. The two pools had a budget of about $300 million a year between them. Each was governed by a cabinet committee of ministers from the three departments, chaired by the foreign secretary (Global Conflict Prevention Pool) and the development secretary (Africa Conflict Prevention Pool). Each department spent money allocated to it under its own arrangements for accountability once the strategy had been approved by the interdepartmental committee.

Initiatives under the pool arrangements included development of new governance and justice systems; disarmament, demobilization, and reintegration of fighters into society and development of alternative livelihoods for them; small arms reduction programs; and training for police, armed forces, and other parts of the security sector in democratic and accountable systems that respect human rights. Most of the money was spent on consultancy and other noncapital support for these objectives.[57]

In Sierra Leone, for example, the Africa Conflict Prevention Pool coordinated a program to retrain and reequip both the army and the police, the creation of a ministry of defense with civilian oversight, funding for an anticorruption unit, and support for a truth and reconciliation commission. The pools were especially successful in promoting coordinated activities in the Balkans, Afghanistan, the Middle East, North Africa, Nepal, and Indonesia.

An evaluation found that the pools promoted significantly better cooperation between the departments concerned, especially in London. The expanded pooled funds acted as an incentive for cooperation. Across the areas of policy, both in the recipient country and in Whitehall, regular formal and informal coordination and information sharing has improved.[58] However, a large part of the spending on these objectives by all the participating departments remained outside the pools.

After the success of the two pools in improving interdepartmental coordination and joining-up of development policy across government, the government also established an interdepartmental unit to coordinate work on postconflict reconstruction, which would help countries to put in place quickly the civilian capabilities needed for a stable environment in the aftermath of war so that reconstruction could begin.

International Development Act 2002

In 2002 Parliament passed the International Development Act 2002, foreshadowed in the 2000 white paper. The act replaced the Overseas Development and Cooperation Act 1980. It enshrined in law the single purpose of aid spending: every development assistance project or program must by law either further sustainable development or promote the welfare of people and be likely to contribute to the reduction of poverty.[59] Exceptions were aid to U.K. overseas territories, humanitarian assistance, and contributions to multilateral development banks. The 2002 Act made it illegal for U.K. aid to be tied to the use of British goods and services. It clarified the purposes for which aid could be given to U.K. overseas territories, gave clearer legal authority for DFID's development awareness work, and provided a wider range of mechanisms through which financial assistance could be provided.

Better Aid Allocation to Increase Value for Money

DFID sought to increase value for money by increasing the proportion of its resources going to very poor countries and by increasing public scrutiny of aid allocation decisions. The new department's emphasis on helping countries achieve the Millennium Development Goals required a greater focus on poor countries because these were furthest from reaching the goals. Analysis by economists at the World Bank implied that aid would have greater impact on economic growth if more of it were spent in countries with large numbers of poor people (as well as in countries with better governments).[60] During the 1990s, however, there had been a significant increase in the proportion of global aid going to richer countries, at the expense of poorer countries (within a roughly constant total for global aid). DFID decided to address this not only by redirecting the allocation of U.K. aid toward the poorest countries but also by drawing attention to the allocation of global aid resources, which were not well targeted to reach the Millennium Development Goals. In 1998 DFID set itself an objective of reversing the trend of European Community aid spending, an increasing proportion of which was going to better-off countries.[61]

In 2002 DFID agreed with the Treasury to set a public target of increasing from 78 to 90 percent the proportion of the department's bilateral program going to low-income countries.[62] This commitment, which demanded a significant shift in resources to the poorest countries, became known as the "90–10 rule."

In 2003 DFID published a technical analysis that looked at the results of studies of aid effectiveness to predict where aid spending would have the most impact in terms of lifting people out of poverty, based on the recipients' income, population, extent of poverty, and the quality of governance.[63] This created a publicly available benchmark allocation of aid spending, optimal in its effect on poverty reduction, from which deviations would have to be justified.

Development and Security: Policy since September 11

After the terrorist attacks of September 11, 2001, U.K. foreign policy increased its focus on identifying and supporting "weak and failing states" and on removing the conditions that create the circumstances in which terrorists could recruit and organize. DFID set out its approach in a policy document in 2005.[64] It argued that lack of security was a significant obstacle to achieving the Millennium Development Goals and that poverty and fragile states created fertile conditions for conflict and the emergence of new security threats, including international crime and terrorism.

Under the International Development Act 2002, DFID could not use development assistance to finance programs whose primary objective was tackling threats to the U.K. or global security. The policy document explained the relationship between aid resources and security: "Nor will DFID open programmes in countries on the basis of U.K. or global security considerations alone—there would have to be a prior and compelling poverty reduction case. But we and other development agencies can support programmes that enhance the human security of the poor in developing countries and, in so doing, benefit everyone's safety, whether rich or poor."[65]

Under the new strategy, DFID committed itself to pay greater attention to regional conflict and insecurity and to countries that were pivotal to regional security. It also committed to expanding safety, security and access to justice programs; refocusing governance work to promote accountability that promotes security; increasing efforts on conflict reduction through the conflict prevention pools; and encouraging transparency of payments for the extraction of natural resources.

There was considerable pressure within the U.K. government to increase DFID spending on reconstruction in Afghanistan and Iraq. However, the 90–10 rule (see above) prevented allocations to the poorest countries from being reduced in order to accommodate increased spending in Iraq (which counted as a middle-income country). In order to increase spending in Iraq without breaching the 90-10 rule, DFID decided to accelerate planned withdrawal from other middle-income countries such as Anguilla, Bulgaria, Croatia, Honduras, Macedonia, Peru, and Romania, and reduce spending in Albania, Bolivia, China, Jamaica, Kosovo, Russia, South Africa, and Sri Lanka.[66]

New Whitehall Environment

Other government departments were predictably nervous at first about the establishment of a new department with such broad responsibilities. Both the Foreign Office and the Department of Trade and Industry had in the past been skeptical of the development agenda, and their policies had reflected the lower political priority of Britain's long-term interest in reducing poverty in favor of shorter-term commercial and political objectives. The Department of Trade and Industry was distrustful of the establishment of a trade policy department within DFID, and there were early disagreements with the Ministry of Defense over military training programs in Africa.[67]

There was inevitably some friction between the new department and the Foreign Office. Clare Short wrote afterwards, "The Foreign Office wanted us to run projects and not interfere in political issues such as the ending of conflict in Africa. Africa came low down the list of Foreign Office priorities, but they certainly did not want DFID poking its nose in."[68] These disagreements mainly took the form of low-intensity bureaucratic warfare on issues such as the sharing of classified documents, the clearing of drafts of UN Security Council resolutions, and responsibility for and wording of policy documents, although some of the disagreements were more substantive, especially relating to the conduct of policy in Africa.[69]

Relations with the Foreign Office improved over time. In April 2002 a joint Foreign Office and DFID unit was established to manage the United Kingdom's relations with Sudan. In May 2004 this team won a public service award for best central government team. There was effective collaboration, especially on conflict resolution and postconflict reconstruction. In 2004 the two departments agreed to an "Action Plan for Collaborative Working," which mainly addressed logistical issues, such as sharing services in the United Kingdom and overseas; estates issues, especially colocation overseas; security; and information technology systems.[70] However, the action plan also allowed for country-level collaboration and the joint planning and delivery of shared government targets.[71]

The new department worked closely from the outset with the Treasury. The independence of the Bank of England in 1997 had liberated senior Treasury officials from short-term worries about the conduct of monetary policy, and they were convinced that progress toward the reduction of world poverty was in the long-term economic interest of the United Kingdom. At the ministerial level, there was an especially good relationship between the secretary of state for international development (Clare Short) and the finance minister (Gordon Brown).

Although relations with the Treasury were generally good, there were some early battles. In 1997 DFID argued that the U.K. executive director of the World Bank should be appointed by the department, separately from the U.K. executive director of the International Monetary Fund (IMF). (The two posts were combined in a single appointment made by the Treasury.) A hard-fought compromise was eventually reached: the secretary of state for international development was designated as the U.K. governor of the World Bank, in place of the finance minister, who would remain Britain's governor of the IMF; but the roles of executive director of the World Bank and the IMF were not split and remained a Treasury appointment.[72]

The new department was given the task of changing attitudes and policies across Whitehall, to bring development policy concerns into the mainstream of U.K. government policymaking. This proved easier than had been expected: other government departments increasingly saw the need to build support among developing countries and civil society organizations for their own policies with an international dimension, and regarded DFID as a potentially useful ally in building international support. In 1999, after the failure of the World Trade Organization Ministerial Conference in Seattle, Clare Short proposed that DFID should publish a second white paper, on the impact of globalization. Although this touched on many areas of other departments' responsibilities, they gave strong support to the idea, in part because they saw that they could better pursue their policy priorities if the government built a broader consensus for its approach to international affairs.

The new department built a good network of relationships across Whitehall and established increasing respect for its effectiveness and for the quality of its thinking. Especially through the process of developing the 2000 white paper on globalization, it formed good working relationships with the Department of Trade and Industry, Foreign Office, Ministry of Defense, and the Department for the Environment, Food and Rural Affairs. These relationships contributed significantly to the evolution of policy. For example, the Department of Trade and Industry championed the designation of the new trade round, launched in Doha in November 2001, as a development agenda. In July 2004 it published a white paper, *Making Globalisation a Force for Good*, which set out a trade policy agenda concentrated on helping the poor.[73]

Objectives of the Changes and Assessment

This section identifies the government's aims in making its institutional changes and discusses whether they have been achieved.

Focus on the Reduction of Poverty

While in opposition the Labour party decided that the new aid department should have as its single purpose the reduction, and eventual elimination, of world poverty. And during this same time, in her role as Labour shadow secretary of state for overseas development, Clare Short determined that the immediate objective of such a department should be to harness the global effort to meeting the 2015 Millennium Development Goals.

There were two significant motives for insisting on this focus. The first was to improve value for money spent: using aid to support British exports or other strategic interests over the years had reduced the effectiveness of the aid program. The second was managerial: by setting a single clear mission, ministers and senior officials could increase the focus and motivation of staff. Sir John Vereker wrote afterwards, "This clarity of purpose, rapidly transmitted through the organisation, has been a powerful motivating, unifying, and guiding force over the last five years."[74]

The government was successful in narrowing the focus of development on the reduction of poverty and eschewing the use of aid for commercial or strategic objectives. The white papers scaled back and then abolished tied aid, and the International Development Act 2002 made it illegal for aid to be used for any purpose other than poverty reduction. However, there was some confusion about what focusing on poverty meant. Some stakeholders, including some of DFID's own staff, officials from other government departments, and other donor countries, misunderstood it to mean that DFID would be focused on poverty relief—that is, addressing needs arising from poverty—rather than tackling the underlying causes. DFID ministers and senior officials always understood that long-term, sustainable poverty reduction involved addressing the causes of poverty, and they interpreted this broadly to include investing in economic growth, conflict reduction, improving governance, fighting corruption, and long-term investments such as research and development and human development. Nonetheless, it was some years before it was widely understood, including within Whitehall, that the focus on poverty reduction extended beyond purely humanitarian objectives.

An instructive example of the impact of limiting the department's resources to poverty reduction occurred in May 2002 when the Home Office drew up proposals to reduce the number of asylum seekers in the United Kingdom, which was (and remains) a very sensitive political issue. One proposal was that aid to some developing countries should be made conditional on accepting the return of asylum seekers. The prime minister attached particular importance to cutting asylum numbers, and Downing Street advisers supported tying bilateral British and European Union (EU) development aid for countries such as Somalia, Sri Lanka, and Turkey to commitments to take back rejected asylum seekers.[75] Clare Short opposed using aid funds to "try to blackmail governments into facilitating the early return of failed asylum seekers."[76] She attended a cabinet meeting chaired by the prime minister to consider the proposals, and argued—successfully—that using aid funds in this way would be a breach of the new act.[77] She told the BBC, "In terms of British aid, it is illegal, because under law we can only spend it for development."[78] The proposal was dropped.

Development Policy, Not Just Aid Policy

The government had decided that the new department should not only be responsible for aid but should also have a role in all the development aspects of U.K. policy, including the environment, trade, conflict, political relationships, international economy, and migration. This had been an aspiration of the first Ministry of Overseas Development as long ago as 1964.

The motive for including all aspects of development policy in the department's purview was the recognition that there were important limits on what aid alone could achieve. A great many other policies pursued by rich nations have as much, or more, impact on the reduction of poverty. Five years after the department was established, the outgoing DFID permanent secretary wrote of the responsibilities of the department:

> As the Accounting Officer for the last eight years of a budget now approaching £3.5 billion [$6 billion], and directly responsible to Parliament, I have to say that I spend surprisingly little of my time transferring resources to developing countries. That's the easy bit; but unthinking aid can do more harm than good. Most of the contents of my in-tray now consist of complex policy issues, spanning different government departments and involving many different international collaborations designed to improve the economy and governance of poor countries. These are areas as diverse as civil-military cooperation in conflict, the developing country voice in international trade negotiations, the coherence of European Union policies towards developing countries, the sustainability of debt, the impact of the global environment on poor people, or the ways of encouraging free and fair election.[79]

One example of DFID's expanded role within government was that it was consulted over the issue of arms export licenses for sales to developing countries, as were the Department of Trade and Industry, Foreign Office, and Ministry of Defense. This did not mean that development interests were always placed above commercial or strategic decisions. In December 2001 DFID unsuccessfully opposed an arms export application from British Aerospace for a £28 million ($48 million) military radar system for Tanzania, on the grounds that it was unnecessary and breached the terms of Tanzania's debt relief. After considerable debate within the government, some of which spilled into the press, the prime minister decided in favor of the Department of Trade and Industry, and the sale was allowed.

More Aid

One of the incoming Labour government's policy commitments was to reverse the decline in total aid spending, with the aim of moving toward the UN target of 0.7 percent of gross national product.[80] In practice, since the UN General Assembly agreed to this goal in 1970, successive U.K. governments have committed themselves to move toward this figure without setting a date by which it would be reached.[81] For example, in its February 1974 manifesto, the Labour party said, that "the next Labour government will seek to implement the United Nations Development Target of 0.7 percent of GNP in official aid and will increase the aid programme to meet it."[82] In the period since 1970, the target acquired considerable political significance as a measure of the willingness of governments to commit resources to development.

However, the new government was also committed to maintaining the public expenditure plans of its predecessor, which constrained its ability to increase aid spending. As a result progress was slow in the early years, and in 2001 the Development Assistance Committee peer review of the U.K. aid program noted that the government's rhetoric had gotten ahead of reality: "The government recognises that a more substantial ODA [overseas development assistance]/GNI performance is necessary to demonstrate the United Kingdom's commitment to tackling world poverty and has reiterated its commitment to the United Nations' ODA/GNI target of 0.7 percent. Although the United Kingdom is one of the few DAC Members committed to raising its official development aid volume and lifting its ODA/GNI ratio, it remains far from reaching this target."[83]

Partly as a result of commitments given by the EU to reverse the decline in aid—commitments made in advance of the International Conference on Financing for Development in March 2002, in Monterrey, Mexico—the government budgeted for a more rapid rise in aid from 2002 onward. In 2004 Secretary of State for International Development Hilary Benn and Finance Minister Gordon Brown agreed on future increases in aid at a rate that would reach the target of 0.7 percent of GDP by 2013, and budgeted for those increases up to 2007–08.[84] As figure 10-1 shows, this would represent the most sustained increase in aid as a share of national income for at least forty years, and it was the first time that any British government had set a timetable for meeting the 0.7 percent target.

Focus on the U.K.'s Long-Term Interests

An important motivation for establishing a separate department in 1997 was to increase the attention paid within government to the U.K.'s long-term strategic interests so that these might be properly balanced against short-term pressures. For example, it was recognized that it was in the U.K.'s long-term commercial interests that Africa should emerge as an

**Figure 10-1 Official Development Aid as Percent of GNI in the
United Kingdom, under Conservative (C) and Labor (L)
Governments, 1960–2007**

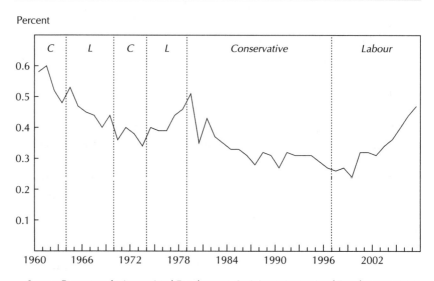

Sources: Department for International Development, *Statistics on International Development* (2004);
HM Treasury, "Further Boost to U.K. Aid Budget," Press Notice, July 12, 2004 (www.hm-treasury.gov.
uk/spending_review/spend_sr04/press/spend_sr04_press09.cfm [January 2006]).

economically strong trading partner, and in the U.K.'s security interests that
there should be reductions in poverty and inequality and improvements in
governance in developing countries. But these long-term interests had not
always been given weight alongside short-term commercial and strategic
concerns. By creating a department with a long-term agenda for global
poverty reduction, the intention was to create institutional pressures within
government to ensure that the U.K.'s long-term interests were taken into
account alongside short-term pressures.

Eight years later, it was apparent that U.K. policy had been substantially
realigned, partly as a result of the collaborative work across Whitehall of
drawing up the two white papers. For example, both trade policy and environmental policy have changed significantly to take account of the U.K.'s
long-term interests in shared economic prosperity and in halting the degra-
dation of the environment.

In 2005 Prime Minister Tony Blair chose two key objectives for the
U.K. presidency of the Group of Eight: the development of Africa and

addressing the impact of climate change. That he chose to focus on these two long-term objectives was a testament to the extent of the change that had occurred in the priorities and time horizons of U.K. policymakers.

Improving the Impact of Aid on Poverty

The reforms of development assistance were intended to enhance the poverty impact of aid by improving both the allocation of aid—especially by targeting it on countries with poor people—and the effectiveness with which it was used. The government completely uncoupled aid from commercial contracts or any requirement that goods and services be bought from U.K. suppliers, which was estimated to increase its effectiveness by between 15 and 30 percent.[85] The government also sought to improve the poverty impact of aid by shifting resources toward poor countries—setting a goal of 90 percent of aid to go to low-income countries—and by using an explicit aid allocation model.

By 2003 DFID estimated that the poverty reduction impact of a marginal dollar of aid had quadrupled since 1990, although some of this was due to changes in aid levels and improvements in governance in developing countries. As a result of improvements in aid allocation, DFID's own estimates showed that it raised more people out of poverty for an extra $1 million than the donor average (it ranked third highest among bilateral donors).[86]

However, the effectiveness of aid depends not only on where it is used but also on how it is spent. Changes in development assistance that were intended to make aid more effective also had the effect of making it more difficult to measure the cost-effectiveness of those aid programs. For example, the move away from supporting individual projects and toward providing financial support more generally to governments committed to poverty reduction plus the increased collaboration and pooling with other donors were changes based on evidence that aid could be more effective when delivered this way. However, these same changes also made it more difficult to attribute particular outputs and outcomes to the U.K. aid program, thus reducing the availability of direct evidence for the effectiveness of aid.

Focus on the Causes of Poverty, Not Just the Symptoms

Because it took a long-term view of its mission, DFID decided to focus on the causes of poverty and not just its symptoms. This brought the new department explicitly into new policy arenas, such as conflict prevention, trade, environment, governance, and security, with the intent to identify and address the causes of poverty. In one sense, the change was less pronounced than it might appear: the previous Overseas Development Administration had been engaged in many of these issues. However, the department's explicitly broad responsibilities for development and not just aid, and its representation in the cabinet, changed government and public perceptions of its role and enabled it to act with considerably greater confidence and effect in these areas.

An example of how DFID began to look at the causes of poverty was the "drivers of change" strategy, which sought to ground development programs in an understanding of the economic, social, and political factors that either drive or block change within a country.[87] The goal of tackling the causes of poverty also led DFID to expand its work on institution building and governance reform, security and access to justice, and governance programs. DFID and the Department of Trade and Industry together argued for a "development round" for the Doha trade talks and for reform of the EU Common Agricultural Policy. With the Ministry of Defense and the Foreign Office, it greatly expanded work on preventing and ending conflict, and on investment in postconflict societies.

Increasing Leverage to Increase Impact

The government made a deliberate effort to work with and through other bilateral and multilateral donors, to leverage the impact of the U.K.'s contribution to development. Starting in 1997 DFID consciously moved away from highlighting U.K. contributions to particular programs (for example, the Union Flag was no longer stenciled onto bags of food aid). In part, this change was intended to facilitate more opportunities to work across the international system as a whole, with other like-minded donors, the European Community, and the international financial institutions. Seeking publicity for the U.K.'s own contribution internationally, it was felt, had been a distraction from, and in some cases an obstacle to, effective collaboration with partners. This change was accompanied by an increased effort within the United Kingdom to explain the purpose and effectiveness of the aid program so as to sustain support as it became less visible on the ground.

One example of the effort to increase leverage was the government's willingness to channel resources through multilateral institutions where they were effective, such as through the World Bank. The United Kingdom gave a higher share of aid as multilateral assistance than the DAC average. From 1996 to 2000, DFID provided on average 41 percent of its aid through multilateral organizations, compared with 36 percent for all DAC donors and 25 percent for the United States. (There is no clear relationship between the size of donor and the multilateral share.) An increased willingness to work with others also led to a very large number of policy collaborations with the World Bank.

In another example, in 2001 DFID's Vietnam program was established with a complete ban on purely bilateral aid projects. All aid was provided in support of projects or programs conducted by or with other development partners, especially the World Bank. This approach was perceived to leverage other resources, help focus other organizations on the achievement of the Millennium Development Goals, discipline project design by requiring all interventions to secure the support of other agencies, and reduce transaction costs for the government of Vietnam.

However, as figure 10-2 shows, although the share of aid going to multilateral institutions remained relatively high, it fell at a time when the department was advocating working through multilateral institutions where possible.

Figure 10-2 Multilateral Aid as a Share of Total Aid, United Kingdom, 1973–2004

Percent

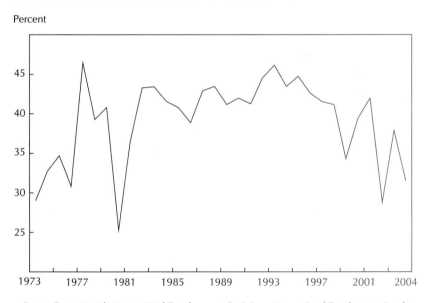

Source: Department for International Development, *Statistics on International Development* (London, 2004), table 2.2.

Evidence-Based Policymaking: Outcomes and Transparency

In line with the new approach across the U.K. government, DFID set itself the task of basing policy on evidence, focusing on outcomes rather than inputs, and increasing the transparency of policymaking and use of resources. Arguably, it was one of the more successful government departments at ensuring that policies were firmly based on evidence.

DFID employed a large number of technical specialists, from economists to anthropologists, and experts in health, engineering, education, statistics, trade, conflict, environment, population, and governance. One important result of DFID's commitment to using evidence was consistent support for the important but politically unglamorous process of building capacity for the collection and analysis of statistics in developing countries.

In line with the aim of basing policy on evidence, both DFID white papers were the result of extensive consultation with experts outside government, including academics and nongovernmental organizations, and were backed by an array of specially commissioned analyses. The 1997 white paper shifted the department's measurement of its performance toward the U.K.'s contribution to meeting the Millennium Development Goals rather than on input-based measures of the U.K.'s contribution. However, in common with other organizations, DFID did not satisfactorily resolve the tension between the two, on the one hand wanting to increase the importance of measuring outcomes, and on the other hand needing to show that those outcomes were attributable to the U.K.'s own contribution. (It was easier to attribute the U.K.'s contribution to inputs, such as total aid given, or to outputs, such as schools built, than it was to outcomes that were the effect of the country's own efforts as well as the combined effects of all the donors.)[88]

Development policy became markedly more transparent. Country assistance plans—which formed the basis of DFID country programs—were published for the first time. Most project documents were made available through the database on the Accessible Information on Development Activities website.[89] And as of 2005, all project documents were opened to public scrutiny under the U.K.'s Freedom of Information Act.

Greater Public Awareness and Political Focus

Finally, an explicit objective of the reforms of U.K. development assistance was to increase the political focus on development. One way this was achieved was by having a high-profile cabinet minister appointed to lead DFID. In addition, the 1997 white paper called for increased public understanding of global mutual dependence and the need for international development. It called for all children to be educated about development issues so that they could understand the key global considerations that would shape their lives.

One consequence of greater collaboration with other donors and more use of resource transfer to recipient governments, rather than project aid, was that U.K. aid was less overtly visible and thus less likely to generate a strong sense of ownership within the United Kingdom. To avoid a decline in support for aid, the government considered it important to explain carefully the rationale for the policy change and highlight the increased impact of British aid that it was expected to produce.

DFID began a low-key but effective public awareness campaign. This included, for example, working with the Department for Education to include "global citizenship" in the new national curriculum, and providing materials and support for teacher training colleges to enable teachers to incorporate development issues into their curriculum. In 2004 the U.K. government teamed up with the Rough Guide, publishers of travel books, to produce *The Rough Guide to a Better World,* which explained what members of the public could do if they wanted to become more involved in supporting developing countries.[90] One effect of these efforts was a steady increase in the proportion of the British public who said that they were "very concerned" about development, from 17 percent in 1999 to 26 percent in 2004.[91]

The Labour government developed an unexpectedly testy relationship, at least at first, with many of the nongovernmental organizations (NGOs). Clare Short, as secretary of state for international development, felt that the development and environmental NGOs had an agenda that would not help developing countries take advantage of globalization, and that funding British NGOs was a "short term political distraction." She wrote: "All of these groups were well intentioned but the most generous possible funding for the best possible U.K. NGOs was not capable of bringing about the massive reductions of poverty that were needed."[92] Relationships with NGOs improved over time, in part because of the introduction of partnership program agreements to fund NGOs on the basis of their strategic objectives. These long-term funding agreements do not restrict the use of their funds to particular projects or activities.[93]

Future Challenges for DFID

By 2005 enormous progress had been made by the new Department for International Development, but considerable challenges remained. In the 2005 edition of the Center for Global Development's authoritative, quantitative annual study of how the policies of rich countries help or hinder poor countries, the United Kingdom ranked about half way, tenth out of twenty-one countries, equal to Canada, just below Germany, and well behind the Scandinavian countries and Australia and New Zealand.[94] A relatively strong performance on aid, trade, and investment was undermined by weak and deteriorating performance on policies such as migration and security. (The United Kingdom, however, along with Spain and Sweden, showed the fastest improvement since the index began in 2003.)

The Department for International Development faces a number of continuing challenges, which will require it to:

—*Maintain a tight focus* on the department's core strengths and limit the number of countries to which Britain gives bilateral aid. Prioritization is more difficult at a time of rapid increases in the aid budget, and arguably one of DFID's weaknesses is that it tries to do too much.

—*Lock in the improvements* in development policy made after the end of the cold war, which enabled aid to be allocated to the poorest countries where it would have most impact and reduced the distortion of aid by short-term strategic, political, and commercial interests. Since September 11 and the heightened focus on security, there will be increasing pressure to use all the government's resources in the fight against terrorism. DFID has, so far, been largely successful in sustaining the argument that the U.K.'s longer-term interests, including its security interests, are best served by preserving the focus of aid on poverty reduction.[95]

—*Restrain, and perhaps reverse, the growth in bilateral aid* by ensuring that the bulk of the anticipated increases in aid are channeled through multilateral institutions—a process more efficient both for donors and recipients—and also by increasing investments in global and regional public goods, such as scientific research, early warning systems, and regional infrastructure, which are currently underfunded.

—Within bilateral aid, make more progress on implementing DFID's rhetorical commitments to *increase program aid,* which increases the recipient's control of resources—thus enhancing effectiveness and accountability—and reduces the administrative burden of projects.

—Improve the department's approach to the *transfer of knowledge and skills,* based on evidence about what works, and thus reduce the proportion of spending on technical cooperation and consultants (which, although declining since the late 1990s, remains high by international standards).

—Expand DFID's influence on *sensitive areas of policy* that have a significant effect on poor countries, including migration, corruption and lack of transparency by transnational corporations, and the configuration of armed forces for humanitarian relief and conflict prevention.

—Build *stronger public support* for the government's role in international development. In an annual survey of U.K. opinion, less than a fifth of people identify the governments of rich countries as making a major contribution to the reduction of international poverty, compared with two-thirds who think that international charities do so.[96] This remains a precarious basis for DFID's long-term survival and influence within government.

Lessons from the U.K. Experience

This final section contains some personal reflections on the main components of the reforms, which I see as having been largely successful.

What Were the Components of Success?

The main ingredients in the successful reform of U.K. development assistance have been:

—Combining *responsibility for all aid in a single government department.* This has been the case in the United Kingdom since 1964 and has made an important contribution to both the coherence and cost-effectiveness of British aid that other countries would do well to emulate.

—Establishing an *integrated development ministry,* with influence over a range of government policies that affect development, has had a significant effect on the conduct of policy. While development interests will not always take precedence over other government objectives, they should at least be identified and taken into account in the design and execution of broader government objectives.

—Setting a *clear purpose and focus on outcomes.* DFID has maintained its long-term strategy in the face of short-term political pressures. This is easier said than done: it requires powerful political leadership to prevent aid budgets being diverted to other priorities. Both the appointment of a separate cabinet minister and legislation delimiting the use of aid resources have enabled the department to resist other pressures.

—Building an understanding among policymakers and commentators of the *relationship between the long-term and short-term interests* of the country.

—Recognizing that development is impossible without security and that *security is impossible without development.* This mutual interdependence has profound implications for government institutions and priorities.

—Accepting that more can be achieved through *partnerships with others* and through leverage of the multilateral system, even if this means a less distinctively high profile for the development program. This includes integrated management of bilateral and multilateral aid to secure the synergies and ensure coherence.

How Did It Happen?

As with most successful revolutions, the changes succeeded in part because they resonated with a long-evolving way of thinking, and in part because they captured the mood of the moment. The unified management of aid by a single government department—unusual internationally—has been a long-standing virtue of the U.K. system, dating back to 1964. The United Kingdom has also consistently argued over many years the importance of assistance to the poorest countries, although its own aid program did not always reflect that priority. Many of the changes that the United Kingdom introduced in 1997 and afterwards were in line with a new international attitude that while increases in aid were an important part of the development agenda, it also was essential to pay attention to the broader set of policies that affect developing countries.

Other elements that enabled these changes to happen and be sustained were:

—High-profile *political leadership* for a new approach to development. The prime minister and the chancellor of the exchequer were willing to back the new department, and Clare Short provided a strong focus for it. One external commentator wrote, "What drove the difference? 'In a word: leadership.' . . . Short imposed focus and drive on her organizations. She believed that DFID should—and could—make a real difference. 'She recruited the best and the brightest' from the U.K. and abroad. She encouraged discussion and debate. She demanded excellence."[97] Subsequent cabinet ministers have ensured that DFID retains a high political profile.

—A *supportive political environment* for improvements in the use of aid, buttressed by investment in public education and development awareness campaigns.

—A supportive environment within the rest of government, including recognition that *reorganizing responsibilities and powers among government agencies is not a zero-sum game.* British government departments learned that they could be more effective and influential if they worked together to deliver coherent policy objectives than if they spent their time and resources fighting for turf. Other government departments were persuaded that they had something to gain from the emergence of a strong, confident agency with responsibility for development assistance.

Appendix 10A: The Pergau Dam

The Pergau Dam is a hydroelectric dam in Malaysia, near the border with Thailand. The dam is the largest aid project ever financed by the United Kingdom. In March 1988 the then defense secretary, Sir George Younger, signed a "defence export protocol" with Malaysia that committed the U.K. government to "bring to bear the resources of its MOD [Ministry of Defence] in order to grant certain facilities, including:—aid in support of nonmilitary aspects under the programme."[98] Lord Younger agreed that Malaysia would receive 20 percent of the value of the arms sales in the form of aid.

In November 1988 an application for aid through the Aid and Trade Provision (ATP) for the Pergau Dam was made to the Department of Trade and Industry (DTI) by a consortium of British companies, led by Balfour Beatty, which had close connections to the governing Conservative party. In March 1989, in the context of a visit to Downing Street by the Malaysian prime minister, Mahathir Mohamad, Prime Minister Margaret Thatcher made an oral offer of a £68.25 million grant, based on a contract price of £316 million.

During the following year, ODA and DTI undertook a joint mission to survey the Malaysian power sector and the possibilities for other projects that might attract British companies. That review indicated that electricity could be produced more cheaply by gas turbine power stations than from the Pergau project dam.

In February 1991 Sir Tim Lankester, the most senior civil servant in the ODA, formally advised the minister for overseas development that funding the Pergau Dam project would not be consistent with policy statements by ministers to Parliament about the basic objectives of the aid program. Ministers at the two departments responsible for the ATP program, Lynda Chalker and Trade Minister Tim Sainsbury, were opposed to providing support for the dam. But Britain's high commissioner to Malaysia, Sir Nicholas Spreckley, and Alan Clark, then minister for defense procurement, argued that to withdraw support for Pergau "would have an adverse impact on U.K. relations with Malaysia in general and on the defence sales relationship in particular." The prime minister, John Major, agreed with their assessment. In July 1991 the then foreign secretary, Douglas Hurd, overruled the objections and authorized expenditure of £234 million (about $400 million) from the aid budget.

At the time officials denied any link between British aid and arms sales to Malaysia. The prime minister's office described the timing of the arms sales as "merely a coincidence." However, in January 1994 Sir Tim Lankester gave evidence to a House of Commons public accounts committee inquiry, and it was clear that there had in fact been a link between the decision to give aid and the arms sales. As a result of this evidence, Douglas Hurd admitted that there had been a "brief entanglement" between aid and arms sales from March to June 1988, which he claimed had been ended by Sir George Younger's letter of June 28, 1988, to the Malaysian finance minister saying that "the linking of aid to projects" would not be possible. But on the same day, the U.K. government offered up to £200 million in ATP and export credit support for future contracts. This amount was the same as the aid expected to accompany the £1 billion of arms sales.

A judicial review sought by a nongovernmental organization led to a High Court ruling in November 1994 that aid for the Pergau Dam was in violation of the Overseas Development Act 1980, which allows the foreign secretary to make payments "for the purpose of promoting the development or maintaining the economy of a country or territories outside the U.K., or the welfare of its people." The High Court ruled that the project was not of economic or humanitarian benefit to the Malaysian people.

After the ruling, the foreign secretary announced that the government would meet its contractual obligation to pay for the three-quarters-built dam. He told the House of Commons in December 1994 that he would not appeal against the court ruling, but the ODA would not be reimbursed for the £24.4 million spent on the Pergau project between July 1991 and March 1994.

Notes

1. Tony Blair, comments regarding engagements, 7 March 2001, *Parliamentary Debates,* Commons, vol. 364 (2000–01), col. 294 (www.publications.parliament. U.K./pa/cm200001/cmhansrd/vo010307/debtext/10307-04.htm [January 2006]).

2. Cabinet ministers are at the top of the three rungs on the ministerial ladder. Ministers immediately below cabinet rank are *ministers of state,* below which there may be one or more *parliamentary undersecretaries of state.* Ministers below cabinet rank are collectively known as *junior ministers.* Junior ministers usually report to a cabinet minister. All ministers are in effect appointed by the prime minister and are nearly always, but not necessarily, members of the House of Commons or the House of Lords. Ministers in charge of large government departments are usually cabinet ministers; there are also other members of the cabinet—such as the chief whip and the leader of the House of Commons—who do not run government departments. The Treasury has two cabinet ministers (the chancellor of the exchequer and the chief secretary). The designation *secretary of state* dates back to before the establishment of cabinet government. It originally meant a minister to whom some of the functions of the monarch were delegated, specifically related to the functioning of the Privy Council. Today the title *secretary of state* is generally given to ministers in charge of departments (although not, for much of the twentieth century, the minister for agriculture), and the term is used almost interchangeably with *cabinet minister.* The designation of secretary of state does not denote seniority within government, as some very senior members of the cabinet are not secretaries of state, such as the prime minister, the chancellor of the exchequer, and, until recently, the lord chancellor.

3. Robert Greenhill, *Making a Difference: External Views on Canada's International Impact. The Interim Report of the External Voices Project* (Toronto: Canadian Institute of International Affairs, January 2005).

4. "Clare Loses It," *Economist,* May 17, 2003.

5. The Colonial Development Act 1929 was passed by a minority Labour government in 1929. Baron Passfield—the former Sidney Webb—was secretary for the colonies and for dominion affairs when it was passed.

6. See William Hare, Earl of Listowel, "Memoirs, Earl of Listowel" (www.redrice. com/listowel/index.html [January 2006]). Hare was minister of state for the colonies from 1948 to 1950.

7. "Planning" was a buzzword in the United Kingdom immediately after the Second World War.

8. The quote is from Hare, "Memoirs."

9. Ibid.

10. A speech given by U.S. Secretary of State George C. Marshall at Harvard University on June 5, 1947, initiated the post-war European Aid Program, more commonly known as the Marshall Plan. For the text of that speech, see Organization for Economic Cooperation and Development, "Marshall Plan Speech" (www.oecd.org/document/10/0,2340,en_2649_201185_1876938_1_1_1_1,00.html [January 2006]). An example of the optimism that the success of the Marshall Plan generated can be found in the inaugural address of President Harry S Truman on January 20, 1949: "Almost a year ago, in company with sixteen free nations of Europe, we launched the greatest cooperative economic program in

history. . . . Our efforts have brought new hope to all mankind. . . . We are moving on with other nations to build an even stronger structure of international order and justice. . . . More than half the people of the world are living in conditions approaching misery. . . . For the first time in history, humanity possesses the knowledge and the skill to relieve the suffering of these people. . . . With the cooperation of business, private capital, agriculture, and labor in this country, this program can greatly increase the industrial activity in other nations and can raise substantially their standards of living." See "Harry S Truman: Inaugural Address" (www.bartleby.com/124/pres53.html [January 2006]).

11. John Bledsoe Bonds, *Bipartisan Strategy: Selling the Marshall Plan* (Westport, Conn.: Praeger, 2002).

12. Personal communication from Sir Brian Barder in September, 2005.

13. Her Majesty's (HM) Treasury, *Assistance from the United Kingdom for Overseas Development,* Cmnd. 974 (London: Her Majesty's Stationery Office [HMSO], March 1960).

14. HM Treasury, *Aid to Developing Countries,* Cmnd. 2147 (London: HMSO, September 1963).

15. See Adrian Hewitt, "British Aid: Policy and Practice," *ODI Review* 2 (1978): 51–66.

16. Barbara Castle (October 18, 1964, to December 23, 1965), Anthony Greenwood (December 23, 1965, to August 11, 1966) and Arthur Bottomley (August 11, 1966, to August 29, 1967) were members of the cabinet. Subsequent ministers of overseas development under this administration, Reginald Prentice (August 1967 to October 1969) and Judith Hart (October 1969 to June 1970) were not members of the cabinet, though the ODM remained a separate department, independent of the Foreign and Commonwealth Office.

17. Ministry of Overseas Development, *Overseas Development: The Work of the New Ministry,* Cmnd. 2736 (London: HMSO, 1965).

18. Ministry of Overseas Development, *Overseas Development: The Work in Hand,* Cmnd. 3180 (London: HMSO, 1967).

19. Technically, the Foreign Office has been called the Foreign and Commonwealth Office since October 1968 but for convenience is referred to as the Foreign Office throughout this chapter. For an explanation of ministerial ranks, see footnote 2.

20. Ministry of Overseas Development, *Overseas Development: The Changing Emphasis in British Aid Policies: More Help for the Poorest.* Cmnd. 6270 (London: HMSO, 1975).

21. From the 1975 white paper, quoted in Hewitt, "British Aid."

22. The foreign secretary formally became minister of overseas development, and hence exercised the powers invested in that office by Parliament, whereas the junior foreign office minister with day-to-day responsibility for official development aid was given the courtesy title of minister for overseas development. Reginald Prentice, who became minister for overseas development from June 1975 until his resignation in December 1976, was a member of the cabinet. His successors, Frank Judd and Judith Hart, were not, and the foreign secretary spoke on development issues in the cabinet on their behalf.

23. French support for the export of railway equipment to Kenya was the case that eventually led the British government to adopt its own program of concessionary export credits.

24. Judith Hart was regarded as having an agenda to the left of the party and had tense relations with the foreign secretary, David Owen. Her successor, Reginald Prentice, sat in the cabinet, but he was becoming increasingly disaffected by the political direction of the Labour Party, from which he resigned when his constituency party deselected him. His successor, Frank Judd, who was not a member of the cabinet, held the post for only a few months before moving to the Foreign Office.

25. John Mitchell, "Public Campaigning on Overseas Aid in the 1980s," in *Britain's Overseas Aid since 1979: Between Idealism and Self-Interest,* edited by Anuradha Bose and Peter Burnell (Manchester University Press, 1991), p. 146.

26. Neil Marten, statement on overseas aid, 20 February 1980, *Parliamentary Debates,* Commons, vol. 979 (1979–80), cols. 464–65. The full text of the statement is reproduced at www.owen.org/musings/marten.php [January 2006].

27. Adrian Hewitt, "Beyond Poverty? The New U.K. Policy on International Development and Globalization," *Third World Quarterly* 22, no. 2 (2001): 291–96.

28. Tony Killick, "Understanding British Aid to Africa: An Historical Perspective" (www.odi.org.uk/RAPID/Projects/RAP0011/docs/Annex2_Killick.pdf [May 2006]).

29. The "Lawson Doctrine" is often known in the United Kingdom as the "Burns Doctrine," after Terry Burns, later Lord Burns, then the chief economic adviser at the Treasury.

30. Peter Montagnon, *Financial Times* (London), June 7, 1990, p. 7.

31. Douglas Hurd, *Memoirs* (London: Little Brown, 2003). Lynda Chalker was the minister for Africa from 1986 to 1997 and contemporaneously minister for overseas development from July 1989 to May 1997.

32. "Labour Party Manifesto, 1997 (www.bbc.co.uk/election97/background/parties/manlab/labmanintro.html [May 2006]). See also Tony Blair interviewed on the Dimbleby program: BBC, "Panorama Leadership Special, April 7—Tony Blair," April 7, 1997 (www.bbc.co.uk/election97/background/parties/panblair2.htm [January 2006]).

33. Vernon Bogdanor, *Joined-Up Government* (Oxford University Press, 2005).

34. The background of the Pergau Dam decision is described in appendix 10A. Labour's foreign affairs spokesman, Robin Cook, called the verdict "an alarming glimpse into the private arrogance of a government who have been there for so long that they no longer even ask whether there are limits to their personal authority." See Robin Cook, Statement regarding foreign affairs and defense, 17 November 1994, *Parliamentary Debates,* Commons, vol. 250 (1994–95), col. 150.

35. John Kampfner, *Blair's Wars* (London: Free Press, 2004), p. 7.

36. From a speech by Robin Cook announcing the new Foreign Office "mission statement." See "Robin Cook's Speech on the Government's Ethical Foreign Policy," *Guardian,* May 12, 1997 (www.guardian.co.uk/indonesia/Story/0,2763,190889,00.html [January 2006]). This is often misquoted as a commitment to an "ethical foreign policy."

37. Willy Brandt, *North-South: A Programme for Survival. Report of the Independent Commission on International Development Issues* (London: Pan Books, 1980).

38. Independent Group on British Aid, *Real Aid: A Strategy for Britain* (London: 1982).

39. Judith Randel and Tony German, *Reality of Aid* (London: ActionAid, ICVA, and EUROSTEP, 1993). *Reality of Aid* reports were also published in 1997, 1998, 2000, 2002, and 2004.

40. Jim Michel, "The Birth of the MDGs," *DACNews*, September–October 2005 (www.oecd.org/document/34/0,2340,en_2649_33721_35295778_1_1_1_1,00.html [January 2006]).

41. Ibid.

42. Development Assistance Committee, *Shaping the 21st Century: The Contribution of Development Cooperation* (Paris: OECD, 1996).

43. UN General Assembly, "United Nations Millennium Declaration," UN A/RES/55/2, September 18, 2000 (www.undp.org/mdg/99-Millennium_Declaration_and_Follow_up_Resolution.pdf [January 2006]).

44. Labour Party, *A Fresh Start for Britain: Labour's Strategy for Britain in the Modern World* (London: 1996). See also "New Labour Because Britain Deserves Better," December 2, 2005 (www.psr.keele.ac.uk/area/uk/man/lab97.htm).

45. Clare Short, *An Honourable Deception? New Labour, Iraq and the Misuse of Power* (London: Free Press, 2004), p. 51.

46. Sir John Vereker, "Blazing the Trail: Eight Years of Change in Handling International Development," *Development Policy Review* 20, no. 2 (2002): 133–140.

47. Kampfner, *Blair's Wars*, p. 64.

48. The ODA Permanent Secretary, Sir John Vereker, had been a member of the OECD committee that drew up *Shaping the 21st Century* in 1996. See note 42.

49. Department for International Development (DFID), *Eliminating World Poverty: A Challenge for the 21st Century*, Cm. 3789 (London: The Stationery Office, 1997).

50. DFID, *Eliminating World Poverty: Making Globalisation Work for the Poor*, Cm. 5006 (London: The Stationery Office, 2000).

51. DFID, *A Challenge for the 21st Century*.

52. The International Development Targets were set out in OECD, *Shaping the 21st Century*.

53. Between 50,000 and 100,000 people demonstrated at the Third World Trade Organization Ministerial Conference in Seattle, Washington, in December 1999.

54. DFID, *A Challenge for the 21st Century*.

55. Ibid.

56. DFID, *The Africa Conflict Prevention Pool: An Information Document* (London: 2004).

57. Bill Rammell, Global Conflict Prevention Pool, Written Answer, 12 Mar 2004, *Parliamentary Debates*, Commons, vol. 418 (2003-04), col. 792W.

58. Greg Austin, "Evaluation of the Conflict Prevention Pools," Report EVSUM EV647 (London: DFID, 2004).

59. For a full text of the act, see Office of Public Sector Information, "International Development Act 2002," April 8, 2002 (www.opsi.gov.uk/acts/acts2002/20020001.htm).

60. See David Dollar and Craig Burnside, "Aid, Policies, and Growth," Policy Research Working Paper 1777 (Washington: World Bank, June 1997); Paul Collier and David Dollar, "Aid Allocation and Poverty Reduction," Policy Research Working Paper 2041 (World Bank, January 1999).

61. DFID, "EU Institutional Strategy Paper" (London: December 1998).

62. DFID, *Public Service Agreement 2003–2006*, July 2002 (www.dfid.gov.uk/pubs/files/publicserviceagreement03-06.pdf [January 2006]). Her Majesty's Treasury (HM Treasury) is the name for the U.K. Finance Ministry, which combines the functions of

an economic ministry and a budget ministry. The finance minister is known as the chancellor of the exchequer.

63. Nick Dyer and others, "Strategic Review of Resource Allocation Priorities," Discussion Paper (London: DFID, January 2003).

64. DFID, *Fighting Poverty to Build a Safer World* (London: 2005).

65. Ibid.

66. DFID, *Achieving the Millennium Development Goals: The Middle-Income Countries. A Strategy for DFID: 2005–2008* (London: 2004).

67. Tom Porteous, "British Government Policy in Sub-Saharan Africa under New Labour," *International Affairs* 81, no. 2 (2005): 281–97; Short, *Honourable Deception*, pp. 78–80.

68. Short, *Honourable Deception*, p. 79.

69. Porteous, "Policy in Sub-Saharan Africa."

70. Unlike other bilateral donors, DFID offices in the partner country were separate from the local British embassy, and the staff reported directly to DFID ministers in London.

71. See DFID, *Departmental Report 2005* (London: 2005), chap. 7, pp. 150–51.

72. Short, *Honourable Deception*, p. 78.

73. Department of Trade and Industry, *Making Globalisation a Force for Good*, Cm. 6278 (London: The Stationery Office, 2004).

74. Vereker, "Blazing the Trail."

75. Seamus Milne and Alan Travis, "Blair's Secret Plan to Crack Down on Asylum Seekers," *Guardian*, May 23, 2002, p. 1.

76. Short, *Honourable Deception*, pp. 130–31.

77. Ibid., p. 134.

78. See BBC, " 'Turn Away Refugees,' Says Tory Leader," May 24, 2002 (news.bbc.co.uk/1/hi/uk_politics/2005605.stm [January 2006]).

79. Vereker, "Blazing the Trail," p. 135.

80. "Each economically advanced country will progressively increase its official development assistance to the developing countries and will exert its best efforts to reach a minimum net amount of 0.7 percent of its gross national product . . . by the middle of the decade." UN General Assembly, "International Development Strategy for the Second United Nations Development Decade," Resolution 2626, 25 sess. (October 24, 1970), paragraph 43.

81. For an account of the history of the 0.7 percent target and a discussion of its rationale as an international goal, see Michael A. Clemens and Todd J. Moss, "Ghost of 0.7 Percent: Origins and Relevance of the International Aid Target," Working Paper 68 (Washington: Center for Global Development, September 6, 2005).

82. See "February 1974 Labour Party Manifesto" (www.labour-party.org.uk/manifestos/1974/Feb/1974-feb-labour-manifesto.shtml [May 2006]).

83. OECD Development Assistance Committee, "United Kingdom (2001), Development Cooperation Review: Main Findings and Recommendations" (www.oecd.org/document/33/0,2340,en_2649_34603_2460513_1_1_1_1,00.html [January 2006]).

84. HM Treasury, "Further Boost to U.K. Aid Budget," Press Notice, July 12, 2004 (www.hm-treasury.gov.uk/spending_review/spend_sr04/press/spend_sr04_press09.cfm [January 2006]).

85. HM Treasury, "Britain in the World," in *2002 Spending Review: New Public Spending Plans 2003–2006* (www.archive2.official-documents.co.uk/document/cm55/5570/5570-05.htm [January 2006]).

86. Dyer and others, "Strategic Review," p. 15.

87. DFID, "Drivers of Change," 2004 (www.grc-exchange.org/docs/doc59.pdf [January 2006]).

88. See OECD Development Assistance Committee, *The DAC Journal Development Cooperation Report 2004,* vol. 6, no. 1 (Paris: 2005).

89. See aida.developmentgateway.org/AidaHome.do [January 2006].

90. Martin Wroe and Malcolm Doney, *The Rough Guide to a Better World and How You Can Make a Difference* (London: Rough Guides, 2004). For an online version, see www.roughguide-betterworld.com [January 2006].

91. Maureen O'Brien, Office of National Statistics, *Public Attitudes towards Development* (London: July 2004). Based on data from the National Statistics Omnibus Survey for the Department for International Development.

92. Short, *Honourable Deception,* p. 81.

93. For case studies see DFID, "Minister Announces 28 Percent Increase in Support to NGO's," press release, February 21, 2005 (www.dfid.gov.uk/news/files/pressreleases/increase-ngo-support.asp [January 2006]).

94. David Roodman, *Foreign Policy* 150 (September-October 2005): 76–83. See also Center for Global Development, "Commitment to Development Index" (www.cgdev.org/section/initiatives/_active/cdi [January 2006]).

95. An example of DFID's success in retaining a focus on poverty is the decision to preserve the 90–10 rule in the face of rising costs in postwar Iraq.

96. O'Brien, "Public Attitudes."

97. It should be noted that this view comes from a report based on interviews with several dozen world leaders, who have a tendency to ascribe most successful changes to leadership above all else. See Greenhill, *Making a Difference.*

98. All quotes and other details of this case can be found in Association for International Water and Forest Studies, "Court Cases in Dam Projects. 5. Pergau (Malaysia)" (www.fivas.org/rettsskr/pergau7.htm [January 2006]).

CHAPTER 11

Conclusion and Recommendations

Lael Brainard

I n the face of unprecedented new global challenges, the hard power assets of the United States—military, economic, and other means of persuasion and coercion—are stretched thin. It has become increasingly critical to leverage foreign aid and other soft power tools in order to grapple with global poverty, pandemics, and other transnational threats. America's fragmented, incoherent foreign assistance infrastructure has diminished the influence and overall effectiveness of these programs, however. While U.S. spending on foreign assistance has recently seen its greatest increase in forty years, the administration of that aid is dispersed between many agencies and branches of government in a manner that inhibits formulation and implementation of an effective strategy.

The imperative for reform can be further underscored by simply scanning the headlines of today's newspapers, which herald the growing impact of private philanthropy on the world's most serious problems: poverty, health, energy, and the environment. Warren Buffet's $37 billion donation in 2006 to the Bill and Melinda Gates Foundation will enable it to disburse roughly $2.8 billion in grants in 2007—more than the Millennium Challenge Corporation will disburse in the same year (which also will be its third year of operation). The quality of U.S. government aid strategies must be improved if we are to keep pace with the coordination, consolidation, and accountability of the philanthropic sector's efforts.

I am grateful to James Pickett for outstanding assistance in writing this chapter.

Taking Reform Step by Step

Previous examples of successful reform make clear that three key conditions are required to tip the scales from proposal to policy: there must be an emergent political consensus regarding the urgency of the mission, the advocacy effort must be compelling, and the president or key congressional champions must be personally committed to change. Moreover, timing is critical. Previous episodes of successful major reform have taken place in the early days of new administrations. This suggests that effective reform will require three parallel processes: improving coordination during the remaining years of an established administration; using hearings, studies, and commissions to lay the groundwork for fundamental reform to be initiated during a presidential transition; and building the political case for reform.

Thus, in the late years of an incumbent administration, the administration should institute a clear system of policy coordination led by the president's staff, with planning and implementation authority delegated to appropriate agency leads. On a parallel track, Congress should use its powers to request analysis, hold hearings, and empower commissions to lay the groundwork for fundamental reform. The process leading to the Goldwater-Nichols Defense Reorganization Act of 1986 can serve as a model, perhaps with the HELP Commission leading the way. Again, timing is a crucial factor: the best opportunity for fundamental reform is in the first year of a new administration. The active support of advocacy groups and nongovernmental organizations (NGOs), in conjunction with nontraditional allies such as military specialists, will be essential to raising the political salience of more effective assistance.

It is clear that reform on the scale proposed in this study will not come easily. It is also clear that the current U.S. strategy of hard power diplomacy is failing to meet strategic interests. A new approach is needed if the United States is to recast itself as a global leader capable of addressing the challenges of the new millennium. The following summary of policy recommendations is provided in support of such a new approach.

Create a Unified Framework

With hard power assets overtaxed and confronting unprecedented global challenges of transnational threats, poverty, and pandemics, the United States must reform its weak aid infrastructure to leverage its soft power more effectively. While foreign assistance funding has seen the greatest increase in four decades, this has brought a proliferation of programs, policy incoherence, and organizational fragmentation. Moving around the organizational boxes or increasing aid will do little to boost impact unless there is broad agreement around a unified framework designed for twenty-first-century challenges.

U.S. foreign assistance should be governed by a unified framework that integrates the national security perspective of foreign assistance as a "soft power tool," intended to achieve diplomatic and strategic ends, with that of a "development tool," allocated according to policy effectiveness and human needs. Development returns are greatest and most durable in countries with transparent and accountable governments that are committed to sound economic policies, removing unnecessary impediments to commerce, and investing in the education and health of their citizens.

This framework should cut across government agencies and be a source of unity rather than division, clarifying the mission rather than confusing it. National security no less than our national interests and national values will be enhanced best by a U.S. foreign aid program with the clear and compelling goals of supporting capable foreign partners and countering security, humanitarian, and transnational threats.

Support Capable Partners

Foreign assistance should be used to strengthen societies with shared values and similar economic and political systems. Such countries are aligned with U.S. interests by virtue of their intrinsic nature rather than because of sometimes short-lived bargains. Assistance to such capable partners is the highest-yielding investment of American soft power, and it merits far greater priority, intelligence in policy design, and constancy of purpose than it currently receives. Only 17 percent of the overall U.S. foreign assistance budget is assigned to capable partners even though they account for the most populous group of countries.

Differentiation

To address this deficiency, foreign assistance must shift from a one-size-fits-all approach and instead be targeted to reinforce recipient practices and goals shared with the United States and to encourage growth. Aid agencies must systematically identify those countries with the greatest needs and best policies and institutions, using a transparent, fact-based system that enables them to allocate aid more effectively and to protect such allocations against political or commercial considerations.

Well-governed countries should receive the largest amount of funding on a per capita basis, have the greatest latitude to set priorities and design aid-financed activities consistent with their own development strategies, and in some cases should be provided with direct budgetary support. This would reduce the need for excessive bureaucracy in Washington and allow more resources to be directed to monitoring and evaluation, which are currently underfunded and underemphasized. Funding can come either from broad development assistance accounts or from specific vertical programs such as the President's Emergency Plan for AIDS Relief (PEPFAR). In some recipient countries, a portion of funds could go directly to national governments, not just to contractors.

Greater U.S. oversight and involvement are necessary for countries with average or poor governance, who should receive less funding per capita. Recipient governments should play an active role in setting priorities and designing projects but should not be given as much flexibility, and the United States should be actively involved in ensuring broad-based participation and technical rigor.

In extremely weak or failing states, aid should be limited to humanitarian relief, establishing security, livelihood generation, and providing basic services to the poor. Emphasis should gradually shift away from direct involvement in implementation to monitoring and evaluation of results. Those responsible for monitoring and evaluation should be involved in the design of projects and programs from the outset to ensure that baseline data are collected and appropriate benchmarks set, and progress should be monitored continuously throughout. A more rigorous evaluation process involving randomized trials or comparisons based on treatment and control groups should be introduced for a small group of projects that are well designed for such evaluations.

Counter Security Threats from Poorly Performing States

Countering security threats that emanate from dysfunctional states is, and shall remain, an important foreign assistance objective. However, the experience of the past decade makes it clear that in the future the United States needs to invest far more systematically in soft power tools for conflict prevention or risk finding its hard security assets increasingly drawn into postconflict stabilization and reconstruction. By using taxpayer dollars more strategically and by taking long-term objectives into account, the United States can solve problems before they become costly. A strategy of prevention demands better coordination and cooperation among agencies and military and civilian units, and with international organizations.

Regional bureaus within the U.S. Agency for International Development (USAID), the Departments of State and Defense, and the intelligence community should coordinate with the Office of the Coordinator for Reconstruction and Stabilization and the National Security Council to identify potential conflicts and to develop and execute conflict prevention strategies. The Office of the Coordinator for Reconstruction and Stabilization is intended to oversee the development of interagency contingency plans, address operational and budgetary requirements, and coordinate interagency actions during operations. The National Security Council can help establish lines of authority between the Departments of Defense and State, USAID, and other relevant agencies in order to promote better cooperation and coordination and can function as an "impartial" facilitator to promote and lead civilian-military cooperation and coordination.

Development in the midst of conflict requires military, political, and economic expertise in equal measure. The U.S. military has the greatest capacity to operate in conflict situations and conduct stabilization and reconstruction operations, but civilians must be trained and prepared to provide leadership and technical capacity in support of transitional governance mechanisms. The creation of a reserve civilian corps capable of providing key expertise, skills, and knowledge would further leverage this untapped potential.

Finally, international partnerships for stabilization and reconstruction operations should be pursued much more frequently, as they are cost effective, increase burden sharing, bolster legitimacy, and increase the likelihood of success.

Counter Security Threats with Foreign Partners

Foreign assistance should also be used to counter security threats by working with governments whose strategic aims are aligned and capabilities are up to the task (rather than working around them, as is necessary with dysfunctional states). However, aid to advance counterterrorism, counternarcotics, counterproliferation, and coalition building often evidences a tension between supporting repressive governments in order to achieve short-term vital interests and promoting open, democratic societies that will better serve U.S. interests over the long term. This internal contradiction calls for a major rethinking of the traditional approach to security and strategic assistance.

In a climate of greater insecurity, advancing strategic interests by working with often repressive regimes will remain a necessity. However, a better and sustainable resolution must be found to the tension between advancing immediate national security objectives and promoting the enduring commitment to human rights and development norms. U.S. efforts must advance lasting political and economic reform while working to achieve a stable security environment. Military counterterrorism efforts, for example, cannot be successful without law and judicial enforcement, nonproliferation, and stabilization and reconstruction initiatives to address the weak states exploited by terrorist groups.

To begin to address this apparent contradiction, a senior director in the National Security Council should be appointed to launch an interagency review of the coherence and effectiveness of military aid programs. Policy guidelines should be developed to deal with conflicts between national security priorities and human rights and development goals in military assistance.

Congressional oversight should similarly be strengthened by adding joint hearings to integrate committees with expertise on military issues and foreign assistance. State and Defense Department field staff should be entrusted with increased spending discretion in return for greater oversight via real-time communication with congressional appropriators. Congress in turn should request a comprehensive administration review of the objectives and performance of security assistance programs on a biennial or quadrennial basis. The administration should be asked to provide evidence that "transformational" diplomacy is the surest means to accomplish U.S. national security objectives, as well as provide detailed country assessments and strategies for implementing security assistance. The State Department may well need new authorities to move funds to different programs, but Congress in turn deserves greater accountability.

The United States must also be more aware of its comparative advantages and recognize the capacities of its donor partners. European allies are often better at certain types of security assistance, such as rule of law and police training, while the United States excels in areas such as health and family planning programs. A robust transatlantic partnership would create a powerful basis for advancing security and development abroad, thus improving American credibility and lessening the financial burden.

Leverage Humanitarian Aid

The U.S. government shines as the biggest humanitarian donor in the world and among the most effective and technically well equipped, contributing to historically low worldwide mortality rates from disaster, famine, and conflict. This is no cause for complacency, however, and humanitarian assistance remains one of the core objectives in the framework proposed by this study. The number of people exposed to catastrophic hazards will rise due to population growth concentrated in areas prone to quakes, floods, and food insecurity. In the face of this, American humanitarian aid suffers from lack of coherence, faulty coordination, competition between agencies, and failure to leverage America's potential international influence. Better internal organization, discipline about directing resources to prevention and objectively assessed need, systematic evaluation, and appropriate use of the military and food aid would make the United States far more effective in addressing the growing demands on humanitarian aid and in leveraging a more effective international response.

The U.S. humanitarian aid system should be reformed to have greater autonomy to direct resources according to humanitarian needs and systematic evaluation rather than political considerations. The best alternative would be to integrate all humanitarian funding, planning, and response into one empowered organization: a merger of USAID's Offices of Foreign Disaster Assistance, Transition Initiatives, and Food for Peace with the State Department's Bureau of Population, Refugees, and Migration and other offices. The combined budget in excess of $1.5 billion would free up resources for neglected crises, internally displaced peoples, and disaster prevention systems.

Most funding currently trails natural disasters, even though the most effective measures for reducing the impact of disasters take place before they occur, particularly when disasters are frequent and extensive. Such measures include prevention, reduction of vulnerability, preparedness, early warning systems, and indigenous surge response capacity. With world-leading expertise in prevention, USAID's Office for Disaster Assistance could effectively absorb increased funding for risk mitigation and should lead a UN-wide effort to establish a 20 percent minimum share of humanitarian assistance aimed at disaster mitigation.

The effectiveness of humanitarian programs can and should be evaluated on the basis of hard evidence. Congress should request a biennial "humanitarian strategy" planning report from the administration and an annual "humanitarian state of affairs" report that assesses what works, what does not, the measured results of humanitarian interventions, and the return on investment. These reports should assess the relative costs and benefits of relief, mitigation, and planning and assess how the United States can more effectively leverage the work of multilaterals and NGOs.

Most of the preventable deaths in emergencies occur in areas that do not generate headlines. Attention should focus on recurring implementation gaps that result in deaths, disability, and suffering. This is especially the case with provision of clean water in emergencies, but it also applies in the areas of hygiene, field communications, early warning networks, practical protection, child survival related to disease, and cold weather threats. Through control of the purse strings, the U.S. government can force corrective action to bolster the skills and refine the orientation of UN agencies and NGOs.

The U.S. military should be deployed only for its *unique* capabilities. The UN and NGOs can lease C-130s and helicopters better than the military in the long term, but the military can respond much faster in the hours and days after the onset of an emergency. Second, the military uniquely possesses capability in real-time assistance at sea. Third, the Defense Department controls a network of laboratory facilities, far beyond the combined capabilities of NGOs, which are useful in identifying the type and drug susceptibility of pathogens encountered in emergencies.

Congress should support USAID's interest in gradually expanding the funding available for the local purchase of food for aid. Congress rejected the administration's fiscal year 2006 budget request for $300 million to procure food within the area of an emergency (if food is available and at a low price) because of opposition from the U.S. agricultural sector. Wherever feasible, local purchases of food can save time—and lives—relative to the traditional approach of procuring, packaging, and shipping food by sea from the United States.

Finally, the crucial link between disaster relief and development must be improved. To reduce the high rate of cycling back into crisis, it is critical to address the economic causes of grievance, conflict, and displacement and to systematically build in sizable economic and governance programs that facilitate the transition from emergency response to reconstruction and ultimately development. The relative effectiveness of humanitarian aid should not lead to complacency, and it should be implemented as a component of the entire aid apparatus, not in isolation.

Eliminate Transnational Threats

Globalization has elevated the profile of transnational threats, making foreign assistance increasingly vital in countering dangers that defy national borders and require concerted action. Nowhere are the consequences of transnational threats more dramatic than in the global AIDS pandemic, which threatens the development prospects, health and education sectors, government capacity, and security of poor nations. The President's Emergency Plan for AIDS Relief is an unprecedented, high-risk presidential foreign policy commitment in the field of global public health. Sustaining U.S. commitment to the global fight against AIDS will require maintaining the president's personal commitment through successive administrations, strong public support for providing lifesaving treatment to a growing population of foreigners for an indefinite period at considerable cost, increasing support for an evidence-based prevention agenda, and tailoring programs to rapidly evolving and complex situations on the ground.

Several elements are essential to maintaining the effectiveness and feasibility of U.S. assistance to address global HIV/AIDS. First, there must be continued strong leadership. Much of the success achieved thus far has rested on the quality and forcefulness of leadership choices made in the start-up phase. Furthermore, presidential leadership must be maintained across administrations. Beyond 2008 a critical test will be whether the next president attaches equal importance to global control of HIV/AIDS, builds that priority explicitly into his or her foreign policy agenda, and makes the case for a more balanced approach that forcefully affirms the U.S. commitment to support both the President's Emergency Plan and the Global Fund.

Prevention efforts must improve. It is critical to elevate the priority of prevention, backed by money, strategy, and political will. Effective prevention will require more than the current 20 percent of resources. Standards and targets need better definition, and the official strategy must be broadened beyond "Abstinence, Be faithful, and Condoms" to encompass a comprehensive approach that addresses the different routes of transmission and gender inequality.

Treatment strategies must be strengthened. This will entail assessing the true input costs and the pressures to increase the U.S. commitment to make treatment available to an expanding foreign population. Retaining public support will require demonstrating results from existing commitments and persuading other donors to contribute an escalating fair share. In the near term, it is critical to expedite procurement contracts and identify reliable producers of generic single-dose therapies that meet U.S. qualifications. In addition, the risk of supply disruptions must be decreased, and investment in the next generation of antiretroviral medications must be encouraged. Furthermore, U.S. investments must be broadened to include prevention and treatment of malaria, tuberculosis, and other acute infectious diseases.

Investment in skilled personnel is critical. A more systematic, far-reaching plan of action is needed in Africa to build up public health systems and offset the drain of medical talent by offering new training and retention programs in concert with African governments, other donors, and the Global Fund and World Bank.

Finally, U.S. capabilities in this arena must be improved. The State Department should create professional incentives and integrate global health issues into foreign policy by establishing a global health career track, strengthening the capacity of the Office of the Global AIDS Coordinator and U.S. embassies, and better integrating the State Department's Office of International Health Affairs.

Organize for Effectiveness

Improving the success of the U.S. aid enterprise requires fundamental organizational and operational transformation. Recent years have witnessed a proliferation of presidential initiatives lodged in a confusing array of new offices. There are now more than fifty separate U.S. government units involved in aid delivery, resulting in duplication and disarray. It is therefore imperative to rationalize agencies, improve cooperation and coordination, and clarify their missions.

Second, the organizational confusion is exacerbated by a concurrent disconnect between budget accounts, policy, and operations. These components of foreign aid must be restructured so that program design is driven by objectives and needs rather than restrictive funding categories.

Third, the current cacophony of actors within the U.S. government undermines American leadership internationally. The United States will only have a strong and effective voice in the international arena if it speaks and acts in a unified manner.

Fourth, to maximize impact and achieve synergies across policies, the United States must deploy all its soft power tools in a coherent manner by creating incentives for interagency coordination of policy and integration of operations and planning. Advancing economic and political modernization in the developing world requires a seamless web of policies encompassing foreign assistance (where appropriate) along with trade and investment, technical assistance, debt relief, and financial stabilization. To increase effectiveness, the United States must achieve coherence not only across foreign assistance but also the full portfolio of policies affecting poor countries.

Fifth, the United States must invest in core foreign assistance competencies, including in the areas of infrastructure and conflict prevention and reconstruction, rather than allowing in-house capacity to erode through reliance on megacontracts and reinventing the wheel with each new crisis. The government should develop this expertise by investing in knowledge critical to the mission, deepen technical expertise, and place much greater emphasis on objective evaluation of results.

Finally, the United States must elevate development as an independent mission alongside defense and diplomacy in practice, not just principle.

An international scan of bilateral donor agencies suggests four possible organizational models: improved coordination while retaining existing decentralization; USAID as the implementation arm of the State Department; merger of USAID and State; and creation of a new "department of global development." Current reform efforts are focused on the second model, improving coordination between the State Department as the policy setter and USAID as the implementer of foreign assistance. Ultimately, a new, empowered department of global development may hold the greatest promise of transforming the U.S. foreign assistance enterprise to address the global challenges of the twenty-first century. It would boost the stature and morale of the development mission, thus attracting the next generation of talent, and realize the president's vision of elevating development as a third pillar of national security alongside diplomacy and defense. However, the greater the potential benefit from transformation, the greater the political hurdle to achieve it.

Effective Partnership with Congress

Historically, successful reform initiatives have come from the White House, but a continuance of the congressional status quo will inhibit effective foreign aid and hinder aid reform as well. Congress has neglected its lawmaking and oversight roles in foreign assistance and overreached in its attempts to manage aid implementation. Congressional interest in foreign assistance is too often limited to areas of concern to one or more members, manifested in the form of earmarks. Three recent trends have compounded these problems: decisionmaking increasingly concentrated in the Executive Office, disinclination to seek permanent legislation to validate major foreign assistance initiatives, and legislative initiatives on behalf of special interest or advocacy groups that are signed into law without due consideration of their cumulative impact.

Congress must reassert its role in foreign assistance, working in tandem with the executive branch. Instead of earmarking for specific areas of concern, Congress should implement authorizing language. Under most circumstances the appropriators should seek to reflect an authorizing committee's recommended modifications to the conditions on foreign assistance in annual and supplemental appropriations bills. Where they do not reflect authorizers' modifications, the appropriators should explicitly explain the discrepancy in their report accompanying the appropriations bill.

Increased transparency regarding congressional intent in foreign assistance appropriations would help reduce the rampant inter- and intra-agency confusion of the present day. The level of detail in most foreign assistance appropriations accounts should be comparable to that for domestic and defense agencies. Senate-House conference agreements should expand the use of account text tables that indicate the purposes for which funds are being appropriated and reconcile inconsistent and contradictory report language. Furthermore, Congress should allow more flexibility to appropriations by abolishing ineffective separate "operating expense" budget accounts, repealing outdated laws requiring annual authorization of appropriations levels, and restoring a small presidential contingency fund solely for unanticipated policy requirements.

Over the longer term, Congress should establish a panel of independent experts to recommend changes within the executive and the legislature to improve the operational efficacy of all foreign assistance and better reflect the constitutional roles of the two branches. The recommendations should be issued in time for consideration by the 110th Congress.

Congress should also reengage the foreign and international relations committees in the allocation of foreign assistance resources by drafting and passing annual or biennial bills authorizing realistic levels for foreign assistance accounts. Until it is possible to enact foreign assistance authorizations, the account levels reported by the committees or passed by each house should be deemed an authorization recommendation to be considered by the appropriations committees. Senate and House rules should be modified to require that committee reports accompanying foreign operations appropriations bills include a detailed explanation of funding in excess of those authorized by law or recommended by the authorizing committee.

Finally, it is important to rationalize the reprogramming notification process by negotiating a more transparent and time-limited process for congressional consideration. Executive branch requests to reprogram funds, including presidential initiatives, for purposes different from those for which the funds were appropriated merit prompt acceptance or modification.

Contributors to the Brookings-CSIS Task Force on Transforming Foreign Assistance in the 21st Century

Lael Brainard and Patrick Cronin

Project Codirectors

The Task Force on Transforming Foreign Assistance in the 21st Century benefited enormously from the community of foreign assistance professionals—policymakers, lawmakers, experts, nongovernmental organizations, and private sector practitioners—who informed and guided its work. We are indebted to the individuals listed below who variously engaged in lengthy conversations and e-mail exchanges, commented on and critiqued papers, presented and participated in Task Force meetings and events, and more generally shared their experience, knowledge, and wisdom on foreign assistance issues. The views expressed in this book are those of the authors alone and do not necessarily represent the views of the individuals listed below. This list does not include a number of people who wished to remain anonymous.

Academia

Lincoln Chen, Global Equity Center, Harvard University
Joe Collins, National Security Strategy, National Defense University
Carol Lancaster, Georgetown University School of Public Service

335

Jeff Levi, Department of Health Policy, George Washington University School of Public Health and Health Services

M. Peter McPherson, National Association of State Universities and Land Grant Colleges

Think Tanks

Carol Adelman, Hudson Institute Center for Science in Public Policy

Jon Alterman, Middle East Program, Center for Strategic and International Studies

Frederick D. Barton, Center for Strategic and International Studies

Colin Bradford, Brookings Institution

Anthony Cordesman, Center for Strategic and International Studies

Peter DeShazo, Americas Program, Center for Strategic and International Studies

Joseph McMillan, Institute for National Strategic Studies, National Defense University

Philip Nieburg, Center for Strategic and International Studies

Stewart Patrick, Center for Global Development

Robert Polk, Institute for Defense Analyses

Susan Rice, Brookings Institution

Gayle Smith, Center for American Progress

Mike Taylor, Resources for the Future

Tamara Cofman Wittes, Brookings Institution

Private Sector

Janet Ballantyne, Abt Associates

Carolyn Bartholomew, Basic Education Coalition

Carole Brookings, formerly of the World Bank

Malcolm Butler, Partners of the Americas

Lawrence Cooley, Management Systems International

Michael Froman, CitiInsurance

Julie Howard, Partnership to Cut Poverty and Hunger in Africa

Ken Isaacs, Samaritan's Purse

Craig Johnstone, Boeing Company, Europe

Jennifer Kates, HIV Policy, Kaiser Family Foundation

Robert Kramer, Humanitarian Response, Chemonics, Inc.

Alan Larson, Covington and Burling
Mark Murray, Piper Rudnick Gray Cary
Don Pressley, Booz Allen Hamilton
Charlie Sykes, formerly CARE International
Julia Taft, InterAction
Rudy von Bernuth, Save the Children

State Department

Richard Behrend, Office of Economic and Development Affairs, Bureau of
   International Organizational Affairs
Lincoln Bloomfield Jr., formerly of Office of Political-Military Affairs
   (currently with Palmer Coates, LLC)
Arthur Eugene Dewey, formerly assistant secretary of state, Bureau of
   Population, Refugees, and Migration
J. Scott Carpenter, Office of the Secretary of State, Bureau of Near Eastern
   Affairs
John Hillen, Office of the Secretary of Political-Military Affairs
Christopher Hoh, Response Strategy and Resource Management, Office of
   the Coordinator for Reconstruction and Stabilization
Stephen Krasner, Policy Planning
Philip Levy, Policy Planning
Carlos Pascual, formerly of Office of Reconstruction and Stabilization
   (currently with Brookings Institution)
Earl Anthony Wayne, Office of Economic and Business Affairs
Philip Zelikow, Counselor

U.S. Congress

David Abramowitz, House Committee on International Relations
Craig Albright, Office of Representative Joe Knollenberg and House Appro-
   priations Subcommittee on Foreign Operations
Rob Blair, Appropriations Subcommittee on Foreign Operations, House
   of Representatives
Reb Brownell, Office of Senator Mitch McConnell
Mark Esper, National Security Affairs, Office of the Majority Leader, U.S.
   Senate
William Hoagland, Office of the Majority Leader, U.S. Senate

Alice Hogans, House Appropriations Committee

Bob Lester, Subcommittee on State, Foreign Operations, and Related Programs, Committee on Appropriations, U.S. Senate

Katherine Maloney, formerly of Senate Foreign Relations Committee (currently with U.S. Trade and Development Agency)

Diana Ohlbaum, Senate Foreign Relations Committee

Robin Roizman, House Committee on International Relations

Paul Oostburg Sanz, House Committee on International Relations

Kim Savit, Senate Foreign Relations Committee

Jeremy Sharp, Congressional Research Service

Beth Tritter, Office of Representative Nita Lowey

U.S. Agency for International Development

Polly Byers, formerly of Office of Policy and Program Coordination (currently with U.S. State Department)

Thomas Fox, Policy and Program Coordination

Gerald Hyman, Office of Democracy and Governance

Don Krumm, Office of Transition Initiatives

Douglas Menarchik, Bureau of Policy and Program Coordination

Andrew Natsios, formerly of USAID (currently with Georgetown University)

Anne Petersen, formerly of Global Health (currently with American Bar Association–Central European and Eurasian Law Initiative)

David Taylor, formerly of Office of Transition Initiatives (currently with World Vision International)

John Tsagronis, Office of the Administrator

U.S. Treasury

Timothy Adams, International Affairs

John Hundley, Development Policy

Overseas Private Investment Corporation

Peter Watson (currently with Dwight Group)

Office of the United States Trade Representative

Mary Ryckman, Trade Capacity Building

Millennium Challenge Corporation

Paul Applegarth (currently with German Marshall Fund of the United States)
John Hewko, Operations
Clay Lowery, formerly Markets and Sector Assessments (currently with U.S.
Department of Treasury)
Frances McNaught, Congressional and Public Affairs
Charles Sethness, Accountability

National Intelligence Council

David Gordon

Department of Defense

Jeffrey "Jeb" Nadaner, Special Operations, Low-Intensity Conflict

White House

Faryar Shirzad, International Economic Affairs
John Simon, formerly with Relief Stabilization and Development for the
National Security Council (currently with Overseas Private Investment
Corporation)

List of Legislation, Strategic Objectives, and Organizations Involved with Foreign Assistance

During the research for this volume, the Brookings Institution conducted a study to determine just how many distinct foreign assistance objectives, laws, initiatives, and organizations exist within the United States government. Although judging what constitutes a distinct objective or organizational entity is inherently subjective, there was little difficulty listing the fifty in each category below, and an exhaustive list would be even longer. The confusion and disorganization are remarkable and illustrate many of the points made in this volume.

Legislation, Presidential Initiatives, and Strategy Papers

Legislation

Agricultural Trade Development and Assistance Act of 1954
Arms Export Control Act of 1976
Assistance for Orphans and Other Vulnerable Children in Developing Countries Act of 2005
Bretton Woods Agreement Act of 1945
Bush Administration Fiscal Year 2003 Budget Request
Fiscal Year 2004 Emergency Supplemental Appropriations Act
Foreign Assistance Act of 1961

Freedom for Russia and Emerging Eurasian Democracies and Open Markets (FREEDOM) Support Act of 1992

Helping Enhance the Livelihood of People (HELP) around the Globe Commission Act

International Security Assistance Act of 1979

Microenterprise Results and Accountability Act of 2004

Migration and Refugee Assistance Act of 1962

Millennium Challenge Act of 2003

National Security Strategy of the USA 2002

National Security Strategy of the USA 2006

President Bush's HIV/AIDS Act of 2003

Special Foreign Assistance Act of 1986

Support for Eastern European Democracy (SEED) Act of 1989

U.S. Leadership against HIV/AIDS, Tuberculosis, and Malaria Act of 2003

USAID White Paper on American Foreign Aid

Presidential Initiatives in USAID

Afghanistan Road Initiative

Africa Education Initiative

Centers for Excellence in Teacher Training

Central American Free Trade Agreement

Clean Energy Initiative

Congo Basin Forest Partnership

Digital Freedom Initiative

Faith-Based and Community Initiatives

Global Fund to Fight AIDS, Tuberculosis, and Malaria

Initiative to End Hunger in Africa

Trade for African Development and Enterprise

Volunteers for Prosperity

Water for the Poor Initiative

Presidential Initiatives outside of USAID's Reporting System

Global Climate Change

Middle East Partnership Initiative

Millennium Challenge Account

President's Emergency Plan for AIDS Relief
President's Initiative against Illegal Logging
Trafficking in Persons

New Initiatives

Accelerating the Fight against Malaria
Business Transformation
Democracy and Governance Strategic Framework
Fragile States Strategy (January 2005)
Mitigating the Development Impacts of HIV/AIDS Foreign Aid in the
    National Interest
Nine Principles, February 2005
Policy Framework for Bilateral Foreign Aid, January 2006
Summary Matrix: Policy Framework for Bilateral Foreign Aid, January 2006
USAID–State Strategic Plan
White Paper: U.S. Foreign Aid: Meeting the Challenges of the Twenty-First
    Century
Women's Justice and Empowerment in Africa

Objectives

Affordable nuclear energy
Agricultural development
Antiterrorism
Biodiversity preservation
Business development
Child survival
Conflict prevention
Conflict resolution
Counternarcotics
Demining operations
Democratization
Disaster relief
Economic growth
Education
Empowerment of women
Encouraging foreign investment

Ensuring water access
Famine relief
Financial technical assistance
Foreign military assistance
Global health
Governance and rule of law
HIV/AIDS
Human resources development
Human rights
Humanitarian assistance
Information technology
Infrastructure construction
International trade
Job creation
Labor reform
Market reform
Media freedom
Migration assistance
Monitoring and evaluation
Natural resource management
Nonproliferation
Peacekeeping operations
Poverty reduction
Prevention of human trafficking
Reconstruction
Refugee assistance
Religious freedom
Scientific and technological innovation
Security
Stabilization
Strengthening civil society
Sustainable forest management
Transparency and accountability
Tuberculosis and malaria

Organizations

African Development Foundation
Department of Agriculture

Bureau of Global Health
Economic Support Fund
Famine Early Warning Systems Network
Food for Peace
International Military Education and Training Program
Nonproliferation, Antiterrorism, Demining, and Related Programs
Office of Democracy and Governance
Office of Transition Initiatives
Office of U.S. Foreign Disaster Assistance and Famine Assistance
U.S. Trade and Development Agency
U.S. Trade Representative (USTR)

OWEN BARDER is director of global development and effectiveness with the U.K. Department for International Development. He previously was head of Africa policy. He has also served as private secretary to the prime minister (Economic Affairs) and private secretary to the chancellor of the exchequer, as well as in a range of roles in the U.K. Treasury. He was also seconded to the South African Finance Ministry, where he helped to develop the medium-term expenditure framework.

LAEL BRAINARD is vice president and director of the Global Economy and Development Program and holds the Bernard L. Schwartz Chair in International Economics at the Brookings Institution. Brainard served as deputy assistant to the president for International Economic Policy and as U.S. sherpa to the G-8 during the Clinton administration. Previously, she served as associate professor of applied economics at MIT Sloan School. Brainard received master's and doctoral degrees in economics from Harvard University as a National Science Foundation Fellow.

PATRICK CRONIN is director of studies for the International Institute for Strategic Studies in London. Previously he served as assistant administrator, Policy and Program Coordination, at the U.S. Agency for International Development. He has served as a director of studies at the National Defense University's Institute for National Strategic Studies, the U.S. Institute of Peace, and, most recently, the Center for Strategic and International Studies. Cronin served as a U.S. Naval Reserve officer and a senior analyst at the Center for Naval Analyses. He received his doctorate and master's degrees at the University of Oxford.

CHARLES FLICKNER has had an extensive career working on Capitol Hill. From 1975 until 1994, he served as a professional staff member with responsibility for international affairs at the Senate Budget Committee. He was clerk (staff director) of the House Appropriations Subcommittee on Foreign Operations from 1995 until 2004.

TAREK GHANI is the special policy assistant to the president of the Center for Global Development. He previously researched UN reform and U.S. security assistance programs for the director of studies at the Center for Strategic and International Studies. A Truman Scholar, Ghani graduated from Stanford University with honors in international security.

STEVEN HANSCH is a senior associate at the Institute for the Study of International Migration at Georgetown University and is also adjunct faculty at American, Columbia, and Johns Hopkins universities. He has conducted field work developing and implementing disaster-response programs with the Refugee Policy Group, Food Aid Management, the International Rescue Committee, CARE, Relief International, and Partners for Development. As senior program officer at the Refugee Policy Group during the 1980s, he led evaluations of NGO field programs and organized numerous interagency conferences to share technical lessons about how to improve collective humanitarian response.

J. STEPHEN MORRISON is trustee fellow and director of the Africa Program and HIV/AIDS Task Force at the Center for Strategic and International Studies, a multiyear project cochaired by Senators Bill Frist (R-Tenn.) and Russ Feingold (D-Wisc.), that aims to strengthen U.S. leadership in battling global HIV/AIDS. From 1996 through 2000, Morrison served on the secretary of state's policy planning staff. From 1993 to 1995, he served as the first deputy director of the Office of Transition Initiatives at USAID, where he created postconflict programs in Angola and Bosnia. Previously, he was senior staff member of the House Foreign Affairs Subcommittee on Africa. Morrison holds a Ph.D. in political science from the University of Wisconsin, has been an adjunct professor at the Johns Hopkins School of Advanced International Studies since 1994, and is a graduate magna cum laude of Yale College.

LARRY NOWELS was a specialist in foreign affairs at the Congressional Research Service. During his thirty-three-year career at CRS, he wrote extensively on U.S. foreign assistance policymaking, including the congressional role in legislating and overseeing American foreign aid programs. He has also specialized in international affairs budget issues, both from a historical and current perspective. Nowels further served on detail assignments to the House Budget Committee and the House Appropriations Foreign Operations Subcommittee. Since retiring from CRS in mid-2006, Nowels consults for several organizations engaged in U.S. foreign aid policy.

STEVEN RADELET is a senior fellow at the Center for Global Development, where he works on issues related to foreign aid, developing country debt, economic growth, and trade between rich and poor countries. He was deputy assistant secretary of the U.S. Treasury for Africa, the Middle East, and Asia from January 2000 through June 2002. He has written numerous articles in economics journals and other publications, is coauthor of *Economics of Development* (a leading undergraduate textbook), and author of *Challenging Foreign Aid: A Policymaker's Guide to the Millennium Challenge Account.*

Index

Accountability, 182–83, 326

Advocacy: for foreign aid, 3, 260; for reform of U.S. aid program, 59, 60, 62, 264–65, 322; special interest in congressional foreign affairs acts, 226, 227; for U.S. HIV/AIDS initiative, 72–73

Afghanistan, 71, 143, 184, 226; aid budget, 15, 116; aid goals, 15–16, 20, 200; aid outcomes, 163; British aid, 298; coordination of aid delivery, 41, 137, 153–54; counternarcotics campaign, 20, 198, 206, 207, 210, 220–21; humanitarian aid, 130–31; postconflict reconstruction and stabilization, 166–67, 181–82, 190, 213, 214–15, 237

Africa: British aid program, 303–05; British conflict reduction program, 295–96; food insecurity, 126–27; HIV/AIDS in, 70, 81; humanitarian relief delivery, 125; infrastructure investment, 48–49; public health spending, 117; sub-Saharan aid spending, 101. *See also* President's Emergency Plan for AIDS Relief (PEPFAR)

African Development Foundation, 269

Agency for International Development (USAID), 42, 138–39; accomplishments, 93–94; administrator as director of U.S. foreign assistance, 4, 189; aid delivery mechanisms, 104–05; allocation of resource by strategic goals, 8–9; counternarcotics efforts, 208; demographic health surveys, 133; development aid outcomes, 94; Famine Early Warning System Network, 124, 135; financial management system, 44–45;

future prospects, 234–35; humanitarian relief efforts, 124, 128–29, 132–35, 138–40, 142, 145, 148, 149–51, 154, 328; Middle East policies and programs, 202; Office of Food for Peace, 134–35; Office of Transition Initiatives, 38, 134, 176; Office of U.S. Foreign Disaster Assistance, 128–29, 133, 139–40, 148, 149–51, 154, 327; operating expense accounting, 242; organizational models for improving aid program, 56–58, 331; origins, 4, 9, 36, 256–57, 262; policy formulation and, 42, 44, 46; postconflict reconstruction efforts, 162, 189–90; procurement system, 49, 183; recommendations for, 325, 331; reform efforts, 234, 259, 273; relations with other aid agencies, 38, 42, 138–39, 331; research capacity and investment, 50, 52; staffing and outsourcing, 46–48, 49, 50; statutory restrictions on programs, 240

Agricultural policy: research investment, 49; responsibility for, 42

Agriculture, Department of, 42, 50, 134, 137–38

AIDS. *See* Human immunodeficiency virus/AIDS

Algeria, 203

Alliance for Progress, 9

Angola, 100, 125–26

Arms Control and Disarmament Agency, 234

Asylum policies, 301

Australia, 185, 310

Avian flu, 21–22

postconflict reconstruction, 190; postwar reconstruction and stabilization operations, 170, 184, 185–86; public awareness of aid sources in, 306, 309
Muskie, Ed, 231

Namibia, 85
Narcotics trade interventions: Afghanistan counternarcotics program, 210; Andean Counterdrug Initiative, 209, 210–11; effectiveness, 210–12; evolution of counternarcotics assistance, 198; governance issues, 207, 211–12; national security and, 20, 206–07; organizational structure of U.S. effort, 208–09; strategies, 207, 220–21; U.S. spending, 208–09, 210
National Commission on International Religious Freedom, 72
National Defense Authorization Act, 219
National Defense Strategy (2005), 212
National Institutes of Health, 50
National security: allocation of aid resources based on, 8–9, 18; conceptual approach to foreign assistance, 5; countering threats from poorly performing states, 15–17, 324–25; countering threats with foreign partners, 17–20, 325–27; counterterrorism policy and, 199; drug trade and, 20, 206–07; foreign assistance rationale, 1–2, 4, 9, 52, 161, 162; significance of weak or failed states, 167–69; status of development mission and, 52, 53–54, 59; support for capable partners as goal of aid, 10; weapons of mass destruction counterproliferation strategies, 19–20, 216–19. See also Security assistance
National Security Council, 180, 188–89, 326
National Security Presidential Directive 44, 38, 175, 176–77, 178, 188
National Security Strategy (2002), 52, 59, 71, 167, 199
Natsios, Andrew, 129, 235

Natural disaster relief, 122; climate change and, 128; disease risk, 131–32; future prospects, 125; mortality, 124; preventive interventions, 124, 127, 148; projected demand, 127, 128; risk insurance, 148. See also Humanitarian relief
New Zealand, 310
Nicaragua, 100
Nigeria, 48, 85
Nixon administration, 242, 257
Nongovernmental organizations, 322; advocacy for aid reform, 60, 62; in British aid program, 208, 209, 289, 290, 309; humanitarian relief role, 328; Middle East Partnership Initiative, 203
North Atlantic Treaty Organization, 40
Norway, 8, 56
Nunn-Lugar Cooperative Threat Reduction Program, 19–20, 197, 216–17
Nunn-Lugar Soviet Nuclear Threat Reduction Act, 36–37

Obey, David, 233, 234
Office of Management and Budget, 183
Office of National Drug Control Policy, 208
Office of the Global AIDS Coordinator, 4, 37, 69, 75, 76–77, 87–88, 330
Office of U.S. Trade Representative, 42
ONE Campaign, 3
Organization for Economic Cooperation and Development, 35, 37, 54–55, 281
Organization for European Economic Cooperation, 280–81
Orr, Robert, 172
Outcomes of aid: assessment of collaborative projects, 305, 308; British strategies to increase aid effectiveness, 305; counternarcotics efforts, 210–12; counterproliferation initiatives, 218–19; donor coordination and, 40; economic development aid, 27, 93–94, 99–100; to Egypt, 204; evidence-based policy formulation, 308; humanitarian relief, 21, 131, 154; information man-

allocation, 100–03; future of PEPFAR, 84–86; governance assessments, 24, 25; involvement in program design and delivery, 40, 96–97; needs assessment, 5–6, 24–25; poorly governed countries, assistance to, 108–10, 324–25; recommendations for reform of aid policy, 323–24, 325–27; strategic world map, 11; strategies for improving aid outcomes, 12–13, 96–97; support for capable partners as goal of aid, 10–13; well-governed countries, assistance to, 105–07

Reform of U.S. aid system: agency realignment issues, 261–62, 268–70; Carlucci Commission, 256, 258, 259–60, 261, 262, 263, 265, 268, 270, 271–72; clarity of message for, 268; composition of reform groups, 261; conditions for, 59–60, 62, 269, 322; congressional–executive branch relations and, 270–71; funding issues, 262–63; Hamilton-Gilman Task Force, 256, 258–59, 260–61, 262, 263, 264, 266, 267, 270, 271, 272; historical outcomes, 255, 272–73; Humphrey initiative, 256, 258, 265, 269; initiators, 260; Kennedy administration, 255, 256–57, 259–60, 261, 262, 264, 265, 267, 271; legislative components, 263, 266; lessons from British experience, 312–13; lessons of historical efforts, 263–72, 273; New Directions legislation, 255, 256, 257, 259–60, 261, 262, 263, 265, 266, 267, 271; obstacles to, 38; organizational models, 35–36, 54–59, 62–63; oversight issues, 263; Peterson Commission, 256, 257, 260, 261–62, 263, 268, 271; politics and, 36, 38, 39, 59, 60; post–World War II efforts, 255, 256; principles for, 35, 37–54, 61–62; prospects for, 35; rationale, 259–60; recent developments, 255; recommendations for, 39, 61–63, 322–33; scope, 260–61, 267–68; stakeholder participation, 265–66; timing, 271–72; Wharton

Report, 256, 259, 260, 261, 262, 263, 264, 265–67, 268, 270–71, 272, 273
Refugee populations, 123, 124; internally displaced persons, 136, 139–40
Research on aid delivery and outcomes, 49–52
Rice, Condoleezza, 13, 70, 196, 205
Rome Declaration on Harmonization, 40
Rough Guide publications, 309
Rusk, Dean, 264
Russia, 217
Rwanda, 85, 125–26

Sainsbury, Tim, 314
Sanctions policies, 42
Saudi Arabia, 200–01, 204
Scowcroft, Brent, 166
Sectoral approach to foreign aid, 7, 97–98
Security assistance: British aid policies, 297–98; coalition building and, 212–16; cold war policies, 195; in conceptual framework for foreign assistance policy, 195–96; counternarcotics campaigns, 206–12; counterproliferation initiatives, 216–19; counterterrorism campaign and, 198–200; current policy, 196; definition and scope, 195; development assistance and, 220; to Egypt, 204–06; Middle East policies, 199–204; military assistance programs, 213–14; opportunities to improve, 196, 219–21; to poorly performing countries, 324–25; post–cold war evolution, 196–98; strategic components, 195. *See also* National security
September *11* terrorist attacks, 1, 4, 15–18, 60, 71, 108, 162, 167, 172, 195, 196, 197, 198, 215, 220, 269, 297, 310
Shaping the 21st Century, 290
Short, Clare, 291, 298, 300, 301, 309, 312
Sierra Leone, 125–26, 295
Somalia, 125–26, 166, 172, 175
South Africa, 85
South Korea, 14
Spreckley, Nicholas, 314
Staffing: British foreign aid programs, 59,

287–88; congressional foreign affairs staff, 230; outsourcing and, 46–48; PEPFAR, 75, 80, 81, 87; trends, 50

State, Department of: Agency for International Development and, 56–58, 139–40, 234–35, 331; Bureau of Political-Military Affairs, 213; Bureau of Population, Refugees, and Migration, 139–40, 142, 149–51; congressional relations, 235–36; coordination of aid policy in, 55–56; counternarcotics efforts, 208–09, 210; counterproliferation programs, 218, 219; director of U.S. foreign assistance, 4, 189; Economic Support Funds, 44, 45, 197, 200, 202, 205; financial management system, 44–45, 326; humanitarian aid, 132–33, 135, 145, 149–51; Humanitarian Information Unit, 138–39; Humanitarian Policy and Planning Bureau, 145; Office of International Health Affairs, 330; Office of Resources, Plans and Policy, 235–36; Office of the Coordinator for Reconstruction and Stabilization, 4, 38, 177, 178, 189; PEPFAR and, 76–77, 87–88; postconflict reconstruction efforts, 162, 176–77, 179–80, 189–90; recommendations for, 325, 326, 330, 331; role in reform of aid system, 264; security assistance policy, 196; security assistance to poorly performing countries, 212–13; separation from policy implementation, 44, 46; status of development mission, 52–53, 58

Sudan, 142, 214, 299

Support for Eastern European Democracy Act, 36, 37

Sweden, 56

Taiwan, 14

Tanzania, 40, 85, 94, 100

Terrorism: British foreign aid and, 297–98, 310; Bush (G. W.) administration policies, 198–99; challenges in formulating policy, 199–200; control of

weapons of mass destruction, 216–19; current U.S. security and strategic assistance policy to prevent, 17–20; drug trade and, 206, 207; as focus of national security concerns, 197, 273; interventions in Middle East to prevent, 201–04; scope of counterterrorism strategy, 199, 200, 201–02, 219–20; state-building rationale, 169–70

Thatcher, Margaret, 286

Thompson, Tommy, 78, 82

Tobias, Randall, 68, 75, 76, 77

Trade and Development Agency, 269

Trade and investment policy: British aid policies and programs, 284–85, 296, 298, 301–02; in Middle East, 204, 206; opportunities for synergy across policy instruments, 41–43

Transformational diplomacy, 13, 17–18, 326

Transparency: aid as direct budget or program support and, 111–12; British aid program, 308; in congressional appropriations, 238–39, 245, 332; in governance, 14–15; strategies for improving aid outcomes, 12

Transparency International, 24, 25

Treasury, Department of the, 42, 44, 235, 269

Truman administration, 48

Tsunami, Southeast Asia (2004), 4, 20, 21, 123, 124

Uganda, 85, 94, 125–26

Ukraine, 217

United Kingdom: aid spending, 302–03; asylum policy, 301; development policy authority, 41; foreign assistance staff, 287–88; influence of Marshall Plan, 280–82; International Development Act (2002), 296, 297, 301; joined-up government, 288, 295; Lawson doctrine, 287; Ministry of Overseas Development, 282–85; Pergau Dam project, 289, 313–14; post–World War II aid policies, 278–82; pre–World War